ANNUAL 1991-92

EDWARD ABELSON

Macdonald
Queen Anne Press

ACKNOWLEDGEMENTS

For this second edition of *Playfair Winners Annual* still thanks to all those who helped last year in the compilation of this book, including: Tony Allom, Guy Attfield, Caroline Williams, Amy Hulley, Celia Kent, Oscar Heini, Lorraine Jerram, Mike Lane, John Tyrrel, Jennifer Kavanagh, Roger Macdonald, Doug Field, Richard Adams, Steve McFerran, John James, Matthew Dodson, Ian Waight and Dave Bond; and for this year Mike Aven, John Milne, Tom Hart, Lucy Hart, Michael Thomas, Jan Carrick, Denise Bull and Julie Kane. Also thanks to all the representatives of the various national and international sports governing bodies who have answered my queries and provided information, and to *The Sporting Life* for horse racing information.

Edward Abelson   October 1991

A QUEEN ANNE PRESS BOOK

© Stamp's Sporting Statistics Ltd, 1991

First published in Great Britain in 1991 by
Queen Anne Press, a division of
Macdonald & Co (Publishers) Ltd
165 Great Dover Street
London SE1 4YA

A member of Maxwell Macmillan Publishing Corporation

All rights reserved. No part of this publication may be reproduced, stored in a retrieval system, or transmitted, in any form or by any means, without the prior permission in writing of the publisher, nor be otherwise circulated in any form of binding or cover other than that in which it is published and without a similar condition including this condition being imposed on the subsequent purchaser.

Cover design: Peter Champion
Cover illustration: David Scutt

A CIP catalogue record for this book is available from the British Library

ISBN 0−356−20319−0

Typeset by Tradespools Ltd, Frome, Somerset
Printed and bound in Great Britain by
BPCC Hazell Books
Aylesbury, Bucks, England
Member of BPCC Ltd.

CONTENTS

American Football 1
Archery 3
Association Football 5
Athletics 17
Australian Rules Football 37

Badminton 38
Baseball 46
Basketball 48
Biathlon 50
Billiards 53
Bobsleighing 55
Bowls 60
Boxing 63

Canoeing 80
Chess 83
Cricket 84
Croquet 99
Cycling 106

Darts 110
Diving 113

Equestrianism 115

Fencing 128

Gaelic Football 135
Golf 136
Greyhound Racing 146
Gymnastics 149

Handball 157
Hockey 158
Horse Racing 161
Hurling 192

Ice Hockey 194
Ice Skating 196

Judo 205

Modern Pentathlon 209
Motor Cycling 211
Motor Racing 219

Orienteering 226

Rackets 227
Rallying 229
Real Tennis 233
Rowing 235
Rugby League 249
Rugby Union 254

Shooting 263
Skiing 265
Snooker 280
Speedway 282
Squash 285
Swimming 287

Table Tennis 298
Tennis 304

Volleyball 335

Water Polo 336
Water Skiing 337
Weightlifting 340
Wrestling 346

Yachting 359

ABBREVIATIONS

Alb	Albania	Fij	Fiji
Alg	Algeria	Fin	Finland
Ant	Antigua	Fra	France
Arg	Argentina	FRG	West Germany
Aus	Australia		
Aut	Austria	Gam	Gambia
		GB	Great Britain
Bah	Bahamas	GDR	East Germany
Bar	Barbados	Ger	Germany
Bel	Belgium	Gha	Ghana
Ber	Bermuda	Gre	Greece
Bhn	Bahrain	Gua	Guatemala
Bol	Bolivia	Guy	Guyana
Bot	Botswana		
Bra	Brazil	Hai	Haiti
Bul	Bulgaria	Haw	Hawaii
Bur	Burma	HK	Hong Kong
		Hon	Honduras
Cam	Cameroon	Hun	Hungary
Camb	Cambodia		
Can	Canada	IC	Ivory Coast
Cha	Chad	Ice	Iceland
Chi	Chile	Ind	India
CI	Channel Islands	Indo	Indonesia
Col	Colombia	Ire	Ireland
Con	Congo	Irn	Iran
CPR	China	Irq	Iraq
CR	Costa Rica	Isr	Israel
Cub	Cuba	Ita	Italy
Cyp	Cyprus		
Cze	Czechoslovakia	Jam	Jamaica
		Jap	Japan
Dah	Dahomey		
Den	Denmark	Ken	Kenya
Dji	Djibouti	Kuw	Kuwait
DPRK	North Korea		
DR	Dominican Republic	Lat	Latvia
		Les	Lesotho
Ecu	Ecuador	Lib	Libya
Egy	Egypt	Lie	Liechtenstein
Eng	England	Lit	Lithuania
Est	Estonia	Lux	Luxembourg
Eth	Ethiopia		

Mex	Mexico	SL	Sierra Leone
Mgl	Mongolia	Som	Somalia
Mlt	Malta	Spa	Spain
Mlw	Malawi	Sri	Sri Lanka
Mly	Malaysia	Sud	Sudan
Mon	Monaco	Sur	Surinam
Mor	Morocco	Swa	Swaziland
		Swe	Sweden
NG	New Guinea	Swi	Switzerland
NI	Northern Ireland	Syr	Syria
Nic	Nicaragua		
Nig	Nigeria	Tan	Tanzania
Nld	Netherlands	Tha	Thailand
Nor	Norway	Tog	Togo
NZ	New Zealand	TT	Trinidad & Tobago
		Tun	Tunisia
Pak	Pakistan	Tur	Turkey
Pan	Panama		
Par	Paraguay	UAR	United Arab Emirates
Per	Peru	Uga	Uganda
Phi	Philippines	Uru	Uruguay
PNG	Papua New Guinea	USA	United States of America
Pol	Poland	USSR	Union of Soviet Socialist Republics
Por	Portugal		
PR	Puerto Rico		
		Ven	Venezuela
Rho	Rhodesia	VI	Virgin Islands
RoC	Taiwan		
RoK	South Korea	Wal	Wales
Rom	Romania	WI	West Indies
Rus	Russia		
		Yug	Yugoslavia
St.V	St Vincent		
SA	South Africa	Zai	Zaire
Sco	Scotland	Zam	Zambia
Sen	Senegal	Zim	Zimbabwe
Sin	Singapore		

OLYMPIC VENUES

Summer

1996	Atlanta, USA
1992	Barcelona, Spain
1988	Seoul, South Korea
1984	Los Angeles, USA
1980	Moscow, USSR
1976	Montreal, Canada
1972	Munich, West Germany
1968	Mexico City, Mexico
1964	Tokyo, Japan
1960	Rome, Italy
1956	Melbourne, Australia
1952	Helsinki, Finland
1948	London, England
1936	Berlin, Germany
1932	Los Angeles, USA
1928	Amsterdam, Netherlands
1924	Paris, France
1920	Antwerp, Belgium
1912	Stockholm, Sweden
1908	London, England
1904	St Louis, USA
1900	Paris, France
1896	Athens, Greece

Winter

1998	Nagano, Japan
1994	Lilliehammer, Norway
1992	Albertville, France
1988	Calgary, Canada
1984	Sarajevo, Yugoslavia
1980	Lake Placid, USA
1976	Innsbruck, Austria
1972	Sapporo, Japan
1968	Grenoble, France
1964	Innsbruck, Austria
1960	Squaw Valley, USA
1956	Cortina, Italy
1952	Oslo, Norway
1948	St Moritz, Switzerland
1936	Garmisch-Partenkirchen, Germany
1932	Lake Placid, USA
1928	St Moritz, Switzerland
1924	Chamonix, France

AMERICAN FOOTBALL

SUPERBOWL CHAMPIONS

FIRST HELD 1967

Year	Winner
1991	New York Giants
1990	San Francisco 49ers
1989	San Francisco 49ers
1988	Washington Redskins
1987	New York Giants
1986	Chicago Bears
1985	San Francisco 49ers
1984	Los Angeles Raiders
1983	Washington Redskins
1982	San Francisco 49ers
1981	Oakland Raiders
1980	Pittsburgh Steelers
1979	Pittsburgh Steelers
1978	Dallas Cowboys
1977	Oakland Raiders
1976	Pittsburgh Steelers
1975	Pittsburgh Steelers
1974	Miami Dolphins
1973	Miami Dolphins
1972	Dallas Cowboys
1971	Baltimore Colts
1970	Kansas City Chiefs
1969	New York Jets
1968	Green Bay Packers
1967	Green Bay Packers

NFC CHAMPIONS

FIRST HELD 1970

Year	Winner
1990	New York Giants
1989	San Francisco 49ers
1988	San Francisco 49ers
1987	Washington Redskins

Year	Winner
1986	New York Giants
1985	Chicago Bears
1984	San Francisco 49ers
1983	Washington Redskins
1982	Washington Redskins
1981	San Francisco 49ers
1980	Philadelphia Eagles
1979	Los Angeles Rams
1978	Dallas Cowboys
1977	Dallas Cowboys
1976	Minnesota Vikings
1975	Dallas Cowboys
1974	Minnesota Vikings
1973	Minnesota Vikings
1972	Washington Redskins
1971	Dallas Cowboys
1970	Dallas Cowboys

AFC CHAMPIONS

FIRST HELD 1970

Year	Winner
1990	Buffalo Bills
1989	Denver Broncos
1988	Cincinnati Bengals
1987	Denver Broncos
1986	Denver Broncos
1985	New England Patriots
1984	Miami Dolphins
1983	Los Angeles Raiders
1982	Miami Dolphins
1981	Cincinnati Bengals
1980	Oakland Raiders
1979	Pittsburgh Steelers
1978	Pittsburgh Steelers
1977	Denver Broncos
1976	Oakland Raiders
1975	Pittsburgh Steelers
1974	Pittsburgh Steelers
1973	Miami Dolphins

Year	Winner
1972	Miami Dolphins
1971	Miami Dolphins
1970	Baltimore Colts

NFL CHAMPIONS

FIRST HELD 1921

Year	Winner
1969	Minnesota Vikings
1968	Baltimore Colts
1967	Green Bay Packers
1966	Green Bay Packers
1965	Green Bay Packers
1964	Cleveland Browns
1963	Chicago Bears
1962	Green Bay Packers
1961	Green Bay Packers
1960	Philadelphia Eagles
1959	Baltimore Colts
1958	Baltimore Colts
1957	Detroit Lions
1956	New York Giants
1955	Cleveland Browns
1954	Cleveland Browns
1953	Detroit Lions
1952	Detroit Lions
1951	Los Angeles Rams
1950	Cleveland Browns
1949	Philadelphia Eagles
1948	Philadelphia Eagles
1947	Chicago Cardinals
1946	Chicago Bears
1945	Cleveland Rams
1944	Green Bay Packers
1943	Chicago Bears
1942	Washington Redskins

Year	Winner
1941	Chicago Bears
1940	Chicago Bears
1939	Green Bay Packers
1938	New York Giants
1937	Washington Redskins
1936	Green Bay Packers
1935	Detroit Lions
1934	New York Giants
1933	Chicago Bears
1932	Chicago Bears
1931	Green Bay Packers
1930	Green Bay Packers
1929	Green Bay Packers
1928	Providence Steamroller
1927	New York Giants
1926	Frankford Yellow Jackets
1925	Chicago Cardinals
1924	Cleveland Bulldogs
1923	Canton Bulldogs
1922	Canton Bulldogs
1921	Chicago Staleys

AFL CHAMPIONS

FIRST HELD 1960

Year	Winner
1969	Kansas City Chiefs
1968	New Yorks Jets
1967	Oakland Raiders
1966	Kansas City Chiefs
1965	Buffalo Bills
1964	Buffalo Bills
1963	San Diego Chargers
1962	Dallas Texans
1961	Houston Oilers
1960	Houston Oilers

ARCHERY

WORLD CHAMPIONS

FIRST HELD 1931

Men's Individual

Year	Winner	
1991	S Fairweather	Aus
1989	S Zabrodsky	USSR
1987	V Asheyez	USSR
1985	R McKinney	USA
1983	R McKinney	USA
1981	K Laasonen	Fin
1979	D Pace	USA
1977	R McKinney	USA
1975	D Pace	USA
1973	V Sidoruk	USSR
1971	J Williams	USA
1969	H Ward	USA
1967	R Rogers	USA
1965	M Haikonen	Fin
1963	C Sandlin	USA
1961	J Thornton	USA
1959	J Caspers	USA
1958	S Thysell	Swe
1957	O Smathers	USA
1955	N Andersson	Swe
1953	B Lundgren	Swe
1952	S Andersson	Swe
1950	H Deutgen	Swe
1949	H Deutgen	Swe
1948	H Deutgen	Swe
1947	H Deutgen	Swe
1946	E Tang Holbek	Den
1945/40	No Competition	
1939	R Beday	Fra
1938	F Hadas	Cze
1937	C de Rons	Bel
1936	E Heilborn	Swe
1935	A van Kohlen	Bel
1934	H Kjellson	Swe
1933	D Mackenzie	USA

Year	Winner	
1932	L Reith	Bel
1931	M Sawicki	Pol

Men's Team

Year	Winner
1991	South Korea
1989	USSR
1987	South Korea
1985	South Korea
1983	United States
1981	United States
1979	United States
1977	United States
1975	United States
1973	United States
1971	United States
1969	United States
1967	United States
1965	United States
1963	United States
1961	United States
1959	United States
1958	Finland
1957	United States
1955	Sweden
1953	Sweden
1952	Sweden
1950	Sweden
1949	Czechoslovakia
1948	Sweden
1947	Czechoslovakia
1946	Denmark
1945/40	No Competition
1939	France
1938	Czechoslovakia
1937	Poland
1936	Czechoslovakia
1935	Belgium
1934	Sweden
1933	Belgium

Year	Winner
1932	Poland
1931	France

Women's Individual

Year	Winner	
1991	Kim Soo-Nyung	RoK
1989	Kim Soo-Nyung	RoK
1987	M Xiagjuan	CPR
1987	M Xiagjuan	CPR
1985	I Soldatova	USSR
1983	Jin-Ho Kim	RoK
1981	N Butusova	USSR
1979	Jin-Ho Kim	RoK
1977	L Ryon	USA
1975	Z Rustamova	USSR
1973	L Myers	USA
1971	E Gapchenko	USSR
1969	D Lidstone	Can
1967	M Mazynska	Pol
1965	M Lindholm	Fin
1963	V Cook	USA
1961	N Vonderheide	USA
1959	A Corby	USA
1958	S Johansson	Swe
1957	C Meinhart	USA
1955	K Wisiniowski	Pol
1953	J Richards	USA
1952	J Lee	USA
1950	J Lee	USA
1949	B Waterhouse	GB
1948	P de Wharton Burr	GB
1947	J Kurkowska	Pol
1946	P de Wharton Burr	GB
1945/40	No Competition	
1939	J Kurkowska	Pol
1938	N Martyr	GB
1937	E Simon	GB
1936	J Kurkowska	Pol
1935	I Catani	Swe
1934	J Kurkowska	Pol
1933	J Kurkowska	Pol
1932	J Kurkowska	Pol
1931	J Kurkowska	Pol

Women's Team

FIRST HELD 1933

Year	Winner
1991	South Korea
1989	South Korea
1987	USSR
1985	USSR
1983	South Korea
1981	USSR
1979	South Korea
1977	United States
1975	USSR
1973	USSR
1971	Poland
1969	USSR
1967	Poland
1965	United States
1963	United States
1961	United States
1959	United States
1958	United States
1957	United States
1955	Great Britain
1953	Finland
1952	United States
1950	Finland
1949	United States
1948	Finland
1947	Great Britain
1946	Czechoslovakia
1945/40	No Competition
1939	Poland
1938	Poland
1937	Great Britain
1936	Poland
1935	Great Britain
1934	Poland
1933	Poland

OLYMPIC CHAMPIONS

Men's Individual

FIRST HELD 1972

Year	Winner	
1988	J Barrs	USA
1984	D Pace	USA
1980	T Poikolainen	Fin
1976	D Pace	USA
1972	J Williams	USA

Men's Team

FIRST HELD 1988

Year	Winner
1988	South Korea

Women's Individual

FIRST HELD 1972

Year	Winner	
1988	Kim Soo-Nyung	RoK
1984	Hyang-Soon Seo	RoK
1980	K Losaberidze	USSR
1976	L Ryon	USA
1972	D Wilber	USA

Women's Team

FIRST HELD 1988

Year	Winner
1988	South Korea

ASSOCIATION FOOTBALL

WORLD CUP

FIRST HELD 1930

Year	Winner
1990	West Germany
1986	Argentina
1982	Italy
1978	Argentina
1974	West Germany
1970	Brazil
1966	England
1962	Brazil
1958	Brazil
1954	West Germany
1950	Uruguay
1938	Italy
1934	Italy
1930	Uruguay

EUROPEAN CHAMPIONS

FIRST HELD 1960

Year	Winner
1988	Netherlands
1984	France
1980	West Germany
1976	Czechoslovakia
1972	West Germany

Year	Winner
1968	Italy
1964	Spain
1960	USSR

EUROPEAN CUP

FIRST HELD 1956

Year	Winner	
1991	Red Star Belgrade	Yug
1990	AC Milan	Ita
1989	AC Milan	Ita
1988	PSV Eindhoven	Nld
1987	FC Porto	Por
1986	Steaua Bucharest	Rom
1985	Juventus	Ita
1984	Liverpool	Eng
1983	SV Hamburg	FRG
1982	Aston Villa	Eng
1981	Liverpool	Eng
1980	Nottingham Forest	Eng
1979	Nottingham Forest	Eng
1978	Liverpool	Eng
1977	Liverpool	Eng
1976	Bayern Munich	FRG
1975	Bayern Munich	FRG
1974	Bayern Munich	FRG
1973	Ajax	Nld
1972	Ajax	Nld
1971	Ajax	Nld
1970	Feyenoord	Nld
1969	AC Milan	Ita
1968	Manchester United	Eng
1967	Celtic	Sco
1966	Real Madrid	Spa
1965	Inter Milan	Ita
1964	Inter Milan	Ita
1963	AC Milan	Ita
1962	Benfica	Por
1961	Benfica	Por
1960	Real Madrid	Spa
1959	Real Madrid	Spa
1958	Real Madrid	Spa
1957	Real Madrid	Spa
1956	Real Madrid	Spa

EUROPEAN CUP WINNERS' CUP

FIRST HELD 1961

Year	Winner	
1991	Manchester United	Eng
1990	Sampdoria	Ita
1989	Barcelona	Spa
1988	Mechelen	Bel
1987	Ajax	Nld
1986	Dynamo Kiev	USSR
1985	Everton	Eng
1984	Juventus	Ita
1983	Aberdeen	Sco
1982	Barcelona	Spa
1981	Dynamo Tbilisi	USSR
1980	Valencia	Spa
1979	Barcelona	Spa
1978	Anderlecht	Bel
1977	SV Hamburg	FRG
1976	Anderlecht	Bel
1975	Dynamo Kiev	USSR
1974	FC Magdeburg	GDR
1973	AC Milan	Ita
1972	Rangers	Sco
1971	Chelsea	Eng
1970	Manchester City	Eng
1969	Slovan Bratislava	Cze
1968	AC Milan	Ita
1967	Bayern Munich	FRG
1966	Borussia Dortmund	FRG
1965	West Ham United	Eng
1964	Sporting Lisbon	Por
1963	Tottenham Hotspur	Eng
1962	Atletico Madrid	Spa
1961	Fiorentina	Ita

UEFA CUP

FIRST HELD 1958

Year	Winner	
1991	Inter Milan	Ita
1990	Juventus	Ita
1989	Napoli	Ita

Year	Winner	
1988	Bayer Leverkusen	FRG
1987	IFK Gothenburg	Swe
1986	Real Madrid	Spa
1985	Real Madrid	Spa
1984	Tottenham Hotspur	Eng
1983	Anderlecht	Bel
1982	IFK Gothenburg	Swe
1981	Ipswich Town	Eng
1980	Eintracht Frankfurt	FRG
1979	Borussia Moen-chengladbach	FRG
1978	PSV Eindhoven	Nld
1977	Juventus	Ita
1976	Liverpool	Eng
1975	Borussia Moen-chengladbach	FRG
1974	Feyenoord	Nld
1973	Liverpool	Eng
1972	Tottenham Hotspur	Eng
1971	Leeds United	Eng
1970	Arsenal	Eng
1969	Newcastle United	Eng
1968	Leeds United	Eng
1967	Dynamo Zagreb	Yug
1966	Barcelona	Spa
1965	Ferencvaros	Hun
1964	Real Zaragoza	Spa
1963	Valencia	Spa
1962	Valencia	Spa
1961	AS Roma	Ita
1960	Barcelona	Spa
1958	Barcelona	Spa

ENGLISH LEAGUE CHAMPIONS

1st Division

FIRST HELD 1888/89

Year	Winner
1990/91	Arsenal
1989/90	Liverpool
1988/89	Arsenal
1987/88	Liverpool

Year	Winner
1986/87	Everton
1985/86	Liverpool
1984/85	Everton
1983/84	Liverpool
1982/83	Liverpool
1981/82	Liverpool
1980/81	Aston Villa
1979/80	Liverpool
1978/79	Liverpool
1977/78	Nottingham Forest
1976/77	Liverpool
1975/76	Liverpool
1974/75	Derby County
1973/74	Leeds United
1972/73	Liverpool
1971/72	Derby County
1970/71	Arsenal
1969/70	Everton
1968/69	Leeds United
1967/68	Manchester City
1966/67	Manchester United
1965/66	Liverpool
1964/65	Manchester United
1963/64	Liverpool
1962/63	Everton
1961/62	Ipswich Town
1960/61	Tottenham Hotspur
1959/60	Burnley
1958/59	Wolverhampton Wanderers
1957/58	Wolverhampton Wanderers
1956/57	Manchester United
1955/56	Manchester United
1954/55	Chelsea
1953/54	Wolverhampton Wanderers
1952/53	Arsenal
1951/52	Manchester United
1950/51	Tottenham Hotspur
1949/50	Portsmouth
1948/49	Portsmouth
1947/48	Arsenal
1946/47	Liverpool
1946/39	No Competition
1938/39	Everton

Year	Winner
1937/38	Arsenal
1936/37	Manchester City
1935/36	Sunderland
1934/35	Arsenal
1933/34	Arsenal
1932/33	Arsenal
1931/32	Everton
1930/31	Arsenal
1929/30	Sheffield Wednesday
1928/29	Sheffield Wednesday
1927/28	Everton
1926/27	Newcastle United
1925/26	Huddersfield Town
1924/25	Huddersfield Town
1923/24	Huddersfield Town
1922/23	Liverpool
1921/22	Liverpool
1920/21	Burnley
1919/20	West Bromwich Albion
1919/15	No Competition
1914/15	Everton
1913/14	Blackburn Rovers
1912/13	Sunderland
1911/12	Blackburn Rovers
1910/11	Manchester United
1909/10	Aston Villa
1908/09	Newcastle United
1907/08	Manchester United
1906/07	Newcastle United
1905/06	Liverpool
1904/05	Newcastle United
1903/04	Sheffield Wednesday
1902/03	Sheffield Wednesday
1901/02	Sunderland
1900/01	Liverpool
1899/00	Aston Villa
1898/99	Aston Villa
1897/98	Sheffield United
1896/97	Aston Villa
1895/96	Aston Villa
1894/95	Sunderland
1893/94	Aston Villa
1892/93	Sunderland
1891/92	Sunderland
1890/91	Everton
1889/90	Preston North End

Year	Winner
1888/89	Preston North End

2nd Division

FIRST HELD 1892/93

Year	Winner
1990/91	Oldham Athletic
1989/90	Leeds United
1988/89	Chelsea
1987/88	Millwall
1986/87	Derby County
1985/86	Norwich City
1984/85	Oxford United
1983/84	Chelsea
1982/83	Queens Park Rangers
1981/82	Luton Town
1980/81	West Ham United
1979/80	Leicester City
1978/79	Crystal Palace
1977/78	Bolton Wanderers
1976/77	Wolverhampton Wanderers
1975/76	Sunderland
1974/75	Manchester United
1973/74	Middlesbrough
1972/73	Burnley
1971/72	Norwich City
1970/71	Leicester City
1969/70	Huddersfield Town
1968/69	Derby County
1967/68	Ipswich Town
1966/67	Coventry City
1965/66	Manchester City
1964/65	Newcastle United
1963/64	Leeds United
1962/63	Stoke City
1961/62	Liverpool
1960/61	Ipswich Town
1959/60	Aston Villa
1958/59	Sheffield Wednesday
1957/58	West Ham United
1956/57	Leicester City
1955/56	Sheffield Wednesday
1954/55	Birmingham City

Year	Winner
1953/54	Leicester City
1952/53	Sheffield United
1951/52	Sheffield Wednesday
1950/51	Preston North End
1949/50	Tottenham Hotspur
1948/49	Fulham
1947/48	Birmingham City
1946/47	Manchester City
1946/39	No Competition
1938/39	Blackburn Rovers
1937/38	Aston Villa
1936/37	Leicester City
1935/36	Manchester United
1934/35	Brentford
1933/34	Grimsby Town
1932/33	Stoke City
1931/32	Wolverhampton Wanderers
1930/31	Everton
1929/30	Blackpool
1928/29	Middlesbrough
1927/28	Manchester City
1926/27	Middlesbrough
1925/26	Sheffield Wednesday
1924/25	Leicester City
1923/24	Leeds United
1922/23	Notts County
1921/22	Nottingham Forest
1920/21	Birmingham
1919/20	Tottenham Hotspur
1919/15	No Competition
1914/15	Derby County
1913/14	Notts County
1912/13	Preston North East
1911/12	Derby County
1910/11	West Bromwich Albion
1909/10	Manchester City
1908/09	Bolton Wanderers
1907/08	Bradford City
1906/07	Nottingham Forest
1905/06	Bristol City
1904/05	Liverpool
1903/04	Preston North End
1902/03	Manchester City
1901/02	West Bromwich Albion
1900/01	Grimsby Town

Year	Winner
1899/00	Sheffield Wednesday
1898/99	Manchester City
1897/98	Burnley
1896/97	Notts County
1895/96	Liverpool
1894/95	Bury
1893/94	Liverpool
1892/93	Small Heath

3rd Division

FIRST HELD 1958/59

Year	Winner
1990/91	Cambridge United
1989/90	Bristol Rovers
1988/89	Wolverhampton Wanderers
1987/88	Sunderland
1986/87	Bournemouth
1985/86	Reading
1984/85	Bradford City
1983/84	Oxford United
1982/83	Portsmouth
1981/82	Burnley
1980/81	Rotherham United
1979/80	Grimsby Town
1978/79	Shrewsbury Town
1977/78	Wrexham
1976/77	Mansfield Town
1975/76	Hereford United
1974/75	Blackburn Rovers
1973/74	Oldham Athletic
1972/73	Bolton Wanderers
1971/72	Aston Villa
1970/71	Preston North End
1969/70	Orient
1968/69	Watford
1967/68	Oxford United
1966/67	Queens Park Rangers
1965/66	Hull City
1964/65	Carlisle United
1963/64	Coventry City
1962/63	Northampton Town
1961/62	Portsmouth

Year	Winner
1960/61	Bury
1959/60	Southampton
1958/59	Plymouth Argyle

4th Division

FIRST HELD 1958/59

Year	Winner
1990/91	Darlington
1989/90	Exeter City
1988/89	Rotherham United
1987/88	Wolverhampton Wanderers
1986/87	Northampton Town
1985/86	Swindon Town
1984/85	Chesterfield
1983/84	York City
1982/83	Wimbledon
1981/82	Sheffield United
1980/81	Southend United
1979/80	Huddersfield Town
1978/79	Reading
1977/78	Watford
1976/77	Cambridge United
1975/76	Lincoln City
1974/75	Mansfield Town
1973/74	Peterborough United
1972/73	Southport
1971/72	Grimsby Town
1970/71	Notts County
1969/70	Chesterfield
1968/69	Doncaster Rovers
1967/68	Luton Town
1966/67	Stockport County
1965/66	Doncaster Rovers
1964/65	Brighton
1963/64	Gillingham
1962/63	Brentford
1961/62	Millwall
1960/61	Peterborough United
1959/60	Walsall
1958/59	Port Vale

3rd Division – North

FIRST HELD 1921/22

Year	Winner
1957/58	Scunthorpe United
1956/57	Derby County
1955/56	Grimsby Town
1954/55	Barnsley
1953/54	Port Vale
1952/53	Oldham Athletic
1951/52	Lincoln City
1950/51	Rotherham United
1949/50	Doncaster Rovers
1948/49	Hull City
1947/48	Lincoln City
1946/47	Doncaster Rovers
1946/39	No Competition
1938/39	Barnsley
1937/38	Tranmere Rovers
1936/37	Stockport County
1935/36	Chesterfield
1934/35	Doncaster Rovers
1933/34	Barnsley
1932/33	Hull City
1931/32	Lincoln City
1930/31	Chesterfield
1929/30	Port Vale
1928/29	Bradford City
1927/28	Bradford Park Avenue
1926/27	Stoke City
1925/26	Grimsby Town
1924/25	Darlington
1923/24	Wolverhampton Wanderers
1922/23	Nelson
1921/22	Stockport County

3rd Division – South

FIRST HELD 1920/21

Year	Winner
1957/58	Brighton
1956/57	Ipswich Town
1955/56	Leyton Orient
1954/55	Bristol City

Year	Winner	Year	Winner
1953/54	Ipswich Town	1980	West Ham United
1952/53	Bristol Rovers	1979	Arsenal
1951/52	Plymouth Argyle	1978	Ipswich Town
1950/51	Nottingham Forest	1977	Manchester United
1949/50	Notts County	1976	Southampton
1948/49	Swansea Town	1975	West Ham United
1947/48	Queens Park Rangers	1974	Liverpool
1946/47	Cardiff City	1973	Sunderland
1946/39	No Competition	1972	Leeds United
1938/39	Newport County	1971	Arsenal
1937/38	Millwall	1970	Chelsea
1936/37	Luton Town	1969	Manchester City
1935/36	Coventry City	1968	West Bromwich Albion
1934/35	Charlton Athletic	1967	Tottenham Hotspur
1933/34	Norwich City	1966	Everton
1932/33	Brentford	1965	Liverpool
1931/32	Fulham	1964	West Ham United
1930/31	Notts County	1963	Manchester United
1929/30	Plymouth Argyle	1962	Tottenham Hotspur
1928/29	Charlton Athletic	1961	Tottenham Hotspur
1927/28	Millwall	1960	Wolverhampton Wanderers
1926/27	Bristol City	1959	Nottingham Forest
1925/26	Reading	1958	Bolton Wanderers
1924/25	Swansea Town	1957	Aston Villa
1923/24	Portsmouth	1956	Manchester City
1922/23	Bristol City	1955	Newcastle United
1921/22	Southampton	1954	West Bromwich Albion
1920/21	Crystal Palace	1953	Blackpool
		1952	Newcastle United

FA CUP

FIRST HELD 1872

Year	Winner	Year	Winner
		1951	Newcastle United
		1950	Arsenal
		1949	Wolverhampton Wanderers
1991	Tottenham Hotspur	1948	Manchester United
1990	Manchester United	1947	Charlton Athletic
1989	Liverpool	1946	Derby County
1988	Wimbledon	1945/40	No Competition
1987	Coventry City	1939	Portsmouth
1986	Liverpool	1938	Preston North End
1985	Manchester United	1937	Sunderland
1984	Everton	1936	Arsenal
1983	Manchester United	1935	Sheffield Wednesday
1982	Tottenham Hotspur	1934	Manchester City
1981	Tottenham Hotspur	1933	Everton
		1932	Newcastle United

Year	Winner
1931	West Bromwich Albion
1930	Arsenal
1929	Bolton Wanderers
1928	Blackburn Rovers
1927	Cardiff City
1926	Bolton Wanderers
1925	Sheffield United
1924	Newcastle United
1923	Bolton Wanderers
1922	Huddersfield Town
1921	Tottenham Hotspur
1920	Aston Villa
1919/16	No Competition
1915	Sheffield United
1914	Burnley
1913	Aston Villa
1912	Barnsley
1911	Bradford City
1910	Newcastle United
1909	Manchester United
1908	Wolverhampton Wanderers
1907	Sheffield Wednesday
1906	Everton
1905	Aston Villa
1904	Manchester City
1903	Bury
1902	Sheffield United
1901	Tottenham Hotspur
1900	Bury
1899	Sheffield United
1898	Nottingham Forest
1897	Aston Villa
1896	Sheffield Wednesday
1895	Aston Villa
1894	Notts County
1893	Wolverhampton Wanderers
1892	West Bromwich Albion
1891	Blackburn Rovers
1890	Blackburn Rovers
1889	Preston North End
1888	West Bromwich Albion
1887	Aston Villa
1886	Blackburn Rovers
1885	Blackburn Rovers

Year	Winner
1884	Blackburn Rovers
1883	Blackburn Olympic
1882	Old Etonians
1881	Old Carthusians
1880	Clapham Rovers
1879	Old Etonians
1878	Wanderers
1877	Wanderers
1876	Wanderers
1875	Royal Engineers
1874	Oxford University
1873	Wanderers
1872	Wanderers

LEAGUE CUP

FIRST HELD 1961

Year	Winner
1991	Sheffield Wednesday
1990	Nottingham Forest
1989	Nottingham Forest
1988	Luton Town
1987	Arsenal
1986	Oxford United
1985	Norwich City
1984	Liverpool
1983	Liverpool
1982	Liverpool
1981	Liverpool
1980	Wolverhampton Wanderers
1979	Nottingham Forest
1978	Nottingham Forest
1977	Aston Villa
1976	Manchester City
1975	Aston Villa
1974	Wolverhampton Wanderers
1973	Tottenham Hotspur
1972	Stoke City
1971	Tottenham Hotspur
1970	Manchester City
1969	Swindon Town
1968	Leeds United
1967	Queen's Park Rangers
1966	West Bromwich Albion

Year	Winner
1965	Chelsea
1964	Leicester City
1963	Birmingham City
1962	Norwich City
1961	Aston Villa

SCOTTISH LEAGUE CHAMPIONS

Premier Division

FIRST HELD 1975/76

Year	Winner
1990/91	Rangers
1989/90	Rangers
1988/89	Rangers
1987/88	Celtic
1986/87	Rangers
1985/86	Celtic
1984/85	Aberdeen
1983/84	Aberdeen
1982/83	Dundee United
1981/82	Celtic
1980/81	Celtic
1979/80	Aberdeen
1978/79	Celtic
1977/78	Rangers
1976/77	Celtic
1975/76	Rangers

1st Division

FIRST HELD 1890/91

Year	Winner
1974/75	Rangers
1973/74	Celtic
1972/73	Celtic
1971/72	Celtic
1970/71	Celtic
1969/70	Celtic
1968/69	Celtic
1967/68	Celtic

Year	Winner
1966/67	Celtic
1965/66	Celtic
1964/65	Kilmarnock
1963/64	Rangers
1962/63	Rangers
1961/62	Dundee
1960/61	Rangers
1959/60	Hearts
1958/59	Rangers
1957/58	Hearts
1956/57	Rangers
1955/56	Rangers
1954/55	Aberdeen
1953/54	Celtic
1952/53	Rangers
1951/52	Hibernian
1950/51	Hibernian
1949/50	Rangers
1948/49	Rangers
1947/48	Hibernian
1946/47	Rangers
1946/39	No Competition
1938/39	Rangers
1937/38	Celtic
1936/37	Rangers
1935/36	Celtic
1934/35	Rangers
1933/34	Rangers
1932/33	Rangers
1931/32	Motherwell
1930/31	Rangers
1929/30	Rangers
1928/29	Rangers
1927/28	Rangers
1926/27	Rangers
1925/26	Celtic
1924/25	Rangers
1923/24	Rangers
1922/23	Rangers
1921/22	Celtic
1920/21	Rangers
1919/20	Rangers
1918/19	Celtic
1917/18	Rangers
1916/17	Celtic
1915/16	Celtic

Year	Winner	Year	Winner
1914/15	Celtic	1977	Celtic
1913/14	Celtic	1976	Rangers
1912/13	Rangers	1975	Celtic
1911/12	Rangers	1974	Celtic
1910/11	Rangers	1973	Rangers
1909/10	Celtic	1972	Celtic
1908/09	Celtic	1971	Celtic
1907/08	Celtic	1970	Aberdeen
1906/07	Celtic	1969	Celtic
1905/06	Celtic	1968	Dunfermline Athletic
1904/05	Celtic	1967	Celtic
1903/04	Third Lanark	1966	Rangers
1902/03	Hibernian	1965	Celtic
1901/02	Rangers	1964	Rangers
1900/01	Rangers	1963	Rangers
1899/00	Rangers	1962	Rangers
1898/99	Rangers	1961	Dunfermline Athletic
1897/98	Celtic	1960	Rangers
1896/97	Hearts	1959	St Mirren
1895/96	Celtic	1958	Clyde
1894/95	Hearts	1957	Falkirk
1893/94	Celtic	1956	Hearts
1892/93	Celtic	1955	Clyde
1891/92	Dumbarton	1954	Celtic
1890/91	Dumbarton Rangers	1953	Rangers
		1952	Motherwell
		1951	Celtic
		1950	Rangers
		1949	Rangers
		1948	Rangers
		1947	Aberdeen
		1946/40	No Competition
		1939	Clyde
		1938	East Fife
		1937	Celtic
		1936	Rangers
		1935	Rangers
		1934	Rangers
		1933	Celtic
		1932	Rangers
		1931	Celtic
		1930	Rangers
		1929	Kilmarnock
		1928	Rangers
		1927	Celtic
		1926	St Mirren

SCOTTISH FA CUP

FIRST HELD 1874

Year	Winner
1991	Motherwell
1990	Aberdeen
1989	Celtic
1988	Celtic
1987	St Mirren
1986	Aberdeen
1985	Celtic
1984	Aberdeen
1983	Aberdeen
1982	Aberdeen
1981	Rangers
1980	Celtic
1979	Rangers
1978	Rangers

Year	Winner	Year	Winner
1925	Celtic	1875	Queen's Park
1924	Airdrieonians	1874	Queen's Park
1923	Celtic		
1922	Morton		
1921	Partick Thistle		
1920	Kilmarnock		
1919/15	No Competition		
1914	Celtic		
1913	Falkirk		
1912	Celtic		
1911	Celtic		
1910	Dundee		
1909	Cup withheld		
1908	Celtic		
1907	Celtic		
1906	Hearts		
1905	Third Lanark		
1904	Celtic		
1903	Rangers		
1902	Hibernian		
1901	Hearts		
1900	Celtic		
1899	Celtic		
1898	Rangers		
1897	Rangers		
1896	Hearts		
1895	St Bernard's		
1894	Rangers		
1893	Queen's Park		
1892	Celtic		
1891	Hearts		
1890	Queen's Park		
1889	Third Lanark		
1888	Renton		
1887	Hibernian		
1886	Queen's Park		
1885	Renton		
1884	Queen's Park		
1883	Dumbarton		
1882	Queen's Park		
1881	Queen's Park		
1880	Queen's Park		
1879	Vale of Leven		
1878	Vale of Leven		
1877	Vale of Leven		
1876	Queen's Park		

SCOTTISH LEAGUE CUP

FIRST HELD 1946/47

Year	Winner
1990/91	Rangers
1989/90	Aberdeen
1988/89	Rangers
1987/88	Rangers
1986/87	Rangers
1985/86	Aberdeen
1984/85	Rangers
1983/84	Rangers
1982/83	Celtic
1981/82	Rangers
1980/81	Dundee United
1979/80	Dundee United
1978/79	Rangers
1977/78	Rangers
1976/77	Aberdeen
1975/76	Rangers
1974/75	Celtic
1973/74	Dundee
1972/73	Hibernian
1971/72	Partick Thistle
1970/71	Rangers
1969/70	Celtic
1968/69	Celtic
1967/68	Celtic
1966/67	Celtic
1965/66	Celtic
1964/65	Rangers
1963/64	Rangers
1962/63	Hearts
1961/62	Rangers
1960/61	Rangers
1959/60	Hearts
1958/59	Hearts
1957/58	Celtic
1956/57	Celtic

Year	Winner
1955/56	Aberdeen
1954/55	Hearts
1953/54	East Fife
1952/53	Dundee
1951/52	Dundee
1950/51	Motherwell
1949/50	East Fife
1948/49	Rangers
1947/48	East Fife
1946/47	Rangers

SOUTH AMERICAN CHAMPIONS

FIRST HELD 1916

Year	Winner
1991	Argentina
1989	Brazil
1987	Uruguay
1983	Uruguay
1979	Paraguay
1975	Peru
1967	Uruguay
1963	Bolivia
1959	Argentina
1959	Uruguay
1957	Argentina
1956	Uruguay
1955	Argentina
1953	Paraguay
1949	Brazil
1947	Argentina
1946	Argentina
1945	Argentina
1942	Uruguay
1941	Argentina
1939	Peru
1937	Argentina
1935	Uruguay
1929	Argentina
1927	Argentina
1926	Uruguay
1925	Argentina
1924	Uruguay

Year	Winner
1923	Uruguay
1922	Brazil
1921	Argentina
1920	Uruguay
1919	Brazil
1917	Uruguay
1916	Uruguay

SOUTH AMERICAN CUP
Copa Libertadores

FIRST HELD 1960

Year	Winner	
1991	Colo Colo	Chi
1990	Olimpia	Par
1989	Nacional	Col
1988	Nacional	Uru
1987	Penarol	Uru
1986	River Plate	Arg
1985	Argentinos Juniors	Arg
1984	Independiente	Arg
1983	Gremio	Bra
1982	Penarol	Uru
1981	Flamengo	Bra
1980	Nacional	Uru
1979	Olimpia	Par
1978	Boca Juniors	Arg
1977	Boca Juniors	Arg
1976	Cruzeiro	Bra
1975	Independiente	Arg
1974	Independiente	Arg
1973	Independiente	Arg
1972	Independiente	Arg
1971	Nacional	Uru
1970	Estudiantes	Arg
1969	Estudiantes	Arg
1968	Estudiantes	Arg
1967	Racing Club	Arg
1966	Penarol	Uru
1965	Independiente	Arg
1964	Independiente	Arg
1963	Santos	Bra

Year	Winner	
1962	Santos	Bra
1961	Penarol	Uru
1960	Penarol	Uru

OLYMPIC CHAMPIONS

FIRST HELD 1908

Year	Winner
1988	USSR
1984	France
1980	Czechoslovakia

Year	Winner
1976	East Germany
1972	Poland
1968	Hungary
1964	Hungary
1960	Yugoslavia
1956	USSR
1952	Hungary
1948	Sweden
1936	Italy
1932	No Tournament
1928	Uruguay
1924	Uruguay
1920	Belgium
1912	England
1908	Great Britain

ATHLETICS

OLYMPIC CHAMPIONS
100 Metres

FIRST HELD 1896

Year	Winner	
1988	C Lewis	USA
1984	C Lewis	USA
1980	A Wells	GB
1976	H Crawford	TT
1972	V Borzov	USSR
1968	J Hines	USA
1964	R Hayes	USA
1960	A Hary	Ger
1956	B Morrow	USA
1952	L Remigino	USA
1948	H Dillard	USA
1936	J Owens	USA
1932	E Tolan	USA
1928	P Williams	Can

Year	Winner	
1924	H Abrahams	GB
1920	C Paddock	USA
1912	R Craig	USA
1908	R Walker	SA
1904	A Hahn	USA
1900	F Jarvis	USA
1896	T Burke	USA

200 Metres

FIRST HELD 1900

Year	Winner	
1988	J DeLoach	USA
1984	C Lewis	USA
1980	P Mennea	Ita
1976	D Quarrie	Jam
1972	V Borzov	USSR
1968	T Smith	USA

Year	Winner	
1964	H Carr	USA
1960	L Berutti	Ita
1956	B Morrow	USA
1952	A Stanfield	USA
1948	M Patton	USA
1936	J Owens	USA
1932	E Tolan	USA
1928	P Williams	Can
1924	J Scholz	USA
1920	A Woodring	USA
1912	R Craig	USA
1908	R Kerr	Can
1904	A Hahn	USA
1900	W Tewksbury	USA

400 Metres

FIRST HELD 1896

Year	Winner	
1988	S Lewis	USA
1984	A Babers	USA
1980	V Markin	USSR
1976	A Juantorena	Cub
1972	V Matthews	USA
1968	L Evans	USA
1964	M Larrabee	USA
1960	O Davis	USA
1956	C Jenkins	USA
1952	G Rhoden	Jam
1948	A Wint	Jam
1936	A Williams	USA
1932	W Carr	USA
1928	R Barbuti	USA
1924	E Liddell	GB
1920	B Rudd	SA
1912	C Reidpath	USA
1908	W Halswelle	GB
1904	H Hillman	USA
1900	M Long	USA
1896	T Burke	USA

800 Metres

FIRST HELD 1896

Year	Winner	
1988	P Ereng	Ken
1984	J Cruz	Bra
1980	S Ovett	GB
1976	A Juantorena	Cub
1972	D Wottle	USA
1968	R Doubell	Aus
1964	P Snell	NZ
1960	P Snell	NZ
1956	T Courtney	USA
1952	M Whitfield	USA
1948	M Whitfield	USA
1936	J Woodruff	USA
1932	T Hampson	GB
1928	D Lowe	GB
1924	D Lowe	GB
1920	A Hill	GB
1912	J Meredith	USA
1908	M Sheppard	USA
1904	J Lightbody	USA
1900	A Tysoe	GB
1896	E Flack	Aus

1500 Metres

FIRST HELD 1896

Year	Winner	
1988	P Rono	Ken
1984	S Coe	GB
1980	S Coe	GB
1976	J Walker	NZ
1972	P Vasala	Fin
1968	K Keino	Ken
1964	P Snell	NZ
1960	H Elliott	Aus
1956	R Delany	Ire
1952	J Barthel	Lux
1948	H Eriksson	Swe
1936	J Lovelock	NZ
1932	L Beccali	Ita
1928	H Larva	Fin
1924	P Nurmi	Fin

Year	Winner	
1920	A Hill	GB
1912	A Jackson	GB
1908	M Sheppard	USA
1904	J Lightbody	USA
1900	C Bennett	GB
1896	E Flack	Aus

5000 Metres

FIRST HELD 1912

Year	Winner	
1988	J Ngugi	Ken
1984	S Aouita	Mor
1980	M Yifter	Eth
1976	L Viren	Fin
1972	L Viren	Fin
1968	M Gammoudi	Tun
1964	R Schul	USA
1960	M Halberg	NZ
1956	V Kuts	USSR
1952	E Zatopek	Cze
1948	G Reiff	Bel
1936	G Hockert	Fin
1932	L Lehtinen	Fin
1928	V Ritola	Fin
1924	P Nurmi	Fin
1920	J Guillemot	Fra
1912	H Kolehmainen	Fin

10,000 Metres

FIRST HELD 1908

Year	Winner	
1988	M B Boutaieb	Mor
1984	A Cova	Ita
1980	M Yifter	Eth
1976	L Viren	Fin
1972	L Viren	Fin
1968	N Temu	Ken
1964	W Mills	USA
1960	P Bolotnikov	USSR
1956	V Kuts	USSR

Year	Winner	
1952	E Zatopek	Cze
1948	E Zatopek	Cze
1936	I Salminen	Fin
1932	J Kusocinski	Pol
1928	P Nurmi	Fin
1924	V Ritola	Fin
1920	P Nurmi	Fin
1912	H Kolehmainen	Fin
1908	E Voight	GB

Marathon

FIRST HELD 1896

Year	Winner	
1988	G Bordin	Ita
1984	C Lopes	Por
1980	W Ceirpinski	GDR
1976	W Ceirpinski	GDR
1972	F Shorter	USA
1968	M Wolde	Eth
1964	A Bikila	Eth
1960	A Bikila	Eth
1956	A Mimoun	Fra
1952	E Zatopek	Cze
1948	D Cabrera	Arg
1936	K Son	Jap
1932	J Zabala	Arg
1928	M El Ouafi	Fra
1924	A Stenroos	Fin
1920	H Kolehmainen	Fin
1912	K McArthur	SA
1908	J Hayes	USA
1904	T Hicks	USA
1900	M Theato	Fra
1896	S Louis	Gre

110 Metres Hurdles

FIRST HELD 1896

Year	Winner	
1988	R Kingdom	USA
1984	R Kingdom	USA

Year	Winner	
1980	T Munkelt	GDR
1976	G Drut	Fra
1972	R Milburn	USA
1968	W Davenport	USA
1964	H Jones	USA
1960	L Calhoun	USA
1956	L Calhoun	USA
1952	H Dillard	USA
1948	W Porter	USA
1936	F Towns	USA
1932	G Saling	USA
1928	S Atkinson	SA
1924	D Kinsey	USA
1920	E Thomson	Can
1912	F Kelly	USA
1908	F Smithson	USA
1904	F Schule	USA
1900	A Kraenzlein	USA
1896	T Curtis	USA

400 Metres Hurdles

FIRST HELD 1900

Year	Winner	
1988	A Phillips	USA
1984	E Moses	USA
1980	V Beck	GDR
1976	E Moses	USA
1972	J Akii-Bua	Uga
1968	D Hemery	GB
1964	W Cawley	USA
1960	G Davis	USA
1956	G Davis	USA
1952	C Moore	USA
1948	R Cochran	USA
1936	G Hardin	USA
1932	R Tisdall	Ire
1928	Lord Burghley	GB
1924	F Taylor	USA
1920	F Loomis	USA
1912	Not held	
1908	C Bacon	USA
1904	H Hillman	USA
1900	W Tewksbury	USA

3000 Metres Steeplechase

FIRST HELD 1900

Year	Winner	
1988	J Kariuki	Ken
1984	J Korir	Ken
1980	B Malinowski	Pol
1976	A Garderud	Swe
1972	K Keino	Ken
1968	A Biwott	Ken
1964	G Roelants	Bel
1960	Z Krzyszkowiak	Pol
1956	C Brasher	GB
1952	H Ashenfelter	USA
1948	T Sjostrand	Swe
1936	V Iso-Holle	Fin
1932	V Iso-Holle	Fin
1928	T Loukola	Fin
1924	V Ritola	Fin
1920	P Hodge	GB
1912	Not held	
1908	A Russell	GB
1904	J Lightbody	USA
1900	J Rimmer	GB
1900	G Orton	Can

4 x 100 Metres Relay

FIRST HELD 1912

Year	Winner
1988	USSR
1984	United States
1980	USSR
1976	United States
1972	United States
1968	United States
1964	United States
1960	Germany
1956	United States
1952	United States
1948	United States
1936	United States
1932	United States
1928	United States
1924	United States

Year	Winner
1920	United States
1912	Great Britain

4 x 400 Metres Relay

FIRST HELD 1908

Year	Winner
1988	United States
1984	United States
1980	USSR
1976	United States
1972	Kenya
1968	United States
1964	United States
1960	United States
1956	United States
1952	Jamaica
1948	United States
1936	Great Britain
1932	United States
1928	United States
1924	United States
1920	Great Britain
1912	United States
1908	United States

20 km Walk

FIRST HELD 1956

Year	Winner	
1988	J Pribilinec	Cze
1984	E Canto	Mex
1980	M Damilano	Ita
1976	D Bautista	Mex
1972	P Frenkel	GDR
1968	V Golubnichiy	USSR
1964	K Matthews	GB
1960	V Golubnichiy	USSR
1956	L Spirin	USSR

50 km Walk

FIRST HELD 1932

Year	Winner	
1988	V Ivanenko	USSR
1984	R Gonzalez	Mex
1980	H Gauder	GDR
1976	Not held	
1972	B Kannenberg	FRG
1968	C Hohne	GDR
1964	A Pamich	Ita
1960	D Thompson	GB
1956	N Read	NZ
1952	G Dordoni	Ita
1948	J Ljunggren	Swe
1936	H Whitlock	GB
1932	T Green	GB

High Jump

FIRST HELD 1896

Year	Winner	
1988	G Avdeyenko	USSR
1984	D Mogenburg	FRG
1980	G Wessig	GDR
1976	J Wszola	Pol
1972	Y Tarmak	USSR
1968	D Fosbury	USA
1964	V Brumel	USSR
1960	R Shavlakadze	USSR
1956	C Dumas	USA
1952	W Davis	USA
1948	J Winter	Aus
1936	C Johnson	USA
1932	D McNaughton	Can
1928	R King	USA
1924	H Osborn	USA
1920	R Landon	USA
1912	A Richards	USA
1908	H Porter	USA
1904	S Jones	USA
1900	I Baxter	USA
1896	E Clark	USA

Long Jump

FIRST HELD 1896

Year	Winner	
1988	C Lewis	USA
1984	C Lewis	USA
1980	L Dombrowski	GDR
1976	A Robinson	USA
1972	R Williams	USA
1968	R Beamon	USA
1964	L Davies	GB
1960	R Boston	USA
1956	G Bell	USA
1952	J Biffle	USA
1948	W Steele	USA
1936	J Owens	USA
1932	E Gordon	USA
1928	E Hamm	USA
1924	W D Hubbard	USA
1920	W Pettersson	Swe
1912	A Gutterson	USA
1908	F Irons	USA
1904	M Prinstein	USA
1900	A Kraenzlein	USA
1896	E Clark	USA

Triple Jump

FIRST HELD 1896

Year	Winner	
1988	H Markov	Bul
1984	A Joyner	USA
1980	J Uudmae	USSR
1976	V Saneyev	USSR
1972	V Saneyev	USSR
1968	V Saneyev	USSR
1964	J Schmidt	Pol
1960	J Schmidt	Pol
1956	A Ferreira da Silva	Bra
1952	A Ferreira da Silva	Bra
1948	A Ahman	Swe
1936	N Tajima	Jap
1932	C Nambu	Jap
1928	M Oda	Jap
1924	A Winter	Aus

Year	Winner	
1920	V Tuulos	Fin
1912	G Lindblom	Swe
1908	T Ahearne	GB
1904	M Prinstein	USA
1900	M Prinstein	USA
1896	J Connolly	USA

Pole Vault

FIRST HELD 1896

Year	Winner	
1988	S Bubka	USSR
1984	P Quinon	Fra
1980	W Kozakiewicz	Pol
1976	T Slusarski	Pol
1972	W Nordwig	GDR
1968	R Seagren	USA
1964	F Hansen	USA
1960	D Bragg	USA
1956	R Richards	USA
1952	R Richards	USA
1948	G Smith	USA
1936	E Meadows	USA
1932	W Miller	USA
1928	S Carr	USA
1924	L Barnes	USA
1920	F Foss	USA
1912	H Babcock	USA
1908	E Cooke	USA
	A Gilbert	USA
1904	C Dvorak	USA
1900	I Baxter	USA
1896	W Hoyt	USA

Shot

FIRST HELD 1896

Year	Winner	
1988	U Timmermann	GDR
1984	A Andrei	Ita
1980	V Kiselyev	USSR
1976	U Beyer	GDR

Year	Winner	
1972	W Komar	Pol
1968	R Matson	USA
1964	D Long	USA
1960	W Nieder	USA
1956	P O'Brien	USA
1952	P O'Brien	USA
1948	W Thompson	USA
1936	H Woellke	Ger
1932	L Sexton	USA
1928	J Kuck	USA
1924	C Houser	USA
1920	V Porhola	Fin
1912	P McDonald	USA
1908	R Rose	USA
1904	R Rose	USA
1900	R Sheldon	USA
1896	R Garrett	USA

Discus

FIRST HELD 1896

Year	Winner	
1988	J Schult	GDR
1984	R Danneberg	FRG
1980	V Rashchupkin	USSR
1976	M Wilkins	USA
1972	L Danek	Cze
1968	A Oerter	USA
1964	A Oerter	USA
1960	A Oerter	USA
1956	A Oerter	USA
1952	S Iness	USA
1948	A Consolini	Ita
1936	K Carpenter	USA
1932	J Anderson	USA
1928	C Houser	USA
1924	C Houser	USA
1920	E Niklander	Fin
1912	A Taipale	Fin
1908	M Sheridan	USA
1904	M Sheridan	USA
1900	R Bauer	Hun
1896	R Garrett	USA

Hammer

FIRST HELD 1900

Year	Winner	
1988	S Litvinov	USSR
1984	J Tiainen	Fin
1980	Y Sedykh	USSR
1976	Y Sedykh	USSR
1972	A Bondarchuk	USSR
1968	G Zsivotzky	Hun
1964	R Klim	USSR
1960	V Rudenkov	USSR
1956	H Connolly	USA
1952	J Csermak	Hun
1948	I Nemeth	Hun
1936	K Hein	Ger
1932	P O'Callaghan	Ire
1928	P O'Callaghan	Ire
1924	F Tootell	USA
1920	P Ryan	USA
1912	M McGrath	USA
1908	J Flanagan	USA
1904	J Flanagan	USA
1900	J Flanagan	USA

Javelin

FIRST HELD 1908

Year	Winner	
1988	T Korjus	Fin
1984	A Harkonen	Fin
1980	D Kula	USSR
1976	M Nemeth	Hun
1972	K Wolfermann	FRG
1968	J Lusis	USSR
1964	P Nevala	Fin
1960	V Tsibulenko	USSR
1956	E Danielsen	Nor
1952	C Young	USA
1948	T Rautavaara	Fin
1936	G Stock	Ger
1932	M Jarvinen	Fin
1928	E Lundkvist	Swe
1924	J Myyra	Fin
1920	J Myyra	Fin

Year	Winner	
1912	E Lemming	Swe
1908	E Lemming	Swe

Decathlon

FIRST HELD 1904

Year	Winner	
1988	C Schenk	GDR
1984	D Thompson	GB
1980	D Thompson	GB
1976	B Jenner	USA
1972	N Avilov	USSR
1968	W Toomey	USA
1964	W Holdorf	Ger
1960	R Johnson	USA
1956	M Campbell	USA
1952	R Mathias	USA
1948	R Mathias	USA
1936	G Morris	USA
1932	J Bausch	USA
1928	P Yrjola	Fin
1924	H Osborn	USA
1920	H Lovland	Nor
1912	H Weislander	Swe
1908	Not held	
1904	T Kiely	Ire

Women's 100 Metres

FIRST HELD 1928

Year	Winner	
1988	F Griffith-Joyner	USA
1984	E Ashford	USA
1980	L Kondratyeva	USSR
1976	A Richter	FRG
1972	R Stecher	GDR
1968	W Tyus	USA
1964	W Tyus	USA
1960	W Rudolph	USA
1956	B Cuthbert	Aus
1952	M Jackson	Aus
1948	F Blankers-Koen	Nld

Year	Winner	
1936	H Stephens	USA
1932	S Walasiewicz	Pol
1928	E Robinson	USA

Women's 200 Metres

FIRST HELD 1948

Year	Winner	
1988	F Griffith-Joyner	USA
1984	V Brisco-Hooks	USA
1980	B Wockel	GDR
1976	B Eckert	GDR
1972	R Stecher	GDR
1968	I Szewinska	Pol
1964	E Maguire	USA
1960	W Rudolph	USA
1956	B Cuthbert	Aus
1952	M Jackson	Aus
1948	F Blankers-Koen	Nld

Women's 400 Metres

FIRST HELD 1964

Year	Winner	
1988	O Bryzgina	USSR
1984	V Brisco-Hooks	USA
1980	M Koch	GDR
1976	I Szewinska	Pol
1972	M Zehrt	GDR
1968	C Besson	Fra
1964	B Cuthbert	Aus

Women's 800 Metres

FIRST HELD 1928

Year	Winner	
1988	S Wodars	GDR
1984	D Melinte	Rom
1980	N Olizarenko	USSR
1976	T Kazankina	USSR

Year	Winner	
1972	H Falck	FRG
1968	M Manning	USA
1964	A Packer	GB
1960	L Shevtsova	USSR
1956/32	Not held	
1928	L Radke	Ger

Women's 1500 Metres

FIRST HELD 1972

Year	Winner	
1988	P Ivan	Rom
1984	G Dorio	Ita
1980	T Kazankina	USSR
1976	T Kazankina	USSR
1972	L Bragina	USSR

Women's 3000 Metres

FIRST HELD 1984

Year	Winner	
1988	T Samolenko	USSR
1984	M Puica	Rom

Women's 10,000 Metres

FIRST HELD 1988

Year	Winner	
1988	O Bondarenko	USSR

Women's Marathon

FIRST HELD 1984

Year	Winner	
1988	R Mota	Por
1984	J Benoit	USA

Women's 100 Metres Hurdles

FIRST HELD 1972

Year	Winner	
1988	J Donkova	Bul
1984	B Fitzgerald-Brown	USA
1980	V Komisova	USSR
1976	J Schaller	GDR
1972	A Ehrhardt	GDR

Women's 80 Metres Hurdles

FIRST HELD 1932

Year	Winner	
1968	M Caird	Aus
1964	K Balzer	Ger
1960	I Press	USSR
1956	S Strickland	Aus
1952	S Strickland	Aus
1948	F Blankers-Koen	Nld
1936	T Valla	Ita
1932	M Didrikson	USA

Women's 400 Metres Hurdles

FIRST HELD 1984

Year	Winner	
1988	D Flintoff-King	Aus
1984	N El Moutawakel	Mor

Women's 4 x 100 Metres Relay

FIRST HELD 1928

Year	Winner
1988	United States
1984	United States
1980	East Germany
1976	East Germany
1972	West Germany

Year	Winner
1968	United States
1964	Poland
1960	United States
1956	Australia
1952	United States
1948	Netherlands
1936	United States
1932	United States
1928	Canada

Women's 4 x 400 Metres Relay

FIRST HELD 1972

Year	Winner
1988	USSR
1984	United States
1980	USSR
1976	East Germany
1972	East Germany

Women's High Jump

FIRST HELD 1928

Year	Winner	
1988	L Ritter	USA
1984	U Meyfarth	FRG
1980	S Simeoni	Ita
1976	R Ackermann	GDR
1972	U Meyfarth	FRG
1968	M Rezkova	Cze
1964	I Balas	Rom
1960	I Balas	Rom
1956	M McDaniel	USA
1952	E Brand	SA
1948	A Coachman	USA
1936	I Csak	Hun
1932	J Shiley	USA
1928	E Catherwood	Can

Women's Long Jump

FIRST HELD 1948

Year	Winner	
1988	J Joyner-Kersee	USA
1984	A Stanciu	Rom
1980	T Kolpakova	USSR
1976	A Voigt	GDR
1972	H Rosendahl	FRG
1968	V Viscopoleanu	Rom
1964	M Rand	GB
1960	V Krepkina	USSR
1956	E Krzesinska	Pol
1952	Y Williams	NZ
1948	O Gyarmati	Hun

Women's Shot

FIRST HELD 1948

Year	Winner	
1988	N Lisovskaya	USSR
1984	C Losch	FRG
1980	I Slupianek	GDR
1976	I Khristova	Bul
1972	N Chizhova	USSR
1968	M Gummel	GDR
1964	T Press	USSR
1960	T Press	USSR
1956	T Tyshkyevich	USSR
1952	G Zybina	USSR
1948	M Ostermeyer	Fra

Women's Discus

FIRST HELD 1928

Year	Winner	
1988	M Hellman	GDR
1984	R Stalman	Nld
1980	E Jahl	GDR
1976	E Schlaak	GDR
1972	F Melnik	USSR
1968	L Manoliu	Rom
1964	T Press	USSR

Year	Winner	
1960	N Ponomaryeva	USSR
1956	O Fikotova	Cze
1952	N Romashkova	USSR
1948	M Ostermeyer	Fra
1936	G Mauermayer	Ger
1932	L Copeland	USA
1928	H Konopacka	Pol

Women's Javelin

FIRST HELD 1932

Year	Winner	
1988	P Felke	GDR
1984	T Sanderson	GB
1980	M Colon	Cub
1976	R Fuchs	GDR
1972	R Fuchs	GDR
1968	A Nemeth	Hun
1964	M Penes	Rom
1960	E Ozolina	USSR
1956	I Jaunzeme	USSR
1952	D Zatopkova	Cze
1948	H Bauma	Aut
1936	T Fleischer	Ger
1932	M Didrikson	USA

Women's Heptathlon

FIRST HELD 1984

Year	Winner	
1988	J Joyner-Kersee	USA
1984	G Nunn	Aus

Women's Pentathlon

FIRST HELD 1964

Year	Winner	
1980	N Tkachenko	USSR
1976	S Siegl	GDR
1972	M Peters	GB
1968	I Becker	FRG
1964	I Press	USSR

WORLD CHAMPIONS

FIRST HELD 1983

100 Metres

Year	Winner	
1991	C Lewis	USA
1987	B Johnson	Can
1983	C Lewis	USA

200 Metres

Year	Winner	
1991	M Johnson	USA
1987	C Smith	USA
1983	C Smith	USA

400 Metres

Year	Winner	
1991	A Pettigrew	USA
1987	T Schoenlebe	GDR
1983	B Cameron	Jam

800 Metres

Year	Winner	
1991	B Konchellah	Ken
1987	B Konchellah	Ken
1983	W Wullbeck	FRG

1500 Metres

Year	Winner	
1991	N Morceli	Alg
1987	A Bile	Som
1983	S Cram	GB

5000 Metres

Year	Winner	
1991	Y Ondieki	Ken
1987	S Aouita	Mor
1983	E Coghlan	Ire

10,000 Metres

Year	Winner	
1991	M Tanui	Ken
1987	P Kipkoech	Ken
1983	A Cova	Ita

Marathon

Year	Winner	
1991	H Taniguchi	Jap
1987	D Wakiihuri	Ken
1983	R de Castella	Aus

110 Metres Hurdles

Year	Winner	
1991	G Foster	USA
1987	G Foster	USA
1983	G Foster	USA

400 Metres Hurdles

Year	Winner	
1991	S Matete	Zam
1987	E Moses	USA
1983	E Moses	USA

3000 Metres Steeplechase

Year	Winner	
1991	M Kiptanui	Ken
1987	F Panetta	Ita
1983	P Ilg	FRG

4 x 100 Metres Relay

Year	Winner
1991	United States
1987	United States
1983	United States

4 x 400 Metres Relay

Year	Winner
1991	Great Britain
1987	United States
1983	USSR

20 km Walk

Year	Winner	
1991	M Damilano	Ita
1987	M Damilano	Ita
1983	E Canto	Mex

50 km Walk

Year	Winner	
1991	A Potashov	USSR
1987	H Gauder	GDR
1983	R Weigel	GDR

High Jump

Year	Winner	
1991	C Austin	USA
1987	P Sjoberg	Swe
1983	G Avdeyenko	USSR

Long Jump

Year	Winner	
1991	M Powell	USA
1987	C Lewis	USA
1983	C Lewis	USA

Triple Jump

Year	Winner	
1991	K Harrison	USA
1987	H Markov	Bul
1983	Z Hoffmann	Pol

Pole Vault

Year	Winner	
1991	S Bubka	USSR
1987	S Bubka	USSR
1983	S Bubka	USSR

Shot

Year	Winner	
1991	W Günthör	Swi
1987	W Günthör	Swi
1983	E Sarul	Pol

Discus

Year	Winner	
1991	L Riedel	Ger
1987	J Schult	GDR
1983	I Bugar	Cze

Hammer

Year	Winner	
1991	Y Sedykh	USSR
1987	S Litvinov	USSR
1983	S Litvinov	USSR

Javelin

Year	Winner	
1991	K Kinnunen	Fin
1987	S Raty	Fin
1983	D Michel	GDR

Decathlon

Year	Winner	
1991	D O'Brien	USA
1987	T Voss	GDR
1983	D Thompson	GB

Women's 100 Metres

Year	Winner	
1991	K Krabbe	Ger
1987	S Gladisch	GDR
1983	M Gohr	GDR

Women's 200 Metres

Year	Winner	
1991	K Krabbe	Ger
1987	S Gladisch	GDR
1983	M Koch	GDR

Women's 400 Metres

Year	Winner	
1991	M-J Perec	Fra
1987	O Bryzgina	USSR
1983	J Kratochvilova	Cze

Women's 800 Metres

Year	Winner	
1991	L Nurutdinova	USSR
1987	S Wodars	GDR
1983	J Kratochvilova	Cze

Women's 1500 Metres

Year	Winner	
1991	H Boulmerka	Alg
1987	T Samolenko	USSR
1983	M Decker	USA

Women's 3000 Metres

Year	Winner	
1991	T Samolenko	USSR
1987	T Samolenko	USSR
1983	M Decker	USA

Women's 10,000 Metres

Year	Winner	
1991	L McColgan	GB
1987	I Kristiansen	Nor
1983	Not held	

Women's Marathon

Year	Winner	
1991	W Panfil	Pol
1987	R Mota	Por
1983	G Waitz	Nor

Women's 100 Metres Hurdles

Year	Winner	
1991	L Narozhilenko	USSR
1987	G Zagorcheva	Bul
1983	B Jahn	GDR

Women's 400 Metres Hurdles

Year	Winner	
1991	T Ledovskaya	USSR
1987	S Busche	GDR
1983	E Fesenko	USSR

Women's 4 x 100 Metres Relay

Year	Winner
1991	Jamaica
1987	United States
1983	East Germany

Women's 4 x 400 Metres Relay

Year	Winner
1991	USSR
1987	East Germany
1983	East Germany

Women's 10 km Walk

Year	Winner	
1991	A Ivanova	USSR
1987	I Strakhova	USSR
1983	Not held	

Women's High Jump

Year	Winner	
1991	H Henkel	Ger
1987	S Kostadinova	Bul
1983	T Bykova	USSR

Women's Long Jump

Year	Winner	
1991	J Joyner-Kersee	USA
1987	J Joyner-Kersee	USA
1983	H Daute	GDR

Women's Shot

Year	Winner	
1991	H Zhihong	CPR
1987	N Lisovskaya	USSR
1983	H Fibingerova	Cze

Women's Discus

Year	Winner	
1991	T Christova	Bul
1987	M Hellman	GDR
1983	M Opitz	GDR

Women's Javelin

Year	Winner	
1991	X Demei	CPR
1987	F Whitbread	GB
1983	T Lillak	Fin

Women's Heptathlon

Year	Winner	
1991	F Braun	Ger
1987	J Joyner-Kersee	USA
1983	R Neubert	GDR

WORLD CUP CHAMPIONS

FIRST HELD 1977

Men

Year	Winner
1989	United States
1985	United States
1981	Europe
1979	United States
1977	East Germany

Women

Year	Winner
1989	East Germany
1985	East Germany
1981	East Germany
1979	East Germany
1977	Europe

EUROPEAN CUP CHAMPIONS

FIRST HELD 1965

Men

Year	Winner
1991	USSR
1989	Great Britain

Year	Winner
1987	USSR
1985	USSR
1983	East Germany
1981	East Germany
1979	East Germany
1977	East Germany
1975	East Germany
1973	USSR
1970	East Germany
1967	USSR
1965	USSR

Women

Year	Winner
1991	Germany
1989	East Germany
1987	East Germany
1985	USSR
1983	East Germany
1981	East Germany
1979	East Germany
1977	East Germany
1975	East Germany
1973	East Germany
1970	East Germany
1967	USSR
1965	USSR

BOSTON MARATHON

FIRST HELD 1897

Year	Winner	
1991	I Hussein	Ken
1990	G Bordin	Ita
1989	A Mekonnen	Eth
1988	I Hussein	Ken
1987	T Seko	Jap
1986	R de Castella	Aus
1985	G Smith	GB
1984	G Smith	GB
1983	G Meyer	USA

Year	Winner		Year	Winner	
1982	A Salazar	USA	1936	E Brown	USA
1981	T Seko	Jap	1935	J A Kelley	USA
1980	B Rodgers	USA	1934	D Komonen	Can
1979	B Rodgers	USA	1933	L Pawson	USA
1978	B Rodgers	USA	1932	P de Bruyn	Ger
1977	J Drayton	Can	1931	J Henigan	USA
1976	J Fultz	USA	1930	C DeMar	USA
1975	B Rodgers	USA	1929	J Miles	Can
1974	N Cusack	Ire	1928	C DeMar	USA
1973	J Anderson	USA	1927	C DeMar	USA
1972	O Suomalainen	Fin	1926	J Miles	Can
1971	A Mejia	Col	1925	C Mellor	USA
1970	R Hill	GB	1924	C DeMar	USA
1969	Y Unetani	Jap	1923	C DeMar	USA
1968	A Burfoot	USA	1922	C DeMar	USA
1967	D McKenzie	NZ	1921	F Zuna	USA
1966	K Kimihara	Jap	1920	P Trivoulidas	Gre
1965	M Shigematsu	Jap	1919	C Linder	USA
1964	A Vandendriessche	Bel	1918	Not held	
1963	A Vandendriessche	Bel	1917	B Kennedy	USA
1962	E Oksanen	Fin	1916	A Roth	USA
1961	E Oksanen	Fin	1915	E Fabre	Can
1960	P Kotila	Fin	1914	J Duffy	Can
1959	E Oksanen	Fin	1913	F Carlson	USA
1958	F Mihalic	Yug	1912	M Ryan	USA
1957	J J Kelley	USA	1911	C DeMar	USA
1956	A Viskari	Fin	1910	F Cameron	Can
1955	H Hamamura	Jap	1909	H Renaud	USA
1954	V Karvonen	Fin	1908	T Morrissey	USA
1953	K Yamada	Jap	1907	T Longboat	Can
1952	D Flores	Gua	1906	T Ford	USA
1951	S Tanaka	Jap	1905	F Lorz	USA
1950	K Yong Ham	RoK	1904	M Spring	USA
1949	G Leandersson	Swe	1903	J Lorden	USA
1948	G Cote	Can	1902	S Mellor	USA
1947	Y Bok Suh	RoK	1901	J Caffrey	Can
1946	S Kyriakidis	Gre	1900	J Caffrey	Can
1945	J A Kelley	USA	1899	L Brignolia	USA
1944	G Cote	Can	1898	R McDonald	USA
1943	G Cote	Can	1897	J McDermott	USA
1942	J Smith	USA			
1941	L Pawson	USA			
1940	G Cote	Can			
1939	E Brown	USA			
1938	L Pawson	USA			
1937	W Young	Can			

Women

FIRST HELD 1972

Year	Winner	
1991	W Panfil	Pol
1990	R Mota	Por
1989	I Kristiansen	Nor
1988	R Mota	Por
1987	R Mota	Por
1986	I Kristiansen	Nor
1985	L Weidenbach	USA
1984	L Moller	NZ
1983	J Benoit	USA
1982	C Teske	FRG
1981	A Roe	NZ
1980	J Gareau	Can
1979	J Benoit	USA
1978	G Barron	USA
1977	M Gorman	USA
1976	K Merritt	USA
1975	L Winter	FRG
1974	M Gorman	USA
1973	J Hansen	USA
1972	N Kuscsik	USA

NEW YORK MARATHON

FIRST HELD 1970

Year	Winner	
1990	D Wakiihuri	Ken
1989	J Ikangaa	Tan
1988	S Jones	GB
1987	I Hussein	Ken
1986	G Poli	Ita
1985	O Pizzolato	Ita
1984	O Pizzolato	Ita
1983	R Dixon	NZ
1982	A Salazar	USA
1981	A Salazar	USA
1980	A Salazar	USA
1979	B Rodgers	USA
1978	B Rodgers	USA
1977	B Rodgers	USA

Year	Winner	
1976	B Rodgers	USA
1975	T Fleming	USA
1974	N Sander	USA
1973	T Fleming	USA
1972	S Karlin	USA
1971	N Higgins	USA
1970	G Muhrcke	USA

Women

FIRST HELD 1971

Year	Winner	
1990	W Panfil	Pol
1989	I Kristiansen	Nor
1988	G Waitz	Nor
1987	P Welch	GB
1986	G Waitz	Nor
1985	G Waitz	Nor
1984	G Waitz	Nor
1983	G Waitz	Nor
1982	G Waitz	Nor
1981	A Roe	NZ
1980	G Waitz	Nor
1979	G Waitz	Nor
1978	G Waitz	Nor
1977	M Gorman	USA
1976	M Gorman	USA
1975	K Merritt	USA
1974	K Switzer	USA
1973	N Kuscsik	USA
1972	N Kuscsik	USA
1971	B Bonner	USA

LONDON MARATHON

FIRST HELD 1981

Year	Winner	
1991	I Tolstikov	USSR
1990	A Hutton	Sco
1989	D Wakiihuri	Ken

Year	Winner	
1988	H Jorgensen	Den
1987	H Taniguchi	Jap
1986	T Seko	Jap
1985	S Jones	GB
1984	C Spedding	GB
1983	M Gratton	GB
1982	H Jones	GB
1981	D Beardsley	USA
	I Simonsen	Nor

Women

Year	Winner	
1991	R Mota	Por
1990	W Panfil	Pol
1989	V Marot	GB
1988	I Kristiansen	Nor
1987	I Kristiansen	Nor
1986	G Waitz	Nor
1985	I Kristiansen	Nor
1984	I Kristiansen	Nor
1983	G Waitz	Nor
1982	J Smith	GB
1981	J Smith	GB

WORLD CROSS COUNTRY CHAMPIONS

FIRST HELD 1903

Men's Individual

Year	Winner	
1991	K Skah	Mor
1990	K Skah	Mor
1989	J Ngugi	Ken
1988	J Ngugi	Ken
1987	J Ngugi	Ken
1986	J Ngugi	Ken
1985	C Lopes	Por
1984	C Lopes	Por

Year	Winner	
1983	B Debele	Eth
1982	M Kedir	Eth
1981	C Virgin	USA
1980	C Virgin	USA
1979	J Treacy	Ire
1978	J Treacy	Ire
1977	L Schots	Bel
1976	C Lopes	Por
1975	I Stewart	Sco
1974	E De Beck	Bel
1973	P Paivarinta	Fin
1972	G Roelants	Bel
1971	D Bedford	Eng
1970	M Tagg	Eng
1969	G Roelants	Bel
1968	M Gammoudi	Tun
1967	G Roelants	Bel
1966	B A El Ghazi	Mor
1965	J Fayolle	Fra
1964	F Arizmendi	Spa
1963	R Fowler	Eng
1962	G Roelants	Bel
1961	B Heatley	Eng
1960	R ben Abdesselem	Mor
1959	F Norris	Eng
1958	S Eldon	Eng
1957	F Sando	Eng
1956	A Mimoun	Fra
1955	F Sando	Eng
1954	A Mimoun	Fra
1953	F Mihalic	Yug
1952	A Mimoun	Fra
1951	G Saunders	Eng
1950	L Theys	Bel
1949	A Mimoun	Fra
1948	J Doms	Bel
1947	R Pujazon	Fra
1946	R Pujazon	Fra
1945/40	No Competition	
1939	J Holden	Eng
1938	J Emery	Eng
1937	J Flockhart	Sco
1936	W Eaton	Eng
1935	J Holden	Eng
1934	J Holden	Eng
1933	J Holden	Eng

Year	Winner	
1932	T Evenson	Eng
1931	T Smythe	Ire
1930	T Evenson	Eng
1929	W Cotterell	Eng
1928	H Eckersley	Eng
1927	L Payne	Eng
1926	E Harper	Eng
1925	J Webster	Eng
1924	W Cotterell	Eng
1923	C Blewitt	Eng
1922	J Guillemot	Fra
1921	W Freeman	Eng
1920	J Wilson	Sco
1919/15	No Competition	
1914	A Nicholls	Eng
1913	J Bouin	Fra
1912	J Bouin	Fra
1911	J Bouin	Fra
1910	E Wood	Eng
1909	E Wood	Eng
1908	A Robertson	Eng
1907	A Underwood	Eng
1906	C Straw	Eng
1905	A Aldridge	Eng
1904	A Shrubb	Eng
1903	A Shrubb	Eng

Men's Team

Year	Winner
1991	Kenya
1990	Kenya
1989	Kenya
1988	Kenya
1987	Kenya
1986	Kenya
1985	Ethiopia
1984	Ethiopia
1983	Ethiopia
1982	Ethiopia
1981	Ethiopia
1980	England
1979	England
1978	France
1977	Belgium

Year	Winner
1976	England
1975	New Zealand
1974	Belgium
1973	Belgium
1972	England
1971	England
1970	England
1969	England
1968	England
1967	England
1966	England
1965	England
1964	England
1963	Belgium
1962	England
1961	Belgium
1960	England
1959	England
1958	England
1957	Belgium
1956	France
1955	England
1954	England
1953	England
1952	France
1951	England
1950	France
1949	France
1948	Belgium
1947	France
1946	France
1945/40	No Competition
1939	France
1938	England
1937	England
1936	England
1935	England
1934	England
1933	England
1932	England
1931	England
1930	England
1929	France
1928	France
1927	France
1926	France

Year	Winner	
1925	England	
1924	England	
1923	France	
1922	France	
1921	England	
1920	England	
1919/15	No Competition	
1914	England	
1913	England	
1912	England	
1911	England	
1910	England	
1909	England	
1908	England	
1907	England	
1906	England	
1905	England	
1904	England	
1903	England	

Year	Winner	
1976	C Valero	Spa
1975	J Brown	USA
1974	P Cacchi	Ita
1973	P Cacchi	Ita
1972	J Smith	Eng
1971	D Brown	USA
1970	D Brown	USA
1969	D Brown	USA
1968	D Brown	USA
1967	D Brown	USA

Women's Team

Year	Winner
1991	Ethiopia
	Kenya
1990	USSR
1989	USSR
1988	USSR
1987	United States
1986	England
1985	United States
1984	United States
1983	United States
1982	USSR
1981	USSR
1980	USSR
1979	United States
1978	Romania
1977	USSR
1976	USSR
1975	United States
1974	England
1973	England
1972	England
1971	England
1970	England
1969	United States
1968	United States
1967	England

FIRST HELD 1967
Women's Individual

Year	Winner	
1991	L Jennings	USA
1990	L Jennings	USA
1989	A Sergent	Fra
1988	I Kristiansen	Nor
1987	A Sergent	Fra
1986	Z Budd	Eng
1985	Z Budd	Eng
1984	M Puica	Rom
1983	G Waitz	Nor
1982	M Puica	Rom
1981	G Waitz	Nor
1980	G Waitz	Nor
1979	G Waitz	Nor
1978	G Waitz	Nor
1977	C Valero	Spa

AUSTRALIAN RULES FOOTBALL

VICTORIA FOOTBALL LEAGUE CHAMPIONS

Grand Final

FIRST HELD 1897

Year	Winner	Year	Winner
		1959	Melbourne
1990	Collingwood	1958	Collingwood
1989	Hawthorn	1957	Melbourne
1988	Hawthorn	1956	Melbourne
1987	Carlton	1955	Melbourne
1986	Hawthorn	1954	Footscray
1985	Essendon	1953	Collingwood
1984	Essendon	1952	Geelong
1983	Hawthorn	1951	Geelong
1982	Carlton	1950	Essendon
1981	Carlton	1949	Essendon
1980	Richmond	1948	Melbourne
1979	Carlton	1947	Carlton
1978	Hawthorn	1946	Essendon
1977	North Melbourne	1945	Carlton
1976	Hawthorn	1944	Fitzroy
1975	North Melbourne	1943	Richmond
1974	Richmond	1942	Essendon
1973	Richmond	1941	Melbourne
1972	Carlton	1940	Melbourne
1971	Hawthorn	1939	Melbourne
1970	Carlton	1938	Carlton
1969	Richmond	1937	Geelong
1968	Carlton	1936	Collingwood
1967	Richmond	1935	Collingwood
1966	St Kilda	1934	Richmond
1965	Essendon	1933	South Melbourne
1964	Melbourne	1932	Richmond
1963	Geelong	1931	Geelong
1962	Essendon	1930	Collingwood
1961	Hawthorn	1929	Collingwood
1960	Melbourne	1928	Collingwood
		1927	Collingwood
		1926	Melbourne
		1925	Geelong
		1924	Essendon
		1923	Essendon
		1922	Fitzroy
		1921	Richmond
		1920	Richmond
		1919	Collingwood

Year	Winner	Year	Winner
1918	South Melbourne	1907	Carlton
1917	Collingwood	1906	Carlton
1916	Fitzroy	1905	Fitzroy
1915	Carlton	1904	Fitzroy
1914	Carlton	1903	Collingwood
1913	Fitzroy	1902	Collingwood
1912	Essendon	1901	Essendon
1911	Essendon	1900	Melbourne
1910	Collingwood	1899	Fitzroy
1909	South Melbourne	1898	Fitzroy
1908	Carlton	1897	Essendon

BADMINTON

WORLD CHAMPIONS

FIRST HELD 1977

Men's Singles

Year	Winner	
1991	Z Jianhua	CPR
1989	Y Yang	CPR
1987	Y Yang	CPR
1985	H Jian	CPR
1983	I Sugiarto	Indo
1980	R Hartono	Indo
1977	F Delfs	Den

Men's Doubles

Year	Winner	
1991	P Joo Bong & K Moon Soo	RoK
1989	T Bingyi & L Yongbo	CPR
1987	T Bingyi & L Yongbo	CPR
1985	P Joo Bong & K Moon Soo	RoK

Year	Winner	
1983	S Fladberg & J Helledie	Den
1980	A Chandra & H Christian	Indo
1977	T Tjun & J Wahjudi	Indo

Women's Singles

Year	Winner	
1991	T Jiuhong	CPR
1989	L Lingwei	CPR
1987	H Aiping	CPR
1985	H Aiping	CPR
1983	L Lingwei	CPR
1980	W Verawaty	Indo
1977	L Koppen	Den

Women's Doubles

Year	Winner	
1991	G Weizhan & N Qunhua	CPR
1989	G Weizhan & L Ying	CPR

Year	Winner	
1987	G Weizhan & L Ying	CPR
1985	H Aiping & L Lingwei	CPR
1983	W Dixi & L Ying	CPR
1980	N Perry & J Webster	GB
1977	E Tuganoo & E Vero	Jap

Mixed Doubles

Year	Winner	
1991	P Joo Bong & C Myung Hee	RoK
1989	P Joo Bong & G Myung Hee	RoK
1987	W Pengrin & S Fangjing	CPR
1985	P Joo Bong & Y Sang Hee	RoK
1983	T Kihlstrom (Swe) & N Perry (GB)	
1980	H Christian & I Wigoeno	Indo
1977	S Stovgaard & L Koppen	Den

ALL-ENGLAND CHAMPIONS

Men's Singles

FIRST HELD 1900

Year	Winner	
1991	A Wiranata	Indo
1990	Z Jianhua	CPR
1989	Y Yang	CPR
1988	I Frederickson	Den
1987	M Frost	Den
1986	M Frost	Den
1985	Z Jianhua	CPR
1984	M Frost	Den
1983	L Jin	CPR
1982	M Frost	Den
1981	L Swie King	Indo
1980	P Padukone	Indo

Year	Winner	
1979	L Swie King	Indo
1978	L Swie King	Indo
1977	F Delfs	Den
1976	R Hartono	Indo
1975	S Pri	Den
1974	R Hartono	Indo
1973	R Hartono	Indo
1972	R Hartono	Indo
1971	R Hartono	Indo
1970	R Hartono	Indo
1969	R Hartono	Indo
1968	R Hartono	Indo
1967	E Kops	Den
1966	T Aik Huang	Mly
1965	E Kops	Den
1964	K Nielsen	Den
1963	E Kops	Den
1962	E Kops	Den
1961	E Kops	Den
1960	E Kops	Den
1959	T Joe Hok	Indo
1958	E Kops	Den
1957	E Choong	Mly
1956	E Choong	Mly
1955	W Peng Soon	Mly
1954	E Choong	Mly
1953	E Choong	Mly
1952	W Peng Soon	Mly
1951	W Peng Soon	Mly
1950	W Peng Soon	Mly
1949	D Freeman	USA
1948	J Skaarup	Den
1947	C Jepsen	Swe
1946/40	No Competition	
1939	T Madsen	Den
1938	R Nichols	GB
1937	R Nichols	GB
1936	R Nichols	GB
1935	R White	GB
1934	R Nichols	GB
1933	R White	GB
1932	R Nichols	GB
1931	F Devlin	Ire
1930	D Hume	GB
1929	F Devlin	Ire
1928	F Devlin	Ire

Year	Winner		Year	Winner	
1927	F Devlin	Ire	1983	S Karlsson &	
1926	F Devlin	Ire		T Kihlstrom	Swe
1925	F Devlin	Ire	1982	R Sidek & J Sidek	Mly
1924	C Mack	Ire	1981	H Kartono &	
1923	G Thomas	GB		R Heryanto	Indo
1922	G Thomas	GB	1980	T Tjun & J Wahjudi	Indo
1921	G Thomas	GB	1979	T Tjun & J Wahjudi	Indo
1920	G Thomas	GB	1978	T Tjun & J Wahjudi	Indo
1919/15	No Competition		1977	T Tjun & J Wahjudi	Indo
1914	G Sautter	GB	1976	B Froman &	
1913	G Sautter	GB		T Kihlstrom	Swe
1912	F Chesterton	GB	1975	T Tjun & J Wahjudi	Indo
1911	G Sautter	GB	1974	T Tjun & J Wahjudi	Indo
1910	F Chesterton	GB	1973	H Christian &	
1909	F Chesterton	GB		A Chandra	Indo
1908	H Marrett	GB	1972	H Christian &	
1907	N Wood	GB		A Chandra	Indo
1906	N Wood	GB	1971	N Boon Bee &	
1905	H Marrett	GB		P Gunalan	Mly
1904	H Marrett	GB	1970	T Bacher &	
1903	R Watling	GB		P Petersen	Den
1902	R Watling	GB	1969	E Kops & H Borch	Den
1901	H Davies	GB	1968	E Kops & H Borch	Den
1900	S Smith	GB	1967	E Kops & H Borch	Den
			1966	N Boon Bee &	
				T Yee Khan	Mly

Men's Doubles

FIRST HELD 1899

Year	Winner		Year	Winner	
1991	L Yongbo &		1965	N Boon Bee &	
	T Bingyi	CPR		T Yee Khan	Mly
1990	K Moon Soo &		1964	F Kobbero &	
	P Joo Bong	RoK		J H Hansen	Den
1989	L Sang Bok &		1963	F Kobbero &	
	P Joo Bong	RoK		J H Hansen	Den
1988	L Yongbo &		1962	F Kobbero &	
	T Bingyi	CPR		J H Hansen	Den
1987	L Yongbo &		1961	F Kobbero &	
	T Bingyi	CPR		J H Hansen	Den
1986	K Moon Soo &		1960	F Kobbero &	
	P Joo Bong	RoK		P Nielsen	Den
1985	K Moon Soo &		1959	L Say Hup &	
	P Joo Bong	RoK		T Kew San	Mly
1984	H Kartono &		1958	E Kops & P Nielsen	Den
	R Heryanto	Indo	1957	J Alston (USA) &	
				H Aun Heah (Mly)	
			1956	F Kobbero &	
				J H Hansen	Den
			1955	F Kobbero &	
				J H Hansen	Den

Year	Winner	
1954	O Teik Hock &	
	O Poh Lim	Mly
1953	E Choong &	
	D Choong	Mly
1952	E Choong &	
	D Choong	Mly
1951	E Choong &	
	D Choong	Mly
1950	P Dabelsteen &	
	J Skaarup	Den
1949	O Teik Hock &	
	T Seng Khoon	Mly
1948	P Dabelsteen &	
	B Frederiksen	Den
1947	T Madsen & P Holm	Den
1946/40	No Competition	
1939	T Boyle & J Rankin	Ire
1938	R Nichols &	
	L Nichols	GB
1937	R Nichols &	
	L Nichols	GB
1936	R Nichols &	
	L Nichols	GB
1935	D Hume & R White	GB
1934	D Hume & R White	GB
1933	D Hume & R White	GB
1932	D Hume & R White	GB
1931	F Devlin & C Mack	Ire
1930	F Devlin & C Mack	Ire
1929	F Devlin & C Mack	Ire
1928	G Thomas & F Hodge	GB
1927	F Devlin & C Mack	Ire
1926	F Devlin & C Mack	Ire
1925	H Uber & A Jones	GB
1924	G Thomas & F Hodge	GB
1923	F Devlin & C Mack	Ire
1922	F Devlin (Ire) &	
	G Sautter (Eng)	
1921	G Thomas & F Hodge	GB
1920	A Engelbach &	
	R du Roveray	GB
1919/15	No Competition	
1914	G Thomas &	
	F Chesterton	GB
1913	G Thomas &	
	F Chesterton	GB

Year	Winner	
1912	G Thomas &	
	H Marrett	GB
1911	G Thomas &	
	H Marrett	GB
1910	P Fitton &	
	E Hawthorn	GB
1909	A Prebble &	
	F Chesterton	GB
1908	G Thomas &	
	H Marrett	GB
1907	A Prebble & N Wood	GB
1906	G Thomas &	
	H Marrett	GB
1905	S Massey & C Barnes	GB
1904	A Prebble &	
	H Marrett	GB
1903	S Massey & E Huson	GB
1902	H Mellersh &	
	F Collier	GB
1901	H Mellersh &	
	F Collier	GB
1900	H Mellersh &	
	F Collier	GB
1899	D Oakes & S Massey	GB

Women's Singles

FIRST HELD 1900

Year	Winner	
1991	S Susanti	Indo
1990	S Susanti	Indo
1989	L Lingwei	CPR
1988	G Jiaming	CPR
1987	K Larsen	Den
1986	K Yun-Ja	RoK
1985	H Aiping	CPR
1984	L Lingwei	CPR
1983	Z Ailing	CPR
1982	Z Ailing	CPR
1981	S A Hwang	RoK
1980	L Koppen	Den
1979	L Koppen	Den
1978	G Gilks	GB
1977	H Yuki	Jap

Year	Winner		Year	Winner	
1976	G Gilks	GB	1924	K McKane	GB
1975	H Yuki	Jap	1923	L Radeglia	GB
1974	H Yuki	Jap	1922	K McKane	GB
1973	M Beck	GB	1921	K McKane	GB
1972	N Nakayama	Jap	1920	K McKane	GB
1971	E Twedberg	Swe	1919/15	No Competition	
1970	E Takenaka	Jap	1914	L Radeglia	GB
1969	H Yuki	Jap	1913	L Radeglia	GB
1968	E Twedberg	Swe	1912	M Tragett	GB
1967	J Hashman	USA	1911	M Larminie	GB
1966	J Hashman	USA	1910	M Lucas	GB
1965	U Smith	GB	1909	M Lucas	GB
1964	J Hashman	USA	1908	M Lucas	GB
1963	J Hashman	USA	1907	M Lucas	GB
1962	J Hashman	USA	1906	E Thomson	GB
1961	J Hashman	USA	1905	M Lucas	GB
1960	J Devlin	USA	1904	E Thomson	GB
1959	H Ward	GB	1903	E Thomson	GB
1958	J Devlin	USA	1902	M Lucas	GB
1957	J Devlin	USA	1901	E Thomson	GB
1956	M Varner	USA	1900	E Thomson	GB
1955	M Varner	USA			
1954	J Devlin	USA			
1953	M Ussing	Den			
1952	T Olsen-Ahm	Den			
1951	A Jacobsen	Den			
1950	T Olsen-Ahm	Den			
1949	A Jacobsen	Den			
1948	K Thorndahl	Den			
1947	M Ussing	Den			
1946/40	No Competition				
1939	D Walton	Can			
1938	D Young	GB			
1937	T Kingsbury	GB			
1936	T Kingsbury	GB			
1935	B Uber	GB			
1934	L Kingsbury	GB			
1933	A Woodroffe	GB			
1932	L Kingsbury	GB			
1931	M Barrett	GB			
1930	M Barrett	GB			
1929	M Barrett	GB			
1928	M Tragett	GB			
1927	M Barrett	GB			
1926	M Barrett	GB			
1925	M Stocks	GB			

Women's Doubles

FIRST HELD 1899

Year	Winner	
1991	C So Young & H Hye Young	RoK
1990	C Myung Hee & H Hye Young	RoK
1989	C Myung Hee & C So Young	RoK
1988	C So Young & K Yun Ja	RoK
1987	C Myung Hee & H Hye Young	RoK
1986	C Myung Hee & H Hye Young	RoK
1985	L Lingwei & H Aiping	CPR
1984	L Ying & W Dixi	CPR
1983	X Rong & W Jianqiu	CPR
1982	L Ying & W Dixi	CPR
1981	N Perry & J Webster	GB

Year	Winner		Year	Winner	
1980	G Gilks & N Perry	GB	1953	I Cooley & J White	GB
1979	W Verawaty & I Wigoeno	Indo	1952	T Olsen-Ahm & A Jacobsen	Den
1978	A Tokuda & M Takada	Jap	1951	T Olsen-Ahm & K Thorndahl	Den
1977	E Tuganoo & E Ueno	Jap	1950	T Olsen-Ahm & K Thorndahl	Den
1976	G Gilks & S Whetnall	GB			
1975	M Aizawa & E Takenaka	Jap	1949	B Uber & Q Allen	GB
			1948	T Olsen-Ahm & K Thorndahl	Den
1974	M Beck & G Gilks	GB	1947	T Olsen-Ahm & K Thorndahl	Den
1973	M Aizawa & E Takenaka	Jap	1946/40	No Competition	
1972	M Aizawa & E Takenaka	Jap	1939	R Dalsgard & T Olsen	Den
1971	N Takagi & H Yuki	Jap	1938	B Uber & D Doveton	GB
1970	M Boxall & S Whetnall	GB	1937	B Uber & D Doveton	GB
			1936	T Kingsbury & M Henderson	GB
1969	M Boxall & S Whetnall	GB	1935	T Kingsbury & M Henderson	GB
1968	R Koestijah & Miss Minarni	Indo	1934	T Kingsbury & M Henderson	GB
1967	I Rietveld & U Strand	Den	1933	T Kingsbury & M Bell	GB
1966	J Hashman (USA) & S Peard (Ire)		1932	M Barrett & L Kingsbury	GB
1965	K Jorgensen & U Rasmussen	Den	1931	B Uber & M Horsley	GB
1964	K Jorgensen & U Rasmussen	Den	1930	M Barrett & V Elton	GB
			1929	M Barrett & V Elton	GB
1963	J Hashman (USA) & S Peard (Ire)		1928	M Barrett & V Elton	GB
1962	J Hashman (USA) & T Holst-Christensen (Den)		1927	M Tragett & H Hogarth	GB
1961	J Hashman (USA) & S Peard (Ire)		1926	A Head & V Elton	GB
			1925	M Tragett & H Hogarth	GB
1960	J Devlin & S Devlin	USA	1924	M Stocks & K McKane	GB
1959	I Rogers & J Timperley	GB	1923	M Tragett & H Hogarth	GB
1958	M Varner (USA) & H Ward (GB)		1922	M Tragett & H Hogarth	GB
1957	K Granlund & A H Hansen	Den	1921	K McKane & M McKane	GB
1956	J Devlin & S Devlin	USA			
1955	I Cooley & J White	GB	1920	L Radeglia & V Elton	GB
1954	J Devlin & S Devlin	USA	1919/15	No Competition	

Year	Winner	
1914	M Tragett &	
	E Peterson	GB
1913	H Hogarth &	
	M Bateman	GB
1912	A Gowenlock &	
	D Cundall	GB
1911	A Gowenlock &	
	D Cundall	GB
1910	M Lucas &	
	& M Bateman	GB
1909	M Lucas & G Murray	GB
1908	M Lucas & G Murray	GB
1907	M Lucas & G Murray	GB
1906	M Lucas &	
	E Thomson	GB
1905	M Lucas &	
	E Thomson	GB
1904	M Lucas &	
	E Thomson	GB
1903	M Hardy &	
	D Douglass	GB
1902	M Lucas &	
	E Thomson	GB
1901	E Moseley &	
	Miss St John	GB
1900	M Lucas &	
	Miss Graeme	GB
1899	M Lucas &	
	Miss Graeme	GB

Mixed Doubles

FIRST HELD 1899

Year	Winner	
1991	P Joo Bong &	
	C Myung Hee	RoK
1990	P Joo Bong &	
	C Myung Hee	RoK
1989	P Joo Bong &	
	C Myung Hee	RoK
1988	W Pengrin &	
	S Fangjiing	CPR
1987	L Deuk Choon &	
	C Myung Hee	RoK

Year	Winner	
1986	P Joo Bong &	
	C Myung Hee	RoK
1985	B Gillibrand &	
	N Perry	GB
1984	M Dew & G Gilks	GB
1983	T Kihlstrom (Swe) &	
	N Perry (GB)	
1982	M Dew & G Gilks	GB
1981	M Tredgett & N Perry	GB
1980	M Tredgett & N Perry	GB
1979	H Christian &	
	I Wigoeno	Indo
1978	M Tredgett & N Perry	GB
1977	D Talbot & G Gilks	GB
1976	D Talbot & G Gilks	GB
1975	E Stuart &	
	N Gardener	GB
1974	D Eddy & S Whetnall	GB
1973	D Talbot & G Gilks	GB
1972	S Prie & U Strand	Den
1971	S Prie & U Strand	Den
1970	P Walsoe &	
	P M Hansen	Den
1969	R Mills & G Perrin	GB
1968	A Jordan & S Pound	GB
1967	S Anderson &	
	U Strand	Den
1966	F Kobbero &	
	U Strand	Den
1965	F Kobbero &	
	U Strand	Den
1964	A Jordan &	
	J Pritchard	GB
1963	F Kobbero &	
	U Rasmussen	Den
1962	F Kobbero &	
	U Rasmussen	Den
1961	F Kobbero &	
	K Granlund	Den
1960	F Kobbero &	
	K Granlund	Den
1959	P Nielsen & I Hansen	Den
1958	A Jordan &	
	J Timperley	GB
1957	F Kobbero &	
	K Granlund	Den

Year	Winner	
1956	A Jordan & J Timperley	GB
1955	F Kobbero & K Thorndahl	Den
1954	J Best & I Cooley	GB
1953	E Choong (Mly) & J White (GB)	
1952	P Holm & T Olsen-Ahm	Den
1951	P Holm & T Olsen-Ahm	Den
1950	P Holm & T Olsen-Ahm	Den
1949	C Stephens & P Stephens	USA
1948	J Skaarup & K Thorndahl	Den
1947	P Holm & T Olsen-Ahm	Den
1946/40	No Competition	
1939	R Nichols & B Staples	GB
1938	R White & B Uber	GB
1937	I Maconachie (Ire) & T Kingsbury (GB)	
1936	D Hume & B Uber	GB
1935	D Hume & B Uber	GB
1934	D Hume & B Uber	GB
1933	D Hume & B Uber	GB
1932	H Uber & B Uber	GB
1931	H Uber & B Uber	GB
1930	H Uber & B Uber	GB
1929	F Devlin (Ire) & M Horsley (GB)	
1928	A Harbot & M Tragett	GB
1927	F Devlin (Ire) & E Peterson (GB)	
1926	F Devlin (Ire) & E Peterson (GB)	
1925	F Devlin (Ire) & K McKane (GB)	
1924	F Devlin (Ire) & K McKane (GB)	
1923	C Mack (Ire) & M Tragett (GB)	

Year	Winner	
1922	G Thomas & H Hogarth	GB
1921	G Thomas & H Hogarth	GB
1920	G Thomas & H Hogarth	GB
1919/15	No Competition	
1914	G Thomas & H Hogarth	GB
1913	G Sautter & M Mayston	GB
1912	E Hawthorn & H Hogarth	GB
1911	G Thomas & M Larminie	GB
1910	G Sautter & D Cundall	GB
1909	A Prebble & D Boothby	GB
1908	N Wood & M Lucas	GB
1907	G Thomas & G Murray	GB
1906	G Thomas & E Thomson	GB
1905	H Marrett & H Hogarth	GB
1904	H Marrett & D Douglass	GB
1903	G Thomas & E Thomson	GB
1902	L Ransford & E Moseley	GB
1901	F Collier & E Stawell-Brown	GB
1900	D Oakes & Miss St John	GB
1899	D Oakes & Miss St John	GB

MEN'S WORLD TEAM CHAMPIONS
Thomas Cup

FIRST HELD 1949

Year	Winner
1990	China
1988	China
1986	China
1984	Indonesia
1982	China
1979	Indonesia
1976	Indonesia
1973	Indonesia
1970	Indonesia
1967	Malaysia
1964	Indonesia
1961	Indonesia
1958	Indonesia
1955	Malaya
1952	Malaya
1949	Malaya

WOMEN'S WORLD TEAM CHAMPIONS
Uber Cup

FIRST HELD 1957

Year	Winner
1990	China
1988	China
1986	China
1984	China
1981	Japan
1978	Japan
1975	Indonesia
1972	Japan
1969	Japan
1966	Japan
1963	United States
1960	United States
1957	United States

BASEBALL

WORLD SERIES CHAMPIONS

FIRST HELD 1903

Year	Winner
1990	Cincinnati Reds
1989	Oakland Athletics
1988	Los Angeles Dodgers
1987	Minnesota Twins
1986	New York Mets
1985	Kansas City Royals
1984	Detroit Tigers
1983	Baltimore Orioles

Year	Winner
1982	St Louis Cardinals
1981	Los Angeles Dodgers
1980	Philadelphia Phillies
1979	Pittsburgh Pirates
1978	New York Yankees
1977	New York Yankees
1976	Cincinnati Reds
1975	Cincinnati Reds
1974	Oakland Athletics
1973	Oakland Athletics
1972	Oakland Athletics
1971	Pittsburgh Pirates
1970	Baltimore Orioles

Year	Winner	Year	Winner
1969	New York Mets	1935	Detroit Tigers
1968	Detroit Tigers	1934	St Louis Cardinals
1967	St Louis Cardinals	1933	New York Giants
1966	Baltimore Orioles	1932	New York Yankees
1965	Los Angeles Dodgers	1931	St Louis Cardinals
1964	St Louis Cardinals	1930	Philadelphia Athletics
1963	Los Angeles Dodgers	1929	Philadelphia Athletics
1962	New York Yankees	1928	New York Yankees
1961	New York Yankees	1927	New York Yankees
1960	Pittsburgh Pirates	1926	St Louis Cardinals
1959	Los Angeles Dodgers	1925	Pittsburgh Pirates
1958	New York Yankees	1924	Washington Senators
1957	Milwaukee Braves	1923	New York Yankees
1956	New York Yankees	1922	New York Giants
1955	Brooklyn Dodgers	1921	New York Giants
1954	New York Giants	1920	Cleveland Indians
1953	New York Yankees	1919	Cincinnati Reds
1952	New York Yankees	1918	Boston Red Sox
1951	New York Yankees	1917	Chicago White Sox
1950	New York Yankees	1916	Boston Red Sox
1949	New York Yankees	1915	Boston Red Sox
1948	Cleveland Indians	1914	Boston Braves
1947	New York Yankees	1913	Philadelphia Athletics
1946	St Louis Cardinals	1912	Boston Red Sox
1945	Detroit Tigers	1911	Philadelphia Athletics
1944	St Louis Cardinals	1910	Philadelphia Athletics
1943	New York Yankees	1909	Pittsburgh Pirates
1942	St Louis Cardinals	1908	Chicago Cubs
1941	New York Yankees	1907	Chicago Cubs
1940	Cincinnati Reds	1906	Chicago White Sox
1939	New York Yankees	1905	New York Giants
1938	New York Yankees	1904	No Competition
1937	New York Yankees	1903	Boston Red Sox
1936	New York Yankees		

BASKETBALL

WORLD CHAMPIONS
Men

FIRST HELD 1950

Year	Winner
1990	Yugoslavia
1986	United States
1982	USSR
1978	Yugoslavia
1974	USSR
1970	Yugoslavia
1967	USSR
1963	Brazil
1959	Brazil
1954	United States
1950	Argentina

Women

FIRST HELD 1953

Year	Winner
1990	United States
1987	United States
1983	USSR
1979	United States
1975	USSR
1971	USSR
1967	USSR
1964	USSR
1959	USSR
1957	United States
1953	United States

OLYMPIC CHAMPIONS
Men

FIRST HELD 1936

Year	Winner
1988	USSR
1984	United States
1980	Yugoslavia
1976	United States
1972	USSR
1968	United States
1964	United States
1960	United States
1956	United States
1952	United States
1948	United States
1936	United States

Women

FIRST HELD 1976

Year	Winner
1988	United States
1984	United States
1980	USSR
1976	USSR

NBA CHAMPIONS

FIRST HELD 1947

Year	Winner
1991	Chicago Bulls
1990	Detroit Pistons
1989	Detroit Pistons
1988	Los Angeles Lakers
1987	Los Angeles Lakers

Year	Winner
1986	Boston Celtics
1985	Los Angeles Lakers
1984	Boston Celtics
1983	Philadelphia 76ers
1982	Los Angeles Lakers
1981	Boston Celtics
1980	Los Angeles Lakers
1979	Seattle Supersonics
1978	Washington Bullets
1977	Portland Trail Blazers
1976	Boston Celtics
1975	Golden State Warriors
1974	Boston Celtics
1973	New York Knicks
1972	Los Angeles Lakers
1971	Milwaukee Bucks
1970	New York Knicks
1969	Boston Celtics
1968	Boston Celtics
1967	Philadelphia 76ers
1966	Boston Celtics
1965	Boston Celtics
1964	Boston Celtics
1963	Boston Celtics
1962	Boston Celtics
1961	Boston Celtics
1960	Boston Celtics
1959	Boston Celtics
1958	St Louis Hawks
1957	Boston Celtics
1956	Philadelphia Warriors
1955	Syracuse Nationals
1954	Minneapolis Lakers
1953	Minneapolis Lakers
1952	Minneapolis Lakers
1951	Rochester Royals
1950	Minneapolis Lakers
1949	Minneapolis Lakers
1948	Baltimore Bullets
1947	Philadelphia Warriors

EUROPEAN CHAMPIONS

Men

FIRST HELD 1935

Year	Winner
1991	Yugoslavia
1989	Yugoslavia
1987	Greece
1985	USSR
1983	Italy
1981	USSR
1979	USSR
1977	Yugoslavia
1975	Yugoslavia
1973	Yugoslavia
1971	USSR
1969	USSR
1967	USSR
1965	USSR
1963	USSR
1961	USSR
1959	USSR
1957	USSR
1955	Hungary
1953	USSR
1951	USSR
1949	Egypt
1947	USSR
1946	Czechoslovakia
1945/40	No Competition
1939	Lithuania
1937	Lithuania
1935	Latvia

Women

FIRST HELD 1938

Year	Winner
1991	USSR
1989	USSR
1987	USSR
1985	USSR
1983	USSR

Year	Winner		Year	Winner
1981	USSR		1964	USSR
1980	USSR		1962	USSR
1978	USSR		1960	USSR
1976	USSR		1958	Bulgaria
1974	USSR		1956	USSR
1972	USSR		1954	USSR
1970	USSR		1952	USSR
1968	USSR		1950	USSR
1966	USSR		1938	Italy

BIATHLON

OLYMPIC CHAMPIONS

10 km

FIRST HELD 1980

Year	Winner	
1988	F Roetsch	GDR
1984	E Kvalfoss	Nor
1980	F Ullrich	GDR

20 km

FIRST HELD 1960

Year	Winner	
1988	F Roetsch	GDR
1984	P Angerer	FRG
1980	A Alyabyev	USSR
1976	N Kruglov	USSR
1972	M Solberg	Nor
1968	M Solberg	Nor
1964	V Melanin	USSR
1960	K Lestander	Swe

4 x 7.5 km Relay

FIRST HELD 1968

Year	Winner
1988	USSR
1984	USSR
1980	USSR
1976	USSR
1972	USSR
1968	USSR

WORLD CHAMPIONS

10 km

FIRST HELD 1974

Year	Winner	
1991	M Kirchner	Ger
1990	M Kirchner	GDR
1989	F Luck	GDR
1987	F Roetsch	GDR
1986	V Medvetsev	USSR
1985	F Roetsch	GDR
1983	E Kvalfoss	Nor

Year	Winner	
1982	E Kvalfoss	Nor
1981	F Ullrich	GDR
1979	F Ullrich	GDR
1978	F Ullrich	GDR
1977	A Tikhonov	USSR
1975	N Kruglov	USSR
1974	J Suutarinen	Fin

20 km

FIRST HELD 1958

Year	Winner	
1991	A Sehmisch	Ger
1990	V Medvetsev	USSR
1989	E Kvalfoss	Nor
1987	F Roetsch	GDR
1986	V Medvetzev	USSR
1985	Y Kashkarov	USSR
1983	F Ullrich	GDR
1982	F Ullrich	GDR
1981	H Ikola	Fin
1979	K Siebert	GDR
1978	O Lirhus	Nor
1977	H Ikola	Fin
1975	H Ikola	Fin
1974	J Suutarinen	Fin
1973	A Tikhonov	USSR
1971	D Speer	USSR
1970	A Tikhonov	USSR
1969	A Tikhonov	USSR
1967	V Mamatov	USSR
1966	J Istad	Nor
1965	O Jordet	Nor
1963	V Melanin	USSR
1962	V Melanin	USSR
1961	K Huuskonen	Fin
1959	V Melanin	USSR
1958	A Wiklund	Swe

4 x 7.5 km Relay

FIRST HELD 1965

Year	Winner
1991	Germany
1990	Italy
1989	East Germany
1987	East Germany
1986	USSR
1985	USSR
1983	USSR
1982	East Germany
1981	East Germany
1979	East Germany
1978	East Germany
1977	USSR
1975	Finland
1974	USSR
1973	USSR
1971	USSR
1970	USSR
1969	USSR
1967	Norway
1966	Norway
1965	Norway

20 km Team

FIRST HELD 1989

Year	Winner
1991	Italy
1990	GDR
1989	USSR

Women's 15 km

FIRST HELD 1989

Year	Winner	
1991	P Schaaf	Ger
1990	S Davydova	USSR
1989	P Schaaf	FRG

Women's 10 km

FIRST HELD 1984

Year	Winner	
1988	A Elvebank	Nor
1987	S Gronlid	Nor
1986	E Korpela	Swe
1985	K Parve	USSR
1984	V Chernyshova	USSR

Women's 7.5 km

FIRST HELD 1989

Year	Winner	
1991	G I Nykkelmo	Nor
1990	A Elvebank	Nor
1989	A Elvebank	Nor

Women's 5 km

FIRST HELD 1984

Year	Winner	
1988	P Schaar	FRG
1987	Y Golovina	USSR
1986	K Parve	USSR
1985	S Gronlid	Nor
1984	V Chernyshova	USSR

Women's 3 x 5 km Relay

FIRST HELD 1984

Year	Winner
1991	USSR
1990	USSR
1989	USSR
1987	USSR
1986	USSR
1985	USSR
1984	USSR

Women's 15 km Team

FIRST HELD 1989

Year	Winner
1991	USSR
1990	USSR
1989	USSR

WORLD CUP CHAMPIONS

FIRST HELD 1978

Year	Winner	
1991	S Tchepikov	USSR
1990	S Tchepikov	USSR
1989	E Kvalfoss	Nor
1988	F Fischer	FRG
1987	F Roetsch	GDR
1986	A Sehmisch	GDR
1985	F Roetsch	GDR
1984	F Roetsch	GDR
1983	P Angerer	FRG
1982	F Ullrich	GDR
1981	F Ullrich	GDR
1980	F Ullrich	GDR
1979	K Siebert	GDR
1978	F Ullrich	GDR

NATIONS CUP CHAMPIONS

FIRST HELD 1988

Year	Winner
1991	Italy
1990	USSR
1989	GDR
1988	FRG

WOMEN'S WORLD CUP CHAMPIONS

FIRST HELD 1988

Year	Winner	
1991	S Davydova	USSR
1990	J Adamichkova	Cze
1989	Y Golovina	USSR
1988	A Elvebank	Nor

WOMEN'S NATIONS CUP CHAMPIONS

FIRST HELD 1989

Year	Winner
1991	Germany
1990	USSR
1989	Norway

BILLIARDS

WORLD PROFESSIONAL CHAMPIONS

FIRST HELD 1870

Year	Winner	
1991	M Russell	Eng
1989	M Russell	Eng
1988	N Dagley	Eng
1987	N Dagley	Eng
1986	R Foldvari	Aus
1985	R Edmonds	Eng
1984	M Wildman	Eng
1983	R Williams	Eng
1982	R Williams	Eng
1980	F Davis	Eng
1974	R Williams	Eng
1973	R Williams	Eng
1971	R Williams	Eng
1971	L Driffield	Eng
1968	R Williams	Eng
1951	C McConachy	NZ
1934	W Lindrum	Aus
1933	W Lindrum	Aus
1932	J Davis	Eng
1930	J Davis	Eng

Year	Winner	
1929	J Davis	Eng
1928	J Davis	Eng
1927	T Newman	Eng
1926	T Newman	Eng
1925	T Newman	Eng
1924	T Newman	Eng
1923	W Smith	Eng
1922	T Newman	Eng
1921	T Newman	Eng
1920	W Smith	Eng
1919	M Inman	Eng
1914	M Inman	Eng
1913	M Inman	Eng
1912	M Inman	Eng
1911	H W Stevenson	Eng
1910	H W Stevenson	Eng
1910	H W Stevenson	Eng
1909	M Inman	Eng
1909	H W Stevenson	Eng
1908	M Inman	Eng
1903	C Dawson	Eng
1901	H W Stevenson	Eng
1901	C Dawson	Eng
1901	H W Stevenson	Eng
1900	C Dawson	Eng
1899	C Dawson	Eng
1885	J Roberts Jnr	Eng

Year	Winner		Year	Winner	
1885	J Roberts Jnr	Eng	1985	G Sethi	Ind
1881	J Bennett	Eng	1983	M Ferreira	Ind
1880	J Bennett	Eng	1981	M Ferreira	Ind
1877	J Roberts Jnr	Eng	1979	P Mifsud	Mlt
1875	J Roberts Jnr	Eng	1977	M Ferreira	Ind
1875	J Roberts Jnr	Eng	1975	N Dagley	Eng
1874	W Cook	Eng	1973	M Lafir	Sri
1872	W Cook	Eng	1971	N Dagley	Eng
1871	W Cook	Eng	1969	J Karnehm	Eng
1871	W Cook	Eng	1967	L Driffield	Eng
1871	J Roberts Jnr	Eng	1964	W Jones	Ind
1870	J Bennett	Eng	1962	R Marshall	Aus
1870	J Roberts Jnr	Eng	1960	H Beetham	Eng
1870	J Roberts Jnr	Eng	1958	W Jones	Ind
1870	W Cook	Eng	1954	T Cleary	Aus
			1952	L Driffield	Eng
			1951	R Marshall	Aus
			1938	R Marshall	Aus
			1936	R Marshall	Aus
			1935	H Coles	Eng
			1933	S Lee	Eng
			1931	L Steeples	Eng
			1929	L Hayes	Aus
			1927	A Prior	SA
			1926	J Earlham	Eng

WORLD AMATEUR CHAMPIONS

FIRST HELD 1926

Year	Winner	
1990	M Kothari	Ind
1987	G Sethi	Ind

BOBSLEIGHING

OLYMPIC CHAMPIONS
Two-Man Bob

FIRST HELD 1932

Year	Winner	
1988	J Kipours & V Kozlov	USSR
1984	W Hoppe & D Schauerhammer	GDR
1980	E Schärer & J Benz	Swi
1976	M Nehmer & B Germeshausen	GDR
1972	W Zimmerer & P Utzschneider	FRG
1968	E Monti & L de Paolis	Ita
1964	T Nash & R Dixon	GB
1956	L Dalla Costa & G Conti	Ita
1952	A Ostler & L Nieberl	FRG
1948	F Endrich & F Waller	Swi
1936	I Brown & A Washbond	USA
1932	H Stevens & C Stevens	USA

Four-Man Bob

FIRST HELD 1924

Year	Winner
1988	Switzerland
1984	East Germany
1980	East Germany
1976	East Germany
1972	Switzerland
1968	Italy
1964	Canada
1956	Switzerland
1952	Germany

Year	Winner
1948	United States
1936	Switzerland
1932	United States
1928	United States
1924	Switzerland

WORLD CHAMPIONS
Two-Man Bob

FIRST HELD 1931

Year	Winner	
1991	R Lochner & M Zimmermann	Ger
1990	G Weder & B Gerber	Swi
1989	W Hoppe & B Musiol	GDR
1987	R Pichler & C Poltera	Swi
1986	W Hoppe & D Schauerhammer	GDR
1985	W Hoppe & D Schauerhammer	GDR
1983	R Pichler & U Leuthold	Swi
1982	E Schärer & J Benz	Swi
1981	B Germeshausen & H Gerhardt	GDR
1979	E Schärer & J Benz	Swi
1978	E Schärer & J Benz	Swi
1977	H Hiltebrand & H Meier	Swi
1975	G Alverà & F Perruquet	Ita
1974	W Zimmerer & P Utzschneider	FRG
1973	W Zimmerer & P Utzschneider	FRG
1971	G Gaspari & M Armano	Ita

Year	Winner	
1970	H Floth & P Bader	FRG
1969	N de Zordo & A Frassinelli	Ita
1967	E Thaler & R Durnthaler	Aut
1966	E Monti & S Siorpaes	Ita
1965	T Nash & R Dixon	GB
1963	E Monti & S Siorpaes	Ita
1962	R Ruatti & E De Lorenzo	Ita
1961	E Monti & S Siorpaes	Ita
1959	E Monti & R Alvera	Ita
1958	E Monti & R Alvera	Ita
1957	E Monti & R Alvera	Ita
1955	F Feierbend & H Warburton	Swi
1954	G Scheibmeier & A Zambelli	Ita
1953	F Endrich & F Stoeckli	Swi
1951	A Osterl & L Nieberl	FRG
1950	F Feierabend & S Waser	Swi
1949	F Endrich & F Waller	Swi
1947	F Feierabend & S Waser	Swi
1946/40	No Competition	
1939	R Lundnen & J Kuffer	Bel
1938	B Fischer & R Thielacke	Ger
1937	F McEnvoy & B Black	GB
1935	R Capadrutt & E Diener	Swi
1934	A Frim & V Dumitrescu	Rom
1933	A Papana & D Hubert	Rom
1931	H Killian & S Huber	Ger

Four-Man Bob

FIRST HELD 1924

Year	Winner
1991	Germany
1990	Switzerland
1989	Switzerland
1988	Switzerland
1987	Switzerland
1986	Switzerland
1985	East Germany
1984	East Germany
1983	Switzerland
1982	Switzerland
1981	East Germany
1980	East Germany
1979	West Germany
1978	East Germany
1977	East Germany
1976	East Germany
1975	Switzerland
1974	West Germany
1973	Switzerland
1972	Switzerland
1971	Switzerland
1970	Italy
1969	West Germany
1968	Italy
1967	Romania
1966	Not held
1965	Canada
1964	Canada
1963	Italy
1962	West Germany
1961	Italy
1960	Italy
1959	United States
1958	West Germany
1957	Switzerland
1956	Switzerland
1955	Switzerland
1954	Switzerland
1953	USA
1952	Germany
1951	Germany
1950	United States
1949	United States

Year	Winner
1948	United States
1947	Switzerland
1946/40	No Competition
1939	Switzerland
1938	Great Britain
1937	Great Britain
1936	Switzerland
1935	Germany
1934	Germany
1933	Not held
1932	United States
1931	Germany
1930	Italy
1929	Not held
1928	United States
1927	Great Britain
1926/25	Not held
1924	Switzerland

WORLD CUP CHAMPIONS

FIRST HELD 1985

Year	Winner	
1991	G Weder	Swi
1990	M Poikans	USSR
1989	G Weder	Swi
1988	I Appelt	Aut
1987	M Roy	USA
1986	E Fasser	Swi
1985	A Fischer	FRG

LUGEING

WORLD CHAMPIONS

FIRST HELD 1955

Singles

Year	Winner	
1991	A Huber	Ita

Year	Winner	
1989	G Hackl	FRG
1987	M Prock	Aut
1985	M Walter	GDR
1983	M Zajonc	Can
1981	S Danilin	USSR
1979	D Günther	GDR
1977	H Rinn	GDR
1975	W Fiedler	GDR
1974	J Fendt	FRG
1973	H Rinn	GDR
1971	K Brunner	Ita
1970	J Fendt	FRG
1969	J Feistmantl	Aut
1967	T Köhler	GDR
1966	Not held	
1965	H Plenk	FRG
1963	F Nachmann	FRG
1962	T Köhler	GDR
1961	J Wojnar	Pol
1960	H Berndt	FRG
1959	H Thaler	Aut
1958	J Wojnar	Pol
1957	H Schaller	FRG
1955	A Salvesen	Nor

Doubles

Year	Winner	
1991	S Krause & J Behrendt	Ger
1989	S Krause & J Behrendt	GDR
1987	J Hoffmann & J Pietzsch	GDR
1985	J Hoffmann & J Pietzsch	GDR
1983	J Hoffmann & J Pietzsch	GDR
1981	B Hann & U Hann	GDR
1980	H Rinn & N Hahn	GDR
1979	H Brandner & B Schwarm	FRG
1978	D Bremse & A Krikis	USSR
1977	H Rinn & N Hahn	GDR

Year	Winner	
1975	B Hann & U Hann	GDR
1974	B Hann & U Hann	GDR
1973	H Hörnlein &	
	R Bredow	GDR
1971	P Hildgartner &	
	W Plaikner	Ita
1970	M Schmid &	
	E Walch	Aut
1969	M Schmid &	
	E Walch	Aut
1967	K Bonsack &	
	T Köhler	GDR
1966	Not held	
1965	W Scheidel &	
	T Köhler	GDR
1963	R Pedrak & L Kudzia	Pol
1962	G Graber &	
	G Ambrosi	Ita
1961	R Pichler & R Prinoth	Ita
1960	R Frosch & E Walch	Aut
1959	Not held	
1958	J Strillinger &	
	F Nachman	FRG
1957	J Strillinger &	
	F Nachman	FRG
1955	H Krausner &	
	H Thaler	Aut

Women's Singles

Year	Winner	
1991	S Erdmann	Ger
1989	S Erdmann	GDR
1987	C Schmidt	GDR
1985	S Martin	GDR
1983	S Martin	GDR
1981	M Sollmann	GDR
1980	V Sosulya	USSR
1979	M Sollmann	GDR
1978	V Sosulya	USSR
1977	M Schumann	GDR
1975	M Schumann	GDR
1974	M Schumann	GDR
1973	M Schumann	GDR
1971	E Demleitner	FRG

Year	Winner	
1970	B Piecha	Pol
1969	P Tierlich	GDR
1967	O Enderlein	GDR
1966	Not held	
1965	O Enderlein	GDR
1963	I Geisler	GDR
1962	I Geisler	GDR
1961	E Nagele	Swi
1960	M Isser	Aut
1959	E Lieber	Aut
1957	M Semczyszak	Pol
1956	M Isser	Aut
1955	K Kienzl	Aut

OLYMPIC CHAMPIONS

FIRST HELD 1964

Singles

Year	Winner	
1988	J Mueller	GDR
1984	P Hildgartner	Ita
1980	B Glass	GDR
1976	D Günther	GDR
1972	W Scheidel	GDR
1968	M Schmid	Aut
1964	T Köhler	Ger

Doubles

Year	Winner	
1988	J Hoffmann &	
	J Pietzsch	GDR
1984	H Stanggasinger &	
	F Wembacher	FRG
1980	H Rinn & N Hahn	GDR
1976	H Rinn & N Hahn	GDR
1972	H Hornlein &	
	R Bredow	GDR
	P Hildgartner &	
	W Plaikner	Ita

Year	Winner	
1968	T Köhler &	
	K Bonsack	GDR
1964	J Feistmantl &	
	M Stengl	Aut

Women's Singles

Year	Winner	
1988	S Walter	GDR
1984	S Martin	GDR
1980	V Sosulya	USSR
1976	M Schumann	GDR
1972	A Muller	GDR
1968	E Lechner	Ita
1964	O Enderlein	Ger

WORLD CUP CHAMPIONS

FIRST HELD 1978

Singles

Year	Winner	
1991	M Prock	Aut
1990	G Hackl	FRG
1989	G Hackl	FRG
1988	M Prock	Aut
1987	N Huber	Ita
1986	N Huber	Ita
1985	N Huber	Ita
1984	M Walter	GDR
1983	P Hildgartner	Ita
1982	E Haspinger	Ita
1981	E Haspinger	Ita
	P Hildgartner	Ita
1980	E Haspinger	Ita
1979	P Hildgartner	Ita
1978	A Winkler	GDR

Doubles

Year	Winner	
1991	H Raffl & N Huber	Ita
1990	H Raffl & N Huber	Ita
1989	H Raffl & N Huber	Ita
1988	E Beloussov &	
	A Beliakov	USSR
1987	T Schwab &	
	W Staudinger	FRG
1986	H Raffl & N Huber	Ita
1985	H Raffl & N Huber	Ita
1984	J Hoffmann &	
	J Pietzsch	GDR
1983	H Raffl & N Huber	Ita
1982	G Lemmerer &	
	R Sulzbacher	Aut
1981	G Lemmerer &	
	R Sulzbacher	Aut
1980	G Lemmerer &	
	R Sulzbacher	Aut
1979	P Gschnitzer &	
	K Brunner	Ita
1978	P Gschnitzer &	
	K Brunner	Ita

Women's Singles

Year	Winner	
1991	S Herdmann	Ger
1990	J Antipova	USSR
1989	G Weissensteiner	Ita
1988	J Antipova	USSR
1987	C Schmidt	GDR
1986	M Rainer	Ita
1985	C Schmidt	GDR
1984	S Martin	GDR
	B Schmidt	GDR
1983	U Weiss	GDR
1982	V Sosulya	USSR
1981	A Schafferer	Aut
1980	A Schafferer	Aut
1979	A Schafferer	Aut
1978	R König	FRG

BOWLS

WORLD OUTDOOR CHAMPIONS

FIRST HELD 1966

Men's Singles

Year	Winner	
1988	D Bryant	Eng
1984	P Belliss	NZ
1980	D Bryant	GB
1976	D Watson	SA
1972	M Evans	Wal
1966	D Bryant	GB

Men's Pairs

Year	Winner	
1988	R Brassey & P Belliss	NZ
1984	G Adrain & S Arculli	USA
1980	A Sandercock & P Rheuben	Aus
1976	D Watson & W Moseley	SA
1972	C Delgado & E Liddell	HK
1966	G Kelly & B Palm	Aus

Men's Triples

Year	Winner
1988	New Zealand
1984	Ireland
1980	England
1976	South Africa
1972	United States
1966	Australia

Men's Fours

Year	Winner
1988	Ireland
1984	England

Year	Winner
1980	Hong Kong
1976	South Africa
1972	England
1966	New Zealand

Team

Year	Winner
1988	England
1984	Scotland
1980	England
1976	South Africa
1972	Scotland
1966	Australia

FIRST HELD 1969

Women's Singles

Year	Winner	
1988	J Ackland	Wal
1985	M Richardson	Aus
1981	N Shaw	GB
1977	E Wilke	NZ
1973	E Wilke	NZ
1969	G Doyle	PNG

Women's Pairs

Year	Winner	
1988	M Johnston & P Nolan	Ire
1985	M Richardson & F Craig	Aus
1981	E Bell & N Allely	Ire
1977	H Wong & E Chok	HK
1973	L Lucas & D Jenkinson	Aus
1969	E McDonald & M Cridlan	SA

Women's Triples

Year	Winner
1988	Australia
1985	Australia
1981	Hong Kong
1977	Wales
1973	New Zealand
1969	South Africa

Women's Fours

Year	Winner
1988	Australia
1985	Scotland
1981	England
1977	Australia
1973	New Zealand
1969	South Africa

Women's Team

Year	Winner
1988	England
1985	Australia
1981	England
1977	Australia
1973	New Zealand
1969	South Africa

WORLD INDOOR CHAMPIONS

Men's Singles

FIRST HELD 1979

Year	Winner	
1991	R Corsie	Sco
1990	J Price	Wal
1989	R Corsie	Sco
1988	H Duff	Sco
1987	A Allcock	GB
1986	A Allcock	GB

Year	Winner	
1985	T Sullivan	Wal
1984	J Baker	Ire
1983	B Sutherland	Sco
1982	J Watson	Sco
1981	D Bryant	GB
1980	D Bryant	GB
1979	D Bryant	GB

Men's Pairs

FIRST HELD 1986

Year	Winner	
1991	D Bryant & A Allcock	Eng
1990	D Bryant & A Allcock	Eng
1989	D Bryant & A Allcock	Eng
1988	J Yates & I Schuback	Aus
1987	D Bryant & A Allcock	Eng
1986	D Bryant & A Allcock	Eng

Women's Singles

FIRST HELD 1988

Year	Winner	
1991	M Price	Eng
1990	F Bougard	CI
1989	M Johnston	Ire
1988	M Johnston	Ire

CROWN GREEN BOWLS

Waterloo Cup

FIRST HELD 1907

Year	Winner
1991	J Eccles
1990	J Bancroft
1989	B Duncan
1988	I Gregory
1987	B Duncan

Year	Winner	Year	Winner
1986	B Duncan	1946	G Parkinson
1985	T Johnstone	1945	W Grace
1984	S Ellis	1944	T Tinkler
1983	S Frith	1943	S Ivell
1982	D Mercer	1942	T Bimson
1981	R Nicholson	1941	W Wilcock
1980	V Lee	1940	A Holden
1979	B Duncan	1939	Abandoned
1978	A Murray	1938	J Whitter
1977	L Barrett	1937	A King
1976	K Illingworth	1936	H Yates
1975	J Collen	1935	C Roberts
1974	W Houghton	1934	W Derbyshire
1973	A Murray	1933	A Ogden
1972	N Burrows	1932	T Booth
1971	J Bradbury	1931	A Gleave
1970	J Everitt	1930	J Chadwick
1969	G Underwood	1929	C Halpin
1968	B Bennett	1928	T Whittle
1967	E Ashton	1927	H Waddecar
1966	R Collier	1926	T Roscoe
1965	J Pepper	1925	J Cox
1964	W Heinkey	1924	R Hill
1963	T Mayor	1923	J Martin
1962	J Collier	1922	W Smith
1961	J Featherstone	1921	J Bagot
1960	H Bury	1920	E Whiteside
1959	W Dawber	1919	L Moss
1958	F Salisbury	1918	W Simms
1957	W Lacy	1917	G Barnes
1956	J Sumner	1916	J Parkinson
1955	J Heyes	1915	W Fairhurst
1954	B Kelly	1914	J Rothwell
1953	B Kelly	1913	G Hart
1952	L Thompson	1912	T Lowe
1951	J Waterhouse	1911	J Peace
1950	H Finch	1910	Not held
1949	J Egan	1909	T Meadows
1948	A Ringrose	1908	G Beatty
1947	W Dalton	1907	J Rothwell

BOXING

WORLD HEAVYWEIGHT CHAMPIONS

FIRST HELD 1892

Undisputed Champions

Year	Winner	
1990	Evander Holyfield	USA
1990	James Douglas	USA
1987	Mike Tyson	USA
1978	Leon Spinks	USA
1974	Muhammad Ali	USA
1973	George Foreman	USA
1970	Joe Frazier	USA
1967	Muhammad Ali	USA
1964	Muhammad Ali	USA
1962	Sonny Liston	USA
1960	Floyd Patterson	USA
1959	Ingemar Johansson	Spa
1956	Floyd Patterson	USA
1952	Rocky Marciano	USA
1951	Jersey Joe Walcott	USA
1949	Ezzard Charles	USA
1937	Joe Louis	USA
1935	James J Braddock	USA
1934	Max Baer	USA
1933	Primo Carnera	Ita
1932	Jack Sharkey	USA
1930	Max Schmeling	Ger
1926	Gene Tunney	USA
1919	Jack Dempsey	USA
1915	Jess Willard	USA
1908	Jack Johnson	USA
1906	Tommy Burns	Can
1905	Marvin Hart	USA
1899	James J Jefferies	USA
1897	Bob Fitzsimmons	GB
1892	James J Corbett	USA

WBC Champions

Year	Winner	
1986	Mike Tyson	USA
1986	Trevor Berbick	Jam
1984	Pinklon Thomas	USA
1984	Tim Witherspoon	USA
1978	Larry Holmes	USA
1968	Joe Frazier	USA
1965	Muhammad Ali	USA

WBA Champions

Year	Winner	
1987	Mike Tyson	USA
1986	James Smith	USA
1986	Tim Witherspoon	USA
1985	Tony Tubbs	USA
1984	Greg Page	USA
1983	Gerrie Coetzee	SA
1982	Michael Dokes	USA
1980	Mike Weaver	USA
1979	John Tate	USA
1978	Muhammad Ali	USA
1978	Leon Spinks	USA
1968	Jimmy Ellis	USA
1965	Ernie Terrell	USA

IBF Champions

Year	Winner	
1987	Mike Tyson	USA
1987	Tony Tucker	USA
1985	Michael Spinks	USA
1984	Larry Holmes	USA

WORLD CRUISERWEIGHT CHAMPIONS

FIRST HELD 1979

Undisputed Champions

Year	Winner	
1988	Evander Holyfield	USA

WBC Champions

Year	Winner	
1991	Anaclet Wamba	Fra
1990	Massimiliano Duran	Ita
1989	Carlos de Leon	PR
1988	Evander Holyfield	USA
1986	Carlos de Leon	PR
1985	Bernard Benton	USA
1985	Alfonso Ratliff	USA
1983	Carlos de Leon	PR
1982	S T Gordon	USA
1980	Carlos de Leon	PR
1979	Marvin Camel	USA

WBA Champions

Year	Winner	
1991	Bobby Czyz	USA
1989	Robert Daniels	USA
1989	Taoufik Belbouli	Fra
1986	Evander Holyfield	USA
1985	Dwight Muhammad Qawi	USA
1984	Piet Crous	SA
1982	Ossie Ocasio	PR

IBF Champions

Year	Winner	
1991	James Warring	USA
1990	Jeff Lampkin	USA
1989	Glenn McCrory	GB
1987	Evander Holyfield	USA
1986	Rickey Parkey	USA
1984	Lee Roy Murphy	USA
1983	Marvin Camel	USA

WORLD LIGHT-HEAVYWEIGHT CHAMPIONS

FIRST HELD 1903

Undisputed Champions

Year	Winner	
1983	Michael Spinks	USA
1972	Bob Foster	USA
1968	Bob Foster	USA
1966	Dick Tiger	Nig
1965	Jose Torres	PR
1963	Willie Pastrano	USA
1962	Harold Johnson	USA
1952	Archie Moore	USA
1950	Joey Maxim	USA
1948	Freddie Mills	GB
1941	Gus Lesnevich	USA
1939	Billy Conn	USA
1935	John Henry Lewis	USA
1934	Bob Olin	USA
1933	Maxie Rosenbloom	USA
1927	Tommy Loughran	USA
1926	Jack Delaney	Can
1925	Paul Berlenbach	USA
1923	Mike McTigue	Ire
1922	Battling Siki	Sen
1920	Georges Carpentier	Fra
1916	Battling Levinsky	USA
1912	Jack Dillon	USA
1905	Jack O'Brien	USA
1903	Bob Fitzsimmons	GB
1903	George Gardner	Ire
1903	Jack Root	Aut

WBC Champions

Year	Winner	
1991	Jeff Harding	Aus
1990	Dennis Andries	GB
1989	Jeff Harding	Aus
1989	Dennis Andries	GB
1988	Sugar Ray Leonard	USA
1987	Don Lalonde	Can
1987	Thomas Hearns	USA
1986	Dennis Andries	GB
1985	J B Williamson	USA
1981	Dwight Muhammad Qawi	USA
1979	Matthew Saad Muhammad	USA
1978	Marvin Johnson	USA
1978	Mate Parlov	Yug
1977	Miguel Cuello	Arg
1974	John Conteh	GB
1971	Bob Foster	USA

WBA Champions

Year	Winner	
1991	Thomas Hearns	USA
1987	Virgil Hill	USA
1987	Leslie Stewart	TT
1986	Marvin Johnson	USA
1981	Michael Spinks	USA
1980	Mustapha Muhammad	USA
1979	Marvin Johnson	USA
1979	Victor Galindez	Arg
1978	Mike Rossman	USA
1974	Victor Galindez	Arg
1971	Vicente Rondon	Ven

IBF Champions

Year	Winner	
1987	Charles Williams	USA
1986	Bobby Czyz	USA
1985	Slobodan Kacar	Yug

WORLD SUPER-MIDDLEWEIGHT CHAMPIONS

FIRST HELD 1984

WBC Champions

Year	Winner	
1990	Mauro Galvano	Ita
1988	Sugar Ray Leonard	USA

WBA Champions

Year	Winner	
1991	Victor Cordova	Pan
1990	Christophe Tiozzo	Fra
1989	In-Chul Baek	RoK
1988	Fully Obelmejias	Ven
1987	Chong-Pal Park	RoK

IBF Champions

Year	Winner	
1991	Darrin Van Horn	USA
1990	Lindell Holmes	USA
1988	Graciano Rocchigiani	FRG
1984	Chong-Pal Park	RoK
1984	Murray Sutherland	GB

WORLD MIDDLEWEIGHT CHAMPIONS

FIRST HELD 1884

Undisputed Champions

Year	Winner	
1980	Marvin Hagler	USA
1980	Alan Minter	GB
1979	Vito Antuofermo	Ita
1978	Hugo Corro	Arg

Year	Winner	
1977	Rodrigo Valdez	Col
1976	Carlos Monzon	Arg
1970	Carlos Monzon	Arg
1968	Nino Benvenuti	Ita
1967	Emile Griffith	VI
1967	Nino Benvenuti	Ita
1966	Emile Griffith	VI
1965	Dick Tiger	Nig
1963	Joey Giardello	USA
1963	Dick Tiger	Nig
1958	Sugar Ray Robinson	USA
1957	Carmen Basilio	USA
1957	Sugar Ray Robinson	USA
1957	Gene Fullmer	USA
1955	Sugar Ray Robinson	USA
1953	Carl Bobo Olson	Haw
1951	Sugar Ray Robinson	USA
1951	Randolph Turpin	GB
1951	Sugar Ray Robinson	USA
1949	Jake la Motta	USA
1948	Marcel Cerdan	Alg
1948	Tony Zale	USA
1947	Rocky Graziano	USA
1941	Tony Zale	USA
1926	Mickey Walker	USA
1926	Tiger Flowers	USA
1923	Harry Greb	USA
1920	Johnny Wilson	USA
1917	Mike O'Dowd	USA
1908	Stanley Ketchel	USA
1908	Billy Papke	USA
1907	Stanley Ketchel	USA
1898	Tommy Ryan	USA
1897	Kid McCoy	USA
1891	Bob Fitzsimmons	GB
1884	Nonpareil Jack Dempsey	Ire

WBC Champions

Year	Winner	
1990	Julian Jackson	VI
1989	Roberto Duran	Pan
1988	Iran Barkley	USA
1987	Thomas Hearns	USA
1987	Sugar Ray Leonard	USA
1986	Marvin Hagler	USA
1974	Rodrigo Valdez	Col

WBA Champions

Year	Winner	
1989	Mike McCallum	Jam
1987	Sumbu Kalambay	Ita
1974	Carlos Monzon	Arg

IBF Champions

Year	Winner	
1991	James Toney	USA
1988	Michael Nunn	USA
1987	Frank Tate	USA

WORLD JUNIOR MIDDLEWEIGHT CHAMPIONS

FIRST HELD 1962

Undisputed Champions

Year	Winner	
1975	Koichi Wajima	Jap
1974	Oscar Albarado	USA
1971	Koichi Wajima	Jap
1970	Carmelo Bossi	Ita
1969	Freddie Little	USA
1968	Sandro Mazzinghi	Ita
1966	Ki-Soo Kim	RoK
1965	Nino Benvenuti	Ita
1963	Sandro Mazzinghi	Ita
1963	Ralph Dupas	USA
1962	Denny Moyer	USA

WBC Champions

Year	Winner	
1990	Terry Norris	USA
1989	John Mugabi	Uga
1989	Rene Jacquot	Fra
1988	Don Curry	USA
1987	Gianfranco Rosi	Ita
1987	Lupe Aquino	Mex
1986	Duane Thomas	USA
1982	Thomas Hearns	USA
1981	Wilfred Benitez	USA
1979	Maurice Hope	GB
1977	Rocky Mattioli	Ita
1976	Eckhard Dagge	FRG
1975	Elisha Obed	Bah
1975	Miguel de Oliveira	Bra

WBA Champions

Year	Winner	
1991	Gilbert Dele	Fra
1987	Julian Jackson	VI
1984	Mike McCallum	Jam
1983	Roberto Duran	Pan
1982	Davey Moore	USA
1981	Tadashi Mihara	Jap
1981	Sugar Ray Leonard	USA
1979	Ayub Kalule	Uga
1978	Masashi Kudo	Jap
1977	Eddie Gazo	Nic
1976	Miguel Castellini	Arg
1976	Jose Duran	Spa
1976	Koichi Wajima	Jap
1975	Jae-Do Yuh	RoK
1975	Koichi Wajima	Jap

IBF Champions

Year	Winner	
1989	Gianfranco Rosi	Ita
1989	Darrin van Horn	USA
1988	Robert Hines	USA
1987	Matthew Hilton	Can
1986	Buster Drayton	USA
1984	Carlos Santos	PR

Year	Winner	
1984	Mark Medal	USA

WORLD WELTERWEIGHT CHAMPIONS

FIRST HELD 1892

Undisputed Champions

Year	Winner	
1986	Lloyd Honeyghan	GB
1985	Don Curry	USA
1981	Sugar Ray Leonard	USA
1971	Jose Napoles	Cub
1970	Billy Backus	USA
1969	Jose Napoles	Cub
1967	Curtis Cokes	USA
1963	Emile Griffith	VI
1963	Luis Rodriguez	Cub
1962	Emile Griffith	VI
1961	Benny Kid Paret	Cub
1961	Emile Griffith	VI
1960	Benny Kid Paret	Cub
1958	Don Jordan	USA
1958	Virgil Akins	USA
1956	Carmen Basilio	USA
1956	Johnny Saxton	USA
1955	Carmen Basilio	USA
1955	Tony de Marco	USA
1954	Johnny Saxton	USA
1952	Kid Gavilan	Cub
1946	Sugar Ray Robinson	USA
1946	Marty Servo	USA
1941	Red Cochrane	USA
1940	Fritzie Zivic	USA
1938	Henry Armstrong	USA
1935	Barney Ross	USA
1934	Jimmy McLarnin	Ire
1934	Barney Ross	USA
1933	Jimmy McLarnin	Ire
1933	Young Corbett III	Ita
1932	Jackie Fields	USA
1931	Lou Brouillard	Can

Year	Winner	
1931	Young Jack Thompson	USA
1930	Tommy Freeman	USA
1930	Young Jack Thompson	USA
1929	Jackie Fields	USA
1927	Joe Dundee	Ita
1926	Pete Latzo	USA
1922	Mickey Walker	USA
1919	Jack Britton	USA
1917	Ted Kid Lewis	GB
1916	Jack Britton	USA
1915	Ted Kid Lewis	GB
1907	Mike Twin Sullivan	USA
1906	Honey Mellody	USA
1904	Dixie Kid	USA
1901	Joe Walcott	Bar
1901	Rube Ferns	USA
1900	Matty Matthews	USA
1900	Rube Ferns	USA
1898	Mysterious Billy Smith	USA
1894	Tommy Ryan	USA
1892	Mysterious Billy Smith	USA

WBC Champions

Year	Winner	
1991	Simon Brown	USA
1990	Maurice Blocker	USA
1989	Marlon Starling	USA
1988	Lloyd Honeyghan	GB
1987	Jorge Vaca	Mex
1986	Lloyd Honeyghan	GB
1983	Milton McCrory	USA
1980	Sugar Ray Leonard	USA
1980	Roberto Duran	Pan
1979	Sugar Ray Leonard	USA
1979	Wilfred Benitez	USA
1976	Carlos Palomino	Mex
1975	John H Stracey	GB
1975	Jose Napoles	Cub

WBA Champions

Year	Winner	
1991	Meldrick Taylor	USA
1990	Aaron Davis	USA
1989	Mark Breland	USA
1988	Tomas Molinares	Col
1987	Marlon Starling	USA
1987	Mark Breland	USA
1983	Don Curry	USA
1980	Thomas Hearns	USA
1976	Pipino Cuevas	Mex
1975	Angel Espada	PR
1966	Curtis Cokes	USA

IBF Champions

Year	Winner	
1988	Simon Brown	USA
1987	Lloyd Honeyghan	GB
1984	Don Curry	USA

WORLD JUNIOR WELTERWEIGHT CHAMPIONS

FIRST HELD 1926

Undisputed Champions

Year	Winner	
1967	Paul Fujii	Haw
1966	Sandro Lopopolo	Ita
1965	Carlos Hernandez	Ven
1965	Eddie Perkins	USA
1962	Duilio Loi	Ita
1962	Eddie Perkins	USA
1960	Duilio Loi	Ita
1959	Carlos Ortiz	PR
1946	Tippy Larkin	USA
1933	Barney Ross	USA
1933	Tony Canzoneri	USA
1933	Battling Shaw	Mex
1932	Johnny Jadick	USA
1931	Tony Canzoneri	USA

Year	Winner	
1930	Jack Kid Berg	GB
1926	Mushy Callahan	USA

WBC Champions

Year	Winner	
1989	Julio Cesar Chavez	Mex
1987	Roger Mayweather	USA
1987	Rene Arredondo	Mex
1986	Tsuyoshi Hamada	Jap
1986	Rene Arredondo	Mex
1985	Lonnie Smith	USA
1984	Billy Costello	USA
1983	Bruce Curry	USA
1982	Leroy Haley	USA
1980	Saoul Mamby	Jam
1978	Sang-Hyun Kim	RoK
1976	Saensak Muangsurin	Tha
1976	Miguel Velasquez	Spa
1975	Saensak Muangsurin	Tha
1974	Perico Fernandez	Spa
1970	Bruno Acari	Ita
1968	Pedro Adigue	Phi

WBA Champions

Year	Winner	
1991	Edwin Rosario	PR
1990	Loreto Garza	USA
1987	Juan Martin Coggi	Arg
1986	Patrizio Oliva	Ita
1985	Ubaldo Sacco	Arg
1984	Gene Hatcher	USA
1984	Johnny Bumphus	USA
1980	Aaron Pryor	USA
1977	Antonio Cervantes	Col
1976	Wilfred Benitez	USA
1972	Antonio Cervantes	Col
1972	Alfonso Frazer	Pan
1968	Nicolino Loche	Arg
1967	Paul Fujii	Haw
1963	Eddie Perkins	USA
1963	Roberto Cruz	Phi

IBF Champions

Year	Winner	
1990	Julio Cesar Chavez	Mex
1988	Meldrick Taylor	USA
1988	James McGirt	USA
1987	Terry Marsh	GB
1986	Joe Manley	USA
1986	Gary Hinton	USA
1984	Aaron Pryor	USA

WORLD LIGHTWEIGHT CHAMPIONS

FIRST HELD 1896

Undisputed Champions

Year	Winner	
1990	Pernell Whitaker	USA
1978	Roberto Duran	Pan
1970	Ken Buchanan	GB
1970	Ismael Laguna	Pan
1969	Mando Ramos	USA
1968	Carlos Teo Cruz	DR
1965	Carlos Ortiz	PR
1965	Ismael Laguna	Pan
1962	Carlos Ortiz	PR
1956	Joe Brown	USA
1955	Wallace Bud Smith	USA
1954	Jimmy Carter	USA
1954	Paddy de Marco	USA
1952	Jimmy Carter	USA
1952	Lauro Salas	Mex
1951	Jimmy Carter	USA
1947	Ike Williams	USA
1941	Sammy Angott	USA
1939	Lou Ambers	USA
1938	Henry Armstrong	USA
1936	Lou Ambers	USA
1935	Tony Canzoneri	USA
1933	Barney Ross	USA
1930	Tony Canzoneri	USA
1930	Al Singer	USA
1926	Sammy Mandell	USA

Year	Winner	
1925	Rocky Kansas	USA
1917	Benny Leonard	USA
1914	Freddie Welsh	GB
1912	Willie Ritchie	USA
1910	Ad Wolgast	USA
1908	Battling Nelson	Den
1902	Joe Gans	USA
1899	Frank Erne	Swi
1896	George Lavigne	USA

WBC Champions

Year	Winner	
1989	Pernell Whitaker	USA
1988	Julio Cesar Chavez	Mex
1987	Jose Luis Ramirez	Mex
1985	Hector Camacho	PR
1984	Jose Luis Ramirez	Mex
1983	Edwin Rosario	PR
1981	Alexis Arguello	Nic
1979	Jim Watt	GB
1976	Esteban de Jesus	PR
1974	Guts Ishimatsu	Jap
1972	Rodolfo Gonzalez	Mex
1972	Chango Carmona	Mex
1972	Mando Ramos	USA
1971	Pedro Carrasco	Spa

WBA Champions

Year	Winner	
1990	Pernell Whitaker	USA
1990	Juan Nazario	PR
1989	Edwin Rosario	PR
1987	Julio Cesar Chavez	Mex
1986	Edwin Rosario	PR
1984	Livingstone Bramble	USA
1982	Ray Mancini	USA
1981	Arturo Frias	USA
1981	Claude Noel	TT
1981	Sean O'Grady	USA
1980	Hilmer Kenty	USA
1979	Ernesto Espana	Ven
1972	Roberto Duran	Pan

Year	Winner	
1971	Ken Buchanan	GB

IBF Champions

Year	Winner	
1989	Pernell Whitaker	USA
1988	Greg Haugen	USA
1987	Vinny Pazienza	USA
1986	Greg Haugen	USA
1985	Jimmy Paul	USA
1984	Harry Arroyo	USA
1984	Charlie Brown	USA

WORLD JUNIOR LIGHTWEIGHT CHAMPIONS

FIRST HELD 1921

Undisputed Champions

Year	Winner	
1967	Hiroshi Kobayashi	Jap
1967	Yoshiaki Numata	Jap
1965	Flash Elorde	Phi
1959	Harold Gomes	USA
1933	Frankie Klick	USA
1931	Kid Chocolate	Cub
1929	Benny Bass	USA
1925	Tod Morgan	USA
1925	Mike Ballerino	USA
1924	Kid Sullivan	USA
1923	Johnny Dundee	Ita
1923	Jack Bernstein	USA
1921	Johnny Dundee	Ita

WBC Champions

Year	Winner	
1988	Azumah Nelson	Gha
1984	Julio Cesar Chavez	Mex
1983	Hector Camacho	PR
1982	Bobby Chacon	USA

Year	Winner	
1982	Rafael Limon	Mex
1981	Rolando Navarrete	Phi
1981	Cornelius Boza-Edwards	Uga
1980	Rafael Limon	Mex
1978	Alexis Arguello	Nic
1975	Alfredo Escalera	PR
1974	Kuniaki Shibata	Jap
1971	Ricardo Arredondo	Mex
1970	Yoshiaki Numati	Jap
1969	Rene Barrientos	Phi

WBA Champions

Year	Winner	
1991	Joey Gamache	USA
1986	Brian Mitchell	SA
1986	Alfredo Layne	Pan
1985	Wilfredo Gomez	PR
1984	Rocky Lockridge	USA
1983	Roger Mayweather	USA
1981	Sam Serrano	PR
1980	Yasutsune Uehara	Jap
1976	Sam Serrano	PR
1973	Ben Villaflor	Phi
1973	Kuniaki Shibata	Jap
1972	Ben Villaflor	Phi
1971	Alfredo Marcano	Ven
1969	Hiroshi Kobayashi	Jap

IBF Champions

Year	Winner	
1991	Brian Mitchell	SA
1990	Tony Lopez	USA
1989	Juan Molina	PR
1988	Tony Lopez	USA
1987	Rocky Lockridge	USA
1985	Barry Michael	GB
1985	Lester Ellis	GB
1984	Hwan-Kil Yuh	RoK

WORLD FEATHERWEIGHT CHAMPIONS

FIRST HELD 1891

Undisputed Champions

Year	Winner	
1964	Vicente Saldivar	Mex
1963	Sugar Ramos	Cub
1959	Davey Moore	USA
1957	Hogan Kid Bassey	Nig
1950	Sandy Saddler	USA
1949	Willie Pep	USA
1948	Sandy Saddler	USA
1946	Willie Pep	USA
1939	Joey Archibald	USA
1937	Henry Armstrong	USA
1929	Battling Battalino	USA
1928	Andre Routis	Fra
1928	Tony Canzoneri	USA
1925	Kid Kaplan	USSR
1923	Johnny Dundee	Ita
1923	Eugene Criqui	Fra
1912	Johnny Kilbane	USA
1906	Abe Attell	USA
1904	Tommy Sullivan	USA
1903	Abe Attell	USA
1901	Young Corbett II	USA
1900	Terry McGovern	USA
1898	George Dixon	Can
1898	Dave Sullivan	Ire
1897	Solly Smith	USA
1891	George Dixon	Can

WBC Champions

Year	Winner	
1990	Marcos Villasana	Mex
1988	Jeff Fenech	Aus
1984	Azumah Nelson	Gha
1984	Wilfredo Gomez	PR
1982	Juan Laporte	PR
1980	Salvador Sanchez	Mex
1976	Danny Lopez	USA

Year	Winner	
1975	David Kotey	Gha
1975	Ruben Olivares	Mex
1974	Bobby Chacon	USA
1973	Eder Jofre	Bra
1972	Jose Legra	Cub
1972	Clemente Sanchez	Mex
1970	Kuniaki Shibata	Jap
1970	Vicente Saldivar	Mex
1969	Johnny Famechon	Fra
1968	Jose Legra	Cub
1968	Howard Winstone	GB

WBA Champions

Year	Winner	
1991	Young-Kyun Park	RoK
1987	Antonio Esparragoza	Ven
1986	Steve Cruz	USA
1985	Barry McGuigan	GB
1978	Eusebio Pedroza	Pan
1977	Cecilio Lastra	Spa
1977	Rafael Ortega	Pan
1974	Alexis Arguello	Nic
1974	Ruben Olivares	Mex
1972	Ernesto Marcel	Pan
1971	Antonio Gomez	Ven
1968	Shozo Saijyo	Jap
1967	Paul Rojas	USA

IBF Champions

Year	Winner	
1991	Manuel Medina	Col
1991	Troy Dorsey	USA
1988	Jorge Paez	Mex
1988	Calvin Grove	USA
1986	Antonio Rivera	PR
1985	Ki-Yung Chung	RoK
1984	Min-Keun Oh	RoK

WORLD JUNIOR FEATHERWEIGHT CHAMPIONS

FIRST HELD 1922

Undisputed Champions

Year	Winner	
1922	Jack Kid Wolfe	USA

WBC Champions

Year	Winner	
1991	Daniel Zaragoza	Mex
1991	Kiyoshi Hatanaka	Jap
1990	Pedro Decima	Arg
1990	Paul Banke	USA
1988	Daniel Zaragoza	Mex
1987	Jeff Fenech	Aus
1986	Samart Payakarun	Tha
1985	Lupe Pintor	Mex
1984	Juan Meza	Mex
1983	Jaime Garza	USA
1977	Wifredo Gomez	PR
1976	Dong-Kyun Yum	RoK
1976	Royal Kobayashi	Jap
1976	Rigoberto Riasco	Pan

WBA Champions

Year	Winner	
1990	Luis Mendoza	Col
1989	Jesus Salud	USA
1988	Juan Jose Estrada	Mex
1988	Bernado Pinango	Ven
1987	Julio Gervacio	DR
1987	Louis Espinoza	USA
1984	Victor Callejas	PR
1984	Loris Stecca	Ita
1982	Leonardo Cruz	DR
1980	Sergio Palma	Arg
1980	Leo Randolph	USA
1978	Ricardo Cardona	Col
1977	Soo-Hwan Hong	RoK

IBF Champions

Year	Winner	
1990	Welcome Ncita	SA
1989	Fabrice Benichou	Fra
1988	Jose Sanabria	Ven
1987	Seung-Hoon Lee	RoK
1985	Ji-Won Kim	RoK
1984	Seung-In Suh	RoK
1983	Bobby Berna	Phi

WORLD BANTAMWEIGHT CHAMPIONS

FIRST HELD 1890

Undisputed Champions

Year	Winner	
1972	Enrique Pinder	Pan
1972	Rafael Herrera	Mex
1971	Ruben Olivares	Mex
1970	Chuchu Castillo	Mex
1969	Ruben Olivares	Mex
1968	Lionel Rose	Aus
1965	Fighting Harada	Jap
1962	Eder Jofre	Bra
1959	Joe Becerra	Mex
1957	Alphonse Halimi	Alg
1954	Robert Cohen	Alg
1952	Jimmy Carruthers	Aus
1950	Vic Toweel	SA
1947	Manuel Ortiz	USA
1947	Harold Dade	USA
1942	Manuel Ortiz	USA
1940	Lou Salica	USA
1938	Sixto Escobar	PR
1937	Harry Jeffra	USA
1936	Sixto Escobar	PR
1936	Tony Marino	USA
1935	Baltazar Sangchilli	Spa
1929	Al Brown	Pan
1925	Charlie Rosenberg	USA
1924	Eddie Martin	USA
1924	Abe Goldstein	USA

Year	Winner	
1922	Joe Lynch	USA
1921	Johnny Buff	USA
1921	Pete Herman	USA
1920	Joe Lynch	USA
1917	Pete Herman	USA
1914	Kid Williams	Den
1910	Johnny Coulon	Can
1905	Jimmy Walsh	USA
1904	Joe Bowker	GB
1903	Frankie Neil	USA
1901	Harry Forbes	USA
1901	Harry Harris	USA
1899	Terry McGovern	USA
1895	Pedlar Palmer	GB
1892	Billy Plimmer	GB
1890	George Dixon	Can

WBC Champions

Year	Winner	
1991	Joichiro Tatsuyoshi	Jap
1991	Greg Richardson	USA
1988	Raul Perez	Mex
1985	Miguel Lora	Col
1985	Daniel Zaragoza	Mex
1983	Albert Davila	USA
1979	Lupe Pintor	Mex
1976	Carlos Zarate	Mex
1974	Rodolfo Martinez	Mex
1973	Rafael Herrera	Mex

WBA Champions

Year	Winner	
1989	Luisito Espinosa	Phi
1989	Kaokor Galaxy	Tha
1988	Sung-Kil Moon	RoK
1988	Kaokor Galaxy	Tha
1987	Wilfredo Vasquez	PR
1987	Chang-Yung Park	RoK
1987	Takuya Muguruma	Jap
1986	Bernardo Pinango	Ven
1986	Gaby Canizales	USA
1984	Richard Sandoval	USA
1980	Jeff Chandler	USA

Year	Winner	
1980	Julian Solis	PR
1977	Jorge Lujan	Pan
1975	Alfonso Zamora	Mex
1974	Soo-Hwan Hong	RoK
1973	Arnold Taylor	SA
1973	Romeo Anaya	Mex
1972	Enrique Pinder	Pan

IBF Champions

Year	Winner	
1988	Orlando Canizales	USA
1987	Kelvin Seabrooks	USA
1985	Jeff Fenech	Aus
1984	Satoshi Shingaki	Jap

WORLD JUNIOR BANTAMWEIGHT CHAMPIONS

FIRST HELD 1980

WBC Champions

Year	Winner	
1990	Sung-Kil Moon	RoK
1989	Nana Konadu	Gha
1988	Gilberto Roman	Mex
1987	Baby Rojas	Col
1987	Santos Laciar	Arg
1986	Gilberto Roman	Mex
1984	Jiro Watanabe	Jap
1983	Payao Poontarat	Tha
1982	Rafael Orono	Ven
1981	Chul-Ho Kim	RoK
1980	Rafael Orono	Ven

WBA Champions

Year	Winner	
1984	Khaosai Galaxy	Tha
1982	Jiro Watanabe	Jap

Year	Winner	
1981	Rafael Pedroza	Pan
1981	Gustavo Ballas	Arg

IBF Champions

Year	Winner	
1990	Robert Quiroga	USA
1989	Juan Polo Perez	Col
1987	Elly Pical	Indo
1987	Tae-Il Chang	RoK
1986	Elly Pical	Indo
1986	Cesar Polanco	PR
1985	Elly Pical	Indo
1983	Joo-Do Chun	RoK

WORLD FLYWEIGHT CHAMPIONS

FIRST HELD 1916

Undisputed Champions

Year	Winner	
1965	Salvatore Burruni	Ita
1964	Pone Kingpetch	Tha
1963	Hiroyuki Ebihara	Jap
1963	Pone Kingpetch	Tha
1962	Fighting Harada	Jap
1960	Pone Kingpetch	Tha
1954	Pascual Perez	Arg
1952	Yoshio Shirai	Jap
1950	Dado Marino	Haw
1950	Terry Allen	GB
1948	Rinty Monaghan	Ire
1943	Jackie Paterson	GB
1938	Peter Kane	GB
1937	Benny Lynch	GB
1927	Fidel la Barba	USA
1923	Pancho Villa	Phi
1916	Jimmy Wilde	GB

WBC Champions

Year	Winner	
1991	Muangchai Kittikasem	Tha
1989	Sot Chitalada	Tha
1988	Yong-Kang Kim	RoK
1984	Sot Chitalada	Tha
1984	Gabriel Bernal	Mex
1984	Koji Kobayashi	Jap
1983	Frank Cedeno	Phi
1983	Charlie Magri	Tun
1982	Eleoncio Mercedes	DR
1982	Freddie Castillo	Mex
1982	Prudencio Cardona	Col
1981	Antonio Avelar	Mex
1980	Shoji Oguma	Jap
1979	Chan-Hee Park	RoK
1975	Miguel Canto	Mex
1974	Shoji Oguma	Jap
1973	Betulio Gonzalez	Ven
1972	Venice Borkorsor	Tha
1972	Betulio Gonzalez	Ven
1970	Erbito Salavarria	Phi
1970	Chartchai Chionoi	Tha
1969	Efren Torres	Mex
1966	Chartchai Chionoi	Tha
1966	Walter McGowan	GB
1965	Salvatore Burruni	Ita

WBA Champions

Year	Winner	
1991	Elvis Alvarez	Col
1990	Leopard Tamakuma	Jap
1990	Yul-Woo Lee	RoK
1989	Jesus Rojas	Ven
1987	Fidel Bassa	Col
1985	Hilario Zapata	Pan
1982	Santos Laciar	Arg
1981	Juan Herrara	Mex
1981	Luis Ibarra	Pan
1981	Santos Laciar	Arg
1980	Peter Mathebula	SA
1980	Tae-Shik Kim	RoK
1979	Luis Ibarra	Pan
1978	Betulio Gonzalez	Ven
1976	Guty Espadas	Mex

Year	Winner	
1976	Alfonso Lopez	Pan
1975	Erbito Salavarria	Phi
1974	Susumu Hanagata	Jap
1973	Chartchai Chionoi	Tha
1970	Masao Ohba	Jap
1970	Berkrerk Chartvanchai	Tha
1969	Bernabe Villacampo	Phi
1969	Hiroyuki Ebihara	Jap
1966	Horacio Accavallo	Arg

IBF Champions

Year	Winner	
1989	Dave McAuley	Ire
1988	Duke McKenzie	GB
1988	Rolando Bohol	Phi
1987	Chang-Ho Choi	RoK
1987	Dodie Penalosa	Phi
1986	Hi-Sup Shin	RoK
1986	Bi-Won Chung	RoK
1985	Chong-Kwan Chung	RoK
1983	Soon-Chun Kwon	RoK

WORLD JUNIOR FLYWEIGHT CHAMPIONS

FIRST HELD 1975

WBC Champions

Year	Winner	
1991	Humberto Gonzalez	Mex
1991	Melchor Cob Castro	Mex
1990	Roland Pascua	Phi
1989	Humberto Gonzalez	Mex
1989	Yul-Woo Lee	RoK
1988	German Torres	Mex
1983	Jung-Koo Chang	RoK
1982	Hilario Zapata	Pan
1982	Tadashi Tomori	Jap
1982	Amado Ursua	Mex

Year	Winner	
1980	Hilario Zapata	Pan
1980	Shigeo Nakajima	Jap
1978	Sung-Jun Kim	RoK
1978	Sor Vorasingh	Tha
1978	Freddie Castillo	Mex
1975	Luis Estaba	Ven
1975	Franco Udella	Ita

WBA Champions

Year	Winner	
1985	Myung-Woo Yuh	RoK
1985	Joey Olivo	USA
1984	Francisco Quiroz	DR
1983	Lupe Madera	Mex
1981	Katsuo Tokashiki	Jap
1981	Hwan-Jin Kim	RoK
1981	Pedro Flores	Mex
1976	Yoko Gushiken	Jap
1976	Juan Guzman	DR
1975	Jaime Rios	Pan

IBF Champions

Year	Winner	
1990	Michael Carbajal	USA
1989	Muangchai Kittikasem	Tha
1988	Tacy Macalos	Phi
1986	Jum-Hwan Choi	RoK
1983	Dodie Penalosa	Phi

WORLD STRAWWEIGHT CHAMPIONS

FIRST HELD 1987

WBC Champions

Year	Winner	
1990	Ricardo Lopez	Mex
1990	Hideyuki Ohashi	Jap

Year	Winner	
1989	Jem-Hwan Choi	RoK
1988	Napa Kiatwanchai	Tha
1987	Hiroki Ioka	Jap

WBA Champions

Year	Winner	
1991	Hi-Yon Choi	RoK
1989	Bong-Jun Kim	RoK
1988	Luis Gamez	Ven

IBF Champions

Year	Winner	
1990	Far-Lan Lookmingkwan	Tha
1989	Eric Chavez	Phi
1989	Nico Thomas	Indo
1988	Samuth Sithnaruepol	Tha
1987	Kyung-Yung Lee	RoK

BRITISH HEAVYWEIGHT CHAMPIONS

FIRST HELD 1894

Year	Winner
1991	Lennox Lewis
1989	Gary Mason
1986	Horace Notice
1985	Hughroy Currie
1983	David Pearce
1981	Gordon Ferris
1981	Neville Meade
1978	John L Gardner
1976	Joe Bugner
1975	Bunny Johnson
1975	Richard Dunn
1972	Danny McAlinden
1971	Joe Bugner
1971	Jack Bodell
1970	Henry Cooper

Year	Winner
1969	Jack Bodell
1959	Henry Cooper
1958	Brian London
1956	Joe Erskine
1953	Don Cockell
1952	Johnny Williams
1950	Jack Gardner
1945	Bruce Woodcock
1944	Jack London
1938	Len Harvey
1937	Tommy Farr
1936	Ben Foord
1934	Jack Petersen
1933	Len Harvey
1932	Jack Petersen
1931	Reggie Meen
1926	Phil Scott
1923	Frank Goddard
1919	Joe Beckett
1919	Frank Goddard
1919	Joe Beckett
1911	Bombardier Billy Wells
1910	P O Curran
1909	Iron Hague
1906	Gunner Moir
1903	Jack Palmer
1897	George Crisp
1895	Jem Smith
1894	Charlie Mitchell

OLYMPIC CHAMPIONS
Super-Heavyweight

FIRST HELD 1984

Year	Winner	
1988	L Lewis	Can
1984	T Biggs	USA

Heavyweight

FIRST HELD 1904

Year	Winner	
1988	R Mercer	USA
1984	H Tillman	USA
1980	T Stevenson	Cub
1976	T Stevenson	Cub
1972	T Stevenson	Cub
1968	G Foreman	USA
1964	J Frazier	USA
1960	F de Piccoli	Ita
1956	P Rademacher	USA
1952	H E Sanders	USA
1948	R Iglesias	Arg
1936	H Runge	Ger
1932	S Lovell	Arg
1928	A R Jurado	Arg
1924	O von Porat	Nor
1920	R Rawson	GB
1912	Not held	
1908	A L Oldham	GB
1904	S Berger	USA

Light-Heavyweight

FIRST HELD 1920

Year	Winner	
1988	A Maynard	USA
1984	A Josipovic	Yug
1980	S Kacar	Yug
1976	L Spinks	USA
1972	M Parlov	Yug
1968	D Poznyak	USSR
1964	C Pinto	Ita
1960	C Clay	USA
1956	J Boyd	USA
1952	N Lee	USA
1948	G Hunter	SA
1936	R Michelot	Fra
1932	D Carstens	SA
1928	V Avendano	Arg
1924	H Mitchell	GB
1920	E Eagan	USA

Middleweight

FIRST HELD 1904

Year	Winner	
1988	H Maske	GDR
1984	Joon-Sup Shin	RoK
1980	J Gomez	Cub
1976	M Spinks	USA
1972	V Lemechev	USSR
1968	C Finnegan	GB
1964	V Popentschenko	USSR
1960	E Crook	USA
1956	G Schatkov	USSR
1952	F Patterson	USA
1948	L Papp	Hun
1936	J Despeaux	Fra
1932	C Barth	USA
1928	P Toscani	Ita
1924	H Mallin	GB
1920	H Mallin	GB
1912	Not held	
1908	J W T Douglas	GB
1904	C Mayer	USA

Light-Middleweight

FIRST HELD 1952

Year	Winner	
1988	Park Si-Hun	RoK
1984	F Tate	USA
1980	A Martinez	Cub
1976	J Rybicki	Pol
1972	D Kottysch	Ger
1968	B Lagutin	USSR
1964	B Lagutin	USSR
1960	W McClure	USA
1956	L Papp	Hun
1952	L Papp	Hun

Welterweight

FIRST HELD 1904

Year	Winner	
1988	R Wangila	Ken
1984	M Breland	USA
1980	A Aldama	Cub
1976	J Bachfeld	GDR
1972	E Correa	Cub
1968	M Wolke	GDR
1964	M Kasprzyk	Pol
1960	G Benvenuti	Ita
1956	N Lince	Rom
1952	Z Chychla	Pol
1948	J Torma	Cze
1936	S Suvio	Fin
1932	E Flynn	USA
1928	E Morgan	NZ
1924	J Delarge	Bel
1920	A Schneider	Can
1912/08	Not held	
1904	A Young	USA

Light-Welterweight

FIRST HELD 1952

Year	Winner	
1988	V Janovski	USSR
1984	J Page	USA
1980	P Oliva	Ita
1976	R Leonard	USA
1972	R Seales	USA
1968	J Kulej	Pol
1964	J Kulej	Pol
1960	B Nemecek	Cze
1956	V Yengibaryan	USSR
1952	C Adkins	USA

Lightweight

FIRST HELD 1904

Year	Winner	
1988	A Zuelow	GDR

Year	Winner	
1984	P Whitaker	USA
1980	A Herrara	Cub
1976	H Davis	USA
1972	J Szczepanski	Pol
1968	R Harris	USA
1964	J Grudzien	Pol
1960	K Pazdzior	Pol
1956	R McTaggart	GB
1952	A Bolognesi	Ita
1948	G Dreyer	SA
1936	I Harangi	Hun
1932	L Stevens	SA
1928	C Orlandi	Ita
1924	H Nielsen	Den
1920	S Mosberg	USA
1912	Not held	
1908	F Grace	GB
1904	H Spanger	USA

Featherweight

FIRST HELD 1904

Year	Winner	
1988	G Parisi	Ita
1984	M Taylor	USA
1980	R Fink	GDR
1976	A Herrera	Cub
1972	B Kuznetsov	USSR
1968	A Roldan	Mex
1964	S Stepashkin	USSR
1960	F Musso	Ita
1956	V Safronov	USSR
1952	J Zachara	Cze
1948	E Formenti	Ita
1936	O Casanovas	Arg
1932	C Robledo	Arg
1928	L van Klaveren	Nld
1924	J Fields	USA
1920	P Fritsch	Fra
1912	Not held	
1908	R Gunn	GB
1904	O Kirk	USA

Bantamweight

FIRST HELD 1904

Year	Winner	
1988	K McKinney	USA
1984	M Stecca	Ita
1980	J Hernandez	Cub
1976	Yong-Jo Gu	DPRK
1972	O Martinez	Cub
1968	V Sokolov	USSR
1964	T Sakurai	Jap
1960	O Grigoryev	USSR
1956	W Behrendt	Ger
1952	P Hamalainen	Fin
1948	T Csik	Hun
1936	U Sergo	Ita
1932	H Gwynne	Can
1928	V Tamagnini	Ita
1924	W Smith	SA
1920	C Walker	SA
1912	Not held	
1908	H Thomas	GB
1904	O Kirk	USA

Flyweight

FIRST HELD 1904

Year	Winner	
1988	Kim Kwang-Sun	RoK
1984	S McCrory	USA
1980	P Lessov	Bul
1976	L Randolph	USA
1972	G Kostadinov	Bul
1968	R Delgado	Mex
1964	F Atzori	Ita
1960	G Torok	Hun
1956	T Spinks	GB
1952	N Brooks	USA
1948	P Perez	Arg
1936	W Kaiser	Ger
1932	I Enekes	Hun
1928	A Kocsis	Hun
1924	F LaBarba	USA
1920	F De Genaro	USA
1912/08	Not held	

Year	Winner	
1904	G Finnegan	USA

Light-Flyweight

FIRST HELD 1968

Year	Winner	
1988	I Hristov	Bul

Year	Winner	
1984	P Gonzales	USA
1980	S Sabirov	USSR
1976	J Hernandez	Cub
1972	G Gedo	Hun
1968	F Rodriguez	Ven

CANOEING

OLYMPIC CHAMPIONS
Kayak Singles
500 metres

FIRST HELD 1976

Year	Winner	
1988	Z Gyulay	Hun
1984	I Ferguson	NZ
1980	V Parfenovich	USSR
1976	V Diba	Rom

Kayak Singles
1000 metres

FIRST HELD 1936

Year	Winner	
1988	G Barton	USA
1984	A Thompson	NZ
1980	R Helm	GDR
1976	R Helm	GDR
1972	A Shaparenko	USSR
1968	M Hesz	Hun

Year	Winner	
1964	R Peterson	Swe
1960	E Hansen	Den
1956	G Fredriksson	Swe
1952	G Fredriksson	Swe
1948	G Fredriksson	Swe
1936	G Hradetzky	Aut

Kayak Doubles
500 metres

FIRST HELD 1976

Year	Winner	
1988	I Ferguson & P McDonald	NZ
1984	I Ferguson & P McDonald	NZ
1980	V Parfenovich & S Chukrai	USSR
1976	J Mattern & B Olbricht	GDR

Kayak Doubles
1000 metres

FIRST HELD 1936

Year	Winner	
1988	G Barton & N Bellingham	USA
1984	H Fisher & A Morris	Can
1980	V Parfenovich & S Chukrai	USSR
1976	S Nargorny & V Romanovsky	USSR
1972	N Gorbachev & V Kratassyuk	USSR
1968	A Shaparenko & V Morozov	USSR
1964	S Sjodelius & N Utterberg	Swe
1960	G Fredriksson & S Sjodelius	Swe
1956	M Scheuer & M Miltenberger	FRG
1952	K Wires & Y Hietanen	Fin
1948	H Berglund & L Klingstrom	Swe
1936	A Kainz & A Dorfner	Aut

Kayak Fours
1000 metres

FIRST HELD 1964

Year	Winner
1988	Hungary
1984	New Zealand
1980	East Germany
1976	USSR
1972	USSR
1968	Norway
1964	USSR

Canadian Singles
500 metres

FIRST HELD 1976

Year	Winner	
1988	O Heudrodt	GDR
1984	L Cain	Can
1980	S Postrekhin	USSR
1976	A Rogov	USSR

Canadian Singles
1000 metres

FIRST HELD 1936

Year	Winner	
1988	I Klementiev	USSR
1984	U Eicke	FRG
1980	L Lubenov	Bul
1976	M Ljubek	Yug
1972	I Patzaichin	Rom
1968	T Tatai	Hun
1964	J Eschert	Ger
1960	J Parti	Hun
1956	L Rotman	Rom
1952	J Holecek	Cze
1948	J Holecek	Cze
1936	F Amyot	Can

Canadian Pairs
500 metres

FIRST HELD 1976

Year	Winner	
1988	V Reineski & N Jouravski	USSR
1984	M Ljubek & M Nisovic	Yug
1980	L Foltan & I Vaskuti	Hun
1976	S Petrenko & A Vinogradov	USSR

Canadian Pairs
1000 metres

FIRST HELD 1936

Year	Winner	
1988	V Reineski & N Jouravski	USSR
1984	I Patzaichin & T Simionov	Rom
1980	I Patzaichin & T Simionov	Rom
1976	S Petrenko & A Vinogradov	USSR
1972	V Chessyunas & Y Lobanov	USSR
1968	I Patzaichin & S Covaliov	Rom
1964	A Khimich & S Oschepkov	USSR
1960	L Geyshtor & S Makarenko	USSR
1956	A Dumitru & S Ismailciuc	Rom
1952	B Peder & F Haunstoft	Den
1948	J Brzak & B Kudrna	Cze
1936	V Syrovatka & J Brzak	Cze

Women's Kayak Singles
500 metres

FIRST HELD 1948

Year	Winner	
1988	V Guecheva	Bul
1984	A Andersson	Swe
1980	B Fischer	GDR
1976	C Zirzow	GDR
1972	Y Ryabchinskaya	USSR
1968	L Pinayeva	USSR

Year	Winner	
1964	L Khvedosyuk	USSR
1960	A Seredina	USSR
1956	E Dementyena	USSR
1952	S Saimo	Fin
1948	K Hoff	Den

Women's Kayak Doubles
500 metres

FIRST HELD 1960

Year	Winner	
1988	B Schmidt & A Nothnagel	GDR
1984	A Andersson & A Olsson	Swe
1980	C Genauss & M Bischof	GDR
1976	N Gopova & G Kreft	USSR
1972	L Pinayeva & Y Kuryshko	USSR
1968	A Zimmermann & R Esser	FRG
1964	A Zimmermann & R Esser	FRG
1960	M Zhubina & Seredina	USSR

Women's Kayak Fours
500 metres

FIRST HELD 1984

Year	Winner
1988	East Germany
1984	Romania

CHESS

WORLD CHAMPIONS

FIRST HELD 1843

Played on a challenge basis

Year	Winner	
1985	G Kasparov	USSR
1975	A Karpov	USSR
1972	R Fischer	USA
1969	B Spassky	USSR
1963	T Petrosian	USSR
1961	M Botvinnik	USSR
1960	M Tal	USSR
1958	M Botvinnik	USSR
1957	V Smyslov	USSR
1948	M Botvinnik	USSR
1937	A Alekhine	Fra
1935	M Euwe	Nld
1927	A Alekhine	Fra
1921	J Capablanca	Cub
1894	E Lasker	Ger
1866	W Steinitz	Aut
1862	A Anderssen	Ger
1858	P Morphy	USA
1851	A Anderssen	Ger
1843	H Staunton	GB

Women's World Champions

FIRST HELD 1927

Played on a challenge basis

Year	Winner	
1978	M Chiburdanidze	USSR
1962	N Gaprindashvili	USSR
1958	E Bykova	USSR
1956	O Rubtsova	USSR
1953	E Bykova	USSR
1950	L Rudenko	USSR
1927	V Menchik	GB

CHESS OLYMPIADS
Men

FIRST HELD 1927

Year	Winner
1990	USSR
1988	USSR
1986	USSR
1984	USSR
1982	USSR
1980	USSR
1978	Hungary
1976	United States
1974	USSR
1972	USSR
1970	USSR
1968	USSR
1966	USSR
1964	USSR
1962	USSR
1960	USSR
1958	USSR
1956	USSR
1956	USSR
1954	USSR
1952	USSR
1950	Yugoslavia
1939	Germany
1937	United States
1935	United States
1933	United States
1931	United States
1928	Hungary
1927	Hungary

Women

FIRST HELD 1957	
Year	Winner
1990	Hungary
1988	Hungary
1986	USSR
1984	USSR
1982	USSR
1980	USSR

Year	Winner
1978	USSR
1976	Israel
1974	USSR
1972	USSR
1969	USSR
1966	USSR
1963	USSR
1957	USSR

CRICKET

WORLD CUP

FIRST HELD 1975	
Year	Winner
1987	Australia
1983	India
1979	West Indies
1975	West Indies

COUNTY CHAMPIONS

FIRST HELD 1864	
Year	Winner
1991	Essex
1990	Middlesex
1989	Worcestershire
1988	Worcestershire
1987	Nottinghamshire
1986	Essex
1985	Middlesex
1984	Essex
1983	Essex

Year	Winner
1982	Middlesex
1981	Nottinghamshire
1980	Middlesex
1979	Essex
1978	Kent
1977	Middlesex
	Kent
1976	Middlesex
1975	Leicestershire
1974	Worcestershire
1973	Hampshire
1972	Warwickshire
1971	Surrey
1970	Kent
1969	Glamorgan
1968	Yorkshire
1967	Yorkshire
1966	Yorkshire
1965	Worcestershire
1964	Worcestershire
1963	Yorkshire
1962	Yorkshire
1961	Hampshire
1960	Yorkshire
1959	Yorkshire
1958	Surrey

Year	Winner	Year	Winner
1957	Surrey	1905	Yorkshire
1956	Surrey	1904	Lancashire
1955	Surrey	1903	Middlesex
1954	Surrey	1902	Yorkshire
1953	Surrey	1901	Yorkshire
1952	Surrey	1900	Yorkshire
1951	Warwickshire	1899	Surrey
1950	Lancashire	1898	Yorkshire
	Surrey	1897	Lancashire
1949	Middlesex	1896	Yorkshire
	Yorkshire	1895	Surrey
1948	Glamorgan	1894	Surrey
1947	Middlesex	1893	Yorkshire
1946	Yorkshire	1892	Surrey
1945/40	No Competition	1891	Surrey
1939	Yorkshire	1890	Surrey
1938	Yorkshire	1889	Surrey
1937	Yorkshire		Nottinghamshire
1936	Derbyshire		Lancashire
1935	Yorkshire	1888	Surrey
1934	Lancashire	1887	Surrey
1933	Yorkshire	1886	Nottinghamshire
1932	Yorkshire	1885	Nottinghamshire
1931	Yorkshire	1884	Nottinghamshire
1930	Lancashire	1883	Nottinghamshire
1929	Nottinghamshire	1882	Nottinghamshire
1928	Lancashire		Lancashire
1927	Lancashire	1881	Lancashire
1926	Lancashire	1880	Nottinghamshire
1925	Yorkshire	1879	Nottinghamshire
1924	Yorkshire		Lancashire
1923	Yorkshire	1878	Undecided
1922	Yorkshire	1877	Gloucestershire
1921	Middlesex	1876	Gloucestershire
1920	Middlesex	1875	Nottinghamshire
1919	Yorkshire	1874	Gloucestershire
1918/15	No Competition	1873	Gloucestershire
1914	Surrey		Nottinghamshire
1913	Kent	1872	Nottinghamshire
1912	Yorkshire	1871	Nottinghamshire
1911	Warwickshire	1870	Yorkshire
1910	Kent	1869	Nottinghamshire
1909	Kent		Yorkshire
1908	Yorkshire	1868	Nottinghamshire
1907	Nottinghamshire	1867	Yorkshire
1906	Kent	1866	Middlesex

Year	Winner
1865	Nottinghamshire
1864	Surrey

NATWEST BANK TROPHY

FIRST HELD 1963

Year	Winner
1991	Hampshire
1990	Lancashire
1989	Warwickshire
1988	Middlesex
1987	Nottinghamshire
1986	Sussex
1985	Essex
1984	Middlesex
1983	Somerset
1982	Surrey
1981	Derbyshire
1980	Middlesex
1979	Somerset
1978	Sussex
1977	Middlesex
1976	Northamptonshire
1975	Lancashire
1974	Kent
1973	Gloucestershire
1972	Lancashire
1971	Lancashire
1970	Lancashire
1969	Yorkshire
1968	Warwickshire
1967	Kent
1966	Warwickshire
1965	Yorkshire
1964	Sussex
1963	Sussex

BENSON & HEDGES CUP

FIRST HELD 1972

Year	Winner
1991	Worcestershire
1990	Lancashire
1989	Nottinghamshire
1988	Hampshire
1987	Yorkshire
1986	Middlesex
1985	Leicestershire
1984	Lancashire
1983	Middlesex
1982	Somerset
1981	Somerset
1980	Northamptonshire
1979	Essex
1978	Kent
1977	Gloucestershire
1976	Kent
1975	Leicestershire
1974	Surrey
1973	Kent
1972	Leicestershire

SUNDAY LEAGUE CHAMPIONS

FIRST HELD 1969

Year	Winner
1991	Nottinghamshire
1990	Derbyshire
1989	Lancashire
1988	Worcestershire
1987	Worcestershire
1986	Hampshire
1985	Essex
1984	Essex
1983	Yorkshire
1982	Sussex
1981	Essex
1980	Warwickshire
1979	Somerset

Year	Winner
1978	Hampshire
1977	Leicestershire
1976	Kent
1975	Hampshire
1974	Leicestershire
1973	Kent
1972	Kent
1971	Worcestershire
1970	Lancashire
1969	Lancashire

REFUGE ASSURANCE CUP

FIRST HELD 1988

Year	Winner
1991	Worcestershire
1990	Middlesex
1989	Essex
1988	Lancashire

LEADING BATSMEN

FIRST HELD 1894

Year	Batsman		
1991	C L Hooper	West Indies	93.81
1990	G A Gooch	Essex	101.70
1989	D M Jones	Australia	88.82
1988	G A Hick	Worcestershire	77.51
1987	M D Crowe	Somerset	66.79
1986	C G Greenidge	Hampshire	67.83
1985	I V A Richards	Somerset	76.50
1984	M W Gatting	Middlesex	68.39
1983	I V A Richards	Somerset	75.25
1982	Zaheer Abbas	Gloucestershire & Pakistan	70.23
1981	Zaheer Abbas	Gloucestershire	88.69
1980	A J Lamb	Northamptonshire	66.55
1979	G Boycott	Yorkshire	102.53
1978	C E B Rice	Nottinghamshire	66.82
1977	G Boycott	Yorkshire	68.04
1976	Zaheer Abbas	Gloucestershire	75.11
1975	R B Kanhai	Warwickshire	82.53
1974	C H Lloyd	Lancashire	63.39
1973	M L C Foster	West Indies	63.69
1972	G Boycott	Yorkshire	72.35
1971	G Boycott	Yorkshire	100.12
1970	T W Graveney	Worcestershire	62.66
1969	J H Eldrich	Surrey	69.93
1968	G Boycott	Yorkshire	64.65
1967	K F Barrington	Surrey	68.63
1966	G S Sobers	West Indies	61.31
1965	M C Cowdrey	Kent	63.42
1964	K F Barrington	Surrey	62.40
1963	G S Sobers	West Indies	47.60

Year	Batsman		
1962	R T Simpson	Nottinghamshire	54.18
1961	W M Lawry	Australia	61.18
1960	R Subba Row	Northamptonshire	55.66
1959	M J K Smith	Warwickshire	54.97
1958	P B H May	Surrey	63.74
1957	P B H May	Surrey	61.76
1956	K D Mackay	Australia	52.52
1955	D J McGlew	South Africa	58.46
1954	D C S Compton	Middlesex	58.62
1953	R N Harvey	Australia	65.80
1952	D S Sheppard	Cambridge Univ. & Sussex	64.62
1951	P B H May	Cambridge Univ. & Surrey	68.79
1950	E Weekes	West Indies	79.65
1949	J Hardstaff Jnr	Nottinghamshire	72.61
1948	D G Bradman	Australia	89.92
1947	D C S Compton	Middlesex	90.85
1946	W R Hammond	Gloucestershire	84.90
1945/40	No Competition		
1939	G Headley	West Indies	72.70
1938	D G Bradman	Australia	115.66
1937	W R Hammond	Gloucestershire	65.04
1936	W R Hammond	Gloucestershire	56.94
1935	W R Hammond	Gloucestershire	49.35
1934	D G Bradman	Australia	84.16
1933	W R Hammond	Gloucestershire	67.81
1932	H Sutcliffe	Yorkshire	74.13
1931	H Sutcliffe	Yorkshire	96.96
1930	D G Bradman	Australia	98.66
1929	J B Hobbs	Surrey	66.55
1928	J B Hobbs	Surrey	82.00
1927	C Hallows	Lancashire	75.58
1926	J B Hobbs	Surrey	77.60
1925	J B Hobbs	Surrey	70.32
1924	A Sandham	Surrey	59.48
1923	E Hendren	Middlesex	77.17
1922	E Hendren	Middlesex	66.83
1921	C P Mead	Hampshire	69.10
1920	E Hendren	Middlesex	61.46
1919	G Gunn	Nottinghamshire	63.08
1918/15	No Competition		
1914	J W Hearne	Middlesex	60.45
1913	C P Mead	Hampshire	50.51
1912	C B Fry	Hampshire	56.85
1911	C B Fry	Hampshire	72.00
1910	J T Tyldesley	Lancashire	46.22
1909	W Bardsley	Australia	47.04

Year	Batsman		
1908	B J T Bosanquet	Middlesex	54.05
1907	C B Fry	Sussex	46.74
1906	C J Burnup	Kent	67.05
1905	C B Fry	Sussex	70.02
1904	K S Ranjitsinhji	Sussex	74.17
1903	C B Fry	Sussex	81.30
1902	A Shrewsbury	Nottinghamshire	50.00
1901	C B Fry	Sussex	78.67
1900	K S Ranjitsinhji	Sussex	87.57
1899	R M Poore	Hampshire	91.23
1898	W G Quaife	Warwickshire	60.95
1897	N F Druce	Surrey	51.55
1896	K S Ranjitsinhji	Sussex	57.91
1895	A C MacLaren	Lancashire	51.20
1894	W Brockwell	Surrey	38.23

LEADING BOWLERS

FIRST HELD 1894

Qualification: 50 wickets

Year	Bowler		
1991	Waqar Younis	Surrey	14.65
1990	I R Bishop	Derbyshire	19.05
1989	T M Alderman	Australia	15.64
1988	S T Clarke	Surrey	14.49
1987	R J Hadlee	Nottinghamshire	12.64
1986	M D Marshall	Hampshire	15.08
1985	R M Ellison	Kent	17.20
1984	R J Hadlee	Nottinghamshire	14.05
1983	J K Lever	Essex	14.57
1982	R J Hadlee	Nottinghamshire	14.57
1981	R J Hadlee	Nottinghamshire	14.89
1980	V A P van der Bijl	Middlesex	14.72
1979	J Garner	Somerset	13.83
1978	D L Underwood	Kent	14.49
1977	M Hendrick	Derbyshire	15.94
1976	M A Holding	West Indies	14.38
1975	A M E Roberts	Hampshire	15.80
1974	A M E Roberts	Hampshire	13.62
1973	T W Cartwright	Somerset	15.84
1972	M J Proctor	Gloucestershire	16.55
1971	G G Arnold	Surrey	17.12

Year	Bowler		
1970	D J Sheppard	Glamorgan	19.16
1969	A Ward	Derbyshire	14.82
1968	O S Wheatley	Glamorgan	12.95
1967	D L Underwood	Kent	12.39
1966	D L Underwood	Kent	13.80
1965	H J Rhodes	Derbyshire	11.05
1964	J A Standen	Worcestershire	13.00
1963	C C Griffith	West Indies	12.83
1962	C Cook	Gloucestershire	17.13
1961	J A Flavell	Worcestershire	17.79
1960	J B Statham	Lancashire	12.31
1959	J B Statham	Lancashire	15.01
1958	H L Jackson	Derbyshire	10.99
1957	G A R Lock	Surrey	12.02
1956	G A R Lock	Surrey	12.46
1955	R Appleyard	Yorkshire	13.01
1954	J B Statham	Lancashire	14.13
1953	H L Jackson	Derbyshire	15.28
1952	F S Trueman	Yorkshire	13.78
1951	R Appleyard	Yorkshire	14.14
1950	R Tattersall	Lancashire	13.59
1949	T W J Goddard	Gloucestershire	19.18
1948	R A Lindwall	Australia	15.68
1947	J C Clay	Glamorgan	16.44
1946	A Booth	Yorkshire	11.61
1945/40	No Competition		
1939	H Verity	Yorkshire	13.13
1938	W E Bowes	Yorkshire	15.23
1937	H Verity	Yorkshire	15.68
1936	H Larwood	Nottinghamshire	12.97
1935	H Verity	Yorkshire	14.36
1934	W J O'Reilly	Australia	17.04
1933	H Verity	Yorkshire	13.43
1932	H Larwood	Nottinghamshire	12.86
1931	H Larwood	Nottinghamshire	12.03
1930	H Verity	Yorkshire	12.42
1929	R Tyldesley	Lancashire	15.57
1928	H Larwood	Nottinghamshire	14.51
1927	H Larwood	Nottinghamshire	16.95
1926	W Rhodes	Yorkshire	14.86
1925	C W L Parker	Gloucestershire	14.91
1924	G Macaulay	Yorkshire	13.23
1923	W Rhodes	Yorkshire	11.54
1922	W Rhodes	Yorkshire	2.19
1921	E R Wilson	Yorkshire	11.19
1920	W Rhodes	Yorkshire	13.18

Year	Bowler		
1919	W Rhodes	Yorkshire	14.42
1918/15	No Competition		
1914	C Blythe	Kent	15.19
1913	B G von Melle	Oxford University	15.90
1912	S F Barnes	Lancashire	11.33
1911	G J Thompson	Northamptonshire	16.71
1910	J T Hearne	Middlesex	12.79
1909	W C Smith	Surrey	12.43
1908	J B King	Philadelphians	11.01
1907	R O Schwarz	South Africa	11.79
1906	W Huddleston	Lancashire	12.26
1905	S Haigh	Yorkshire	15.37
1904	W C Smith	Surrey	17.90
1903	W Mead	Essex	13.67
1902	S Haigh	Yorkshire	12.55
1901	W Rhodes	Yorkshire	15.12
1900	W Rhodes	Yorkshire	13.81
1899	A E Trott	Middlesex	17.09
1898	J T Hearne	Middlesex	14.05
1897	A E Trott	Middlesex	13.84
1896	T R McKibbin	Australia	14.26
1895	C L Townsend	Gloucestershire	13.94
1894	A D Pougher	Leicestershire	9.3

ENGLAND V AUSTRALIA

Test Series

FIRST HELD 1876/77

ASHES FIRST HELD 1882/83

Year	Winner
1990/91	Australia
1989	Australia
1987/88	Drawn
1986/87	England
1985	England
1982/83	Australia
1981	England
1980	Drawn
1979/80	Australia
1978/79	England
1977	England

Year	Winner
1976/77	Australia
1975	Australia
1974/75	Australia
1972	Drawn
1970/71	England
1968	Drawn
1965/66	Drawn
1964	Australia
1962/63	Drawn
1961	Australia
1958/59	Australia
1956	England
1954/55	England
1953	England
1950/51	Australia
1948	Australia
1946/47	Australia
1938	Drawn
1936/37	Australia

Year	Winner
1934	Australia
1932/33	England
1930	Australia
1928/29	England
1926	England
1924/25	Australia
1921	Australia
1920/21	Australia
1912	England
1911/12	England
1909	Australia
1907/08	Australia
1905	England
1903/04	England
1902	Australia
1901/02	Australia
1899	Australia
1897/98	Australia
1896	England
1894/95	England
1893	England
1891/92	Australia
1890	England
1888	England
1887/88	England
1886/87	England
1886	England
1884/85	England
1884	England
1882/83	England
1882	Australia
1881/82	Australia
1880	England
1878/79	Australia
1876/77	Drawn

ENGLAND V SOUTH AFRICA

Test Series

FIRST HELD 1888/89

Year	Winner
1965	South Africa
1964/65	England
1960	England
1956/57	Drawn
1955	England
1951	England
1948/49	England
1947	England
1938/39	England
1935	South Africa
1930/31	South Africa
1929	England
1927/28	Drawn
1924	England
1922/23	England
1913/14	England
1912	England
1909/10	South Africa
1907	England
1905/06	South Africa
1898/99	England
1895/96	England
1891/92	England
1888/89	England

ENGLAND V WEST INDIES

Test Series

FIRST HELD 1928

Year	Winner
1991	Drawn
1990	West Indies
1988	West Indies
1985/86	West Indies
1984	West Indies

Year	Winner		Year	Winner
1980/81	West Indies		1950/51	England
1980	West Indies		1949	Drawn
1976	West Indies		1946/47	Drawn
1973/74	Drawn		1937	England
1973	West Indies		1932/33	Drawn
1969	England		1931	England
1967/68	England		1929/30	England
1966	West Indies			
1963	West Indies			
1959/60	England			
1957	England			
1953/54	Drawn			
1950	West Indies			
1947/48	West Indies			
1939	England			
1934/35	West Indies			
1933	England			
1929/30	Drawn			
1928	England			

ENGLAND V NEW ZEALAND

Test Series

FIRST HELD 1929/30

Year	Winner
1990	England
1987/88	Drawn
1986	New Zealand
1983/84	New Zealand
1983	England
1978	England
1977/78	Drawn
1974/75	England
1973	England
1970/71	England
1969	England
1965/66	Drawn
1965	England
1962/63	England
1958/59	England
1958	England
1954/55	England

ENGLAND V INDIA

Test Series

FIRST HELD 1932

Year	Winner
1990	England
1986	India
1984/85	England
1982	England
1981/82	India
1979/80	England
1979	England
1976/77	England
1974	England
1972/73	India
1971	India
1967	England
1963/64	Drawn
1961/62	India
1959	England
1952	England
1951/52	Drawn
1946	England
1936	England
1933/34	England
1932	England

ENGLAND V PAKISTAN

Test Series

FIRST HELD 1954

Year	Winner
1987/88	Pakistan
1987	Pakistan
1983/84	Pakistan
1982	England
1978	England
1977/78	Drawn
1974	Drawn
1972/73	Drawn
1971	England
1968/69	Drawn
1967	England
1962	England
1961/62	England
1954	Drawn

ENGLAND V SRI LANKA

Test Series

FIRST HELD 1981/82

Year	Winner
1991	England
1988	England
1984	Drawn
1981/82	England

AUSTRALIA V WEST INDIES

Test Series

FIRST HELD 1930/31

Year	Winner
1990/91	West Indies

Year	Winner
1988/89	West Indies
1984/85	West Indies
1983/84	West Indies
1981/82	Drawn
1979/80	West Indies
1977/78	West Indies
1975/76	Australia
1972/73	Australia
1968/69	Australia
1964/65	West Indies
1960/61	Australia
1954/55	Australia
1951/52	Australia
1930/31	Australia

SHEFFIELD SHIELD

FIRST HELD 1892/93

Year	Winner
1990/91	Victoria
1989/90	New South Wales
1988/89	Western Australia
1987/88	Western Australia
1986/87	Western Australia
1985/86	New South Wales
1984/85	New South Wales
1983/84	Western Australia
1982/83	New South Wales
1981/82	South Australia
1980/81	Western Australia
1979/80	Victoria
1978/79	Victoria
1977/78	Western Australia
1976/77	Western Australia
1975/76	South Australia
1974/75	Western Australia
1973/74	Victoria
1972/73	Western Australia
1971/72	Western Australia
1970/71	South Australia
1969/70	Victoria
1968/69	South Australia
1967/68	Western Australia
1966/67	Victoria

Year	Winner
1965/66	New South Wales
1964/65	New South Wales
1963/64	South Australia
1962/63	Victoria
1961/62	New South Wales
1960/61	New South Wales
1959/60	New South Wales
1958/59	New South Wales
1957/58	New South Wales
1956/57	New South Wales
1955/56	New South Wales
1954/55	New South Wales
1953/54	New South Wales
1952/53	South Australia
1951/52	New South Wales
1950/51	Victoria
1949/50	New South Wales
1948/49	New South Wales
1947/48	Western Australia
1946/47	Victoria
1946/40	No Competition
1939/40	New South Wales
1938/39	South Australia
1937/38	New South Wales
1936/37	Victoria
1935/36	South Australia
1934/35	Victoria
1933/34	Victoria
1932/33	New South Wales
1931/32	New South Wales
1930/31	Victoria
1929/30	Victoria
1928/29	New South Wales
1927/28	Victoria
1926/27	South Australia
1925/26	New South Wales
1924/25	Victoria
1923/24	Victoria
1922/23	New South Wales
1921/22	Victoria
1920/21	New South Wales
1919/20	New South Wales
1919/15	No Competition
1914/15	Victoria
1913/14	New South Wales
1912/13	South Australia

Year	Winner
1911/12	New South Wales
1910/11	New South Wales
1909/10	South Australia
1908/09	New South Wales
1907/08	Victoria
1906/07	New South Wales
1905/06	New South Wales
1904/05	New South Wales
1903/04	New South Wales
1902/03	New South Wales
1901/02	New South Wales
1900/01	Victoria
1899/00	New South Wales
1898/99	Victoria
1897/98	Victoria
1896/97	New South Wales
1895/96	New South Wales
1894/95	Victoria
1893/94	South Australia
1892/93	Victoria

FAI INSURANCE CUP

FIRST HELD 1969/70

Year	Winner
1990/91	Western Australia
1989/90	Western Australia
1988/89	Queensland
1987/88	New South Wales
1986/87	South Australia
1985/86	Western Australia
1984/85	New South Wales
1983/84	South Australia
1982/83	Western Australia
1981/82	Queensland
1980/81	Queensland
1979/80	Victoria
1978/79	Tasmania
1977/78	Western Australia
1976/77	Western Australia
1975/76	Queensland
1974/75	New Zealand
1973/74	Western Australia
1972/73	New Zealand

Year	Winner
1971/72	Victoria
1970/71	Western Australia
1969/70	New Zealand

CURRIE CUP

FIRST HELD 1889/90

Year	Winner
1990/91	Western Province
1989/90	Western Province
1988/89	Eastern Province
1987/88	Transvaal
1986/87	Transvaal
1985/86	Western Province
1984/85	Transvaal
1983/84	Transvaal
1982/83	Transvaal
1981/82	Western Province
1980/81	Natal
1979/80	Transvaal
1978/79	Transvaal
1977/78	Western Province
1976/77	Natal
1975/76	Natal
1974/75	Western Province
1973/74	Natal
1972/73	Transvaal
1971/72	Transvaal
1970/71	Transvaal
1969/70	Transvaal
	Western Province
1968/69	Transvaal
1967/68	Natal
1966/67	Natal
1965/66	Natal
	Transvaal
1963/64	Natal
1962/63	Natal
1960/61	Natal
1959/60	Natal
1958/59	Transvaal
1955/56	Western Province
1954/55	Natal
1952/53	Western Province

Year	Winner
1951/52	Natal
1950/51	Transvaal
1947/48	Natal
1946/47	Natal
1946/38	No Competition
1937/38	Natal
	Transvaal
1936/37	Natal
1934/35	Transvaal
1933/34	Natal
1931/32	Western Province
1929/30	Transvaal
1926/27	Transvaal
1925/26	Transvaal
1923/24	Transvaal
1921/22	Transvaal
	Natal
	Western Province
1920/21	Western Province
1920/13	No Competition
1912/13	Natal
1910/11	Natal
1908/09	Western Province
1906/07	Transvaal
1904/05	Transvaal
1903/04	Transvaal
1902/03	Transvaal
1897/98	Western Province
1896/97	Western Province
1894/95	Transvaal
1893/94	Western Province
1892/93	Western Province
1890/91	Griqualand West
1889/90	Transvaal

RED STRIPE CUP

FIRST HELD 1965/66

Year	Winner
1990/91	Barbados
1989/90	Leeward Islands
1988/89	Jamaica
1987/88	Jamaica
1986/87	Guyana

Year	Winner	Year	Winner
1985/86	Barbados	1972/73	Wellington
1984/85	Trinidad & Tobago	1971/72	Otago
1983/84	Barbados	1970/71	Central Districts
1982/83	Guyana	1969/70	Otago
1981/82	Barbados	1968/69	Auckland
1980/81	Combined Islands	1967/68	Central Districts
1979/80	Barbados	1966/67	Central Districts
1978/79	Barbados	1965/66	Wellington
1977/78	Barbados	1964/65	Canterbury
1976/77	Barbados	1963/64	Auckland
1975/76	Trinidad	1962/63	Northern Districts
	Barbados	1961/62	Wellington
1974/75	Guyana	1960/61	Wellington
1973/74	Barbados	1959/60	Canterbury
1972/73	Guyana	1958/59	Auckland
1971/72	Barbados	1957/58	Otago
1970/71	Trinidad	1956/57	Wellington
1969/70	Trinidad	1955/56	Canterbury
1968/69	Jamaica	1954/55	Wellington
1966/67	Barbados	1953/54	Central Districts
1965/66	Barbados	1952/53	Otago
		1951/52	Canterbury
		1950/51	Otago

SHELL TROPHY

FIRST HELD 1921/22

Year	Winner	Year	Winner
		1949/50	Wellington
		1948/49	Canterbury
		1947/48	Otago
		1946/47	Auckland
1990/91	Auckland	1945/46	Canterbury
1989/90	Wellington	1945/40	No Competition
1988/89	Auckland	1939/40	Auckland
1987/88	Otago	1938/39	Auckland
1986/87	Central Districts	1937/38	Auckland
1985/86	Otago	1936/37	Auckland
1984/85	Wellington	1935/36	Wellington
1983/84	Canterbury	1934/35	Canterbury
1982/83	Wellington	1933/34	Auckland
1981/82	Wellington	1932/33	Otago
1980/81	Auckland	1931/32	Wellington
1979/80	Northern Districts	1930/31	Canterbury
1978/79	Otago	1929/30	Wellington
1977/78	Auckland	1928/29	Auckland
1976/77	Otago	1927/28	Wellington
1975/76	Canterbury	1926/27	Auckland
1974/75	Otago	1925/26	Wellington
1973/74	Wellington	1924/25	Otago
		1923/24	Wellington

Year	Winner
1922/23	Canterbury
1921/22	Auckland

RANJI TROPHY

FIRST HELD 1934/35

Year	Winner
1990/91	Haryana
1989/90	Bengal
1988/89	Delhi
1987/88	Tamil Nadu
1986/87	Hyderabad
1985/86	Delhi
1984/85	Bombay
1983/84	Bombay
1982/83	Karnataka
1981/82	Delhi
1980/81	Bombay
1979/80	Delhi
1978/79	Delhi
1977/78	Karnataka
1976/77	Bombay
1975/76	Bombay
1974/75	Bombay
1973/74	Karnataka
1972/73	Bombay
1971/72	Bombay
1970/71	Bombay
1969/70	Bombay
1968/69	Bombay
1967/68	Bombay
1966/67	Bombay
1965/66	Bombay
1964/65	Bombay
1963/64	Bombay
1962/63	Bombay
1961/62	Bombay
1960/61	Bombay
1959/60	Bombay
1958/59	Bombay
1957/58	Baroda
1956/57	Bombay
1955/56	Bombay
1954/55	Madras

Year	Winner
1953/54	Bombay
1952/53	Holkar
1951/52	Bombay
1950/51	Holkar
1949/50	Baroda
1948/49	Bombay
1947/48	Holkar
1946/47	Baroda
1945/46	Holkar
1944/45	Bombay
1943/44	Western India
1942/43	Baroda
1941/42	Bombay
1940/41	Maharashtra
1939/40	Maharashtra
1938/39	Bengal
1937/38	Hyderabad
1936/37	Nawanagar
1935/36	Bombay
1934/35	Bombay

QUAID-E-AZAM TROPHY

FIRST HELD 1953/54

Year	Winner
1990/91	Karachi
1989/90	PIA
1988/89	ADBP
1987/88	PIA
1986/87	National Bank
1985/86	Karachi
1984/85	United Bank
1983/84	National Bank
1982/83	United Bank
1981/82	National Bank
1980/81	United Bank
1979/80	PIA
1978/79	National Bank
1977/78	Habib Bank
1976/77	United Bank
1975/76	National Bank
1974/75	Punjab A
1973/74	Railways

Year	Winner	Year	Winner
1972/73	Railways	1962/63	Karachi A
1971/72	Not held	1961/62	Karachi Blues
1970/71	Karachi Blues	1960/61	Not held
1969/70	PIA	1959/60	Karachi
1968/69	Lahore	1958/59	Karachi
1967/68	Not held	1957/58	Bahawalpur
1966/67	Karachi	1956/57	Punjab
1965/66	Not held	1955/56	Not held
1964/65	Karachi Blues	1954/55	Karachi
1963/64	Karachi Blues	1953/54	Bahawalpur

CROQUET

WORLD CHAMPIONS

FIRST HELD 1989

Year	Winner	
1991	J Walters	GB
1990	R Fulford	GB
1989	J Hogan	NZ

OPEN CHAMPIONS

FIRST HELD 1867

Year	Winner	
1991	R Fulford	GB
1990	S Mulliner	GB
1989	J Hogan	NZ
1988	S Mulliner	GB
1987	M Avery	GB
1986	J Hogan	NZ
1985	D Openshaw	GB
1984	G N Aspinall	GB
1983	G N Aspinall	GB
1982	G N Aspinall	GB

Year	Winner	
1981	D Openshaw	GB
1980	W de Prichard	GB
1979	D Openshaw	GB
1978	G N Aspinall	GB
1977	M Heap	GB
1976	G N Aspinall	GB
1975	G N Aspinall	GB
1974	G N Aspinall	GB
1973	Prof B Neal	GB
1972	Prof B Neal	GB
1971	K Wylie	GB
1970	K Wylie	GB
1969	G N Aspinall	GB
1968	J Solomon	GB
1967	J Solomon	GB
1966	J Solomon	GB
1965	J Solomon	GB
1964	J Solomon	GB
1963	J Solomon	GB
1962	E Cotter	GB
1961	J Solomon	GB
1960	Mrs E Rotherham	GB
1959	J Solomon	GB
1958	E Cotter	GB
1957	Dr W Wiggins	GB
1956	J Solomon	GB

Year	Winner		Year	Winner	
1955	E Cotter	GB	1902	C Corbally	GB
1954	A Ross	NZ	1901	R Roper	GB
1953	J Solomon	GB	1900	J Austin	GB
1952	H Hicks	GB	1899	B Evelegh	GB
1951	G Reckitt	GB	1898	Rev C Powell	GB
1950	H Hicks	GB	1897	C Willis	GB
1949	H Hicks	GB	1882	A Spong	GB
1948	H Hicks	GB	1881	A Spong	GB
1947	H Hicks	GB	1880	A Spong	GB
1946	D Hamilton-Miller	GB	1879	B Evelegh	GB
1945/40	No Competition		1878	A Spong	GB
1939	H Hicks	GB	1877	B Evelegh	GB
1938	D Hamilton-Miller	GB	1876	Colonel Busk	GB
1937	C Colman	GB	1875	R Gray	GB
1936	Miss D Steel	GB	1874	J Heath	GB
1935	Miss D Steel	GB	1873	J Heath	GB
1934	Lt Col W Du Pre	GB	1872	C Black	GB
1933	Miss D Steel	GB	1871	W H Peel	GB
1932	H Hicks	GB	1870	W H Peel	GB
1931	B Apps	GB	1869	G C Joad	GB
1930	B Apps	GB	1868	W H Peel	GB
1929	Lt Col W Du Pre	GB	1867	W J Whitmore	GB
1928	Captain K Coxe	GB			
1927	P Mathews	GB			
1926	B Apps	GB			
1925	Miss D Steel	GB			
1924	D Joseph	GB			
1923	H Snell	GB			
1922	C Pepper	GB			
1921	Captain C O'Callaghan	GB			
1920	P Mathews	GB			
1919	P Mathews	GB			
1918/15	No Competition				
1914	P Mathews	GB			
1913	C Corbally	GB			
1912	C O'Callaghan	GB			
1911	E Whitaker	GB			
1910	C O'Callaghan	GB			
1909	G Ashmore	GB			
1908	C Corbally	GB			
1907	R Beaton	GB			
1906	C Corbally	GB			
1905	Miss L Gower	GB			
1904	R Beaton	GB			
1903	C Corbally	GB			

OPEN DOUBLES CHAMPIONS

FIRST HELD 1924

Year	Winner	
1991	R Fulford & C Clarke	GB
1990	R Fulford & C Clarke	GB
1989	J Hogan & R Jackson	NZ
1988	G N Aspinall & S Mulliner	GB
1987	D Openshaw & M Avery	GB
1986	G N Aspinall & S Mulliner	GB
1985	D Openshaw & M Avery	GB
1984	G N Aspinall & S Mulliner	GB
1983	J McCullough & P Cordingley	GB

Year	Winner	
1982	Dr M Murray & A Hope	GB
1981	S Mulliner & M Ormerod	GB
1980	W de B Prichard & S Mulliner	GB
1979	Prof B Neal & S Hemsted	GB
1978	G N Aspinall & Dr W Ormerod	GB
1977	M Heap & S Wright	GB
1976	G N Aspinall & Dr W Ormerod	GB
1975	G N Aspinall & Dr W Ormerod	GB
1974	J Prince & G Rowling	NZ
1973	H Hicks & J Soutter	GB
1972	G N Aspinall & Dr W Ormerod	GB
1971	G N Aspinall & Dr W Ormerod	GB
1970	G N Aspinall & J Simon	GB
1969	J Solomon & E Cotter	GB
1968	G N Aspinall & J Simon	GB
1967	D Hamilton & P Hallett	GB
1966	G N Aspinall & J Simon	GB
1965	J Solomon & E Cotter	GB
1964	J Solomon & E Cotter	GB
1963	J Solomon & E Cotter	GB
1962	J Solomon & E Cotter	GB
1961	J Solomon & E Cotter	GB
1960	H Hicks & W Ormerod	GB
1959	J Solomon & E Cotter	GB
1958	J Solomon & E Cotter	GB
1957	H Hicks & Dr W Wiggins	GB
1956	Major G Stone & L Kirk-Greene	GB
1955	J Solomon & E Cotter	GB
1954	J Solomon & E Cotter	GB

Year	Winner	
1953	H Hicks & Dr W Wiggins	GB
1952	H Hicks & Dr W Wiggins	GB
1951	H Hicks & D Hamilton-Miller	GB
1950	M Reckitt & G Reckitt	GB
1949	H Hicks & D Hamilton-Miller	GB
1948	H Hicks & D Hamilton-Miller	GB
1947	Major R Tingey & Colonel J Clarke	GB
1946	M Reckitt & Miss D Lintern	GB
1945/40	No Competition	
1939	R Tingey & Captain K Coxe	GB
1938	C Colman & Mrs R Beaton	GB
1937	Lord Tollemache & Sir G Burke	GB
1936	Rev G Elvey & Mrs G Elvey	GB
1935	H Poulter & E Ward-Petley	GB
1934	B Klein & M Reckitt	GB
1933	B Klein & M Reckitt	GB
1932	Col C Wilson & W Windsor Richards	GB
1931	Lt Col W Du Pre & Miss D Steel	GB
1930	Lt Col W Du Pre & Miss D Steel	GB
1929	B Klein & C Wentworth Reeve	GB
1928	Miss D Steel & Mrs de la Mothe	GB
1927	Miss D Steel & Mrs de la Mothe	GB
1926	Col C Wilson & Mrs R Beaton	GB
1925	P Mathews & T Williams	GB
1924	T Dickson & Miss D Steel	GB

MEN'S CHAMPIONS

FIRST HELD 1925

Year	Winner	
1991	D Openshaw	GB
1990	R Fulford	GB
1989	K Aiton	GB
1989	K Aiton	GB
1988	M Saurin	GB
1987	K Aiton	GB
1986	D Foulser	GB
1985	S Mulliner	GB
1984	S Mulliner	GB
1983	G N Aspinall	GB
1982	Dr M Murray	GB
1981	D Openshaw	GB
1980	Dr M Murray	GB
1979	G Noble	GB
1978	P W Hands	GB
1977	G Jackson	GB
1976	Dr M Murray	GB
1975	G Jackson	GB
1974	Dr M Murray	GB
1973	G N Aspinall	GB
1972	J Solomon	GB
1971	J Solomon	GB
1970	Dr W Ormerod	GB
1969	E Cotter	GB
1968	K Wylie	GB
1967	Prof B Neal	GB
1966	H Hicks	GB
1965	J Solomon	GB
1964	J Solomon	GB
1963	A Cotter	GB
1962	J Solomon	GB
1961	H Hicks	GB
1960	J Solomon	GB
1959	J Solomon	GB
1958	J Solomon	GB
1957	Dr W Wiggins	GB
1956	H Hicks	GB
1955	H Hicks	GB
1954	E Cotter	GB
1953	J Solomon	GB
1952	E Cotter	GB
1951	J Solomon	GB

Year	Winner	
1950	H Hicks	GB
1949	H Hicks	GB
1948	H Hicks	GB
1947	E Ward Petley	GB
1946	M Reckitt	GB
1945/40	No Competition	
1939	R Tingey	GB
1938	C Colman	GB
1937	J McMordie	GB
1936	Lt Col W Du Pre	GB
1935	M Reckitt	GB
1934	J Lovett	GB
1933	Lt Col W Du Pre	GB
1932	H Hicks	GB
1931	B Apps	GB
1930	H Hicks	GB
1929	B Apps	GB
1928	B Klein	GB
1927	Lt Col W Du Pre	GB
1926	C Corbally	GB
1925	C Elwes	GB

WOMEN'S CHAMPIONS

FIRST HELD 1869

Year	Winner	
1991	G Curry	GB
1990	F Ransom	GB
1989	B Harris	GB
1988	D Cornelius	GB
1987	M Collin	GB
1986	W Wiggins	NZ
1985	M Collin	GB
1984	H Carlisle	GB
1983	W Wiggins	NZ
1982	W Wiggins	NZ
1981	H Carlisle	GB
1980	B Meachem	GB
1979	B Meachem	GB
1978	H Carlisle	GB
1977	F Joly	GB
1976	B Meachem	GB

Year	Winner		Year	Winner	
1975	G T Wheeler	GB	1924	M Bryan	GB
1974	K Sessions	GB	1923	C Strickland	GB
1973	K Sessions	GB	1922	D Steel	GB
1972	J Jarden	NZ	1921	N S Gilchrist	GB
1971	B Sundius-Smith	GB	1920	W Hope	GB
1970	J Jarden	NZ	1919	D Steel	GB
1969	E Warwick	GB	1918/15	No Competition	
1968	E Warwick	GB	1914	E Bramwell	GB
1967	E Lightfoot	GB	1913	Lady J Parr	GB
1966	E Warwick	GB	1912	E Simeon	GB
1965	E Warwick	GB	1911	E Reid	GB
1964	E Rotherham	GB	1910	B Willis	GB
1963	E Rotherham	GB	1909	N J Beausire	GB
1962	E Warwick	GB	1908	E Bramwell	GB
1961	I M Roe	GB	1907	E Bramwell	GB
1960	E Warwick	GB	1906	J Preston	GB
1959	E Rotherham	GB	1905	N Coote	GB
1958	D Lintern	GB	1904	V Rowley	GB
1957	D Lintern	GB	1903	N Coote	GB
1956	L Kirk	NZ	1902	M Glyn	GB
1955	E Rotherham	GB	1901	L Gower	GB
1954	D Lintern	GB	1900	L Gower	GB
1953	E Rotherham	GB	1899	L Gower	GB
1952	E Rotherham	GB	1898	O Henry	GB
1951	D Lintern	GB	1897	M Drummond	GB
1950	M Claughton	NZ	1882	K Philbrick	GB
1949	D Lintern	GB	1881	K Philbrick	GB
1948	G Elvey	GB	1880	Miss Walsh	GB
1947	G Elvey	GB	1879	Miss Walsh	GB
1946	B Wiggins	GB	1878	Miss Walsh	GB
1945/40	No Competition		1877	K Philbrick	GB
1939	D Steel	GB	1876	K Philbrick	GB
1938	D Steel	GB	1875	Mrs Hallowes	GB
1937	D Steel	GB	1874	Miss Williamson	GB
1936	D Steel	GB	1873	Mrs Walsh	GB
1935	D Steel	GB	1872	Mrs Walsh	GB
1934	D Steel	GB	1871	Mrs Walsh	GB
1933	D Steel	GB	1870	Miss Walter	GB
1932	D Steel	GB	1869	G Joad	GB
1931	A Ionides	GB			
1930	D Steel	GB			
1929	D Steel	GB			
1928	R Beaton	GB			
1927	D Steel	GB			
1926	D Steel	GB			
1925	D Steel	GB			

MIXED DOUBLES CHAMPIONS

FIRST HELD 1899

Year	Winner	
1991	R Ransom & F Ransom	GB
1990	M Saurin & F McCoig	GB
1989	F Maugham & B Harris	GB
1988	P Smith & Lady Bazley	GB
1987	G N Aspinall & D Cornelius	GB
1986	T Griffith & J Macleod	GB
1985	K Aiton & M Collin	GB
1984	I Bond & H Carlisle	GB
1983	Dr M Murray & K Yeoman	GB
1982	G N Aspinall & C Knox	GB
1981	Dr M Murray & B Meachem	GB
1980	B Sykes & B Sykes	GB
1979	Dr M Murray & B Meachem	GB
1978	A Hope & E A Thomas	GB
1977	G Jackson & J Povey	GB
1976	C Prichard & D Prichard	GB
1975	C Prichard & D Prichard	GB
1974	P W Hands & K Sessions	GB
1973	G N Aspinall (GB) & N Dodd (Aus)	
1972	Prof B Neal & J Jarden	GB
1971	B Perry & E Warwick	GB
1970	B Perry & E Warwick	GB
1969	W de Prichard & D Prichard	GB
1968	J Bolton & B Duthie	GB
1967	Lt Col D Prichard & E Warwick	GB

Year	Winner	
1966	H Hicks & J Neville-Rolfe	GB
1965	D Hamilton-Miller & E Rotherham	GB
1964	D Hamilton-Miller & E Rotherham	GB
1963	D Hamilton-Miller & E Rotherham	GB
1962	J Warwick & E Warwick	GB
1961	J Hollweg & A Mills	GB
1960	Lt Col G Cave & E Reeve	GB
1959	Dr W Wiggins & E Rotherham	GB
1958	M Reckitt & D Lintern	GB
1957	E Cotter & E Rotherham	GB
1956	G Rowling & Mrs Mackenzie-Smartt	NZ
1955	H Hicks & E Rotherham	GB
1954	J Solomon & N Oddie	GB
1953	Dr W Wiggins & E Rotherham	GB
1952	M Reckitt & D Lintern	GB
1951	E Cotter & G Turkentine	GB
1950	H Hicks & E Rotherham	GB
1949	A Heenan (NZ) & E Kingsford (GB)	
1948	M Reckitt & D Lintern	GB
1947	E Ward-Petley & D Steel	GB
1946	M Reckitt & D Lintern	GB
1945/40	No Competition	
1939	E Ward-Petley & D Steel	GB
1938	Lt Col W Du Pre & R Beaton	GB
1937	M Reckitt & B Apps	GB

Year	Winner	
1936	Lt Col W Du Pre & D Steel	GB
1935	Lt Col W Du Pre & D Steel	GB
1934	Lt Col W Du Pre & D Steel	GB
1933	T Williams & A Ionides	GB
1932	Lt Col W Du Pre & D Steel	GB
1931	H Hicks & F White	GB
1930	E T Hardman & T Clarkson	GB
1929	Lt Col W Du Pre & Mrs R Beaton	GB
1928	D Joseph & W Heap	GB
1927	B Apps & C Strickland	GB
1926	B Apps & C Strickland	GB
1925	R Leetham-Jones & M Haslam	GB
1924	D Joseph & W Heap	GB
1923	Lord Tollemache & D Steel	GB
1922	Major R O'Callaghan & N Gilchrist	GB
1921	Captain C O'Callaghan & E Bramwell	GB
1920	R Beaton & Mrs R Beaton	GB
1919	C Barry & W Hope	GB
1918/15	No Competition	

Year	Winner	
1914	C O'Callaghan & G Lockett	GB
1913	H Corbally & E Reid	GB
1912	C O'Callaghan & G Lockett	GB
1911	C Corbally & N Barlow	GB
1910	C O'Callaghan & H Johnson-Houghton	GB
1909	C O'Callaghan & H Johnson-Houghton	GB
1908	T Considine & N Coote	GB
1907	R Beaton & Mrs R Beaton	GB
1906	R Beaton & Mrs R Beaton	GB
1905	H Corbally & M Coote	GB
1904	R Beaton & L Gower	GB
1903	C Corbally & L Gower	GB
1902	G Woolston & V Rowley	GB
1901	R Roper & Miss Cowie	GB
1900	R Roper & Miss Cowie	GB
1899	B Evelegh & M Drummond	GB

CYCLING

WORLD PROFESSIONAL CHAMPIONS
Road Race

FIRST HELD 1927

Year	Winner	
1991	G Bugno	Ita
1990	R Dhaenens	Bel
1989	G LeMond	USA
1988	M Fondriest	Ita
1987	S Roche	Ire
1986	M Argentin	Ita
1985	J Zoetemelk	Nld
1984	C Criquielon	Bel
1983	G LeMond	USA
1982	G Saronni	Ita
1981	F Maertens	Bel
1980	B Hinault	Fra
1979	J Raas	Nld
1978	G Knetemann	Nld
1977	F Moser	Ita
1976	F Maertens	Bel
1975	H Kuiper	Nld
1974	E Merckx	Bel
1973	F Gimondi	Ita
1972	M Basso	Ita
1971	E Merckx	Bel
1970	J-P Monsere	Bel
1969	H Ottenbros	Nld
1968	V Adorni	Ita
1967	E Merckx	Bel
1966	R Altig	FRG
1965	T Simpson	GB
1964	J Janssen	Nld
1963	R Beheyt	Bel
1962	J Stablinski	Fra
1961	R van Looy	Bel
1960	R van Looy	Bel
1959	A Darrigade	Fra
1958	E Baldini	Ita

Year	Winner	
1957	R van Steenbergen	Bel
1956	R van Steenbergen	Bel
1955	S Ockers	Bel
1954	L Bobet	Fra
1953	F Coppi	Ita
1952	H Muller	Ger
1951	F Kubler	Swi
1950	A Schotte	Bel
1949	R van Steenbergen	Bel
1948	A Schotte	Bel
1947	T Middlekamp	Nld
1946	H Knecht	Swi
1945/39	No Race	
1938	M Kint	Bel
1937	A Meulenberg	Bel
1936	A Magne	Fra
1935	J Aerts	Bel
1934	K Kaers	Bel
1933	G Speicher	Fra
1932	A Binda	Ita
1931	L Guerra	Ita
1930	A Binda	Ita
1929	G Ronsse	Bel
1928	G Ronsse	Bel
1927	A Binda	Ita

TOUR DE FRANCE

FIRST HELD 1903

Year	Winner	
1991	M Indurain	Spa
1990	G LeMond	USA
1989	G LeMond	USA
1988	P Delgado	Spa
1987	S Roche	Ire
1986	G LeMond	USA
1985	B Hinault	Fra
1984	L Fignon	Fra
1983	L Fignon	Fra
1982	B Hinault	Fra

Year	Winner	
1981	B Hinault	Fra
1980	J Zoetemelk	Nld
1979	B Hinault	Fra
1978	B Hinault	Fra
1977	B Thevenet	Bel
1976	L van Impe	Bel
1975	B Thevenet	Fra
1974	E Merckx	Bel
1973	L Ocana	Spa
1972	E Merckx	Bel
1971	E Merckx	Bel
1970	E Merckx	Bel
1969	E Merckx	Bel
1968	J Janssen	Nld
1967	R Pingeon	Fra
1966	L Aimar	Fra
1965	F Gimondi	Ita
1964	J Anquetil	Fra
1963	J Anquetil	Fra
1962	J Anquetil	Fra
1961	J Anquetil	Fra
1960	G Nencini	Ita
1959	F Bahamontes	Spa
1958	C Gaul	Lux
1957	J Anquetil	Fra
1956	R Walkowiak	Fra
1955	L Bobet	Fra
1954	L Bobet	Fra
1953	L Bobet	Fra
1952	F Coppi	Ita
1951	H Koblet	Swi
1950	F Kubler	Swi
1949	F Coppi	Ita
1948	G Bartali	Ita
1947	J Robic	Fra
1946/40	No Race	
1939	S Maes	Bel
1938	G Bartali	Ita
1937	R Lapebie	Fra
1936	S Maes	Bel
1935	R Maes	Bel
1934	A Magne	Fra
1933	G Speicher	Fra
1932	A Leducq	Fra
1931	A Magne	Fra
1930	A Leducq	Fra

Year	Winner	
1929	M de Waele	Bel
1928	N Frantz	Lux
1927	N Frantz	Lux
1926	L Buysse	Bel
1925	O Bottecchia	Ita
1924	O Bottecchia	Ita
1923	H Pelissier	Fra
1922	F Lambot	Bel
1921	L Scieur	Bel
1920	P Thys	Bel
1919	F Lambot	Bel
1918/15	No Race	
1914	P Thys	Bel
1913	P Thys	Bel
1912	O Defraye	Bel
1911	G Garrigou	Fra
1910	O Lapize	Fra
1909	F Faber	Lux
1908	L Petit-Breton	Fra
1907	L Petit-Breton	Fra
1906	R Pottier	Fra
1905	L Trousselier	Fra
1904	H Cornet	Fra
1903	M Garin	Fra

OLYMPIC CHAMPIONS

1000 Metre Time Trial

FIRST HELD 1896

Year	Winner	
1988	A Kirchenko	USSR
1984	F Schmidtke	FRG
1980	L Thoms	GDR
1976	K Grunke	GDR
1972	N Fredborg	Den
1968	P Trentin	Fra
1964	P Sercu	Bel
1960	S Gaiardoni	Ita
1956	L Faggin	Ita
1952	R Mockridge	Aus
1948	J Dupont	Fra
1936	A van Vliet	Nld

Year	Winner	
1932	E Gray	Aus
1928	W Falck-Hansen	Den
1924/00	Not held	
1896	P Masson	Fra

1000 Metres Sprint

FIRST HELD 1896

Year	Winner	
1988	L Hesslich	GDR
1984	M Gorski	USA
1980	L Hesslich	GDR
1976	A Tkac	Cze
1972	D Morelon	Fra
1968	D Morelon	Fra
1964	G Pettenella	Ita
1960	S Gaiardoni	Ita
1956	M Rousseau	Fra
1952	E Sacchi	Ita
1948	M Ghella	Ita
1936	T Merkens	Ger
1932	J van Egmond	Nld
1928	R Beaufrand	Fra
1924	L Michard	Fra
1920	M Peeters	Nld
1912	Not held	
1908	No gold medal awarded	
1904	Not held	
1900	G Taillandier	Fra
1896	P Masson	Fra

4000 Metres Individual Pursuit

FIRST HELD 1964

Year	Winner	
1988	G Umarus	USSR
1984	S Hegg	USA
1980	R Dill-Bundi	Swi
1976	G Braun	GDR
1972	K Knudsen	Nor
1968	D Rebillard	Fra

Year	Winner	
1964	J Daler	Cze

4000 Metres Team Pursuit

FIRST HELD 1908

Year	Winner
1988	USSR
1984	Australia
1980	USSR
1976	West Germany
1972	West Germany
1968	Denmark
1964	West Germany
1960	Italy
1956	Italy
1952	Italy
1948	France
1936	France
1932	Italy
1928	Italy
1924	Italy
1920	Italy
1912	Not held
1908	Great Britain

100 km Team Time Trial

FIRST HELD 1912

Year	Winner
1988	East Germany
1984	Italy
1980	USSR
1976	USSR
1972	USSR
1968	Netherlands
1964	Netherlands
1960	Italy
1956	France
1952	Belgium
1948	Belgium
1936	France
1932	Italy

Year	Winner
1928	Denmark
1924	France
1920	France
1912	Sweden

Individual Road Race

FIRST HELD 1896

Year	Winner	
1988	O Ludwig	GDR
1984	A Grewal	USA
1980	S Sukhoruchenkov	USSR
1976	B Johansson	Swe
1972	H Kuiper	Nld
1968	P Vianelli	Ita
1964	M Zanin	Ita
1960	V Kapitonov	USSR
1956	E Baldini	Ita
1952	A Noyelle	Bel
1948	J Beyaert	Fra
1936	R Charpentier	Fra
1932	A Pavesi	Ita
1928	H Hansen	Den
1924	A Blanchonnet	Fra
1920	H Stenqvist	Swe
1912	R Lewis	SA
1908/00	Not held	
1896	A Konstantinidis	Gre

Women's 1000 Metres Sprint

FIRST HELD 1988

Year	Winner	
1988	E Saloumiae	USSR

Women's Individual Road Race

FIRST HELD 1984

Year	Winner	
1988	M Knol	Nld
1984	C Carpenter-Phinney	USA

TOUR OF BRITAIN CHAMPIONS
Milk Race

FIRST HELD 1951

Year	Winner	
1991	C Walker	GB
1990	S Sutton	Aus
1989	B Walton	Can
1988	V Zhdanov	USSR
1987	M Elliott	GB
1986	J McLoughlin	GB
1985	E van Lancker	Bel
1984	O Czougeda	USSR
1983	M Eaton	USA
1982	Y Kashirin	USSR
1981	S Krivocheyev	USSR
1980	I Mitchtenko	USSR
1979	Y Kashirin	USSR
1978	J Brzezny	Pol
1977	S Gusseinov	USSR
1976	B Nickson	GB
1975	B Johansson	Swe
1974	R Schuiten	Nld
1973	P Van Katwijk	Nld
1972	H Kuiper	Nld
1971	F Den Hertog	Nld
1970	J Mainus	Cze
1969	F Den Hertog	Nld
1968	G Petterson	Swe
1967	L West	GB
1966	J Gawliczek	Pol
1965	L West	GB
1964	A Metcalfe	GB
1963	P Chisman	GB

Year	Winner		Year	Winner	
1962	E Pokorny	Pol	1955	A Hewson	GB
1961	W Holmes	GB	1954	E Tamburlini	Fra
1960	W Bradley	GB	1953	G Thomas	GB
1959	W Bradley	GB	1952	K Russell	GB
1958	R Durlacher	Aut	1951	I Steel	GB
1957/56	Not held				

DARTS

WORLD PROFESSIONAL CHAMPIONS

FIRST HELD 1978

Year	Winner	
1991	D Priestley	Eng
1990	P Taylor	Eng
1989	J Wilson	Sco
1988	B Anderson	Eng
1987	J Lowe	Eng
1986	E Bristow	Eng
1985	E Bristow	Eng
1984	E Bristow	Eng
1983	K Deller	Eng
1982	J Wilson	Sco
1981	E Bristow	Eng
1980	E Bristow	Eng
1979	J Lowe	Eng
1978	L Rees	Wal

WORLD MASTERS

FIRST HELD 1974

Year	Winner	
1990	P Taylor	Eng
1989	P Evison	Eng

Year	Winner	
1988	B Anderson	Eng
1987	B Anderson	Eng
1986	B Anderson	Eng
1985	D Whitcombe	Eng
1984	E Bristow	Eng
1983	E Bristow	Eng
1982	D Whitcombe	Eng
1981	E Bristow	Eng
1980	J Lowe	Eng
1979	E Bristow	Eng
1978	R Davies	Wal
1977	E Bristow	Eng
1976	J Lowe	Eng
1975	A Evans	Wal
1974	C Inglis	Eng

BRITISH OPEN CHAMPIONS

FIRST HELD 1975

Year	Winner	
1991	M Gregory	Eng
1990	A Warriner	Eng
1989	B Cairns	Eng
1988	J Lowe	Eng
1987	B Anderson	Eng
1986	E Bristow	Eng

Year	Winner	
1985	E Bristow	Eng
1984	J Cusnett	Eng
1983	E Bristow	Eng
1982	J Wilson	Sco
1981	E Bristow	Eng
1980	C Lazarenko	Eng
1979	A Brown	Eng
1978	E Bristow	Eng
1977	J Lowe	Eng
1976	J North	Eng
1975	A Evans	Wal

NEWS OF THE WORLD CHAMPIONS

FIRST HELD 1948

Year	Winner	
1991	Not held	
1990	P Cook	GB
1989	D Whitcombe	GB
1988	M Gregory	GB
1987	M Gregory	GB
1986	B George	GB
1985	D Lee	GB
1984	E Bristow	GB
1983	E Bristow	GB
1982	R Morgan	GB
1981	J Lowe	GB
1980	S Lord	Swe
1979	B George	GB
1978	S Lord	Swe
1977	M Norris	GB
1976	B Lennard	GB
1975	D White	GB
1974	P Chapman	GB
1973	I Hodgkinson	GB
1972	B Netherton	GB
1971	D Filkins	GB
1970	H Barney	GB
1969	B Twomlow	GB
1968	B Duddy	GB
1967	W Seaton	GB

Year	Winner	
1966	W Ellis	GB
1965	T Barrett	GB
1964	T Barrett	GB
1963	R Rumney	GB
1962	E Brown	GB
1961	A Adamson	GB
1960	T Reddington	GB
1959	A Welch	GB
1958	T Gibbons	GB
1957	A Mullins	GB
1956	T Peachey	GB
1955	T Reddington	GB
1954	O James	GB
1953	J Carr	GB
1952	T Gibbons	GB
1951	H Perryman	GB
1950	D Newberry	GB
1949	J Boyce	GB
1948	H Leadbetter	GB

WORLD CUP CHAMPIONS

Individual

FIRST HELD 1977

Year	Winner	
1989	E Bristow	Eng
1987	E Bristow	Eng
1985	E Bristow	Eng
1983	E Bristow	Eng
1981	J Lowe	Eng
1979	N Virachkul	USA
1977	L Rees	Wal

Team

FIRST HELD 1977

Year	Winner
1989	England
1987	England
1985	England

Year	Winner
1983	England
1981	England
1979	England
1977	Wales

Women's World Masters

FIRST HELD 1982

Year	Winner	
1990	R Speed	Wal
1989	M Solomons	Eng
1988	M Solomons	Eng
1987	A Thomas	Wal
1986	K Wones	Eng
1985	L Barnett	NZ
1984	K Wones	Eng
1983	S Ralphs	Eng
1982	A Davies	Wal

Women's British Open

FIRST HELD 1979

Year	Winner	
1991	P Dyer	Eng
1990	S Colclough	Eng
1989	K McCullough	Sco
1988	J Stubbs	Eng
1987	S Colclough	Eng
1986	G Sutton	Eng

Year	Winner	
1985	L Batten	Eng
1984	A Davies	Wal
1983	S Earnshaw	Eng
1982	M Flowers	Eng
1981	A Davies	Wal
1980	L Batten	Eng
1979	J Campbell	Sco

WOMEN'S WORLD CUP CHAMPIONS
Individual

FIRST HELD 1983

Year	Winner	
1989	E Grisby	USA
1987	V Maycum	Nld
1985	L Batten	Eng
1983	S Reitan	USA

Team

FIRST HELD 1983

Year	Winner
1989	England
1987	United States
1985	England
1983	England

DIVING

WORLD CHAMPIONS

FIRST HELD 1973

Highboard

Year	Winner	
1991	S Shuwei	CPR
1986	G Louganis	USA
1982	G Louganis	USA
1978	G Louganis	USA
1975	K Dibiasi	Ita
1973	K Dibiasi	Ita

Springboard

Year	Winner	
1991	K Ferguson	USA
1986	G Louganis	USA
1982	G Louganis	USA
1978	P Boggs	USA
1975	P Boggs	USA
1973	P Boggs	USA

One-metre Springboard

FIRST HELD 1991

Year	Winner	
1991	E Jongejans	Nld

FIRST HELD 1973

Women's Highboard

Year	Winner	
1991	F Mingxia	CPR
1986	L Chen	CPR
1982	W Wyland	USA

Year	Winner	
1978	I Kalinina	USSR
1975	J Ely	USA
1973	U Knape	Swe

Women's Springboard

Year	Winner	
1991	G Min	CPR
1986	G Min	CPR
1982	M Neyer	USA
1978	I Kalinina	USSR
1975	I Kalinina	USSR
1973	C Kohler	GDR

Women's One-metre Springboard

FIRST HELD 1991

Year	Winner	
1991	G Min	CPR

OLYMPIC CHAMPIONS

Highboard

FIRST HELD 1904

Year	Winner	
1988	G Louganis	USA
1984	G Louganis	USA
1980	F Hoffman	GDR
1976	K Dibiasi	Ita
1972	K Dibiasi	Ita
1968	K Dibiasi	Ita
1964	R Webster	USA
1960	R Webster	USA
1956	J C Perez	Mex
1952	S Lee	USA

Year	Winner	
1948	S Lee	USA
1936	M Wayne	USA
1932	H Smith	USA
1928	P Desjardins	USA
1924	A White	USA
1920	C Pinkston	USA
1912	E Adlerz	Swe
1908	H Johansson	Swe
1904	G Sheldon	USA

Springboard

FIRST HELD 1908

Year	Winner	
1988	G Louganis	USA
1984	G Louganis	USA
1980	A Portnov	USSR
1976	P Boggs	USA
1972	V Vasin	USSR
1968	B Wrightson	USA
1964	K Sitzberger	USA
1960	G Tobian	USA
1956	R Clotworthy	USA
1952	D Browning	USA
1948	B Harlan	USA
1936	R Degener	USA
1932	M Galitzen	USA
1928	P Desjardins	USA
1924	A White	USA
1920	L Kuehn	USA
1912	P Gunther	Ger
1908	A Zurner	Ger

Women's Highboard

FIRST HELD 1912

Year	Winner	
1988	X Yanmei	CPR
1984	J Zhou	CPR
1980	M Jaschke	GDR
1976	E Vaytsekhovskaya	USSR
1972	U Knape	Swe

Year	Winner	
1968	M Duchkova	Cze
1964	L Bush	USA
1960	I Kramer	Ger
1956	P McCormick	USA
1952	P McCormick	USA
1948	V Draves	USA
1936	D Hill	USA
1932	D Poynton	USA
1928	E Pinkston	USA
1924	C Smith	USA
1920	S Fryland-Clausen	Den
1912	G Johansson	Swe

Women's Springboard

FIRST HELD 1920

Year	Winner	
1988	G Min	CPR
1984	S Bernier	Can
1980	I Kalinina	USSR
1976	J Chandler	USA
1972	M King	USA
1968	S Gossick	USA
1964	I Kramer-Engel	Ger
1960	I Kramer	Ger
1956	P McCormick	USA
1952	P McCormick	USA
1948	V Draves	USA
1936	M Gestring	USA
1932	G Coleman	USA
1928	H Meany	USA
1924	E Becker	USA
1920	A Riggin	USA

EQUESTRIANISM

SHOW JUMPING
WORLD CHAMPIONS
Individual

FIRST HELD 1953

Year	Winner		
1990	Eric Navet	Fra	Quito de Baussy
1986	Gail Greenhough	Can	Mr.T
1982	Norbert Koof	FRG	Fire II
1978	Gerd Wiltfang	FRG	Roman
1974	Hartwig Steenken	FRG	Simona
1970	David Broome	GB	Beethoven
1966	Pierre d'Oriola	Fra	Pomone
1960	Raimondo d'Inzeo	Ita	Gowran Girl
1956	Raimondo d'Inzeo	Ita	Merano
1955	Hans-Gunter Winkler	FRG	Halla
1954	Hans-Gunter Winkler	FRG	Halla
1953	Francisco Goyoago	Spa	Quorom

Team

FIRST HELD 1978

Year	Winner
1990	France
1986	United States
1982	France
1978	Great Britain

WOMEN'S WORLD CHAMPIONS

FIRST HELD 1965

Year	Winner		
1974	Janou Tissot	Fra	Rocket
1970	Janou Lefebvre	Fra	Rocket
1965	Marion Coakes	GB	Stroller

OLYMPIC CHAMPIONS
Individual

FIRST HELD 1900

Year	Winner		
1988	Pierre Durand	Fra	Jappeloup
1984	Joe Fargis	USA	Touch of Class
1980	Jan Kowalczyk	Pol	Artemor
1976	Alwin Schockemohle	FRG	Warwick Rex
1972	Graziano Mancinelli	Ita	Ambassador
1968	William Steinkraus	USA	Snowbound
1964	Pierre d'Oriola	Fra	Lutteur B
1960	Raimondo d'Inzeo	Ita	Posillipo
1956	Hans-Gunter Winkler	Ger	Halla
1952	Pierre d'Oriola	Fra	Ali Baba
1948	Humberto Cortes	Mex	Arete
1936	Kurt Hasse	Ger	Tora
1932	Takeichi Nishi	Jap	Uranus
1928	Frantisek Ventura	Cze	Eliot
1924	Alphonse Gemuseus	Swi	Lucette
1920	Tommaso Lequio	Ita	Trebecco
1912	Jean Cariou	Fra	Mignon
1908/04	Not held		
1900	Aime Haegeman	Bel	Benton II

Team

FIRST HELD 1912

Year	Winner
1988	West Germany
1984	United States
1980	USSR
1976	France
1972	West Germany
1968	Canada
1964	West Germany

Year	Winner
1960	West Germany
1956	West Germany
1952	Great Britain
1948	Mexico
1936	Germany
1932	No medals awarded
1928	Spain
1924	Sweden
1920	Sweden
1912	Sweden

EUROPEAN CHAMPIONS
Individual

FIRST HELD 1957

Year	Winner		
1991	Eric Navet	Fra	Quito de Baussy
1989	John Whitaker	GB	Milton
1987	Pierre Durand	Fra	Jappeloup
1985	Paul Schockemohle	FRG	Deister
1983	Paul Schockemohle	FRG	Deister
1981	Paul Schockemohle	FRG	Deister
1979	Gerhard Wiltfang	FRG	Roman
1977	Johan Heins	Nld	Seven Valleys
1975	Alwin Schockemohle	FRG	Warwick
1973	Paddy McMahon	GB	Penwood Forge Mill
1971	Hartwig Steenken	FRG	Simona
1969	David Broome	GB	Mister Softee
1967	David Broome	GB	Mister Softee
1966	Nelson Pessoa	Bra	Gran Geste
1965	Herman Schridde	FRG	Dozent
1963	Graziano Mancinelli	Ita	Rockette
1962	David Barker	GB	Mister Softee
1961	David Broome	GB	Sunsalve
1959	Piero d'Inzeo	Ita	Uruguay
1958	Fritz Thiedemann	FRG	Meteor
1957	Hans-Gunter Winkler	FRG	Sonnenglanz

Team

FIRST HELD 1975

Year	Winner
1991	Netherlands
1989	Great Britain
1987	Great Britain

Year	Winner
1985	Great Britain
1983	Switzerland
1981	West Germany
1979	Great Britain
1977	Netherlands
1975	West Germany

WOMEN'S EUROPEAN CHAMPIONS

FIRST HELD 1957

Year	Winner		
1973	Ann Moore	GB	Psalm
1971	Ann Moore	GB	Psalm
1969	Iris Kellett	Ire	Morning Light

Year	Winner		
1968	Anneli Drummond-Hay	GB	Merely-a-Monarch
1967	Kathy Kusner	USA	Untouchable
1966	Janou Lefebvre	Fra	Kenavo
1963	Pat Smythe	GB	Flanagan
1962	Pat Smythe	GB	Flanagan
1961	Pat Smythe	GB	Flanagan
1960	Susan Cohen	GB	Clare Castle
1959	Ann Townsend	GB	Bandit
1958	Guilia Serventi	Ita	Doly
1957	Pat Smythe	GB	Flanagan

KING GEORGE V GOLD CUP

FIRST HELD 1911

Year	Winner		
1991	David Broome	GB	Lannegan
1990	John Whitaker	GB	Milton
1989	Michael Whitaker	GB	Didi
1988	Robert Smith	GB	Boysie
1987	Malcolm Pyrah	GB	Towerlands Anglezark
1986	John Whitaker	GB	Ryan's Son
1985	Malcolm Pyrah	GB	Towerlands Anglezark
1984	Nick Skelton	GB	St James
1983	Paul Schockemohle	FRG	Deister
1982	Michael Whitaker	GB	Disney Way
1981	David Broome	GB	Mr Ross
1980	David Bowen	GB	Scorton
1979	Robert Smith	GB	Video
1978	Jeff McVean	Aus	Claret
1977	David Broome	GB	Philco
1976	Michael Saywell	GB	Chain Bridge
1975	Alwin Schockemohle	FRG	Rex the Robber
1974	Frank Chapot	USA	Main Spring
1973	Paddy McMahon	GB	Penwood Forge Mill
1972	David Broome	GB	Sportsman
1971	Gerhard Wiltfang	FRG	Askan
1970	Harvey Smith	GB	Mattie Brown
1969	Ted Edgar	GB	Uncle Max
1968	Hans-Gunter Winkler	FRG	Enigk
1967	Peter Robeson	GB	Firecrest
1966	David Broome	GB	Mister Softee
1965	Han-Gunter Winkler	FRG	Fortun
1964	Bill Steinkraus	USA	Sinjon
1963	Thomas Wade	Ire	Dundrum

Year	Winner		
1962	Piero d'Inzeo	Ita	The Rock
1961	Piero d'Inzeo	Ita	The Rock
1960	David Broome	GB	Sunsalve
1959	Hugh Wiley	USA	Nautical
1958	Hugh Wiley	USA	Master William
1957	Piero d'Inzeo	Ita	Uruguay
1956	Bill Steinkraus	USA	First Boy
1955	Luigi Cartesegua	Ita	Brando
1954	Fritz Thiedemann	FRG	Meteor
1953	Harry Llewellyn	GB	Foxhunter
1952	Don Carlos Figueroa	Spa	Gracieux
1951	Kevin Barry	Ire	Ballyneety
1950	Harry Llewellyn	GB	Foxhunter
1949	Brian Butler	GB	Tankard
1948	Harry Llewellyn	GB	Foxhunter
1947	Pierre d'Oriola	Fra	Marquis III
1946/40	No Competition		
1939	Conte A Bettoni-Cazzago	Ita	Adigrat
1938	John Friedberger	GB	Derek
1937	Xavier Bizard	Fra	Honduras
1936	Jed O'Dwyer	Ire	Limerick Lace
1935	John Lewis	Ire	Tramore Bay
1934	Jack Talbot-Ponsonby	GB	Best Girl
1933	No Competition		
1932	Jack Talbot-Ponsonby	GB	Chelsea
1931	Jacques Misonne	Bel	The Parson
1930	Jack Talbot-Ponsonby	GB	Chelsea
1929	Hubert Gibault	Fra	Mandarin
1928	A G Martyr	GB	Forty-Six
1927	Xavier Bizard	Fra	Quinine
1926	Fred Bontecou	USA	Ballymacshane
1925	Malise Graham	GB	Broncho
1924	Conte Giulio B di Rifferdo	Ita	Con Chisciotte
1923	Auguste de Laissardiere	Fra	Grey Fox
1922	Conte Giacomo Antonelli	Ita	Bluff
1921	Geoffrey Brooke	GB	Combined Training
1920	Auguste de Laissardiere	Fra	Dignite
1919/15	No Competition		
1914	Baron de Meslon	Fra	Amazone
1913	Baron de Meslon	Fra	Amazone
1912	Lt Delvoie	Bel	Murat
1911	Dimitri d'Exe	Rus	Piccolo

QUEEN ELIZABETH II CUP

FIRST HELD 1949

Year	Winner		
1991	Janet Hunter	GB	Lisnamarrow
1990	Emma-Jane Mac	GB	Oyster
1989	Janet Hunter	GB	Lisnamarrow
1988	Janet Hunter	GB	Lisnamarrow
1987	Gillian Greenwood	GB	Monsanta
1986	Liz Edgar	GB	Rapier
1985	Sue Pountain	GB	Ned Kelly VI
1984	Veronique Whitaker	GB	Jingo
1983	Jean Germany	GB	Mandingo
1982	Liz Edgar	GB	Forever
1981	Liz Edgar	GB	Forever
1980	Caroline Bradley	GB	Tigre
1979	Liz Edgar	GB	Forever
1978	Caroline Bradley	GB	Marius
1977	Liz Edgar	GB	Wallaby
1976	Marion Mould	GB	Elizabeth Ann
1975	Jean Davenport	GB	Hang On
1974	Jean Davenport	GB	All Trumps
1973	Ann Moore	GB	Psalm
	Alison Dawes	GB	Mr Banbury
1972	Ann Moore	GB	Psalm
1971	Marion Mould	GB	Stroller
1970	Anneli Drummond-Hay	GB	Merely-a-Monarch
1969	Alison Westwood	GB	The Maverick VII
1968	Mary Chapot	USA	White Lightning
1967	Betty Jennaway	GB	Grey Leg
1966	Althea Roger Smith	GB	Havana Royal
1965	Marion Coakes	GB	Stroller
1964	Gillian Makin	GB	Jubilant
1963	Julie Nash	GB	Trigger Hill
1962	Judy Crago	GB	Spring Fever
1961	Lady Sarah FitzAlan Howard	GB	Oorskiet
1960	Susan Cohen	GB	Clare Castle
1959	Anna Clement	Ger	Nico
1958	Pat Smythe	GB	Mr Pollard
1957	Elizabeth Anderson	GB	Sunsalve
1956	Dawn Palethorpe	GB	Earlsrath Rambler
1955	Dawn Palethorpe	GB	Earlsrath Rambler
1954	Jose Bonnaud	Fra	Charleston
1953	Marie Delfosse	GB	Fanny Rosa
1952	Gill Rich	GB	Quicksilver III
1951	Iris Kellett	Ire	Rusty
1950	Gill Palethorpe	GB	Silver Cloud

Year	Winner		
1949	Iris Kellett	Ire	Rusty

BRITISH SHOW JUMPING DERBY

FIRST HELD 1961

Year	Winner		
1991	Michael Whitaker	GB	Monsanta
1990	Joe Turi	GB	Vital
1989	Nick Skelton	GB	Apollo
1988	Nick Skelton	GB	Apollo
1987	Nick Skelton	GB	Raffles
1986	Paul Schockemohle	FRG	Deister
1985	Paul Schockemohle	FRG	Lorenzo
1984	John Ledingham	Ire	Gabhram
1983	John Whitaker	GB	Ryan's Son
1982	Paul Schockemohle	FRG	Deister
1981	Harvey Smith	GB	Sanyo Video
1980	Michael Whitaker	GB	Owen Gregory
1979	Eddie Macken	Ire	Boomerang
1978	Eddie Macken	Ire	Boomerang
1977	Eddie Macken	Ire	Boomerang
1976	Eddie Macken	Ire	Boomerang
1975	Paul Darragh	Ire	Pele
1974	Harvey Smith	GB	Salvador
1973	Alison Dawes	GB	Mr Banbury
1972	Hendrick Snoek	FRG	Shirokko
1971	Harvey Smith	GB	Mattie Brown
1970	Harvey Smith	GB	Mattie Brown
1969	Anneli Drummond-Hay	GB	Xanthos
1968	Alison Westwood	GB	The Maverick VII
1967	Marion Coakes	GB	Stroller
1966	David Broome	GB	Mister Softee
1965	Nelson Pessoa	Bra	Gran Geste
1964	Seamus Hayes	Ire	Goodbye III
1963	Nelson Pessoa	Bra	Gran Geste
1962	Pat Smythe	GB	Flanagan
1961	Seamus Hayes	Ire	Goodbye III

3-DAY EVENT
OLYMPIC CHAMPIONS
FIRST HELD 1912

Individual

Year	Winner		
1988	Mark Todd	NZ	Charisma
1984	Mark Todd	NZ	Charisma
1980	Federico Roman	Ita	Rossinan
1976	Edmund Coffin	USA	Bally-Cor
1972	Richard Meade	GB	Laurieston
1968	Jean-Jacques Guyon	Fra	Pitou
1964	Mauro Checcoli	Ita	Surbean
1960	Lawrence Morgan	USA	Salad Days
1956	Petrus Kastenman	Swe	Iluster
1952	Hans von Blixen-Finecke	Swe	Jubal
1948	Bernard Chevallier	Fra	Aiglonne
1936	Ludwig Stubbendorff	Ger	Nurmi
1932	Charles Pahud de Mortanges	Nld	Marcroix
1928	Charles Pahud de Mortanges	Nld	Marcroix
1924	Adolph van der Voort van Zijp	Nld	Silver Piece
1920	Helmer Morner	Swe	Germania
1912	Axel Nordlander	Swe	Lady Artist

Team

Year	Winner
1988	West Germany
1984	United States
1980	USSR
1976	United States
1972	Great Britain
1968	Great Britain
1964	Italy
1960	Australia
1956	Great Britain
1952	Sweden
1948	United States
1936	Germany
1932	United States
1928	Netherlands
1924	Netherlands
1920	Sweden
1912	Sweden

WORLD CHAMPIONS

FIRST HELD 1966

Individual

Year	Winner		
1990	Blyth Tait	NZ	Messiah
1986	Virginia Leng	GB	Priceless
1982	Lucinda Green	GB	Regal Realm
1978	Bruce Davidson	USA	Might Tango
1974	Bruce Davidson	USA	Irish Cap
1970	Mary Gordon-Watson	GB	Cornishman V
1966	Carlos Moratorio	Arg	Chalon

Team

Year	Winner	Year	Winner
1990	New Zealand	1978	Canada
1986	Great Britain	1974	United States
1982	Great Britain	1970	Great Britain
		1966	Ireland

EUROPEAN CHAMPIONS

FIRST HELD 1953

Individual

Year	Winner		
1991	Ian Stark	GB	Glenburnie
1989	Virginia Leng	GB	Master Craftsmen
1987	Virginia Leng	GB	Night Cap
1985	Virginia Holgate	GB	Priceless
1983	Rachel Bayliss	GB	Mystic Minstrel
1981	Hansueli Schmutz	Swi	Oran
1979	Nils Haagensen	Den	Monaco
1977	Lucinda Prior-Palmer	GB	George
1975	Lucinda Prior-Palmer	GB	Be Fair
1973	Aleksandr Yevdokimov	USSR	Jeger
1971	HRH Princess Anne	GB	Doublet
1969	Mary Gordon-Watson	GB	Cornishman V
1967	Eddie Boylan	Ire	Durlas Eile
1965	Marian Babirecki	Pol	Volt
1962	James Templar	GB	M'Lord Connolly
1959	Hans Schwarzenbach	Swi	Burn Trout
1957	Sheila Willcox	GB	High and Mighty

Year	Winner		
1955	Frank Weldon	GB	Kilbarry
1954	Albert Hill	GB	Crispin
1953	Lawrence Rook	GB	Starlight

Team

Year	Winner		Year	Winner
			1971	Great Britain
1991	Great Britain		1969	Great Britain
1989	Great Britain		1967	Great Britain
1987	Great Britain		1965	USSR
1985	Great Britain		1962	USSR
1983	Sweden		1959	West Germany
1981	Great Britain		1957	Great Britain
1979	Ireland		1955	Great Britain
1977	Great Britain		1954	Great Britain
1975	USSR		1953	Great Britain
1973	West Germany			

BADMINTON HORSE TRIALS

FIRST HELD 1949

Year	Winner		
1991	Rodney Powell	GB	The Irishman II
1990	Nicola McIrvine	GB	Middle Road
1989	Virginia Leng	GB	Master Craftsman
1988	Ian Stark	GB	Sir Wattie
1987	Not held		
1986	Ian Stark	GB	Sir Wattie
1985	Virginia Holgate	GB	Priceless
1984	Lucinda Green	GB	Beagle Bay
1983	Lucinda Green	GB	Regal Realm
1982	Richard Meade	GB	Speculator III
1981	Mark Phillips	GB	Lincoln
1980	Mark Todd	NZ	Southern Comfort
1979	Lucinda Prior-Palmer	GB	Killaire
1978	Jane Holderness-Roddam	GB	Warrior
1977	Lucinda Prior-Palmer	GB	George
1976	Lucinda Prior-Palmer	GB	Wideawake
1975	Cancelled after dressage		
1974	Mark Phillips	GB	Columbus
1973	Lucinda Prior-Palmer	GB	Be Fair
1972	Mark Phillips	GB	Great Ovation
1971	Mark Phillips	GB	Great Ovation

Year	Winner		
1970	Richard Meade	GB	The Poacher
1969	Richard Walker	GB	Pasha
1968	Jane Bullen	GB	Our Nobby
1967	Celia Ross-Taylor	GB	Jonathan
1966	Not held		
1965	Eddie Boylan	Ire	Durlas Eile
1964	James Templer	GB	M'Lord Connolly
1963	Susan Fleet	GB	Gladiator
1962	Anneli Drummond-Hay	GB	Merely-a-Monarch
1961	Lawrence Morgan	Aus	Salad Days
1960	Bill Roycroft	Aus	Our Solo
1959	Sheila Waddington	GB	Airs and Graces
1958	Sheila Willcox	GB	High and Mighty
1957	Sheila Willcox	GB	High and Mighty
1956	Frank Weldon	GB	Kilbarry
1955	Frank Weldon	GB	Kilbarry
1954	Margaret Hough	GB	Bambi
1953	Lawrence Rook	GB	Starlight
1952	Mark Darley	Ire	Emily Little
1951	Hans Schwarzenbach	Swi	Vae Victus
1950	Tony Collings	GB	Remus
1949	John Shedden	GB	Golden Willow

BURGHLEY HORSE TRIALS

FIRST HELD 1961

Year	Winner		
1991	Mark Todd	NZ	Welton Greylag
1990	Mark Todd	NZ	Face the Music
1988	Jane Thelwall	GB	Kings Jester
1987	Mark Todd	NZ	Wilton Fair
1986	Virginia Leng	GB	Murphy Himself
1984	Virginia Holgate	GB	Night Cap
1983	Virginia Holgate	GB	Priceless
1982	Richard Walker	GB	Ryan's Cross
1981	Lucinda Prior-Palmer	GB	Beagle Bay
1980	Richard Walker	GB	John of Gaunt
1979	Andrew Hoy	Aus	Davy
1978	Lorna Clarke	GB	Greco
1977	Lucinda Prior-Palmer	GB	George
1976	Jane Holderness-Roddam	GB	Warrior
1975	Aly Pattinson	GB	Carawich
1973	Mark Phillips	GB	Maid Marion
1972	Janet Hodgson	GB	Larkspur

Year	Winner		
1970	Judy Bradwell	GB	Don Camillo
1969	Gillian Watson	GB	Shaitan
1968	Sheila Willcox	GB	Fair and Square
1967	Lorna Sutherland	GB	Popadom
1965	Jeremy Beale	GB	Victoria Bridge
1964	Richard Meade	GB	Barberry
1963	Harry Freeman-Jackson	Ire	St Finbar
1961	Anneli Drummond-Hay	GB	Merely-a-Monarch

DRESSAGE
OLYMPIC CHAMPIONS
Individual

FIRST HELD 1912

Year	Winner		
1988	Nicole Uphoff	FRG	Rembrandt
1984	Reiner Klimke	FRG	Ahlerich
1980	Elisabeth Theurer	Aut	Mon Cherie
1976	Christine Stuckelberger	Swi	Granat
1972	Liselott Linsenhoff	FRG	Piaff
1968	Ivan Kizimov	USSR	Ichor
1964	Henri Chammartin	Swi	Woermann
1960	Sergey Filatov	USSR	Absent
1956	Henri St Cyr	Swe	Juli
1952	Henri St Cyr	Swe	Master Rufus
1948	Hans Moser	Swi	Hummer
1936	Heinz Pollay	Ger	Kronos
1932	Xavier Lesage	Fra	Taine
1928	Carl von Langen	Ger	Draufganger
1924	Ernst Linder	Swe	Piccolomini
1920	Janne Lundblad	Swe	Uno
1912	Carl Bonde	Swe	Emperor

Team

FIRST HELD 1928

Year	Winner
1988	West Germany
1984	West Germany
1980	USSR
1976	West Germany

Year	Winner
1972	USSR
1968	West Germany
1964	West Germany
1960	Not held
1956	Sweden
1952	Sweden
1948	France

Year	Winner
1936	Germany
1932	France
1928	Germany

WORLD CHAMPIONS

FIRST HELD 1966

Individual

Year	Winner		
1990	Nicole Uphoff	FRG	Rembrandt
1986	Anne Grethe Jensen	Den	Marzog
1982	Reiner Klimke	FRG	Ahlerich
1978	Christine Stuckelberger	Swi	Granat
1974	Reiner Klimke	FRG	Mehmed
1970	Yelena Petouchkova	USSR	Pepel
1966	Josef Neckermann	FRG	Mariano

Team

Year	Winner	Year	Winner
1990	West Germany	1978	West Germany
1986	West Germany	1974	West Germany
1982	West Germany	1970	USSR
		1966	West Germany

EUROPEAN CHAMPIONS

FIRST HELD 1963

Individual

Year	Winner		
1991	Isabell Werth	Ger	Gigolo
1989	Nicole Uphoff	FRG	Rembrandt
1987	Margrit Otto-Crepin	Fra	Corlandus
1985	Reiner Klimke	FRG	Ahlerich
1983	Anne Grethe Jensen	Den	Marzog
1981	Uwe Schulten-Baumer	FRG	Madras
1979	Elisabeth Theurer	Aut	Mon Cherie
1977	Christine Stuckelberger	Swi	Granat
1975	Christine Stuckelberger	Swi	Granat
1973	Reiner Klimke	FRG	Mehmed

Year	Winner		
1971	Liselott Linsenhoff	FRG	Piaff
1969	Liselott Linsenhoff	FRG	Piaff
1967	Reiner Klimke	FRG	Dux
1965	Henri Chammartin	Swi	Wolfdietrich
1963	Henri Chammartin	Swi	Wolfdietrich

Team

Year	Winner
1991	Germany
1989	West Germany
1987	West Germany
1985	West Germany
1983	West Germany
1981	West Germany
1979	West Germany

Year	Winner
1977	West Germany
1975	West Germany
1973	West Germany
1971	West Germany
1969	West Germany
1967	West Germany
1965	West Germany
1963	Great Britain

FENCING

WORLD CHAMPIONS

FIRST HELD 1937

Men's Foil

Year	Winner	
1991	I Weissenborn	Ger
1990	P Omnes	Fra
1989	A Koch	FRG
1987	M Gey	FRG
1986	A Borella	Ita
1985	M Numa	Ita
1983	A Romankov	USSR
1982	A Romankov	USSR
1981	V Smirnov	USSR
1979	A Romankov	USSR
1978	D Flament	Fra
1977	A Romankov	USSR

Year	Winner	
1975	C Noel	Fra
1974	A Romankov	USSR
1973	C Noel	Fra
1971	V Stankovich	USSR
1970	F Wessel	FRG
1969	F Wessel	FRG
1967	V Putyatin	USSR
1966	G Sveshnikov	USSR
1965	J-C Magnan	Fra
1963	J-C Magnan	Fra
1962	G Sveshnikov	USSR
1961	R Parulski	Pol
1959	A Jay	GB
1958	G Bergamini	Ita
1957	M Fulop	Hun
1955	R Gyuricza	Hun
1954	C d'Oriola	Fra
1953	C d'Oriola	Fra

Year	Winner	
1951	M Di Rosa	Ita
1950	R Nostino	Ita
1949	C d'Oriola	Fra
1947	C d'Oriola	Fra
1946/39	No Competition	
1938	G Guaragna	Ita
1937	G Marzi	Ita

Men's Epee

Year	Winner	
1991	A Shuvalov	USSR
1990	T Garull	FRG
1989	M Pereira	Spa
1987	V Fischer	FRG
1986	P Riboud	Fra
1985	P Boisse	Fra
1983	E Bormann	FRG
1982	J Pap	Hun
1981	Z Szekely	Hun
1979	P Riboud	Fra
1978	A Pusch	FRG
1977	J Harmenberg	Swe
1975	A Pusch	FRG
1974	R Edling	Swe
1973	R Edling	Swe
1971	G Kriss	USSR
1970	A Nikanchikov	USSR
1969	B Andrzejewski	Pol
1967	A Nikanchikov	USSR
1966	A Nikanchikov	USSR
1965	Z Nemere	Hun
1963	R Losert	Aut
1962	I Kausz	Hun
1961	J Guittet	Fra
1959	B Khabarov	USSR
1958	W Hoskyns	GB
1957	A Mouyal	Fra
1955	G Anglesio	Ita
1954	E Mangiarotti	Ita
1953	J Sakovics	Hun
1951	E Mangiarotti	Ita
1950	M Luchow	Den
1949	D Mangiarotti	Ita
1947	E Artigas	Fra

Year	Winner	
1946/39	No Competition	
1938	M Pecheux	Fra
1937	B Schmetz	Fra

Men's Sabre

Year	Winner	
1991	G Kirienko	USSR
1990	G Nebald	Hun
1989	G Kirienko	USSR
1987	J Lamour	Fra
1986	S Mindirgassov	USSR
1985	G Nebald	Hun
1983	V Etropolski	Bul
1982	V Krovopuskov	USSR
1981	M Wodke	Pol
1979	V Nazlimov	USSR
1978	V Krovopuskov	USSR
1977	P Gerevich	Hun
1975	V Nazlimov	USSR
1974	M Monttano	Ita
1973	M Monttano	Ita
1971	M Maffei	Ita
1970	T Pezsa	Hun
1969	V Sidiak	USSR
1967	M Rakita	USSR
1966	J Pawlowski	Pol
1965	J Pawlowski	Pol
1963	Y Rylsky	USSR
1962	Z Horvath	Hun
1961	Y Rylsky	USSR
1959	R Karpati	Hun
1958	Y Rylsky	USSR
1957	J Pawlowski	Pol
1955	A Gerevich	Hun
1954	R Karpati	Hun
1953	P Kovacs	Hun
1951	A Gerevich	Hun
1950	J Levavasseur	Fra
1949	G Dare	Ita
1947	A Montano	Ita
1946/39	No Competition	
1938	A Montano	Ita
1937	P Kovacs	Hun

Men's Team Foil

Year	Winner
1991	Cuba
1990	Italy
1989	USSR
1987	USSR
1986	Italy
1985	Italy
1983	West Germany
1982	USSR
1981	USSR
1979	USSR
1978	Poland
1977	West Germany
1975	France
1974	USSR
1973	USSR
1971	France
1970	USSR
1969	USSR
1967	Romania
1966	USSR
1965	USSR
1963	USSR
1962	USSR
1961	USSR
1959	USSR
1958	France
1957	Hungary
1955	Italy
1954	Italy
1953	France
1951	France
1950	Italy
1949	Italy
1947	France
1946/39	No Competition
1938	Italy
1937	Italy

Year	Winner
1987	West Germany
1986	West Germany
1985	West Germany
1983	France
1982	France
1981	USSR
1979	USSR
1978	Hungary
1977	Sweden
1975	Sweden
1974	Sweden
1973	West Germany
1971	Hungary
1970	Hungary
1969	USSR
1967	USSR
1966	France
1965	France
1963	Poland
1962	France
1961	USSR
1959	Hungary
1958	Italy
1957	Italy
1955	Italy
1954	Italy
1953	Italy
1951	France
1950	Italy
1949	Italy
1947	France
1946/39	No Competition
1938	France
1937	Italy

Men's Team Epee

Year	Winner
1991	USSR
1990	Italy
1989	Italy

Men's Team Sabre

Year	Winner
1991	Hungary
1990	USSR
1989	USSR
1987	USSR
1986	USSR
1985	USSR
1983	USSR

Year	Winner
1982	Hungary
1981	Hungary
1979	USSR
1978	Hungary
1977	USSR
1975	USSR
1974	USSR
1973	Hungary
1971	USSR
1970	USSR
1969	USSR
1967	USSR
1966	Hungary
1965	USSR
1963	Poland
1962	Poland
1961	Poland
1959	Poland
1958	Hungary
1957	Hungary
1955	Hungary
1954	Hungary
1953	Hungary
1951	Hungary
1950	Italy
1949	Italy
1947	Italy
1946/39	No Competition
1938	Italy
1937	Hungary

Women's Foil

Year	Winner	
1991	G Trillini	Ita
1990	A Fichtel	FRG
1989	O Velitchko	USSR
1987	E Tufan	Rom
1986	A Fichtel	FRG
1985	C Hanisch	FRG
1983	D Vaccaroni	Ita
1982	N Giliazova	USSR
1981	C Hanisch	FRG
1979	C Hanisch	FRG
1978	V Sidorova	USSR

Year	Winner	
1977	V Sidorova	USSR
1975	E Stahl	Rom
1974	I Bobis	Hun
1973	V Nikonova	USSR
1971	M Demaille	Fra
1970	G Gorokhova	USSR
1969	Y Novikova	USSR
1967	A Zabelina	USSR
1966	T Samusenko	USSR
1965	G Gorokhova	USSR
1963	I Ujlaki-Rejto	Hun
1962	O Szabo-Orban	Rom
1961	H Schmid	FRG
1959	Y Yefimova	USSR
1958	V Kiselyeva	USSR
1957	A Zabelina	USSR
1955	L Domolki	Hun
1954	K Lachman	Den
1953	I Camber	Ita
1951	I Elek	Hun
1950	E Muller-Preiss	Aut
	R Garilhe	Fra
1949	E Muller-Preiss	Aut
1947	E Muller-Preiss	Aut
1946/39	No Competition	
1938	M Sediva	Cze
1937	H Mayer	Ger

Women's Epee

FIRST HELD 1989

Year	Winner	
1991	M Horvath	Hun
1990	T Chappe	Cub
1989	A Straub	Swi

Women's Team Foil

FIRST HELD 1937

Year	Winner
1991	Italy
1990	Italy

Year	Winner
1989	West Germany
1987	Hungary
1986	USSR
1985	West Germany
1983	Italy
1982	Italy
1981	USSR
1979	USSR
1978	USSR
1977	USSR
1975	USSR
1974	USSR
1973	Hungary
1971	USSR
1970	USSR
1969	Romania
1967	Hungary
1966	USSR
1965	USSR
1963	USSR
1962	Hungary
1961	USSR
1959	Hungary
1958	USSR
1957	Italy
1956	USSR
1955	Hungary
1954	Hungary
1953	Hungary
1952	Hungary
1951	France
1950	France
1949	Not held
1948	Denmark
1947	Denmark
1946/38	No Competition
1937	Hungary

Women's Team Epee

FIRST HELD 1989

Year	Winner
1991	Hungary
1990	West Germany

Year	Winner
1989	Hungary

OLYMPIC CHAMPIONS

Men's Foil

FIRST HELD 1896

Year	Winner	
1988	S Cerioni	Ita
1984	M Numa	Ita
1980	V Smirnov	USSR
1976	F Dal Zotto	Ita
1972	W Woyda	Pol
1968	I Drimba	Rom
1964	E Franke	Pol
1960	V Zhdanovich	USSR
1956	C d'Oriola	Fra
1952	C d'Oriola	Fra
1948	J Buhan	Fra
1936	G Gaudini	Ita
1932	G Marzi	Ita
1928	L Gaudin	Fra
1924	R Ducret	Fra
1920	N Nadi	Ita
1912	N Nadi	Ita
1908	Not held	
1904	R Fonst	Cub
1900	E Coste	Fra
1896	E Gravelotte	Fra

Men's Epee

FIRST HELD 1900

Year	Winner	
1988	A Schmitt	FRG
1984	P Boisse	Fra
1980	J Harmenberg	Swe
1976	A Pusch	FRG
1972	C Fenyvesi	Hun
1968	G Kulcsar	Hun
1964	G Kriss	USSR

Year	Winner	
1960	G Delfino	Ita
1956	C Pavesi	Ita
1952	E Mangiarotti	Ita
1948	L Cantone	Ita
1936	F Riccardi	Ita
1932	G Cornaggia-Medici	Ita
1928	L Gaudin	Fra
1924	C Delporte	Bel
1920	A Massard	Fra
1912	P Anspach	Bel
1908	G Alibert	Fra
1904	R Fonst	Cub
1900	R Fonst	Cub

Men's Sabre

FIRST HELD 1896

Year	Winner	
1988	J Lamour	Fra
1984	J Lamour	Fra
1980	V Krovopouskov	USSR
1976	V Krovopouskov	USSR
1972	V Sidiak	USSR
1968	J Pawlowski	Pol
1964	T Pezsa	Hun
1960	R Karpati	Hun
1956	R Karpati	Hun
1952	P Kovacs	Hun
1948	A Gerevich	Hun
1936	E Kabos	Hun
1932	G Piller	Hun
1928	O Tersztyanszky	Hun
1924	S Posta	Hun
1920	N Nadi	Ita
1912	J Fuchs	Aut
1908	J Fuchs	Hun
1904	M Diaz	Cub
1900	G de la Falaise	Fra
1896	J Georgiadis	Gre

Men's Team Foil

FIRST HELD 1904

Year	Winner
1988	USSR
1984	Italy
1980	France
1976	West Germany
1972	Poland
1968	France
1964	USSR
1960	USSR
1956	Italy
1952	France
1948	France
1936	Italy
1932	France
1928	Italy
1924	France
1920	Italy
1912/08	Not held
1904	Cuba

Men's Team Epee

FIRST HELD 1908

Year	Winner
1988	France
1984	West Germany
1980	France
1976	Sweden
1972	Hungary
1968	Hungary
1964	Hungary
1960	Italy
1956	Italy
1952	Italy
1948	France
1936	Italy
1932	France
1928	Italy
1924	France
1920	Italy
1912	Belgium
1908	France

Men's Team Sabre

FIRST HELD 1908

Year	Winner
1988	Hungary
1984	Italy
1980	USSR
1976	USSR
1972	Italy
1968	USSR
1964	USSR
1960	Hungary
1956	Hungary
1952	Hungary
1948	Hungary
1936	Hungary
1932	Hungary
1928	Hungary
1924	Italy
1920	Italy
1912	Hungary
1908	Hungary

Women's Foil

FIRST HELD 1924

Year	Winner	
1988	A Fichtel	FRG
1984	Luan Jujie	CPR
1980	P Trinquet	Fra
1976	I Schwarczenberger	Hun
1972	A Ragno-Lonzi	Ita
1968	E Novikova	USSR
1964	I Ujlaki-Rejto	Hun
1960	H Schmid	Ger
1956	G Sheen	GB
1952	I Camber	Ita
1948	I Elek	Hun
1936	I Elek	Hun
1932	E Preis	Aut
1928	H Mayer	Ger
1924	E Osier	Den

Women's Team Foil

FIRST HELD 1960

Year	Winner
1988	West Germany
1984	West Germany
1980	France
1976	USSR
1972	USSR
1968	USSR
1964	Hungary
1960	USSR

GAELIC FOOTBALL

ALL-IRELAND CHAMPIONS

FIRST HELD 1887

Year	Winner
1991	Down
1990	Cork
1989	Cork
1988	Meath
1987	Meath
1986	Kerry
1985	Kerry
1984	Kerry
1983	Dublin
1982	Offaly
1981	Kerry
1980	Kerry
1979	Kerry
1978	Kerry
1977	Dublin
1976	Dublin
1975	Kerry
1974	Dublin
1973	Cork
1972	Offaly
1971	Offaly
1970	Kerry
1969	Kerry
1968	Down
1967	Meath
1966	Galway
1965	Galway
1964	Galway
1963	Dublin
1962	Kerry
1961	Down
1960	Down
1959	Kerry
1958	Dublin
1957	Louth
1956	Galway
1955	Kerry

Year	Winner
1954	Meath
1953	Kerry
1952	Cavan
1951	Mayo
1950	Mayo
1949	Meath
1948	Cavan
1947	Cavan
1946	Kerry
1945	Cork
1944	Roscommon
1943	Roscommon
1942	Dublin
1941	Kerry
1940	Kerry
1939	Kerry
1938	Galway
1937	Kerry
1936	Mayo
1935	Cavan
1934	Galway
1933	Cavan
1932	Kerry
1931	Kerry
1930	Kerry
1929	Kerry
1928	Kildare
1927	Kildare
1926	Kerry
1925	Galway
1924	Kerry
1923	Dublin
1922	Dublin
1921	Dublin
1920	Tipperary
1919	Kildare
1918	Wexford
1917	Wexford
1916	Wexford
1915	Wexford
1914	Kerry
1913	Kerry

Year	Winner	Year	Winner
1912	Louth	1899	Dublin
1911	Cork	1898	Dublin
1910	Louth	1897	Dublin
1909	Kerry	1896	Limerick
1908	Dublin	1895	Tipperary
1907	Dublin	1894	Dublin
1906	Dublin	1893	Wexford
1905	Kildare	1892	Dublin
1904	Kerry	1891	Dublin
1903	Kerry	1890	Cork
1902	Dublin	1889	Tipperary
1901	Dublin	1888	Not completed
1900	Tipperary	1887	Limerick

GOLF

BRITISH OPEN CHAMPIONS

FIRST HELD 1860

Year	Winner		
1991	I Baker-Finch	Aus	Royal Birkdale
1990	N Faldo	GB	St Andrews
1989	M Calcavecchia	USA	Royal Troon
1988	S Ballesteros	Spa	Royal Lytham
1987	N Faldo	GB	Muirfield
1986	G Norman	Aus	Turnberry
1985	S Lyle	GB	Sandwich
1984	S Ballesteros	Spa	St Andrews
1983	T Watson	USA	Royal Birkdale
1982	T Watson	USA	Royal Troon
1981	W Rogers	USA	Sandwich
1980	T Watson	USA	Muirfield
1979	S Ballesteros	Spa	Royal Lytham
1978	J Nicklaus	USA	St Andrews
1977	T Watson	USA	Turnberry
1976	J Miller	USA	Royal Birkdale
1975	T Watson	USA	Carnoustie
1974	G Player	SA	Royal Lytham

Year	Winner		
1973	T Weiskopf	USA	Troon
1972	L Trevino	USA	Muirfield
1971	L Trevino	USA	Royal Birkdale
1970	J Nicklaus	USA	St Andrews
1969	A Jacklin	GB	Royal Lytham
1968	G Player	SA	Carnoustie
1967	R de Vicenzo	Arg	Hoylake
1966	J Nicklaus	USA	Muirfield
1965	P Thomson	Aus	Royal Birkdale
1964	A Lema	USA	St Andrews
1963	R Charles	NZ	Royal Lytham
1962	A Palmer	USA	Troon
1961	A Palmer	USA	Royal Birkdale
1960	K Nagle	Aus	St Andrews
1959	G Player	SA	Muirfield
1958	P Thomson	Aus	Royal Lytham
1957	R Locke	SA	St Andrews
1956	P Thomson	Aus	Hoylake
1955	P Thomson	Aus	St Andrews
1954	P Thomson	Aus	Royal Birkdale
1953	B Hogan	USA	Carnoustie
1952	R Locke	SA	Royal Lytham
1951	M Faulkner	GB	Portrush
1950	R Locke	SA	Troon
1949	R Locke	SA	Sandwich
1948	H Cotton	GB	Muirfield
1947	F Daly	GB	Hoylake
1946	S Snead	USA	St Andrews
1945/40	No Competition		
1939	D Burton	GB	St Andrews
1938	R Whitcombe	GB	Sandwich
1937	H Cotton	GB	Carnoustie
1936	A Padgham	GB	Hoylake
1935	A Perry	GB	Muirfield
1934	H Cotton	GB	Sandwich
1933	D Shute	USA	St Andrews
1932	G Sarazen	USA	Prince's
1931	T Armour	USA	Carnoustie
1930	R Jones	USA	Hoylake
1929	W Hagen	USA	Muirfield
1928	W Hagen	USA	Sandwich
1927	R Jones	USA	St Andrews
1926	R Jones	USA	Royal Lytham
1925	J Barnes	USA	Prestwick
1924	W Hagen	USA	Hoylake
1923	A Havers	GB	Troon

Year	Winner		
1922	W Hagen	USA	Sandwich
1921	J Hutchinson	USA	St Andrews
1920	G Duncan	GB	Deal
1919/15	No Competition		
1914	H Vardon	. GB	Prestwick
1913	J H Taylor	GB	Hoylake
1912	E Ray	GB	Muirfield
1911	H Vardon	GB	Sandwich
1910	J Braid	GB	St Andrews
1909	J H Taylor	GB	Deal
1908	J Braid	GB	Prestwick
1907	A Massy	Fra	Hoylake
1906	J Braid	GB	Muirfield
1905	J Braid	GB	St Andrews
1904	J White	GB	Sandwich
1903	H Vardon	GB	Prestwick
1902	S Herd	GB	Hoylake
1901	J Braid	GB	Muirfield
1900	J H Taylor	GB	St Andrews
1899	H Vardon	GB	Sandwich
1898	H Vardon	GB	Prestwick
1897	H H Hilton	GB	Hoylake
1896	H Vardon	GB	Muirfield
1895	J H Taylor	GB	St Andrews
1894	J H Taylor	GB	Sandwich
1893	W Auchterlonie	GB	Prestwick
1892	H H Hilton	GB	Muirfield
1891	H Kirkaldy	GB	St Andrews
1890	J Ball	GB	Prestwick
1889	W Park Jnr	GB	Musselburgh
1888	J Burns	GB	St Andrews
1887	W Park Jnr	GB	Prestwick
1886	D Brown	GB	Musselburgh
1885	R Martin	GB	St Andrews
1884	J Simpson	GB	Prestwick
1883	W Fernie	GB	Musselburgh
1882	R Ferguson	GB	St Andrews
1881	R Ferguson	GB	Prestwick
1880	R Ferguson	GB	Musselburgh
1879	J Anderson	GB	St Andrews
1878	J Anderson	GB	Prestwick
1877	J Anderson	GB	Musselburgh
1876	R Martin	GB	St Andrews
1875	W Park Snr	GB	Prestwick
1874	M Park	GB	Musselburgh
1873	T Kidd	GB	St Andrews

Year	Winner		
1872	T Morris Jnr	GB	Prestwick
1870	T Morris Jnr	GB	Prestwick
1869	T Morris Jnr	GB	Prestwick
1868	T Morris Jnr	GB	Prestwick
1867	T Morris Snr	GB	Prestwick
1866	W Park Snr	GB	Prestwick
1865	A Strath	GB	Prestwick
1864	T Morris Snr	GB	Prestwick
1863	W Park Snr	GB	Prestwick
1862	T Morris Snr	GB	Prestwick
1861	T Morris Snr	GB	Prestwick
1860	W Park Snr	GB	Prestwick

US OPEN CHAMPIONS

FIRST HELD 1895

Year	Winner		
1991	P Stewart	USA	Hazeltine
1990	H Irwin	USA	Medinah
1989	C Strange	USA	Oak Hill
1988	C Strange	USA	Brookline
1987	S Simpson	USA	Olympic
1986	R Floyd	USA	Shinnecock Hills
1985	A North	USA	Oakland Hills
1984	F Zoeller	USA	Winged Foot
1983	L Nelson	USA	Oakmont
1982	T Watson	USA	Pebble Beach
1981	D Graham	Aus	Merion
1980	J Nicklaus	USA	Baltusrol
1979	H Irwin	USA	Inverness
1978	A North	USA	Cherry Hills
1977	H Green	USA	Southern Hills
1976	J Pate	USA	Atlanta
1975	L Graham	USA	Medinah
1974	H Irwin	USA	Winged Foot
1973	J Miller	USA	Oakmont
1972	J Nicklaus	USA	Pebble Beach
1971	L Trevino	USA	Merion
1970	A Jacklin	GB	Hazeltine
1969	O Moody	USA	Champions
1968	L Trevino	USA	Oak Hill
1967	J Nicklaus	USA	Baltusrol
1966	W Casper	USA	Olympic
1965	G Player	SA	Bellerive

Year	Winner		
1964	K Venturi	USA	Congressional
1963	J Boros	USA	Brookline
1962	J Nicklaus	USA	Oakmont
1961	G Littler	USA	Oakland Hills
1960	A Palmer	USA	Cherry Hills
1959	W Casper	USA	Winged Foot
1958	T Bolt	USA	Southern Hills
1957	R Mayer	USA	Inverness
1956	C Middlecoff	USA	Oak Hill
1955	J Fleck	USA	Olympic
1954	E Furgol	USA	Baltusrol
1953	B Hogan	USA	Oakmont
1952	J Boros	USA	Northwood
1951	B Hogan	USA	Oakland Hills
1950	B Hogan	USA	Merion
1949	C Middlecoff	USA	Medinah
1948	B Hogan	USA	Riviera
1947	L Worsham	USA	St Louis
1946	L Mangrum	USA	Canterbury
1945/42	No Competition		
1941	C Wood	USA	Colonial
1940	L Little	USA	Canterbury
1939	B Nelson	USA	Philadelphia
1938	R Guldahl	USA	Cherry Hills
1937	R Guldahl	USA	Oakland Hills
1936	T Manero	USA	Baltusrol
1935	S Parks	USA	Oakmont
1934	O Dutra	USA	Merion
1933	J Goodman	USA	North Shore
1932	G Sarazen	USA	Fresh Meadow
1931	W Burke	USA	Inverness
1930	R Jones	USA	Interlachen
1929	R Jones	USA	Winged Foot
1928	J Farrell	USA	Olympia Fields
1927	T Armour	USA	Oakmont
1926	R Jones	USA	Scioto
1925	W Macfarlane	USA	Worcester
1924	C Walker	USA	Oakland Hills
1923	R Jones	USA	Inwood
1922	G Sarazen	USA	Skokie
1921	J Barnes	USA	Columbia
1920	E Ray	GB	Inverness
1919	W Hagen	USA	Brae Burn
1918/17	No Competition		
1916	C Evans Jnr	USA	Minikahda
1915	J Travers	USA	Baltusrol

Year	Winner		
1914	W Hagen	USA	Midlothian
1913	F Ouimet	USA	Brookline
1912	J McDermott	USA	Buffalo
1911	J McDermott	USA	Chicago
1910	A Smith	USA	Philadelphia
1909	G Sargent	USA	Englewood
1908	F McLeod	USA	Myopia Hunt
1907	A Ross	USA	Philadelphia
1906	A Smith	USA	Onwentsia
1905	W Anderson	USA	Myopia Hunt
1904	W Anderson	USA	Glen View
1903	W Anderson	USA	Baltusrol
1902	L Auchterlonie	USA	Garden City
1901	W Anderson	USA	Myopia Hunt
1900	H Vardon	GB	Chicago
1899	W Smith	USA	Baltimore
1898	F Herd	USA	Myopia Hunt
1897	J Lloyd	USA	Chicago
1896	J Foulis	USA	Shinnecock Hills
1895	H Rawlins	USA	Newport

US PGA CHAMPIONS

FIRST HELD 1916

Year	Winner		
1991	J Daly	USA	Crooked Stick
1990	W Grady	Aus	Shoal Creek
1989	P Stewart	USA	Kemper Lakes
1988	J Sluman	USA	Oaktree
1987	L Nelson	USA	Palm Beach
1986	B Tway	USA	Toledo
1985	H Green	USA	Cherry Hills
1984	L Trevino	USA	Shoal Creek
1983	H Sutton	USA	Riviera
1982	R Floyd	USA	Southern Hills
1981	L Nelson	USA	Atlanta
1980	J Nicklaus	USA	Oak Hill
1979	D Graham	Aus	Oakland Hills
1978	J Mahaffey	USA	Oakmont
1977	L Wadkins	USA	Pebble Beach
1976	D Stockton	USA	Congressional
1975	J Nicklaus	USA	Firestone
1974	L Trevino	USA	Tanglewood
1973	J Nicklaus	USA	Canterbury

Year	Winner		
1972	G Player	SA	Oakland Hills
1971	J Nicklaus	USA	PGA National
1970	D Stockton	USA	Southern Hills
1969	R Floyd	USA	NCR Dayton
1968	J Boros	USA	Pecan Valley
1967	D January	USA	Columbine
1966	A Geiberger	USA	Firestone
1965	D Marr	USA	Laurel Valley
1964	R Nichols	USA	Columbus
1963	J Nicklaus	USA	Dallas
1962	G Player	SA	Aronmink
1961	J Barber	USA	Olympia Fields
1960	J Hebert	USA	Firestone
1959	B Rosburg	USA	Minneapolis
1958	D Finsterwald	USA	Llanerch
1957	L Hebert	USA	Miami Valley
1956	J Burke	USA	Blue Hill
1955	D Ford	USA	Meadowbrook
1954	C Harbert	USA	Keller
1953	W Burkemo	USA	Birmingham
1952	J Turnesa	USA	Big Spring
1951	S Snead	USA	Oakmont
1950	C Harper	USA	Scioto
1949	S Snead	USA	Hermitage
1948	B Hogan	USA	Norwood Hills
1947	J Ferrier	USA	Plum Hollow
1946	B Hogan	USA	Portland
1945	B Nelson	USA	Morraine
1944	R Hamilton	USA	Manito
1943	Not held		
1942	S Snead	USA	Sea View
1941	V Ghezzi	USA	Cherry Hills
1940	B Nelson	USA	Hershey
1939	H Picard	USA	Pomonok
1938	P Runyan	USA	Shawnee
1937	D Shute	USA	Pittsburgh
1936	D Shute	USA	Pinehurst
1935	J Revolta	USA	Twin Hills
1934	P Runyan	USA	Park
1933	G Sarazen	USA	Blue Mound
1932	O Dutra	USA	Keller
1931	T Creavy	USA	Wannamoisett
1930	T Armour	USA	Fresh Meadow
1929	L Diegel	USA	Hill Crest
1928	L Diegel	USA	Five Farms
1927	W Hagen	USA	Cedar Crest

Year	Winner		
1926	W Hagen	USA	Salisbury
1925	W Hagen	USA	Olympia Fields
1924	W Hagen	USA	French Lick
1923	G Sarazen	USA	Pelham
1922	G Sarazen	USA	Oakmont
1921	W Hagen	USA	Inwood
1920	J Hutchinson	USA	Flossmoor
1919	J Barnes	USA	Engineers
1916	J Barnes	USA	Siwanoy

US MASTERS CHAMPIONS

Played at Augusta National

FIRST HELD 1934

Year	Winner	
1991	I Woosnam	GB
1990	N Faldo	GB
1989	N Faldo	GB
1988	S Lyle	GB
1987	L Mize	USA
1986	J Nicklaus	USA
1985	B Langer	FRG
1984	B Crenshaw	USA
1983	S Ballesteros	Spa
1982	C Stadler	USA
1981	T Watson	USA
1980	S Ballesteros	Spa
1979	F Zoeller	USA
1978	G Player	SA
1977	T Watson	USA
1976	R Floyd	USA
1975	J Nicklaus	USA
1974	G Player	SA
1973	T Aaron	USA
1972	J Nicklaus	USA
1971	C Coody	USA
1970	W Casper	USA
1969	G Archer	USA
1968	R Goalby	USA
1967	G Brewer	USA
1966	J Nicklaus	USA
1965	J Nicklaus	USA

Year	Winner	
1964	A Palmer	USA
1963	J Nicklaus	USA
1962	A Palmer	USA
1961	G Player	SA
1960	A Palmer	USA
1959	A Wall Jnr	USA
1958	A Palmer	USA
1957	D Ford	USA
1956	J Burke Jnr	USA
1955	C Middlecoff	USA
1954	S Snead	USA
1953	B Hogan	USA
1952	S Snead	USA
1951	B Hogan	USA
1950	J Demaret	USA
1949	S Snead	USA
1948	C Harmon	USA
1947	J Demaret	USA
1946	H Keiser	USA
1945/43	No Competition	
1942	B Nelson	USA
1941	C Wood	USA
1940	J Demaret	USA
1939	R Guldahl	USA
1938	H Picard	USA
1937	B Nelson	USA
1936	H Smith	USA
1935	G Sarazen	USA
1934	H Smith	USA

WORLD MATCH-PLAY CHAMPIONS

Played at Wentworth

FIRST HELD 1964

Year	Winner	
1990	I Woosnam	GB
1989	N Faldo	GB
1988	S Lyle	GB
1987	I Woosnam	GB
1986	G Norman	Aus
1985	S Ballesteros	Spa
1984	S Ballesteros	Spa
1983	G Norman	Aus
1982	S Ballesteros	Spa
1981	S Ballesteros	Spa
1980	G Norman	Aus

Year	Winner	
1979	W Rogers	USA
1978	I Aoki	Jap
1977	G Marsh	Aus
1976	D Graham	Aus
1975	H Irwin	USA
1974	H Irwin	USA
1973	G Player	SA
1972	T Weiskopf	USA
1971	G Player	SA
1970	J Nicklaus	USA
1969	R Charles	NZ
1968	G Player	SA
1967	A Palmer	USA
1966	G Player	SA
1965	G Player	SA
1964	A Palmer	USA

RYDER CUP

FIRST HELD 1927

Year	Winner	
1991	United States	Kiawah Island
1989	Drawn	The Belfry
1987	Europe	Muirfield Village
1985	Europe	The Belfry
1983	United States	PGA National, Florida
1981	United States	Walton Heath, Surrey
1979	United States	Greenbrier
1977	United States	Royal Lytham & St Annes
1975	United States	Laurel Valley, Penn.
1973	Drawn	Muirfield, Scotland
1971	United States	St Louis, Missouri
1969	United States	Royal Birkdale
1967	United States	Houston, Texas
1965	United States	Royal Birkdale
1963	United States	Atlanta, Georgia
1961	United States	Royal Lytham & St Annes
1959	United States	Eldorado CC, California
1957	Great Britain	Lindrick Club, Yorkshire
1955	United States	Thunderbird, California
1953	United States	Wentworth, Surrey
1951	United States	Pinehurst, North Carolina

Year	Winner	
1949	United States	Ganton, Yorkshire
1947	United States	Portland, Oregon
1937	United States	Southport & Ainsdale
1935	United States	Ridgewood, New Jersey
1933	Great Britain	Southport & Ainsdale
1931	United States	Scioto, Ohio
1929	Great Britain	Moortown, Yorkshire
1927	United States	Worcester, Massachusetts

WALKER CUP

FIRST HELD 1922

Year	Winner	
1991	United States	Portmarnock, Ireland
1989	Great Britain	Peachtree, Georgia
1987	United States	Sunningdale, England
1985	United States	Pine Valley, Philadelphia
1983	United States	Royal Liverpool, England
1981	United States	Cypress Point, California
1979	United States	Muirfield, Scotland
1977	United States	Shinnecock Hills, New York
1975	United States	St Andrews, Scotland
1973	United States	Brookline, Massachusetts
1971	Great Britain	St Andrews, Scotland
1969	United States	Milwaukee, Wisconsin
1967	United States	Royal St George's
1965	Drawn	Baltimore, Maryland
1963	United States	Turnberry, Scotland
1961	United States	Seattle, Washington
1959	United States	Muirfield, Scotland
1957	United States	Minikhada, Minnesota
1955	United States	St Andrews, Scotland
1953	United States	Kittansett, Massachusetts
1951	United States	Royal Birkdale
1949	United States	Winged Foot, New York
1947	United States	St Andrews, Scotland
1938	Great Britain	St Andrews, Scotland
1936	United States	Pine Valley, New Jersey
1934	United States	St Andrews, Scotland
1932	United States	Brookline, Massachusetts
1930	United States	Royal St George's
1928	United States	Chicago, Illinois
1926	United States	St Andrews, Scotland
1924	United States	Garden City, New York

Year	Winner	
1923	United States	St Andrews, Scotland
1922	United States	Long Island, New York

GREYHOUND RACING

THE GREYHOUND DERBY

FIRST HELD 1927

Year	Winner
1991	Ballinderry Ash
1990	Slippy Blue
1989	Lartigue Note
1988	Hit the Lid
1987	Signal Spark
1986	Tico
1985	Pagan Swallow
1984	Whisper Wishes
1983	I'm Slippy
1982	Laurie's Panther
1981	Parkdown Jet
1980	Indian Joe
1979	Sarah's Bunny
1978	Lacca Champion
1977	Ballinska Band
1976	Mutts Silver
1975	Tartan Khan
1974	Jimsun
1973	Patricia's Hope
1972	Patricia's Hope
1971	Dolores Rocket
1970	John Silver
1969	Sand Star
1968	Camira Flash
1967	Tric-Trac
1966	Faithful Hope
1965	Chittering Clapton
1964	Hack Up Chieftan
1963	Lucky Boy Boy

Year	Winner
1962	The Grand Canal
1961	Palm's Printer
1960	Duleek Dandy
1959	Mile Bush Pride
1958	Pigalle Wonder
1957	Ford Spartan
1956	Dunmore King
1955	Rushton Mac
1954	Paul's Fun
1953	Daw's Dancer
1952	Endless Gossip
1951	Ballylanigan Tanist
1950	Ballymac Ball
1949	Narrogar Ann
1948	Priceless Border
1947	Trev's Perfection
1946	Monday's News
1945	Ballyhennesy Seal
1944/41	Not run
1940	G.R. Archduke
1939	Highland Rum
1938	Lone Keel
1937	Wattle Bark
1936	Fine Jubilee
1935	Greta Ranee
1934	Davesland
1933	Future Cutlet
1932	Wild Woolley
1931	Seldom Led
1930	Mick the Miller
1929	Mick the Miller
1928	Boher Ash
1927	Entry Badge

THE WATERLOO CUP

FIRST HELD 1836

Year	Winner
1991	Evening Mail
1990	Sam the Man
1989	React Fagan
1988	React Fraggl
1987	Mousetail
1986	Not run
1985	Hear and There
1984	Tobertelly Queen
1983	Luda Hussar
1982	Play Solo
1981	Timworth Edward
1980/78	Not run
1977	Minnesota Yank
1976	Minnesota Miller
1975	Hardly Ever
1974	Not run
1973	Modest Newdown
1972	Linden Eland
1971	So Clever
1970	Rodney Magnet
1969/68	Not run
1967	Haich Bee
1966	Just Better
1965	Nicelya Head
1964	Latin Lover
1963	Himalayan Climber
1962	Best Champagne
1961	Dubedoon
1960	Jonquil
1959	Mutual Friend
1958	Holystone Elf
1957	Old Kentucky Minstrel
1956	Magical Lore
1955	Full Pete
1954	Cotton King
1953	Holystone Lifelong
1952	Dew Whaler
1951	Peter's Poet
1950	Roving Minstrel
1949	Life Line
1948	Noted Sunlight

Year	Winner
1947	Constable
1946	Maesydd Michael
1945	Bryn Tritoma
1944	Dutton Swordfish
1943	Countryman
1942	Swinging Light
1941	Swinging Light
1940	Dee Flint
1939	Delightful Devon
1938	Perambulate
1937	Rotten Row
1936	Hand Grenade
1935	Dee Rock
1934	Bryn Truthful
1933	Genial Nobleman
1932	Ben Tinto
1931	Conversion
1930	Church Street
1929	Golden Surprise
1928	White Collar
1927	Golden Seal
1926	Jovial Judge
1925	Pentonville
1924	Cushey Job
1923	Latto
1922	Guard's Brigade
1921	Shortcoming
1920	Fighting Force
1919/17	Not run
1916	Harmonicon
1915	Winning Number
1914	Dilwyn
1913	Hung Well
1912	Tide Time
1911	Jabberwock
1910	Heavy Weapon
1909	Dendraspis
1908	Hallow Eve
1907	Long Span
1906	Hoprend
1905	Pistol II
1904	Homfray
1903	Father Flint
1902	Farndon Ferry
1901	Fearless Footsteps
1900	Fearless Footsteps

Year	Winner	Year	Winner
1899	Black Fury	1867	Lobelia
1898	Wild Night	1866	Brigadier
1897	Gallant	1865	Meg
1896	Fabulous Fortune	1864	King Death
1895	Thoughtless Beauty	1863	Chloe
1894	Texture	1862	Roaring Meg
1893	Character	1861	Canaradzo
1892	Fullerton	1860	Maid of the Mill
1891	Fullerton	1859	Clive
1890	Fullerton	1858	Neville
1889	Fullerton	1857	King Lear
1888	Burnaby	1856	Protest
1887	Greater Scot	1855	Judge
1886	Miss Glendyne	1854	Sackcloth
1885	Bit of Fashion	1853	Cerito
1884	Mineral Water	1852	Cerito
1883	Wild Mint	1851	Hughie Graham
1882	Snowflight	1850	Cerito
1881	Princess Dagmar	1849	Magician
1880	Honeywood	1848	Shade
1879	Misterton	1847	Senate
1878	Coomassie	1846	Harlequin
1877	Coomassie	1845	Titania
1876	Donald	1844	Speculation
1875	Honeymoon	1843	Major
1874	Magnano	1842	Priam
1873	Muriel	1841	Bloomsbury
1872	Bed of Stone	1840	Earwig
1871	Master M'Grath	1839	Empress
1870	Sea Cove	1838	Bugle
1869	Master M'Grath	1837	Fly
1868	Master M'Grath	1836	Milanie

GYMNASTICS

WORLD CHAMPIONS

FIRST HELD 1903

Combined

Year	Winner	
1991	G Misutin	USSR
1989	I Korobchinski	USSR
1987	D Belozerchev	USSR
1985	Y Korolev	USSR
1983	D Belozerchev	USSR
1981	Y Korolev	USSR
1979	A Ditatin	USSR
1978	N Andrianov	USSR
1974	S Kasamatsu	Jap
1970	E Kenmotsu	Jap
1966	M Voronin	USSR
1962	Y Titov	USSR
1958	B Shakhlin	USSR
1954	W Chukarin	USSR
1950	W Lehmann	Swi
1946/42	No Competition	
1938	J Gajdos	Cze
1934	E Mack	Swi
1930	J Primozic	Yug
1926	P Sumi	Yug
1922	P Sumi	Yug
	F Pechacek	Cze
1918/15	No Competition	
1913	M Torres	Fra
1911	F Steiner	Cze
1909	M Torres	Fra
1907	J Cada	Cze
1905	M Lalu	Fra
1903	J Martinez	Fra

Team

Year	Winner
1991	USSR

Year	Winner
1989	USSR
1987	USSR
1985	USSR
1983	China
1981	USSR
1979	USSR
1978	Japan
1974	Japan
1970	Japan
1966	Japan
1962	Japan
1958	USSR
1954	USSR
1950	Switzerland
1938	Czechoslovakia
1934	Not held
1930	Czechoslovakia
1926	Czechoslovakia
1922	Czechoslovakia
1918/15	No Competition
1913	Czechoslovakia
1911	Czechoslovakia
1909	France
1907	Czechoslovakia
1905	France
1903	France

Parallel Bars

Year	Winner	
1991	J Li	CPR
1989	V Artemov	USSR
1987	V Artemov	USSR
1985	S Kroll	GDR
	V Moguilni	USSR
1983	V Artemov	USSR
	L Yun	CPR
1981	A Ditiatin	USSR
	K Gushiken	Jap

Year	Winner	
1979	B Conner	USA
1978	E Kenmotsu	Jap
1974	E Kenmotsu	Jap
1970	A Nakayama	Jap
1966	S Diomidov	USSR
1962	M Cerar	Yug
1958	B Shakhlin	USSR
1954	V Chukarin	USSR
1950	H Eugster	Swi
1946/42	No Competition	
1938	M Reusch	Swi
1934	E Mack	Swi
1930	J Primozic	Yug
1926	L Vacha	Cze
1922	L Stukelj	Yug
	S Derganc	Yug
	V Simoncic	Yug
	N Jindrich	Cze
	M Klinger	Cze
1918/15	No Competition	
1913	G Zampori	Ita
	G Boni	Ita
1911	G Zampori	Ita
1909	J Martinez	Fra
1907	J Lux	Fra
1905	J Martinez	Fra
1903	J Martinez	Fra
	F Hentges	Lux

High Bar

Year	Winner	
1991	C Li	CPR
1989	C Li	CPR
1987	D Belozerchev	USSR
1985	T Fei	CPR
1983	D Belozerchev	USSR
1981	A Tkachev	USSR
1979	K Thomas	USA
1978	S Kasamatsu	Jap
1974	E Gienger	FRG
1970	E Kenmotsu	Jap
1966	A Nakayama	Jap
1962	T Ono	Jap
1958	B Shakhlin	USSR

Year	Winner	
1954	V Mouratov	USSR
1950	P Aaltonen	Fin
1946/38	No Competition	
1934	R Winter	Ger
1930	I Pelle	Hun
1926	L Stukelj	Yug
1922	M Klinger	Cze
1918/15	No Competition	
1913	J Cada	Cze
1911	J Cada	Cze
1909	J Martinez	Fra
	J Cada	Cze
1907	G Charmoille	Fra
	F Erben	Cze
1905	M Lalu	Fra
1903	J Martinez	Fra
	N Pissie	Fra

Rings

Year	Winner	
1991	G Misutin	USSR
1989	A Aguilar	FRG
1987	Y Korolev	USSR
1985	L Ning	CPR
	Y Korolev	USSR
1983	D Belozerchev	USSR
	K Gushiken	Jap
1981	A Ditiatin	USSR
1979	A Ditiatin	USSR
1978	N Andrianov	USSR
1974	N Andrianov	USSR
	D Grecu	Rom
1970	A Nakayama	Jap
1966	M Voronin	USSR
1962	Y Titov	USSR
1958	A Azarian	USSR
1954	A Azarian	USSR
1950	W Lehmann	Swi
1946/42	No Competition	
1938	A Hudec	Cze
1934	A Hudec	Cze
1930	E Loffler	Cze
1926	L Stukelj	Yug

Year	Winner	
1922	L Karasek	Cze
	N Maly	Cze
	L Stukelj	Yug
	P Sumi	Yug
1918/15	No Competition	
1913	L Grech	Fra
	M Torres	Fra
	G Zampori	Ita
	G Boni	Ita
1911	F Steiner	Cze
	D Follacci	Fra
	P Bianchi	Ita
1909	G Romano	Ita
	M Torres	Fra
1907/05	Not held	
1903	J Martinez	Fra
	J Lux	Fra

Vault

Year	Winner	
1991	You Ok Youl	RoK
1989	J Behrend	GDR
1987	S Kroll	GDR
	L Yun	CPR
1985	Y Korolev	USSR
1983	A Akopian	USSR
1981	R-P Hemmann	GDR
1979	A Ditiatin	USSR
1978	J Shimizu	Jap
1974	S Kasamatsu	Jap
1970	M Tsukahara	Jap
1966	H Matsuda	Jap
1962	P Krbec	Cze
1958	Y Titov	USSR
1954	L Sotornik	Cze
1950	E Gebendinger	Swi
1946/38	No Competition	
1934	E Mack	Swi
1930/15	No Competition	
1913	K Stary	Cze
	B Sadoun	Fra
	O Palazzi	Ita
	S Vidmar	Yug
1911/09	Not held	

Year	Winner	
1907	F Erben	Cze
1905	N Dejaeghere	Fra
1903	N Dejaeghere	Fra
	J Lux	Fra
	N Thysen	Nld

Pommel Horse

FIRST HELD 1911

Year	Winner	
1991	V Belenki	USSR
1989	V Moguilni	USSR
1987	D Belozerchev	USSR
	Z Borkai	Hun
1985	V Moguilni	USSR
1983	D Belozerchev	USSR
1981	M Nikolay	GDR
	L Xiaoping	CPR
1979	Z Magyar	Hun
1978	Z Magyar	Hun
1974	Z Magyar	Hun
1970	M Cerar	Yug
1966	M Cerar	Yug
1962	M Cerar	Yug
1958	B Shakhlin	USSR
1954	G Chaginyan	USSR
1950	J Stalder	Swi
1946/42	No Competition	
1938	M Reusch	Swi
	V Petracek	Cze
1934	E Mack	Swi
1930	J Primozic	Yug
1926	N Karafiat	Cze
1922	M Klinger	Cze
	N Jindrich	Cze
	L Stukelj	Yug
1918/15	No Competition	
1913	G Zampori	Ita
	O Palazzi	Ita
	N Aubrey	Fra
1911	O Palazzi	Ita

Floor

FIRST HELD 1913

Year	Winner	
1991	I Korobchinski	USSR
1989	I Korobchinski	USSR
1987	L Yun	CPR
1985	T Fei	CPR
1983	T Fei	CPR
1981	Y Korolev	USSR
	L Yuejiu	CPR
1979	K Thomas	USA
	R Bruckner	GDR
1978	K Thomas	USA
1974	S Kasamatsu	Jap
1970	A Nakayama	Jap
1966	A Nakayama	Jap
1962	N Aihara	Jap
	Y Endo	Jap
1958	M Takemoto	Jap
1954	V Mouratov	USSR
	M Takemoto	Jap
1950	J Stadler	Swi
1946/42	No Competition	
1938	J Gajdos	Cze
1934	G Miez	Swi
1930	J Primozic	Yug
1926/15	No Competition	
1913	G Zampori	Ita
	V Rabic	Cze

FIRST HELD 1934

Women's Combined

Year	Winner	
1991	K Zmeskal	USA
1989	S Boguinskaia	USSR
1987	A Dobre	Rom
1985	O Omelianchuk	USSR
	E Chouchounova	USSR
1983	N Yurchenko	USSR
1981	O Bicherova	USSR
1979	N Kim	USSR
1978	Y Mukhina	USSR
1974	L Tourischeva	USSR

Year	Winner	
1970	L Tourischeva	USSR
1966	V Caslavska	Cze
1962	L Latynina	USSR
1958	L Latynina	USSR
1954	G Roudiko	USSR
1950	H Rakoczy	Pol
1946/42	No Competition	
1938	V Dekanova	Cze
1934	V Dekanova	Cze

Women's Team

Year	Winner
1991	USSR
1989	USSR
1987	Romania
1985	USSR
1983	USSR
1981	USSR
1979	Romania
1978	USSR
1974	USSR
1970	USSR
1966	Czechoslovakia
1962	USSR
1958	USSR
1954	USSR
1950	Sweden
1938	Czechoslovakia
1934	Czechoslovakia

FIRST HELD 1938

Women's Beam

Year	Winner	
1991	S Boguinskaia	USSR
1989	D Silivas	Rom
1987	A Dobre	Rom
1985	D Silivas	Rom
1983	O Mostepanova	USSR
1981	M Gnauck	GDR
1979	V Cerna	Cze
1978	N Comaneci	Rom

Year	Winner	
1974	L Tourischeva	USSR
1970	E Zuchold	GDR
1966	N Kuchinskaya	USSR
1962	E Bosakova	Cze
1958	L Latynina	USSR
1954	K Tanaka	Jap
1950	H Rakoczy	Pol
1946/42	No Competition	
1938	V Dekanova	Cze

Women's Floor

Year	Winner	
1991	C Bontas	Rom
1989	S Boguinskaia	USSR
	D Silivas	Rom
1987	E Chouchounova	USSR
	D Silivas	Rom
1985	O Omelianchuk	USSR
1983	E Szabo	Rom
1981	N Ilyenko	USSR
1979	E Eberle	Rom
1978	N Kim	USSR
	Y Mukhina	USSR
1974	L Tourischeva	USSR
1970	L Tourischeva	USSR
1966	N Kuchinskaya	USSR
1962	L Latynina	USSR
1958	E Bosakova	Cze
1954	T Manina	USSR
1950	H Rakoczy	Pol
1946/42	No Competition	
1938	M Palfyova	Cze

Women's Vault

Year	Winner	
1991	L Milosovici	Rom
1989	O Dudnik	USSR
1987	E Chouchounova	USSR
1985	E Chouchounova	USSR
1983	B Stoyanova	Bul
1981	M Gnauck	GDR
1979	D Turner	Rom

Year	Winner	
1978	N Kim	USSR
1974	O Korbut	USSR
1970	E Zuchold	GDR
1966	V Caslavska	Cze
1962	V Caslavska	Cze
1958	L Latynina	USSR
1954	T Manina	USSR
	A Peterson	Swe
1950	H Rakoczy	Pol
1946/42	No Competition	
1938	M Palfyova	Cze
	M Majowska	Pol

Women's Asymmetrical Bars

FIRST HELD 1950

Year	Winner	
1991	Gwang Suk	RoK
1989	D Silivas	Rom
	D Fan	CPR
1987	D Silivas	Rom
	D Thumler	GDR
1985	G Fahnrich	GDR
1983	M Gnauck	GDR
1981	M Gnauck	GDR
1979	M Y Hong	CPR
	M Gnauck	GDR
1978	M Frederick	USA
1974	A Zinke	GDR
1970	K Janz	GDR
1962	I Pervuschina	USSR
1958	L Latynina	USSR
1954	A Kaleti	Hun
1950	H Rakoczy	Pol

OLYMPIC CHAMPIONS

Combined

FIRST HELD 1900

Year	Winner	
1988	V Artemov	USSR
1984	K Gushiken	Jap
1980	A Ditiatin	USSR
1976	N Andrianov	USSR
1972	S Kato	Jap
1968	S Kato	Jap
1964	Y Endo	Jap
1960	B Shakhlin	USSR
1956	V Chukarin	USSR
1952	V Chukarin	USSR
1948	V Huhtanen	Fin
1936	A Schwarzmann	Ger
1932	R Neri	Ita
1928	G Miez	Swi
1924	L Stukelj	Yug
1920	G Zampori	Ita
1912	A Braglia	Ita
1908	A Braglia	Ita
1904	J Lenhart	Aut
1900	G Sandras	Fra

Team

FIRST HELD 1924

Year	Winner
1988	USSR
1984	United States
1980	USSR
1976	Japan
1972	Japan
1968	Japan
1964	Japan
1960	Japan
1956	USSR
1952	USSR
1948	Finland
1936	Germany
1932	Italy

Year	Winner	
1928	Switzerland	
1924	Italy	

FIRST HELD 1896

Parallel Bars

Year	Winner	
1988	V Artemov	USSR
1984	B Conner	USA
1980	A Tkachev	USSR
1976	S Kato	Jap
1972	S Kato	Jap
1968	A Nakayama	Jap
1964	Y Endo	Jap
1960	B Shakhlin	USSR
1956	V Chukarin	USSR
1952	H Eugster	Swi
1948	M Reusch	Swi
1936	K Frey	Ger
1932	R Neri	Ita
1928	L Vacha	Cze
1924	A Guttinger	Swi
1920/08	Not held	
1904	G Eyser	USA
1900	Not held	
1896	A Flatow	Ger

Pommel Horse

Year	Winner	
1988	L Gueraskov	Bul
	Z Borkai	Hun
	D Belozerchev	USSR
1984	L Ning	CPR
	P Vidmar	USA
1980	Z Magyar	Hun
1976	Z Magyar	Hun
1972	V Klimenko	USSR
1968	M Cerar	Yug
1964	M Cerar	Yug
1960	E Ekman	Fin
	B Shakhlin	USSR
1956	B Shakhlin	USSR
1952	V Chukarin	USSR

Year	Winner	
1948	V Huhtanen	Fin
	H Savolainen	Fin
	P Aaltonen	Fin
1936	K Frey	Ger
1932	I Pelle	Hun
1928	H Hanggi	Swi
1924	J Wilhelm	Swi
1920/08	Not held	
1904	A Heida	USA
1900	Not held	
1896	L Zutter	Swi

Rings

Year	Winner	
1988	H Behrendt	GDR
	D Belozerchev	USSR
1984	K Gushiken	Jap
	L Ning	CPR
1980	A Ditiatin	USSR
1976	N Andrianov	USSR
1972	A Nakayama	Jap
1968	A Nakayama	Jap
1964	T Hayata	Jap
1960	A Azaryan	USSR
1956	A Azaryan	USSR
1952	G Shaginyan	USSR
1948	K Frei	Swi
1936	A Hudec	Cze
1932	G Gulack	USA
1928	L Stukelj	Yug
1924	F Martino	Ita
1920/08	Not held	
1904	H Glass	USA
1900	Not held	
1896	I Mitropoulos	Gre

Horizontal Bar

Year	Winner	
1988	V Artemov	USSR
	V Lioukine	USSR
1984	S Morisue	Jap
1980	S Deltchev	Bul

Year	Winner	
1976	M Tsukahara	Jap
1972	M Tsukahara	Jap
1968	M Voronin	USSR
	A Nakayama	Jap
1964	B Shakhlin	USSR
1960	T Ono	Jap
1956	T Ono	Jap
1952	J Gunthard	Swi
1948	J Stadler	Swi
1936	A Saarvala	Fin
1932	D Bixler	USA
1928	G Miez	Swi
1924	L Stukelj	Yug
1920/08	Not held	
1904	A Heida	USA
	E Hennig	USA
1900	Not held	
1896	H Weingartner	Ger

Vault

Year	Winner	
1988	L Yun	CPR
1984	L Yun	CPR
1980	N Andrianov	USSR
1976	N Andrianov	USSR
1972	K Koste	GDR
1968	M Voronin	USSR
1964	H Yamashita	Jap
1960	T Ono	Jap
	B Shakhlin	USSR
1956	H Bantz	Ger
	V Muratov	USSR
1952	V Chukarin	USSR
1948	P Aaltonen	Fin
1936	A Schwarzmann	Ger
1932	S Guglielmetti	Ita
1928	E Mack	Swi
1924	F Kriz	USA
1920/08	Not held	
1904	A Heida	USA
	G Eyser	USA
1900	Not held	
1896	C Schumann	Ger

Floor

FIRST HELD 1932

Year	Winner	
1988	S Kharikov	USSR
1984	L Ning	CPR
1980	R Bruckner	GDR
1976	N Andrianov	USSR
1972	N Andrianov	USSR
1968	S Kato	Jap
1964	F Menichelli	Ita
1960	N Aihara	Jap
1956	V Muratov	USSR
1952	W Thoresson	Swe
1948	F Pataki	Hun
1936	G Miez	Swi
1932	I Pelle	Hun

Women's Combined

FIRST HELD 1952

Year	Winner	
1988	E Chouchounova	USSR
1984	M L Retton	USA
1980	E Davydova	USSR
1976	N Comaneci	Rom
1972	L Tourischeva	USSR
1968	V Caslavska	Cze
1964	V Caslavska	Cze
1960	L Latynina	USSR
1956	L Latynina	USSR
1952	M Gorokhovskaya	USSR

Women's Team

FIRST HELD 1928

Year	Winner
1988	USSR
1984	Romania
1980	USSR
1976	USSR
1972	USSR

Year	Winner
1968	USSR
1964	USSR
1960	USSR
1956	USSR
1952	USSR
1948	Czechoslovakia
1936	Germany
1932	Not held
1928	Netherlands

FIRST HELD 1952

Women's Beam

Year	Winner	
1988	D Silivas	Rom
1984	S Pauca	Rom
	E Szabo	Rom
1980	N Comaneci	Rom
1976	N Comaneci	Rom
1972	O Korbut	USSR
1968	N Kuchinskaya	USSR
1964	V Caslavska	Cze
1960	E Bosakova	Cze
1956	A Keleti	Hun
1952	N Bocharova	USSR

Women's Floor

Year	Winner	
1988	D Silivas	Rom
1984	E Szabo	Rom
1980	N Kim	USSR
	N Comaneci	Rom
1976	N Kim	USSR
1972	O Korbut	USSR
1968	L Petrik	USSR
	V Caslavska	Cze
1964	L Latynina	USSR
1960	L Latynina	USSR
1956	L Latynina	USSR
	A Keleti	Hun
1952	A Keleti	Hun

Women's Asymmetrical Bars

Year	Winner	
1988	D Silivas	Rom
1984	M Y Hong	CPR
	J McNamara	USA
1980	M Gnauck	GDR
1976	N Comaneci	Rom
1972	K Janz	GDR
1968	V Caslavska	Cze
1964	P Astakhova	USSR
1960	P Astakhova	USSR
1956	A Keleti	Hun
1952	M Korondi	Hun

Women's Vault

Year	Winner	
1988	S Boguinskaia	Rom
1984	E Szabo	Rom
1980	N Shaposhnikova	USSR
1976	N Kim	USSR
1972	K Janz	GDR
1968	V Caslavska	Cze
1964	V Caslavska	Cze
1960	M Nikolayeva	USSR
1956	L Latynina	USSR
1952	Y Kalinchuk	USSR

HANDBALL

WORLD CHAMPIONS
Men

FIRST HELD 1938

Year	Winner
1990	Sweden
1986	Yugoslavia
1982	USSR
1978	West Germany
1974	Romania
1970	Romania
1967	Czechoslovakia
1964	Romania
1961	Romania
1958	Sweden
1954	Sweden
1938	Germany

Women

FIRST HELD 1957

Year	Winner
1990	USSR
1986	USSR
1982	USSR
1979	East Germany
1975	East Germany
1973	Yugoslavia
1971	East Germany
1965	Hungary
1962	Romania
1957	Czechoslovakia

OLYMPIC CHAMPIONS
Men

FIRST HELD 1936

Year	Winner
1988	USSR
1984	Yugoslavia
1980	East Germany
1976	USSR
1972	Yugoslavia
1968/48	Not held
1936	Germany

Women

FIRST HELD 1976

Year	Winner
1988	South Korea
1984	Yugoslavia
1980	USSR
1976	USSR

HOCKEY

OLYMPIC CHAMPIONS

FIRST HELD 1908

Year	Winner
1988	Great Britain
1984	Pakistan
1980	India
1976	New Zealand
1972	West Germany
1968	Pakistan
1964	India
1960	Pakistan
1956	India
1952	India
1948	India
1936	India
1932	India
1928	India
1924	Not held
1920	Great Britain
1912	Not held

Year	Winner
1908	England

Women

FIRST HELD 1980

Year	Winner
1988	Australia
1984	Netherlands
1980	Zimbabwe

WORLD CUP

FIRST HELD 1971

Year	Winner
1990	Netherlands
1986	Australia
1982	Pakistan

Year	Winner
1978	Pakistan
1975	India
1973	Netherlands
1971	Pakistan

Women

FIRST HELD 1974

Year	Winner
1990	Netherlands
1986	Netherlands
1983	Netherlands
1981	West Germany
1978	Netherlands
1976	West Germany
1974	Netherlands

CHAMPIONS TROPHY

FIRST HELD 1978

Year	Winner
1991	Germany
1990	Australia
1989	Australia
1988	West Germany
1987	West Germany
1986	West Germany
1985	Australia
1984	Australia
1983	Australia
1982	Netherlands
1981	Netherlands
1980	Pakistan
1978	Pakistan

EUROPEAN CLUBS CUP CHAMPIONS

FIRST HELD 1971

Year	Winner	
1991	Uhlenhorst	Ger
1990	Uhlenhorst	FRG
1989	Uhlenhorst	FRG
1988	Uhlenhorst	FRG
1987	Bloemendaal	Nld
1986	Kampong Utrecht	Nld
1985	Atletico Terrasa	Spa
1984	TG 1846 Frankental	FRG
1983	Dinamo Alma-Ata	USSR
1982	Dinamo Alma-Ata	USSR
1981	Klein Zwitserland	Nld
1980	Slough	GB
1979	Klein Zwitserland	Nld
1978	Southgate	GB
1977	Southgate	GB
1976	Southgate	GB
1975	Frankfurt 1880	FRG
1974	Frankfurt 1880	FRG
1973	Frankfurt 1880	FRG
1972	Frankfurt 1880	FRG
1971	Frankfurt 1880	FRG

Women

FIRST HELD 1974

Year	Winner	
1991	HGC Wassenaar	Nld
1990	Amsterdam	Nld
1989	Amsterdam	Nld
1988	Amsterdam	Nld
1987	HGC Wassenaar	Nld
1986	HGC Wassenaar	Nld
1985	HGC Wassenaar	Nld
1984	HGC Wassenaar	Nld
1983	HGC Wassenaar	Nld
1982	Amsterdam	Nld
1981	Amsterdam	Nld
1980	Amsterdam	Nld
1979	Amsterdam	Nld

Year	Winner	
1978	Amsterdam	Nld
1977	Amsterdam	Nld
1976	Amsterdam	Nld
1975	Amsterdam	Nld
1974	Harvetschuder Hamburg	FRG

ENGLISH LEAGUE CHAMPIONS

FIRST HELD 1975

Year	Winner
1991	Havant
1990	Hounslow
1989	Southgate
1988	Southgate
1987	Slough
1986	East Grinstead
1985	East Grinstead
1984	Neston
1983	Slough
1982	Slough
1981	Slough
1980	Slough
1979	ISCA
1978	Southgate
1977	Southgate
1976	Slough
1975	Bedfordshire Eagles

HOCKEY ASSOCIATION CUP

FIRST HELD 1972

Year	Winner
1991	Hounslow
1990	Havant
1989	Hounslow
1988	Southgate
1987	Southgate

Year	Winner
1986	Southgate
1985	Southgate
1984	East Grinstead
1983	Neston
1982	Southgate
1981	Slough
1980	Slough
1979	Slough
1978	Guildford
1977	Slough
1976	Nottingham
1975	Southgate
1974	Southgate
1973	Hounslow
1972	Hounslow

ENGLISH WOMEN'S CLUB CHAMPIONS

FIRST HELD 1979

Year	Winner
1991	Sutton Coldfield
1990	Sutton Coldfield
1989	Ealing
1988	Ealing
1987	Ealing
1986	Slough
1985	Ipswich
1984	Sheffield
1983	Slough
1982	Slough
1981	Sutton Coldfield
1980	Norton
1979	Chelmsford

HORSE RACING

THE DERBY

Run at Epsom over 1 mile 4 furlongs

FIRST RUN 1780

Year	Winner
1991	Generous
1990	Quest for Fame
1989	Nashwan
1988	Kahyasi
1987	Reference Point
1986	Shahrastani
1985	Slip Anchor
1984	Secreto
1983	Teenoso
1982	Golden Fleece
1981	Shergar
1980	Henbit
1979	Troy
1978	Shirley Heights
1977	The Minstrel
1976	Empery
1975	Grundy
1974	Snow Knight
1973	Morston
1972	Roberto
1971	Mill Reef
1970	Nijinsky
1969	Blakeney
1968	Sir Ivor
1967	Royal Palace
1966	Charlottown
1965	Sea Bird II
1964	Santa Claus
1963	Relko
1962	Larkspur
1961	Psidium
1960	St Paddy
1959	Parthia
1958	Hard Ridden
1957	Crepello
1956	Lavandin

Year	Winner
1955	Phil Drake
1954	Never Say Die
1953	Pinza
1952	Tulyar
1951	Arctic Prince
1950	Galcador
1949	Nimbus
1948	My Love
1947	Pearl Diver
1946	Airborne
1945	Dante
1944	Ocean Swell
1943	Straight Deal
1942	Watling Street
1941	Owen Tudor
1940	Pont l'Eveque
1939	Blue Peter
1938	Bois Roussel
1937	Mid-day Sun
1936	Mahmoud
1935	Bahram
1934	Windsor Lad
1933	Hyperion
1932	April the Fifth
1931	Cameronian
1930	Blenheim
1929	Trigo
1928	Felstead
1927	Call Boy
1926	Coronach
1925	Manna
1924	Sansovino
1923	Papyrus
1922	Captain Cuttle
1921	Humorist
1920	Spion Kop
1919	Grand Parade
1918	Gainsborough
1917	Gay Crusader
1916	Fifinella
1915	Pommern
1914	Durbar II

Year	Winner	Year	Winner
1913	Aboyeur	1868	Blue Gown
1912	Tagalie	1867	Hermit
1911	Sunstar	1866	Lord Lyon
1910	Lemberg	1865	Gladiateur
1909	Minoru	1864	Blair Athol
1908	Signorinetta	1863	Macaroni
1907	Orby	1862	Caractacus
1906	Spearmint	1861	Kettledrum
1905	Cicero	1860	Thormanby
1904	St Amant	1859	Musjid
1903	Rock Sand	1858	Beadsman
1902	Ard Patrick	1857	Blink Bonny
1901	Volodyovski	1856	Ellington
1900	Diamond Jubilee	1855	Wild Dayrell
1899	Flying Fox	1854	Andover
1898	Jeddah	1853	West Australian
1897	Galtee More	1852	Daniel O'Rourke
1896	Persimmon	1851	Teddington
1895	Sir Visto	1850	Voltigeur
1894	Ladas	1849	The Flying Dutchman
1893	Isinglass	1848	Surplice
1892	Sir Hugo	1847	Cossack
1891	Common	1846	Pyrrhus the First
1890	Sainfoin	1845	The Merry Monarch
1889	Donovan	1844	Orlando
1888	Ayrshire	1843	Cotherstone
1887	Merry Hampton	1842	Attila
1886	Ormonde	1841	Coronation
1885	Melton	1840	Little Wonder
1884	St Gatien	1839	Bloomsbury
	Harvester	1838	Amato
1883	St Blaise	1837	Phosphorus
1882	Shotover	1836	Bay Middleton
1881	Iroquois	1835	Mundig
1880	Bend Or	1834	Plenipotentiary
1879	Sir Bevys	1833	Dangerous
1878	Sefton	1832	St Giles
1877	Silvio	1831	Spaniel
1876	Kisber	1830	Priam
1875	Galopin	1829	Frederick
1874	George Frederick	1828	Cadland
1873	Doncaster	1827	Mameluke
1872	Cremorne	1826	Lapdog
1871	Favonius	1825	Middleton
1870	Kingcraft	1824	Cedric
1869	Pretender	1823	Emilius

Year	Winner
1822	Moses
1821	Gustavus
1820	Sailor
1819	Tiresias
1818	Sam
1817	Azor
1816	Prince Leopold
1815	Whisker
1814	Blucher
1813	Smolensko
1812	Octavius
1811	Phantom
1810	Whalebone
1809	Pope
1808	Pan
1807	Election
1806	Paris
1805	Cardinal Beaufort
1804	Hannibal
1803	Ditto
1802	Tyrant
1801	Eleanor
1800	Champion
1799	Archduke
1798	Sir Harry
1797	c by Fidget
1796	Didelot
1795	Spread Eagle
1794	Daedalus
1793	Waxy
1792	John Bull
1791	Eager
1790	Rhadamanthus
1789	Skyscraper
1788	Sir Thomas
1787	Sir Peter Teazle
1786	Noble
1785	Aimwell
1784	Serjeant
1783	Saltram
1782	Assassin
1781	Young Eclipse
1780	Diomed

THE OAKS

Run at Epsom over 1 mile 4 furlongs

FIRST RUN 1779

Year	Winner
1991	Jet Ski Lady
1990	Salsabil
1989	Snow Bride
1988	Diminuendo
1987	Unite
1986	Midway Lady
1985	Oh So Sharp
1984	Circus Plume
1983	Sun Princess
1982	Time Charter
1981	Blue Wind
1980	Bireme
1979	Scintillate
1978	Fair Salinia
1977	Dunfermline
1976	Pawneese
1975	Juliette Marny
1974	Polygamy
1973	Mysterious
1972	Ginevra
1971	Altesse Royale
1970	Lupe
1969	Sleeping Partner
1968	La Lagune
1967	Pia
1966	Valoris
1965	Long Look
1964	Homeward Bound
1963	Noblesse
1962	Monade
1961	Sweet Solera
1960	Never Too Late II
1959	Petite Etoile
1958	Bella Paola
1957	Carrozza
1956	Sicarelle
1955	Meld
1954	Sun Cap
1953	Ambiguity
1952	Frieze

Year	Winner	Year	Winner
1951	Neasham Belle	1905	Cherry Lass
1950	Asmena	1904	Pretty Polly
1949	Musidora	1903	Our Lassie
1948	Masaka	1902	Sceptre
1947	Imprudence	1901	Cap and Bells II
1946	Steady Aim	1900	La Roche
1945	Sun Stream	1899	Musa
1944	Hycilla	1898	Airs and Graces
1943	Why Hurry	1897	Limasol
1942	Sun Chariot	1896	Canterbury Pilgrim
1941	Commotion	1895	La Sagesse
1940	Godiva	1894	Amiable
1939	Galatea II	1893	Mrs Butterwick
1938	Rockfel	1892	La Fleche
1937	Exhibitionist	1891	Mimi
1936	Lovely Rosa	1890	Memoir
1935	Quashed	1889	L'Abbesse de Jouarre
1934	Light Brocade	1888	Seabreeze
1933	Chatelaine	1887	Reve d'Or
1932	Udaipur	1886	Miss Jummy
1931	Brulette	1885	Lonely
1930	Rose of England	1884	Busybody
1929	Pennycomequick	1883	Bonny Jean
1928	Toboggan	1882	Geheimniss
1927	Beam	1881	Thebais
1926	Short Story	1880	Jenny Howlet
1925	Saucy Sue	1879	Wheel of Fortune
1924	Straitlace	1878	Jannette
1923	Brownhylda	1877	Placida
1922	Pogrom	1876	Camelia
1921	Love in Idleness		Enguerrande
1920	Charlebelle	1875	Spinaway
1919	Bayuda	1874	Apology
1918	My Dear	1873	Marie Stuart
1917	Sunny Jane	1872	Reine
1916	Fifinella	1871	Hannah
1915	Snow Marten	1870	Gamos
1914	Princess Dorrie	1869	Brigantine
1913	Jest	1868	Formosa
1912	Mirska	1867	Hippia
1911	Cherimoya	1866	Tormentor
1910	Rosedrop	1865	Regalia
1909	Perola	1864	Fille de l'Air
1908	Signorinetta	1863	Queen Bertha
1907	Glass Doll	1862	Feu de Joie
1906	Keystone II	1861	Brown Duchess

Year	Winner
1860	Butterfly
1859	Summerside
1858	Governess
1857	Blink Bonny
1856	Mincepie
1855	Marchioness
1854	Mincemeat
1853	Catherine Hayes
1852	Songstress
1851	Iris
1850	Rhedycina
1849	Lady Evelyn
1848	Cymbra
1847	Miami
1846	Mendicant
1845	Refraction
1844	The Princess
1843	Poison
1842	Our Nell
1841	Ghuznee
1840	Crucifix
1839	Deception
1838	Industry
1837	Miss Letty
1836	Cyprian
1835	Queen of Trumps
1834	Pussy
1833	Vespa
1832	Galata
1831	Oxygen
1830	Variation
1829	Green Mantle
1828	Turquoise
1827	Gulnare
1826	Lilias
1825	Wings
1824	Cobweb
1823	Zinc
1822	Pastille
1821	Augusta
1820	Caroline
1819	Shoveler
1818	Corinne
1817	Neva
1816	Landscape
1815	Minuet

Year	Winner
1814	Medora
1813	Music
1812	Manuella
1811	Sorcery
1810	Oriana
1809	Maid of Orleans
1808	Morel
1807	Briseïs
1799	Bellina
1798	Bellissima
1797	Niké
1796	Parissot
1795	Platina
1794	Hermione
1793	Caelia
1792	Volantè
1791	Portia
1790	Hippolyta
1789	Tag
1788	Nightshade
1787	Annette
1786	Yellow Filly
1785	Trifle
1784	Stella
1783	Maid of the Oaks
1782	Ceres
1781	Faith
1780	Teetotum
1779	Bridget

TWO THOUSAND GUINEAS

Run at Newmarket over 1 mile

FIRST RUN 1809

Year	Winner
1991	Mystiko
1990	Tirol
1989	Nashwan
1988	Doyoun
1987	Don't Forget Me
1986	Dancing Brave

Year	Winner	Year	Winner
1985	Shadeed	1939	Blue Peter
1984	El Gran Senor	1938	Pasch
1983	Lomond	1937	Le Ksar
1982	Zino	1936	Pay Up
1981	To-Agori-Mou	1935	Bahram
1980	Known Fact	1934	Colombo
1979	Tap on Wood	1933	Rodosto
1978	Roland Gardens	1932	Orwell
1977	Nebbiolo	1931	Cameronian
1976	Wollow	1930	Diolite
1975	Bolkonski	1929	Mr Jinks
1974	Nonoalco	1928	Flamingo
1973	Mon Fils	1927	Adam's Apple
1972	High Top	1926	Colorado
1971	Brigadier Gerard	1925	Manna
1970	Nijinsky	1924	Diophon
1969	Right Tack	1923	Ellangowan
1968	Sir Ivor	1922	St Louis
1967	Royal Palace	1921	Craig an Eran
1966	Kashmir II	1920	Tetratema
1965	Niksar	1919	The Panther
1964	Baldric II	1918	Gainsborough
1963	Only for Life	1917	Gay Crusader
1962	Privy Councillor	1916	Clarissimus
1961	Rockavon	1915	Pommern
1960	Martial	1914	Kennymore
1959	Taboun	1913	Louvois
1958	Pall Mall	1912	Sweeper II
1957	Crepello	1911	Sunstar
1956	Gilles de Retz	1910	Neil Gow
1955	Our Babu	1909	Minoru
1954	Darius	1908	Norman III
1953	Nearula	1907	Slieve Gallion
1952	Thunderhead II	1906	Gorgos
1951	Ki Ming	1905	Vedas
1950	Palestine	1904	St Amant
1949	Nimbus	1903	Rock Sand
1948	My Babu	1902	Sceptre
1947	Tudor Minstrel	1901	Handicapper
1946	Happy Knight	1900	Diamond Jubilee
1945	Court Martial	1899	Flying Fox
1944	Garden Path	1898	Disraeli
1943	Kingsway	1897	Galtee More
1942	Big Game	1896	St Frusquin
1941	Lambert Simnel	1895	Kirkconnel
1940	Djebel	1894	Ladas

Year	Winner
1893	Isinglass
1892	Bonavista
1891	Common
1890	Surefoot
1889	Enthusiast
1888	Ayrshire
1887	Enterprise
1886	Ormonde
1885	Paradox
1884	Scot Free
1883	Galliard
1882	Shotover
1881	Peregrine
1880	Petronel
1879	Charibert
1878	Pilgrimage
1877	Chamant
1876	Petrarch
1875	Camballo
1874	Atlantic
1873	Gang Forward
1872	Prince Charlie
1871	Bothwell
1870	Macgregor
1869	Pretender
1868	Moslem
	Formosa
1867	Vauban
1866	Lord Lyon
1865	Gladiateur
1864	General Peel
1863	Macaroni
1862	The Marquis
1861	Diophantus
1860	The Wizard
1859	The Promised Land
1858	Fitz-Roland
1857	Vedette
1856	Fazzoletto
1855	Lord of the Isles
1854	The Hermit
1853	West Australian
1852	Stockwell
1851	Hernandez
1850	Pitsford
1849	Nunnykirk

Year	Winner
1848	Flatcatcher
1847	Conyngham
1846	Sir Tatton Sykes
1845	Idas
1844	The Ugly Buck
1843	Cotherstone
1842	Meteor
1841	Ralph
1840	Crucifix
1839	The Corsair
1838	Grey Momus
1837	Achmet
1836	Bay Middleton
1835	Ibrahim
1834	Glencoe
1833	Clearwell
1832	Archibald
1831	Riddlesworth
1830	Augustus
1829	Patron
1828	Cadland
1827	Turcoman
1826	Dervise
1825	Enamel
1824	Schahriar
1823	Nicolo
1822	Pastille
1821	Reginald
1820	Pindarrie
1819	Antar
1818	Interpreter
1817	Manfred
1816	Nectar
1815	Tigris
1814	Olive
1813	Smolensko
1812	Cwrw
1811	Trophonius
1810	Hephestion
1809	Wizard

ONE THOUSAND GUINEAS

Run at Newmarket over 1 mile

FIRST RUN 1814

Year	Winner
1991	Shadayid
1990	Salsabil
1989	Musical Bliss
1988	Ravinella
1987	Miesque
1986	Midway Lady
1985	Oh So Sharp
1984	Pebbles
1983	Ma Biche
1982	On the House
1981	Fairy Footsteps
1980	Quick as Lightning
1979	One in a Million
1978	Enstone Spark
1977	Mrs McArdy
1976	Flying Water
1975	Nocturnal Spree
1974	Highclere
1973	Mysterious
1972	Waterloo
1971	Altesse Royale
1970	Humble Duty
1969	Full Dress II
1968	Caergwrle
1967	Fleet
1966	Glad Rags
1965	Night Off
1964	Pourparler
1963	Hula Dancer
1962	Abermaid
1961	Sweet Solera
1960	Never Too Late II
1959	Petite Etoile
1958	Bella Paola
1957	Rose Royale II
1956	Honeylight
1955	Meld
1954	Festoon
1953	Happy Laughter

Year	Winner
1952	Zabara
1951	Belle of All
1950	Camaree
1949	Musidora
1948	Queenpot
1947	Imprudence
1946	Hypericum
1945	Sun Stream
1944	Picture Play
1943	Herringbone
1942	Sun Chariot
1941	Dancing Time
1940	Godiva
1939	Galatea II
1938	Rockfel
1937	Exhibitionist
1936	Tide-way
1935	Mesa
1934	Campanula
1933	Brown Betty
1932	Kandy
1931	Four Course
1930	Fair Isle
1929	Taj Mah
1928	Scuttle
1927	Cresta Run
1926	Pillion
1925	Saucy Sue
1924	Plack
1923	Tranquil
1922	Silver Urn
1921	Bettina
1920	Cinna
1919	Roseway
1918	Ferry
1917	Diadem
1916	Canyon
1915	Vaucluse
1914	Princess Dorrie
1913	Jest
1912	Tagalie
1911	Atmah
1910	Winkipop
1909	Electra
1908	Rhodora
1907	Witch Elm

Year	Winner	Year	Winner
1906	Flair	1860	Sagitta
1905	Cherry Lass	1859	Mayonaise
1904	Pretty Polly	1858	Governess
1903	Quintessence	1857	Imperieuse
1902	Sceptre	1856	Manganese
1901	Aida	1855	Habena
1900	Winifreda	1854	Virago
1899	Sibola	1853	Mentmore Lass
1898	Nun Nicer	1852	Kate
1897	Chelandry	1851	Aphrodite
1896	Thais	1850	f by Slane
1895	Galeottia	1849	Flea
1894	Amiable	1848	Canezou
1893	Siffleuse	1847	Clementina
1892	La Fleche	1846	Mendicant
1891	Mimi	1845	Picnic
1890	Semolina	1844	Sorella
1889	Minthe	1843	Extempore
1888	Briar-root	1842	Firebrand
1887	Rêve d'Or	1841	Potentia
1886	Miss Jummy	1840	Crucifix
1885	Farewell	1839	Cara
1884	Busybody	1838	Barcarolle
1883	Hauteur	1837	Chapeau d'Espagne
1882	St Marguerite	1836	Destiny
1881	Thebais	1835	Preserve
1880	Elizabeth	1834	May Day
1879	Wheel of Fortune	1833	Tarantella
1878	Pilgrimage	1832	Galata
1877	Belphoebe	1831	Galantine
1876	Camelia	1830	Charlotte West
1875	Spinaway	1829	f out of Mouse
1874	Apology	1828	Zoè
1873	Cecilia	1827	Arab
1872	Reine	1826	Problem
1871	Hannah	1825	Tontine
1870	Hester	1824	Cobweb
1869	Scottish Queen	1823	Zinc
1868	Formosa	1822	Whizgig
1867	Achievement	1821	Zeal
1866	Repulse	1820	Rowena
1865	Siberia	1819	Catgut
1864	Tomato	1818	Corinne
1863	Lady Augusta	1817	Neva
1862	Hurricane	1816	Rhoda
1861	Nemesis	1815	f by Selim

Year	Winner
1814	Charlotte

ST LEGER

Run at Doncaster over 1 mile 6 furlongs 127 yds

FIRST RUN 1776

Year	Winner
1991	Toulon
1990	Snurge
1989	Michelozzo
1988	Minster Son
1987	Reference Point
1986	Moon Madness
1985	Oh So Sharp
1984	Commanche Run
1983	Sun Princess
1982	Touching Wood
1981	Cut Above
1980	Light Cavalry
1979	Son of Love
1978	Julio Mariner
1977	Dunfermline
1976	Crow
1975	Bruni
1974	Bustino
1973	Peleid
1972	Boucher
1971	Athens Wood
1970	Nijinsky
1969	Intermezzo
1968	Ribero
1967	Ribocco
1966	Sodium
1965	Provoke
1964	Indiana
1963	Ragusa
1962	Hethersett
1961	Aurelius
1960	St Paddy
1959	Cantelo
1958	Alcide
1957	Ballymoss

Year	Winner
1956	Cambremer
1955	Meld
1954	Never Say Die
1953	Premonition
1952	Tulyar
1951	Talma II
1950	Scratch II
1949	Ridge Wood
1948	Black Tarquin
1947	Sayajirao
1946	Airborne
1945	Chamossaire
1944	Tehran
1943	Herringbone
1942	Sun Chariot
1941	Sun Castle
1940	Turkhan
1939	No Race
1938	Scottish Union
1937	Chulmleigh
1936	Boswell
1935	Bahram
1934	Windsor Lad
1933	Hyperion
1932	Firdaussi
1931	Sandwich
1930	Singapore
1929	Trigo
1928	Fairway
1927	Book Law
1926	Coronach
1925	Solario
1924	Salmon-Trout
1923	Tranquil
1922	Royal Lancer
1921	Polemarch
1920	Caligula
1919	Keysoe
1918	Gainsborough
1917	Gay Crusader
1916	Hurry On
1915	Pommern
1914	Black Jester
1913	Night Hawk
1912	Tracery
1911	Prince Palatine

Year	Winner	Year	Winner
1910	Swynford	1864	Blair Athol
1909	Bayardo	1863	Lord Clifden
1908	Your Majesty	1862	The Marquis
1907	Wool Winder	1861	Caller Ou
1906	Troutbeck	1860	St Albans
1905	Challacombe	1859	Gamester
1904	Pretty Polly	1858	Sunbeam
1903	Rock Sand	1857	Imperieuse
1902	Sceptre	1856	Warlock
1901	Doricles	1855	Saucebox
1900	Diamond Jubilee	1854	Knight of St George
1899	Flying Fox	1853	West Australian
1898	Wildfowler	1852	Stockwell
1897	Galtee More	1851	Newminster
1896	Persimmon	1850	Voltigeur
1895	Sir Visto	1849	The Flying Dutchman
1894	Throstle	1848	Surplice
1893	Isinglass	1847	Van Tromp
1892	La Fleche	1846	Sir Tatton Sykes
1891	Common	1845	The Baron
1890	Memoir	1844	Faugh-a-Ballagh
1889	Donovan	1843	Nutwith
1888	Seabreeze	1842	Blue Bonnet
1887	Kilwarlin	1841	Satirist
1886	Ormonde	1840	Launcelot
1885	Melton	1839	Charles the Twelfth
1884	The Lambkin	1838	Don John
1883	Ossian	1837	Mango
1882	Dutch Oven	1836	Elis
1881	Iroquois	1835	Queen of Trumps
1880	Robert the Devil	1834	Touchstone
1879	Rayon d'Or	1833	Rockingham
1878	Jannette	1832	Margrave
1877	Silvio	1831	Chorister
1876	Petrarch	1830	Birmingham
1875	Craig Millar	1829	Rowton
1874	Apology	1828	The Colonel
1873	Marie Stuart	1827	Matilda
1872	Wenlock	1826	Tarrare
1871	Hannah	1825	Memnon
1870	Hawthornden	1824	Jerry
1869	Pero Gomez	1823	Barefoot
1868	Formosa	1822	Theodore
1867	Achievement	1821	Jack Spigot
1866	Lord Lyon	1820	St Patrick
1865	Gladiateur	1819	Antonio

Year	Winner
1818	Reveller
1817	Ebor
1816	The Duchess
1815	Filho da Puta
1814	William
1813	Altisidora
1812	Otterington
1811	Soothsayer
1810	Octavian
1809	Ashton
1808	Petronius
1807	Paulina
1806	Fyldener
1805	Staveley
1804	Sancho
1803	Remembrancer
1802	Orville
1801	Quiz
1800	Champion
1799	Cockfighter
1798	Symmetry
1797	Lounger
1796	Ambrosio
1795	Hambletonian
1794	Beningbrough
1793	Ninety-three
1792	Tartar
1791	Young Traveller
1790	Ambidexter
1789	Pewett
1788	Young Flora
1787	Spadille
1786	Paragon
1785	Cowslip
1784	Omphale
1783	Phoenomenon
1782	Imperatrix
1781	Serina
1780	Ruler
1779	Tommy
1778	Hollandaise
1777	Bourbon
1776	Allabaculia

ASCOT GOLD CUP

Run at Ascot over 2 miles 4 furlongs

FIRST RUN 1807

Year	Winner
1991	Indian Queen
1990	Ashal
1989	Sadeem
1988	Sadeem
1987	Paean
1986	Longboat
1985	Gildoran
1984	Gildoran
1983	Little Wolf
1982	Ardross
1981	Ardross
1980	Le Moss
1979	Le Moss
1978	Shangamuzo
1977	Sagaro
1976	Sagaro
1975	Sagaro
1974	Ragstone
1973	Lassalle
1972	Erimo Hawk
1971	Random Shot
1970	Precipice Wood
1969	Levmoss
1968	Pardallo II
1967	Parbury
1966	Fighting Charlie
1965	Fighting Charlie
1964	No Race
1963	Twilight Alley
1962	Balto
1961	Pandofell
1960	Sheshoon
1959	Wallaby II
1958	Gladness
1957	Zarathustra
1956	Macip
1955	Botticelli
1954	Elpenor
1953	Souepi
1952	Aquino II

Year	Winner	Year	Winner
1951	Pan II	1904	Throwaway
1950	Supertello	1903	Maximum II
1949	Alycidon	1902	William the Third
1948	Arbar	1901	Santoi
1947	Souverain	1900	Merman
1946	Caracalla II	1899	Cyllene
1945	Ocean Swell	1898	Elf II
1944	Umiddad	1897	Persimmon
1943	Ujiji	1896	Love Wisely
1942	Owen Tudor	1895	Isinglass
1941	Finis	1894	La Fleche
1940	No Race	1893	Marcion
1939	Flyon	1892	Buccaneer
1938	Flares	1891	Morion
1937	Precipitation	1890	Gold
1936	Quashed	1889	Trayles
1935	Tiberius	1888	Timothy
1934	Felicitation	1887	Bird of Freedom
1933	Foxhunter	1886	Althorp
1932	Trimdon	1885	St Gatien
1931	Trimdon	1884	St Simon
1930	Bosworth	1883	Tristan
1929	Invershin	1882	Foxhall
1928	Invershin	1881	Robert the Devil
1927	Foxlaw	1880	Isonomy
1926	Solario	1879	Isonomy
1925	Santorb	1878	Verneuil
1924	Massine	1877	Petrach
1923	Happy Man	1876	Apology
1922	Golden Myth	1875	Doncaster
1921	Periosteum	1874	Boiard
1920	Tangiers	1873	Cremorne
1919	By Jingo	1872	Henry
1918	Gainsborough	1871	Mortemer
1917	Gay Crusader	1870	Sabinus
1916/15	No Race	1869	Brigantine
1914	Aleppo	1868	Blue Gown
1913	Prince Palatine	1867	Lecturer
1912	Prince Palatine	1866	Gladiateur
1911	Willonyx	1865	Ely
1910	Bayardo	1864	Scottish Chief
1909	Bomba	1863	Buckstone
1908	The White Knight	1862	Asteroid
1907	The White Knight	1861	Thormanby
1906	Bachelor's Button	1860	Rupee
1905	Zinfandel	1859	Fisherman

Year	Winner
1858	Fisherman
1857	Skirmisher
1856	Winkfield
1855	Fandango
1854	West Australian
1853	Teddington
1852	Joe Miller
1851	Woolwich
1850	The Flying Dutchman
1849	Van Tromp
1848	The Hero
1847	The Hero
1846	Alarm
1845	The Emperor
1844	The Emperor
1843	Ralph
1842	Bee's Wing
1841	Lanercost
1840	St Francis
1839	Caravan
1838	Grey Momus
1837	Touchstone
1836	Touchstone
1835	Glencoe
1834	Glaucus
1833	Galata
1832	Camarine
1831	Cetus
1830	Lucetta
1829	Zingaree
1828	Bobadilla
1827	Memnon
1826	Chateau Margaux
1825	Bizarre
1824	Bizarre
1823	Marcellus
1822	Sir Huldibrand
1821	Banker
1820	Champignon
1819	Anticipation
1818	Belville
1817	Sir Richard
1816	Anticipation
1815	Aladdin
1814	Pranks
1813	Lutzen

Year	Winner
1812	Flash
1811	Smallhopes
1810	Loiterer
1809	Anderida
1808	Brighton
1807	Master Jackey

KING GEORGE VI & QUEEN ELIZABETH STAKES

Run at Ascot over 1 mile 4 furlongs

FIRST RUN 1951

Year	Winner
1991	Generous
1990	Belmez
1989	Nashwan
1988	Mtoto
1987	Reference Point
1986	Dancing Brave
1985	Petoski
1984	Teenoso
1983	Time Charter
1982	Kalaglow
1981	Shergar
1980	Ela-Mana-Mou
1979	Troy
1978	Ile de Bourbon
1977	The Minstrel
1976	Pawneese
1975	Grundy
1974	Dahlia
1973	Dahlia
1972	Brigadier Gerard
1971	Mill Reef
1970	Nijinsky
1969	Park Top
1968	Royal Palace
1967	Busted
1966	Aunt Edith
1965	Meadow Court

Year	Winner
1964	Nasram II
1963	Ragusa
1962	Match III
1961	Right Royal V
1960	Aggressor
1959	Alcide
1958	Ballymoss
1957	Montaval
1956	Ribot
1955	Vimy
1954	Aureole
1953	Pinza
1952	Tulyar
1951	Supreme Court

ECLIPSE STAKES

Run at Sandown Park over 1 mile 2 furlongs

FIRST RUN 1886

Year	Winner
1991	Environment Friend
1990	Elmaamul
1989	Nashwan
1988	Mtoto
1987	Mtoto
1986	Dancing Brave
1985	Pebbles
1984	Sadlers Wells
1983	Solford
1982	Kalaglow
1981	Master Willie
1980	Ela-Mana-Mou
1979	Dickens Hill
1978	Gunner B
1977	Artaius
1976	Wollow
1975	Star Appeal
1974	Coup de Feu
1973	Scottish Rifle
1972	Brigadier Gerard
1971	Mill Reef

Year	Winner
1970	Connaught
1969	Wolver Hollow
1968	Royal Palace
1967	Busted
1966	Pieces of Eight
1965	Canisbay
1964	Ragusa
1963	Khalkis
1962	Henry the Seventh
1961	St Paddy
1960	Javelot
1959	Saint Crespin III
1958	Ballymoss
1957	Arctic Explorer
1956	Tropique
1955	Darius
1954	King of the Tudors
1953	Argur
1952	Tulyar
1951	Mystery IX
1950	Flocon
1949	Djeddah
1948	Petition
1947	Migoli
1946	Gulf Stream
1945/40	No Race
1939	Blue Peter
1938	Pasch
1937	Boswell
1936	Rhodes Scholar
1935	Windsor Lad
1934	King Salmon
1933	Loaningdale
1932	Miracle
1931	Caerleon
1930	Rustom Pasha
1929	Royal Minstrel
1928	Fairway
1927	Colorado
1926	Coronach
1925	Polyphontes
1924	Polyphontes
1923	Saltash
1922	Golden Myth
1921	Craig an Eran
1920	Buchan

Year	Winner	Year	Winner
1919	Buchan	1987	Sir Harry Lewis
1918/15	No Race	1986	Shahrastani
1914	Hapsburg	1985	Law Society
1913	Tracery	1984	El Gran Senor
1912	Prince Palatine	1983	Shareef Dancer
1911	Swynford	1982	Assert
1910	Lemberg	1981	Shergar
	Neil Gow	1980	Tyrnavos
1909	Bayardo	1979	Troy
1908	Your Majesty	1978	Shirley Heights
1907	Lally	1977	The Minstrel
1906	Llangibby	1976	Malacate
1905	Val d'Or	1975	Grundy
1904	Darley Dale	1974	English Prince
1903	Ard Patrick	1973	Weavers' Hall
1902	Cheers	1972	Steel Pulse
1901	Epsom Lad	1971	Irish Ball
1900	Diamond Jubilee	1970	Nijinsky
1899	Flying Fox	1969	Prince Regent
1898	Velasquez	1968	Ribero
1897	Persimmon	1967	Ribocco
1896	St Frusquin	1966	Sodium
1895	Le Justicier	1965	Meadow Court
1894	Isinglass	1964	Santa Claus
1893	Orme	1963	Ragusa
1892	Orme	1962	Tambourine II
1891	Surefoot	1961	Your Highness
1890	No Race	1960	Chamour
1889	Ayrshire	1959	Fidalgo
1888	Orbit	1958	Sindon
1887	No Race	1957	Ballymoss
1886	Bendigo	1956	Talgo
		1955	Panaslipper
		1954	Zarathustra

IRISH DERBY

Run at The Curragh over 1
mile 4 furlongs

FIRST RUN 1866

Year	Winner	Year	Winner
		1953	Chamier
		1952	Thirteen of Diamonds
		1951	Fraise du Bois II
		1950	Dark Warrior
		1949	Hindostan
		1948	Nathoo
		1947	Sayajirao
		1946	Bright News
1991	Generous	1945	Piccadilly
1990	Salsabil	1944	Slide On
1989	Old Vic	1943	The Phoenix
1988	Kahyasi	1942	Windsor Slipper

Year	Winner	Year	Winner
1941	Sol Oriens	1897	Wales
1940	Turkhan	1896	Gulsalberk
1939	Mondragon	1895	Portmarnock
1938	Rosewell	1894	Blairfinde
1937	Phideas	1893	Bowline
1936	Raeburn	1892	Roy Neil
1935	Museum	1891	Narraghmore
1934	Primero	1890	Kentish Fire
	Patriot King	1889	Tragedy
1933	Harinero	1888	Theodolite
1932	Dastur	1887	Pet Fox
1931	Sea Serpent	1886	Theodemir
1930	Rock Star	1885	St Kevin
1929	Kopi	1884	Theologian
1928	Baytown	1883	Sylph
1927	Knight of the Grail	1882	Sortie
1926	Embargo	1881	Master Ned
1925	Zionist	1880	King of the Bees
1924	Haine	1879	Soulouque
	Zodiac	1878	Madame Dubarry
1923	Waygood	1877	Redskin
1922	Spike Island	1876	Umpire
1921	Ballyheron	1875	Innishowen
1920	He Goes	1874	Ben Battle
1919	Loch Lomond	1873	Kyrle Daly
1918	King John	1872	Trickstress
1917	First Flier	1871	Maid of Athens
1916	Furore	1870	Billy Pitt
1915	Ballaghtobin	1869	The Scout
1914	Land of Song	1868	Madeira
1913	Bachelor's Wedding	1867	Golden Plover
1912	Civility	1866	Selim
1911	Shanballymore
1910	Aviator
1909	Bachelor's Double
1908	Wild Bouquet
1907	Orby
1906	Killeagh
1905	Flax Park
1904	Royal Arch
1903	Lord Rossmore
1902	St Brendan
1901	Carrigavalla
1900	Gallinaria
1899	Oppressor
1898	Noble Howard

PRIX DE L'ARC DE TRIOMPHE

Run at Longchamp, Paris over 2,400 metres

FIRST RUN 1920

Year	Winner
1990	Saumarez

Year	Winner	Year	Winner
1989	Carroll House	1943	Verso II
1988	Tony Bin	1942	Djebel
1987	Trempolino	1941	Le Pacha
1986	Dancing Brave	1940/39	No Race
1985	Rainbow Quest	1938	Eclair au Chocolat
1984	Sagace	1937	Corrida
1983	All Along	1936	Corrida
1982	Akiyda	1935	Samos
1981	Gold River	1934	Brantome
1980	Detroit	1933	Crapom
1979	Three Troikas	1932	Motrico
1978	Alleged	1931	Pearl Cap
1977	Alleged	1930	Motrico
1976	Ivanjica	1929	Ortello
1975	Star Appeal	1928	Kantar
1974	Allez France	1927	Mon Talisman
1973	Rheingold	1926	Biribi
1972	San San	1925	Priori
1971	Mill Reef	1924	Massine
1970	Sassafras	1923	Parth
1969	Levmoss	1922	Ksar
1968	Vaguely Noble	1921	Ksar
1967	Topyo	1920	Comrade
1966	Bon Mot		
1965	Sea Bird II		
1964	Prince Royal II		
1963	Exbury		
1962	Soltikoff		
1961	Molvedo		
1960	Puissant Chef		
1959	Saint Crespin III		
1958	Ballymoss		
1957	Oroso		
1956	Ribot		
1955	Ribot		
1954	Sica Boy		
1953	La Sorellina		
1952	Nuccio		
1951	Tantieme		
1950	Tantieme		
1949	Coronation V		
1948	Migoli		
1947	Le Paillon		
1946	Caracalla		
1945	Nikellora		
1944	Ardan		

KENTUCKY DERBY

Run at Louisville, Kentucky over 1 mile 2 furlongs

FIRST RUN 1875

Year	Winner
1991	Strike The Gold
1990	Unbridled
1989	Sunday Silence
1988	Winning Colors
1987	Alysheba
1986	Ferdinand
1985	Spend a Buck
1984	Swale
1983	Sunny's Halo
1982	Gato Del Sol
1981	Pleasant Colony
1980	Genuine Risk
1979	Spectacular Bid

Year	Winner	Year	Winner
1978	Affirmed	1932	Burgoo King
1977	Seattle Slew	1931	Twenty Grand
1976	Bold Forbes	1930	Gallant Fox
1975	Foolish Pleasure	1929	Clyde Van Dusen
1974	Cannonade	1928	Reigh Count
1973	Secretariat	1927	Whiskery
1972	Riva Ridge	1926	Bubbling Over
1971	Canonero II	1925	Flying Ebony
1970	Dust Commander	1924	Black Gold
1969	Majestic Prince	1923	Zev
1968	Forward Pass	1922	Morvich
1967	Proud Clarion	1921	Behave Yourself
1966	Kauai King	1920	Paul Jones
1965	Lucky Debonair	1919	Sir Barton
1964	Northern Dancer	1918	Exterminator
1963	Chateaugay	1917	Omar Khayyam
1962	Decidedly	1916	George Smith
1961	Carry Back	1915	Regret
1960	Venetian Way	1914	Old Rosebud
1959	Tomy Lee	1913	Donerail
1958	Tim Tam	1912	Worth
1957	Iron Liege	1911	Meridian
1956	Needles	1910	Donau
1955	Swaps	1909	Wintergreen
1954	Determine	1908	Stone Street
1953	Dark Star	1907	Pink Star
1952	Hill Gail	1906	Sir Huon
1951	Count Turf	1905	Agile
1950	Middleground	1904	Elwood
1949	Ponder	1903	Judge Himes
1948	Citation	1902	Alan-a-Dale
1947	Jet Pilot	1901	His Eminence
1946	Assault	1900	Lieut. Gibson
1945	Hoop Jr	1899	Manuel
1944	Pensive	1898	Plaudit
1943	Count Fleet	1897	Typhoon II
1942	Shut Out	1896	Ben Brush
1941	Whirlaway	1895	Halma
1940	Gallahadion	1894	Chant
1939	Johnstown	1893	Lookout
1938	Lawrin	1892	Azra
1937	War Admiral	1891	Kingman
1936	Bold Venture	1890	Riley
1935	Omaha	1889	Spokane
1934	Cavalcade	1888	Macbeth II
1933	Brokers Tip	1887	Montrose

Year	Winner
1886	Ben Ali
1885	Joe Cotton
1884	Buchanan
1883	Leonatus
1882	Apollo
1881	Hindoo
1880	Fonso
1879	Lord Murphy
1878	Day Star
1877	Baden Baden
1876	Vagrant
1875	Aristides

PREAKNESS STAKES

Run at Pimlico, Maryland
over 1 mile 1¹/₂ furlongs

FIRST RUN 1873

Year	Winner
1991	Hansel
1990	Summer Squall
1989	Sunday Silence
1988	Risen Star
1987	Alysheba
1986	Snow Chief
1985	Tank's Prospect
1984	Gate Dancer
1983	Deputed Testamony
1982	Aloma's Ruler
1981	Pleasant Colony
1980	Codex
1979	Spectacular Bid
1978	Affirmed
1977	Seattle Slew
1976	Elocutionist
1975	Master Derby
1974	Little Current
1973	Secretariat
1972	Bee Bee Bee
1971	Canonero II
1970	Personality
1969	Majestic Prince
1968	Forward Pass

Year	Winner
1967	Damascus
1966	Kuai King
1965	Tom Rolfe
1964	Northern Dancer
1963	Candy Spots
1962	Greek Money
1961	Carry Back
1960	Bally Ache
1959	Royal Orbit
1958	Tim Tam
1957	Bold Ruler
1956	Fabius
1955	Nashua
1954	Hasty Road
1953	Native Dancer
1952	Blue Man
1951	Bold
1950	Hill Prince
1949	Capot
1948	Citation
1947	Faultless
1946	Assault
1945	Polynesian
1944	Pensive
1943	Count Fleet
1942	Alsab
1941	Whirlaway
1940	Bimelech
1939	Challedon
1938	Dauber
1937	War Admiral
1936	Bold Venture
1935	Omaha
1934	High Quest
1933	Head Play
1932	Burgoo King
1931	Mate
1930	Gallant Fox
1929	Dr Freeland
1928	Victorian
1927	Bostonian
1926	Display
1925	Coventry
1924	Nellie Morse
1923	Vigil
1922	Pillory

Year	Winner
1921	Broomspun
1920	Man o'War
1919	Sir Barton
1918	Jack Hare Jr
1918	War Cloud
1917	Kalitan
1916	Damrosch
1915	Rhine Maiden
1914	Holiday
1913	Buskin
1912	Colonel Holloway
1911	Watervale
1910	Layminster
1909	Effendi
1908	Royal Tourist
1907	Don Enrique
1906	Whimsical
1905	Cairngorm
1904	Bryn Mawr
1903	Flocarline
1902	Old England
1901	The Parader
1900	Hindus
1899	Half Time
1898	Sly Fox
1897	Paul Kauvar
1896	Margrave
1895	Belmar
1894	Assignee
1893/91	No Race
1890	Montague
1889	Buddhist
1888	Refund
1887	Dunboyne
1886	The Bard
1885	Tecumseh
1884	Knight of Ellerslie
1883	Jacobus
1882	Vanguard
1881	Saunterer
1880	Grenada
1879	Harold
1878	Duke of Magenta
1877	Claverbrook
1876	Shirley
1875	Tom Ochiltree

Year	Winner
1874	Culpepper
1873	Survivor

BELMONT STAKES

Run at Belmont Park, New York over 1 mile 4 furlongs

FIRST RUN 1867

Year	Winner
1991	Hansel
1990	Go and Go
1989	Easy Goer
1988	Risen Star
1987	Bet Twice
1986	Danzig Connection
1985	Creme Fraiche
1984	Swale
1983	Caveat
1982	Conquistador Cielo
1981	Summing
1980	Temperence Hill
1979	Coastal
1978	Affirmed
1977	Seattle Slew
1976	Bold Forbes
1975	Avatar
1974	Little Current
1973	Secretariat
1972	Riva Ridge
1971	Pass Catcher
1970	High Echelon
1969	Arts and Letters
1968	Stage Door Johnny
1967	Damascus
1966	Amberoid
1965	Hail to All
1964	Quadrangle
1963	Chateaugay
1962	Jaipur
1961	Sherluck
1960	Celtic Ash
1959	Sword Dancer
1958	Cavan

Year	Winner	Year	Winner
1957	Gallant Man	1910	Sweep
1956	Needles	1909	Joe Madden
1955	Nashua	1908	Colin
1954	High Gun	1907	Peter Pan
1953	Native Dancer	1906	Burgomaster
1952	One Count	1905	Tanya
1951	Counterpoint	1904	Delhi
1950	Middleground	1903	Africander
1949	Capot	1902	Masterman
1948	Citation	1901	Commando
1947	Phalanx	1900	Ildrim
1946	Assault	1899	Jean Bereaud
1945	Pavot	1898	Bowling Brook
1944	Bounding Home	1897	Scottish Chieftain
1943	Count Fleet	1896	Hastings
1942	Shut Out	1895	Belmar
1941	Whirlaway	1894	Henry of Navarre
1940	Bimelech	1893	Commanche
1939	Johnstown	1892	Patron
1938	Pasteurized	1891	Foxford
1937	War Admiral	1890	Burlington
1936	Granville	1889	Eric
1935	Omaha	1888	Sir Dixon
1934	Peace Chance	1887	Hanover
1933	Hurryoff	1886	Inspector B
1932	Faireno	1885	Tyrant
1931	Twenty Grand	1884	Panique
1930	Gallant Fox	1883	George Kinney
1929	Blue Larkspur	1882	Forester
1928	Vito	1881	Saunterer
1927	Chance Shot	1880	Grenada
1926	Crusader	1879	Spendthrift
1925	American Flag	1878	Duke of Magenta
1924	Mad Play	1877	Cloverbrook
1923	Zev	1876	Algerine
1922	Pillory	1875	Calvin
1921	Grey Lag	1874	Saxon
1920	Man o'War	1873	Springbok
1919	Sir Barton	1872	Joe Daniels
1918	Johren	1871	Harry Bassett
1917	Hourless	1870	Kingfisher
1916	Friar Rock	1869	Fenian
1915	The Finn	1868	General Duke
1914	Luke McLuke	1867	Ruthless
1913	Prince Eugene		
1912/11	No Race		

MELBOURNE CUP

Run at Flemington,
Melbourne over 2 miles

FIRST RUN 1861

Year	Winner
1990	Kingston Blue
1989	Tawrrific
1988	Empire Rose
1987	Kensei
1986	At Talaq
1985	What a Nuisance
1984	Black Knight
1983	Kiwi
1982	Gurner's Lane
1981	Just a Dash
1980	Beldale Ball
1979	Hyperno
1978	Arwon
1977	Gold and Black
1976	Van Der Hum
1975	Think Big
1974	Think Big
1973	Gala Supreme
1972	Piping Lane
1971	Silver Knight
1970	Baghdad Note
1969	Rain Lover
1968	Rain Lover
1967	Red Handed
1966	Galilee
1965	Light Fingers
1964	Polo Prince
1963	Gatum Gatum
1962	Even Stevens
1961	Lord Fury
1960	Hi Jinx
1959	MacDougal
1958	Baystone
1957	Straight Draw
1956	Evening Peal
1955	Toparoa
1954	Rising Fast
1953	Wodalla
1952	Dalray
1951	Delta

Year	Winner
1950	Comic Court
1949	Foxzami
1948	Rimfire
1947	Hiraji
1946	Russia
1945	Rainbird
1944	Sirius
1943	Dark Felt
1942	Colonus
1941	Skipton
1940	Old Rowley
1939	Rivette
1938	Catalogue
1937	The Trump
1936	Wotan
1935	Marabou
1934	Peter Pan
1933	Hall Mark
1932	Peter Pan
1931	White Nose
1930	Phar Lap
1929	Nightmarch
1928	Statesman
1927	Trivalve
1926	Spearfelt
1925	Windbag
1924	Backwood
1923	Bitalli
1922	King Ingoda
1921	Sister Olive
1920	Poitrel
1919	Artilleryman
1918	Night Watch
1917	Westcourt
1916	Sasanof
1915	Patrobas
1914	Kingsburgh
1913	Posinatus
1912	Piastre
1911	The Parisian
1910	Comedy King
1909	Prince Foote
1908	Lord Nolan
1907	Apologue
1906	Poseidon
1905	Blue Spec

Year	Winner
1904	Acrasia
1903	Lord Cardigan
1902	The Victory
1901	Revenue
1900	Clean Sweep
1899	Merriwee
1898	The Grafter
1897	Gaulus
1896	Newhaven
1895	Auraria
1894	Patron
1893	Tarcoola
1892	Glenloth
1891	Malvolio
1890	Carbine
1889	Bravo
1888	Mentor
1887	Dunlop
1886	Arsenal
1885	Sheet Anchor
1884	Malua
1883	Martini Henry
1882	The Assyrian
1881	Zulu
1880	Grand Flaneur
1879	Darriwell
1878	Calamia
1877	Chester
1876	Briseis
1875	Wollomai
1874	Haricot
1873	Don Juan
1872	The Quack
1871	The Pearl
1870	Nimblefoot
1869	Warrior
1868	Glencoe
1867	Tim Whiffler
1866	The Barb
1865	Toryboy
1864	Lantern
1863	Banker
1862	Archer
1861	Archer

THE GRAND NATIONAL

Run at Aintree, Liverpool over 4 miles 856 yards

FIRST RUN 1837

Year	Winner
1991	Seagram
1990	Mr Frisk
1989	Little Polveir
1988	Rhyme'N'Reason
1987	Maori Venture
1986	West Tip
1985	Last Suspect
1984	Hallo Dandy
1983	Corbiere
1982	Grittar
1981	Aldaniti
1980	Ben Nevis
1979	Rubstic
1978	Lucius
1977	Red Rum
1976	Rag Trade
1975	L'Escargot
1974	Red Rum
1973	Red Rum
1972	Well To Do
1971	Specify
1970	Gay Trip
1969	Highland Wedding
1968	Red Alligator
1967	Foinavon
1966	Anglo
1965	Jay Trump
1964	Team Spirit
1963	Ayala
1962	Kilmore
1961	Nicolaus Silver
1960	Merryman II
1959	Oxo
1958	Mr What
1957	Sundew
1956	E.S.B.
1955	Quare Times
1954	Royal Tan
1953	Early Mist

Year	Winner	Year	Winner
1952	Teal	1902	Shannon Lass
1951	Nickel Coin	1901	Grudon
1950	Freebooter	1900	Ambush II
1949	Russian Hero	1899	Manifesto
1948	Sheila's Cottage	1898	Drogheda
1947	Caughoo	1897	Manifesto
1946	Lovely Cottage	1896	The Soarer
1945/41	No Race	1895	Wild Man from Borneo
1940	Bogskar	1894	Why Not
1939	Workman	1893	Cloister
1938	Battleship	1892	Father O'Flynn
1937	Royal Mail	1891	Come Away
1936	Reynoldstown	1890	Ilex
1935	Reynoldstown	1889	Frigate
1934	Golden Miller	1888	Playfair
1933	Kellsboro' Jack	1887	Gamecock
1932	Forbra	1886	Old Joe
1931	Grakle	1885	Roquefort
1930	Shaun Goilin	1884	Voluptuary
1929	Gregalach	1883	Zoedone
1928	Tipperary Tim	1882	Seaman
1927	Sprig	1881	Woodbrook
1926	Jack Horner	1880	Empress
1925	Double Chance	1879	The Liberator
1924	Master Robert	1878	Shifnal
1923	Sergeant Murphy	1877	Austerlitz
1922	Music Hall	1876	Regal
1921	Shaun Spadah	1875	Pathfinder
1920	Troytown	1874	Reugny
1919	Poethlyn	1873	Disturbance
1918	Poethlyn	1872	Casse Tete
1917	Ballymacad	1871	The Lamb
1916	Vermouth	1870	The Colonel
1915	Ally Sloper	1869	The Colonel
1914	Sunloch	1868	The Lamb
1913	Covertcoat	1867	Cortolvin
1912	Jerry M	1866	Salamander
1911	Glenside	1865	Alcibiade
1910	Jenkinstown	1864	Emblematic
1909	Lutteur III	1863	Emblem
1908	Rubio	1862	Huntsman
1907	Eremon	1861	Jealousy
1906	Ascetic's Silver	1860	Anatis
1905	Kirkland	1859	Half Caste
1904	Moifaa	1858	Little Charley
1903	Drumcree	1857	Emigrant

Year	Winner
1856	Freetrader
1855	Wanderer
1854	Bourton
1853	Peter Simple
1852	Miss Mowbray
1851	Abd-el-Kader
1850	Abd-el-Kader
1849	Peter Simple
1848	Chandler
1847	Matthew
1846	Pioneer
1845	Cure-All
1844	Discount
1843	Vanguard
1842	Gay Lad
1841	Charity
1840	Jerry
1839	Lottery
1838	Sir Henry
1837	The Duke

CHELTENHAM GOLD CUP

Run at Cheltenham over 3 miles 2 furlongs

FIRST RUN 1924

Year	Winner
1991	Garrison Savannah
1990	Norton's Coin
1989	Desert Orchid
1988	Charter Party
1987	The Thinker
1986	Dawn Run
1985	Forgive'N'Forget
1984	Burrough Hill Lad
1983	Bregawn
1982	Silver Buck
1981	Little Owl
1980	Master Smudge
1979	Alverton
1978	Midnight Court
1977	Davy Lad

Year	Winner
1976	Royal Frolic
1975	Ten Up
1974	Captain Christy
1973	The Dikler
1972	Glencaraig Lady
1971	L'Escargot
1970	L'Escargot
1969	What a Myth
1968	Fort Leney
1967	Woodland Venture
1966	Arkle
1965	Arkle
1964	Arkle
1963	Mill House
1962	Mandarin
1961	Saffron Tartan
1960	Pas Seul
1959	Roddy Owen
1958	Kerstin
1957	Linwell
1956	Limber Hill
1955	Gay Donald
1954	Four Ten
1953	Knock Hard
1952	Mont Tremblant
1951	Silver Fame
1950	Cottage Rake
1949	Cottage Rake
1948	Cottage Rake
1947	Fortina
1946	Prince Regent
1945	Red Rower
1944/43	No Race
1942	Medoc II
1941	Poet Prince
1940	Roman Hackle
1939	Brendan's Cottage
1938	Morse Code
1937	No Race
1936	Golden Miller
1935	Golden Miller
1934	Golden Miller
1933	Golden Miller
1932	Golden Miller
1931	No Race
1930	Easter Hero

Year	Winner
1929	Easter Hero
1928	Patron Saint
1927	Thrown In
1926	Koko
1925	Ballinode
1924	Red Splash

CHAMPION HURDLE

Run at Cheltenham over 2 miles 200 yds

FIRST RUN 1927

Year	Winner
1991	Morley Street
1990	Kribensis
1989	Beech Road
1988	Celtic Shot
1987	See You Then
1986	See You Then
1985	See You Then
1984	Dawn Run
1983	Gaye Brief
1982	For Auction
1981	Sea Pigeon
1980	Sea Pigeon
1979	Monksfield
1978	Monksfield
1977	Night Nurse
1976	Night Nurse
1975	Comedy of Errors
1974	Lanzarote
1973	Comedy of Errors
1972	Bula
1971	Bula
1970	Persian War
1969	Persian War
1968	Persian War
1967	Saucy Kit
1966	Salmon Spray
1965	Kirriemuir
1964	Magic Court
1963	Winning Fair

Year	Winner
1962	Anzio
1961	Eborneezer
1960	Another Flash
1959	Fare Time
1958	Bandalore
1957	Merry Deal
1956	Doorknocker
1955	Clair Soleil
1954	Sir Ken
1953	Sir Ken
1952	Sir Ken
1951	Hatton's Grace
1950	Hatton's Grace
1949	Hatton's Grace
1948	National Spirit
1947	National Spirit
1946	Distel
1945	Brains Trust
1944/43	No Race
1942	Forestation
1941	Seneca
1940	Solford
1939	African Sister
1938	Our Hope
1937	Free Fare
1936	Victor Norman
1935	Lion Courage
1934	Chenango
1933	Insurance
1932	Insurance
1931	No Race
1930	Brown Tony
1929	Royal Falcon
1928	Brown Jack
1927	Blaris

QUEEN MOTHER CHAMPION CHASE

Run at Cheltenham over 2 miles

FIRST RUN 1959

Year	Winner
1991	Katabatic
1990	Barnbrook Again
1989	Barnbrook Again
1988	Pearlyman
1987	Pearlyman
1986	Buck House
1985	Badsworth Boy
1984	Badsworth Boy
1983	Badsworth Boy
1982	Rathgorman
1981	Drumgora
1980	Another Dolly
1979	Hilly Way
1978	Hilly Way
1977	Skymas
1976	Skymas
1975	Lough Inagh
1974	Royal Relief
1973	Inkslinger
1972	Royal Relief
1971	Crisp
1970	Straight Fort
1969	Muir
1968	Drinny's Double
1967	Drinny's Double
1966	Flyingbolt
1965	Dunkirk
1964	Ben Stack
1963	Sandy Abbot
1962	Piperton
1961	Fortria
1960	Fortria
1959	Quita Que

KING GEORGE VI CHASE

Run at Kempton over 3 miles

FIRST RUN 1947

Year	Winner
1990	Desert Orchid
1989	Desert Orchid
1988	Desert Orchid
1987	Nupsala
1986	Desert Orchid
1985	Wayward Lad
1984	Burrough Hill Lad
1983	Wayward Lad
1982	Wayward Lad
1981	No Race
1980	Silver Buck
1979	Silver Buck
1978	Gay Spartan
1977	Bachelor's Hall
1976	Royal Marshall II
1975	Captain Christy
1974	Captain Christy
1973	Pendil
1972	Pendil
1971	The Dikler
1970	No Race
1969	Titus Oates
1968/67	No Race
1966	Dormant
1965	Arkle
1964	Frenchman's Cove
1963	Mill House
1962/61	No Race
1960	Saffron Tartan
1959	Mandarin
1958	Lochroe
1957	Mandarin
1956	Rose Park
1955	Limber Hill
1954	Halloween
1953	Galloway Braes
1952	Halloween
1951	Statecraft
1950	Manicou
1949	Finnure

Year	Winner	Year	Winner
1948	Cottage Rake	1958	Taxidermist
1947	Rowland Roy	1957	Much Obliged

WHITBREAD GOLD CUP

Run at Sandown over 3 miles 5 furlongs 18 yds

FIRST RUN 1957

Year	Winner
1991	Docklands Express
1990	Mr Frisk
1989	Brown Windsor
1988	Desert Orchid
1987	Lean Ar Aghaidh
1986	Plundering
1985	By the Way
1984	Special Cargo
1983	Drumlargen
1982	Shady Deal
1981	Diamond Edge
1980	Royal Mail
1979	Diamond Edge
1978	Strombolus
1977	Andy Pandy
1976	Otter Way
1975	April Seventh
1974	The Dikler
1973	Charlie Potheen
1972	Grey Sombrero
1971	Titus Oates
1970	Royal Toss
1969	Larbawn
1968	Larbawn
1967	Mill House
1966	What a Myth
1965	Arkle
1964	Dormant
1963	Hoodwinked
1962	Frenchman's Cove
1961	Pas Seul
1960	Plummers Plain
1959	Done Up

ENGLISH CHAMPION JOCKEYS

Flat Racing

FROM 1840

Year	Winner	
1990	P Eddery	209
1989	P Eddery	171
1988	P Eddery	183
1987	S Cauthen	197
1986	P Eddery	177
1985	S Cauthen	195
1984	S Cauthen	130
1983	W Carson	159
1982	L Piggott	188
1981	L Piggott	179
1980	W Carson	165
1979	J Mercer	164
1978	W Carson	182
1977	P Eddery	176
1976	P Eddery	162
1975	P Eddery	164
1974	P Eddery	148
1973	W Carson	163
1972	W Carson	132
1971	L Piggott	162
1970	L Piggott	162
1969	L Piggott	163
1968	L Piggott	139
1967	L Piggott	117
1966	L Piggott	191
1965	L Piggott	166
1964	L Piggott	140
1963	A Breasley	176
1962	A Breasley	179
1961	A Breasley	171
1960	L Piggott	170
1959	D Smith	157
1958	D Smith	165

Year	Winner		Year	Winner	
1957	A Breasley	173	1912	F Wootton	118
1956	D Smith	155	1911	F Wootton	187
1955	D Smith	168	1910	F Wootton	137
1954	D Smith	129	1909	F Wootton	165
1953	G Richards	191	1908	D Maher	139
1952	G Richards	231	1907	W Higgs	146
1951	G Richards	227	1906	W Higgs	149
1950	G Richards	201	1905	E Wheatley	124
1949	G Richards	261	1904	O Madden	161
1948	G Richards	224	1903	O Madden	154
1947	G Richards	269	1902	W Lane	170
1946	G Richards	212	1901	O Madden	130
1945	G Richards	104	1900	L Reiff	143
1944	G Richards	88	1899	S Loates	160
1943	G Richards	65	1898	O Madden	161
1942	G Richards	67	1897	M Cannon	145
1941	H Wragg	71	1896	M Cannon	164
1940	G Richards	68	1895	M Cannon	184
1939	G Richards	155	1894	M Cannon	167
1938	G Richards	206	1893	T Loates	222
1937	G Richards	214	1892	M Cannon	182
1936	G Richards	177	1891	M Cannon	137
1935	G Richards	210	1890	T Loates	147
1934	G Richards	212	1889	T Loates	167
1933	G Richards	259	1888	F Barrett	108
1932	G Richards	190	1887	C Wood	151
1931	G Richards	145	1886	F Archer	170
1930	F Fox	129	1885	F Archer	246
1929	G Richards	135	1884	F Archer	241
1928	G Richards	148	1883	F Archer	232
1927	G Richards	164	1882	F Archer	210
1926	T Weston	95	1881	F Archer	220
1925	G Richards	118	1880	F Archer	120
1924	C Elliott	106	1879	F Archer	197
1923	S Donoghue	89	1878	F Archer	229
	C Elliott	89	1877	F Archer	218
1922	S Donoghue	102	1876	F Archer	207
1921	S Donoghue	141	1875	F Archer	172
1920	S Donoghue	143	1874	F Archer	147
1919	S Donoghue	129	1873	H Constable	110
1918	S Donoghue	66	1872	T Cannon	87
1917	S Donoghue	42	1871	G Fordham	86
1916	S Donoghue	43		C Maidment	86
1915	S Donoghue	62	1870	W Grey	76
1914	S Donoghue	129		C Maidment	76
1913	D Maher	115	1869	G Fordham	95

Year	Winner	
1868	G Fordham	110
1867	G Fordham	143
1866	S Kenyon	123
1865	G Fordham	142
1864	J Grimshaw	164
1863	G Fordham	103
1862	G Fordham	166
1861	G Fordham	106
1860	G Fordham	146
1859	G Fordham	118
1858	G Fordham	91
1857	G Fordham	84
1856	G Fordham	108
1855	G Fordham	70
1854	J Wells	82
1853	J Wells	86
1852	E Flatman	92
1851	E Flatman	78
1850	E Flatman	88
1849	E Flatman	94
1848	E Flatman	104
1847	E Flatman	89
1846	E Flatman	81
1845	E Flatman	81
1844	E Flatman	64
1843	E Flatman	60
1842	E Flatman	42
1841	E Flatman	68
1840	E Flatman	50

National Hunt

FROM 1900

Year	Winner	
1990/91	P Scudamore	141
1989/90	P Scudamore	170
1988/89	P Scudamore	221
1987/88	P Scudamore	132
1986/87	P Scudamore	123
1985/86	P Scudamore	91
1984/85	J Francome	101
1983/84	J Francome	131
1982/83	J Francome	106
1981/82	J Francome	120

Year	Winner	
	P Scudamore	120
1980/81	J Francome	105
1979/80	J J O'Neill	117
1978/79	J Francome	95
1977/78	J J O'Neill	149
1976/77	T Stack	97
1975/76	J Francome	96
1974/75	T Stack	82
1973/74	R Barry	94
1972/73	R Barry	125
1971/72	B Davies	89
1970/71	G Thorner	74
1969/70	B Davies	91
1968/69	B Davies	77
	T Biddlecombe	77
1967/68	J Gifford	82
1966/67	J Gifford	122
1965/66	T Biddlecombe	102
1964/65	T Biddlecombe	114
1963/64	J Gifford	94
1962/63	J Gifford	70
1961/62	S Mellor	80
1960/61	S Mellor	118
1959/60	S Mellor	68
1958/59	T Brookshaw	83
1957/58	F Winter	82
1956/57	F Winter	80
1955/56	F Winter	74
1954/55	T Molony	67
1953/54	R Francis	76
1952/53	F Winter	121
1951/52	T Molony	99
1950/51	T Molony	83
1949/50	T Molony	95
1948/49	T Molony	60
1947/48	B Marshall	66
1946/47	J Dowdeswell	58
1945/46	T Rimell	54
1944/45	H Nicholson	15
	T Rimell	15
1942/44	Not held	
1941/42	R Smyth	12
1940/41	G Wilson	22
1939/40	T Rimell	24
1938/39	T Rimell	61
1937/38	G Wilson	59

Year	Winner		Year	Winner	
1936/37	G Wilson	45	1918	G Duller	17
1935/36	G Wilson	57	1917	W Smith	15
1934/35	G Wilson	73	1916	C Hawkins	17
1933/34	G Wilson	56	1915	E Piggott	44
1932/33	G Wilson	61	1914	Mr J R Anthony	60
1931/32	W Stott	77	1913	E Piggott	60
1930/31	W Stott	81	1912	I Anthony	78
1929/30	W Stott	77	1911	W Payne	76
1928/29	W Stott	65	1910	E Piggott	67
1927/28	W Stott	88	1909	R Gordon	45
1926/27	F Rees	59	1908	P Cowley	65
1925/26	T Leader	61	1907	F Mason	59
1925	E Foster	76	1906	F Mason	58
1924	F Rees	108	1905	F Mason	73
1923	F Rees	64	1904	F Mason	59
1922	J Anthony	78	1903	P Woodland	54
1921	F Rees	65	1902	F Mason	67
1920	F Rees	64	1901	F Mason	58
1919	Mr H Brown	48	1900	Mr H Sidney	53

HURLING

ALL-IRELAND CHAMPIONS

FIRST HELD 1887

Year	Winner		Year	Winner
1991	Tipperary		1979	Kilkenny
1990	Cork		1978	Cork
1989	Tipperary		1977	Cork
1988	Galway		1976	Cork
1987	Galway		1975	Kilkenny
1986	Cork		1974	Kilkenny
1985	Offaly		1973	Limerick
1984	Cork		1972	Kilkenny
1983	Kilkenny		1971	Tipperary
1982	Kilkenny		1970	Cork
1981	Offaly		1969	Kilkenny
1980	Galway		1968	Wexford
			1967	Kilkenny
			1966	Cork
			1965	Tipperary
			1964	Tipperary
			1963	Kilkenny

Year	Winner	Year	Winner
1962	Tipperary	1924	Dublin
1961	Tipperary	1923	Galway
1960	Wexford	1922	Kilkenny
1959	Waterford	1921	Limerick
1958	Tipperary	1920	Dublin
1957	Kilkenny	1919	Cork
1956	Wexford	1918	Limerick
1955	Wexford	1917	Dublin
1954	Cork	1916	Tipperary
1953	Cork	1915	Laois
1952	Cork	1914	Clare
1951	Tipperary	1913	Kilkenny
1950	Tipperary	1912	Kilkenny
1949	Tipperary	1911	Kilkenny
1948	Waterford	1910	Wexford
1947	Kilkenny	1909	Kilkenny
1946	Cork	1908	Tipperary
1945	Tipperary	1907	Kilkenny
1944	Cork	1906	Tipperary
1943	Cork	1905	Kilkenny
1942	Cork	1904	Kilkenny
1941	Cork	1903	Cork
1940	Limerick	1902	Cork
1939	Kilkenny	1901	London Irish
1938	Dublin	1900	Tipperary
1937	Tipperary	1899	Tipperary
1936	Limerick	1898	Tipperary
1935	Kilkenny	1897	Limerick
1934	Limerick	1896	Tipperary
1933	Kilkenny	1895	Tipperary
1932	Kilkenny	1894	Cork
1931	Cork	1893	Cork
1930	Tipperary	1892	Cork
1929	Cork	1891	Kerry
1928	Cork	1890	Cork
1927	Dublin	1889	Dublin
1926	Cork	1888	Not completed
1925	Tipperary	1887	Tipperary

ICE HOCKEY

OLYMPIC CHAMPIONS

FIRST HELD 1920

Year	Winner
1988	USSR
1984	USSR
1980	United States
1976	USSR
1972	USSR
1968	USSR
1964	USSR
1960	United States
1956	USSR
1952	Canada
1948	Canada
1936	Great Britain
1932	Canada
1928	Canada
1924	Canada
1920	Canada

WORLD CHAMPIONS

FIRST HELD 1930

Year	Winner
1991	Sweden
1990	USSR
1989	USSR
1988	USSR
1987	Sweden
1986	USSR
1985	Czechoslovakia
1984	USSR
1983	USSR
1982	USSR
1981	USSR
1979	USSR

Year	Winner
1978	USSR
1977	Czechoslovakia
1976	Czechoslovakia
1975	USSR
1974	USSR
1973	USSR
1972	Czechoslovakia
1971	USSR
1970	USSR
1969	USSR
1967	USSR
1966	USSR
1965	USSR
1963	USSR
1962	Sweden
1961	Canada
1959	Canada
1958	Canada
1957	Sweden
1955	Canada
1954	USSR
1953	Sweden
1951	Canada
1950	Canada
1949	Czechoslovakia
1947	Czechoslovakia
1946/40	No Competition
1939	Canada
1938	Canada
1937	Canada
1935	Canada
1934	Canada
1933	United States
1931	Canada
1930	Canada

STANLEY CUP CHAMPIONS

FIRST HELD 1893/94

Year	Winner
1990/91	Pittsburgh Penguins
1989/90	Edmonton Oilers
1988/89	Calgary Flames
1987/88	Edmonton Oilers
1986/87	Edmonton Oilers
1985/86	Montreal Canadiens
1984/85	Edmonton Oilers
1983/84	Edmonton Oilers
1982/83	New York Islanders
1981/82	New York Islanders
1980/81	New York Islanders
1979/80	New York Islanders
1978/79	Montreal Canadiens
1977/78	Montreal Canadiens
1976/77	Montreal Canadiens
1975/76	Montreal Canadiens
1974/75	Philadelphia Flyers
1973/74	Philadelphia Flyers
1972/73	Montreal Canadiens
1971/72	Boston Bruins
1970/71	Montreal Canadiens
1969/70	Boston Bruins
1968/69	Montreal Canadiens
1967/68	Montreal Canadiens
1966/67	Toronto Maple Leafs
1965/66	Montreal Canadiens
1964/65	Montreal Canadiens
1963/64	Toronto Maple Leafs
1962/63	Toronto Maple Leafs
1961/62	Toronto Maple Leafs
1960/61	Chicago Black Hawks
1959/60	Montreal Canadiens
1958/59	Montreal Canadiens
1957/58	Montreal Canadiens
1956/57	Montreal Canadiens
1955/56	Montreal Canadiens
1954/55	Detroit Red Wings
1953/54	Detroit Red Wings
1952/53	Montreal Canadiens
1951/52	Detroit Red Wings
1950/51	Toronto Maple Leafs

Year	Winner
1949/50	Detroit Red Wings
1948/49	Toronto Maple Leafs
1947/48	Toronto Maple Leafs
1946/47	Toronto Maple Leafs
1945/46	Montreal Canadiens
1944/45	Toronto Maple Leafs
1943/44	Montreal Canadiens
1942/43	Detroit Red Wings
1941/42	Toronto Maple Leafs
1940/41	Boston Bruins
1939/40	New York Rangers
1938/39	Boston Bruins
1937/38	Chicago Black Hawks
1936/37	Detroit Red Wings
1935/36	Detroit Red Wings
1934/35	Montreal Maroons
1933/34	Chicago Black Hawks
1932/33	New York Rangers
1931/32	Toronto Maple Leafs
1930/31	Montreal Canadiens
1929/30	Montreal Canadiens
1928/29	Boston Bruins
1927/28	New York Rangers
1925/26	Montreal Maroons
1924/25	Victoria Cougars
1923/24	Montreal Canadiens
1922/23	Ottawa Senators
1921/22	Toronto St Patricks
1920/21	Ottawa Senators
1919/20	Ottawa Senators
1918/19	No Competition
1917/18	Toronto Arenas
1916/17	Seattle Metropolitans
1915/16	Montreal Canadiens
1914/15	Vancouver Millionaires
1913/14	Toronto Ontarios
1912/13	Quebec Bulldogs
1911/12	Quebec Bulldogs
1910/11	Ottawa Senators
1909/10	Montreal Wanderers
1908/09	Ottawa Senators
1907/08	Montreal Wanderers
1906/07	Montreal Wanderers
1906/07	Kenora Thistles
1905/06	Montreal Wanderers
1904/05	Ottawa Silver Seven

Year	Winner	Year	Winner
1903/04	Ottawa Silver Seven	1897/98	Montreal Victorias
1902/03	Ottawa Silver Seven	1896/97	Montreal Victorias
1901/02	Montreal AAA	1895/96	Montreal Victorias
1900/01	Winnipeg Victorias	1894/95	Montreal Victorias
1899/00	Montreal Shamrocks	1893/94	Montreal AAA
1898/99	Montreal Victorias		

ICE SKATING

FIGURE SKATING

WORLD CHAMPIONS

Men's Individual

FIRST HELD 1896

Year	Winner	
1991	K Browning	Can
1990	K Browning	Can
1989	K Browning	Can
1988	B Boitano	USA
1987	B Orser	Can
1986	B Boitano	USA
1985	A Fadeyev	USSR
1984	S Hamilton	USA
1983	S Hamilton	USA
1982	S Hamilton	USA
1981	S Hamilton	USA
1980	J Hoffman	GDR
1979	V Kovalyev	USSR
1978	C Tickner	USA
1977	V Kovalyev	USSR
1976	J Curry	GB
1975	S Volkov	USSR
1974	J Hoffman	GDR
1973	O Nepela	Cze
1972	O Nepela	Cze
1971	O Nepela	Cze
1970	T Wood	USA

Year	Winner	
1969	T Wood	USA
1968	E Danzer	Aut
1967	E Danzer	Aut
1966	E Danzer	Aut
1965	A Calmat	Fra
1964	M Schnelldorfer	FRG
1963	D McPherson	Can
1962	D Jackson	Can
1961	Not held	
1960	A Giletti	Fra
1959	D Jenkins	USA
1958	D Jenkins	USA
1957	D Jenkins	USA
1956	H A Jenkins	USA
1955	H A Jenkins	USA
1954	H A Jenkins	USA
1953	H A Jenkins	USA
1952	R Button	USA
1951	R Button	USA
1950	R Button	USA
1949	R Button	USA
1948	R Button	USA
1947	H Gerschwiler	Swi
1946/40	No Competition	
1939	G Sharp	GB
1938	F Kaspar	Aut
1937	F Kaspar	Aut
1936	K Schafer	Aut
1935	K Schafer	Aut
1934	K Schafer	Aut

Year	Winner		Year	Winner	
1933	K Schafer	Aut	1984	K Witt	GDR
1932	K Schafer	Aut	1983	R Sumners	USA
1931	K Schafer	Aut	1982	E Zayak	USA
1930	K Schafer	Aut	1981	D Biellmann	Swi
1929	G Grafstrom	Swe	1980	A Potzsch	GDR
1928	W Bockl	Aut	1979	L Fratianne	USA
1927	W Bockl	Aut	1978	A Potzsch	GDR
1926	W Bockl	Aut	1977	L Fratianne	USA
1925	W Bockl	Aut	1976	D Hamill	USA
1924	G Grafstrom	Swe	1975	D De Leeuw	Nld
1923	F Kachler	Aut	1974	C Errath	GDR
1922	G Grafstrom	Swe	1973	K Magnussen	Can
1921/15	No Competition		1972	B Schuba	Aut
1914	G Sandahl	Swe	1971	B Schuba	Aut
1913	F Kachler	Aut	1970	G Seyfert	GDR
1912	F Kachler	Aut	1969	G Seyfert	GDR
1911	U Salchow	Swe	1968	P Fleming	USA
1910	U Salchow	Swe	1967	P Fleming	USA
1909	U Salchow	Swe	1966	P Fleming	USA
1908	U Salchow	Swe	1965	P Burka	Can
1907	U Salchow	Swe	1964	S Dijkstra	Nld
1906	G Fuchs	Ger	1963	S Dijkstra	Nld
1905	U Salchow	Swe	1962	S Dijkstra	Nld
1904	U Salchow	Swe	1961	Not held	
1903	U Salchow	Swe	1960	C Heiss	USA
1902	U Salchow	Swe	1959	C Heiss	USA
1901	U Salchow	Swe	1958	C Heiss	USA
1900	G Hugel	Aut	1957	C Heiss	USA
1899	G Hugel	Aut	1956	C Heiss	USA
1898	H Grenander	Swe	1955	T Albright	USA
1897	G Hugel	Aut	1954	G Busch	FRG
1896	G Fuchs	Ger	1953	T Albright	USA
			1952	J du Bief	Fra
			1951	J Altwegg	GB

Women's Individual

FIRST HELD 1906

Year	Winner		Year	Winner	
			1950	A Vrzanova	Cze
			1949	A Vrzanova	Cze
			1948	B A Scott	Can
			1947	B A Scott	Can
1991	K Yamaguchi	USA	1946/40	No Competition	
1990	J Trennary	USA	1939	M Taylor	GB
1989	M Ito	Jap	1938	M Taylor	GB
1988	K Witt	GDR	1937	C Colledge	GB
1987	K Witt	GDR	1936	S Henie	Nor
1986	D Thomas	USA	1935	S Henie	Nor
1985	K Witt	GDR	1934	S Henie	Nor
			1933	S Henie	Nor

Year	Winner	
1932	S Henie	Nor
1931	S Henie	Nor
1930	S Henie	Nor
1929	S Henie	Nor
1928	S Henie	Nor
1927	S Henie	Nor
1926	H Jaross	Aut
1925	H Jaross	Aut
1924	H Szabo	Aut
1923	H Szabo	Aut
1922	H Szabo	Aut
1921/15	No Competition	
1914	O von M Horvath	Hun
1913	O von M Horvath	Hun
1912	O von M Horvath	Hun
1911	L Kronberger	Hun
1910	L Kronberger	Hun
1909	L Kronberger	Hun
1908	L Kronberger	Hun
1907	M Syers	GB
1906	M Syers	GB

Pairs

FIRST HELD 1908

Year	Winner	
1991	N Mishkuteniok & A Dmitriev	USSR
1990	Y Gordeyeva & S Grinkov	USSR
1989	Y Gordeyeva & S Grinkov	USSR
1988	Y Valova & O Vasiliev	USSR
1987	Y Gordeyeva & S Grinkov	USSR
1986	Y Gordeyeva & S Grinkov	USSR
1985	Y Valova & O Vasiliev	USSR
1984	B Underhill & P Martini	Can
1983	Y Valova & O Vasiliev	USSR
1982	S Baess & T Thierbach	GDR
1981	I Vorobyeva & I Lissovsky	USSR
1980	M Tcherkassova & S Shakrai	USSR
1979	T Babilonia & R Gardner	USA
1978	I Rodnina & A Zaitsev	USSR
1977	I Rodnina & A Zaitsev	USSR
1976	I Rodnina & A Zaitsev	USSR
1975	I Rodnina & A Zaitsev	USSR
1974	I Rodnina & A Zaitsev	USSR
1973	I Rodnina & A Zaitsev	USSR
1972	I Rodnina & A Ulanov	USSR
1971	I Rodnina & A Ulanov	USSR
1970	I Rodnina & A Ulanov	USSR
1969	I Rodnina & A Ulanov	USSR
1968	L Belousova & O Protopopov	USSR
1967	L Belousova & O Protopopov	USSR
1966	L Belousova & O Protopopov	USSR
1965	L Belousova & O Protopopov	USSR
1964	M Kilius & H Baumler	FRG
1963	M Kilius & H Baumler	FRG
1962	M Jelinek & O Jelinek	Can
1961	Not held	
1960	B Wagner & R Paul	Can
1959	B Wagner & R Paul	Can
1958	B Wagner & R Paul	Can
1957	B Wagner & R Paul	Can

Year	Winner	
1956	E Schwarz & K Oppelt	Aut
1955	F Dafoe & N Bowden	Can
1954	F Dafoe & N Bowden	Can
1953	J Nicks & J Nicks	GB
1952	R Falk & P Falk	FRG
1951	R Falk & P Falk	FRG
1950	K Kennedy & P Kennedy	USA
1949	A Kekesy & E Kiraly	Hun
1948	M Lannoy & P Baugniet	Bel
1947	M Lannoy & P Baugniet	Bel
1946/40	No Competition	
1939	M Herber & E Baier	Ger
1938	M Herber & E Baier	Ger
1937	M Herber & E Baier	Ger
1936	M Herber & E Baier	Ger
1935	E Rotter & L Szollas	Hun
1934	E Rotter & L Szollas	Hun
1933	E Rotter & L Szollas	Hun
1932	A Brunet & P Brunet	Fra
1931	E Rotter & L Szollas	Hun
1930	A Brunet & P Brunet	Fra
1929	L Scholz & O Kaiser	Aut
1928	A Joly & P Brunet	Fra
1927	H Szabo & L Wrede	Aut
1926	A Joly & P Brunet	Fra
1925	H Szabo & L Wrede	Aut
1924	H Engelman & A Berger	Aut
1923	L Jakobsson & W Jakobsson	Fin
1922	H Engelman & A Berger	Aut
1921/15	No Competition	
1914	L Eilers & W Jakobsson	Fin
1913	H Engelman & K Mejstrick	Aut
1912	P Johnson & J Johnson	GB
1911	L Eilers & W Jakobsson	Fin
1910	A Hubler & H Burger	Ger
1909	P Johnson & J Johnson	GB

Year	Winner	
1908	A Hubler & G Burger	Ger

Ice Dance

FIRST HELD 1952

Year	Winner	
1991	I Duchesnay & P Duchesnay	Fra
1990	M Klimova & S Ponomarenko	USSR
1989	M Klimova & S Ponomarenko	USSR
1988	N Bestemianova & A Bukin	USSR
1987	N Bestemianova & A Bukin	USSR
1986	N Bestemianova & A Bukin	USSR
1985	N Bestemianova & A Bukin	USSR
1984	J Torvill & C Dean	GB
1983	J Torvill & C Dean	GB
1982	J Torvill & C Dean	GB
1981	J Torvill & C Dean	GB
1980	K Regoczy & A Sallay	Hun
1979	N Linichuk & G Karponosov	USSR
1978	N Linichuk & G Karponosov	USSR
1977	I Moiseyeva & A Minenkov	USSR
1976	L Pakhomova & A Gorshkov	USSR
1975	I Moiseyeva & A Minenkov	USSR
1974	L Pakhomova & A Gorshkov	USSR
1973	L Pakhomova & A Gorshkov	USSR
1972	L Pakhomova & A Gorshkov	USSR
1971	L Pakhomova & A Gorshkov	USSR

Year	Winner	
1970	L Pakhomova &	
	A Gorshkov	USSR
1969	D Towler & B Ford	GB
1968	D Towler & B Ford	GB
1967	D Towler & B Ford	GB
1966	D Towler & B Ford	GB
1965	E Romanova &	
	P Roman	Cze
1964	E Romanova &	
	P Roman	Cze
1963	E Romanova &	
	P Roman	Cze
1962	E Romanova &	
	P Roman	Cze
1961	Not held	
1960	D Denny & C Jones	GB
1959	D Denny & C Jones	GB
1958	J Markham & C Jones	GB
1957	J Markham & C Jones	GB
1956	P Weight & P Thomas	GB
1955	J Westwood &	
	L Demmy	GB
1954	J Westwood &	
	L Demmy	GB
1953	J Westwood &	
	L Demmy	GB
1952	J Westwood &	
	L Demmy	GB

OLYMPIC CHAMPIONS

FIRST HELD 1908

Men's Individual

Year	Winner	
1988	B Boitano	USA
1984	S Hamilton	USA
1980	R Cousins	GB
1976	J Curry	GB
1972	O Nepela	Cze
1968	W Schwarz	Aut
1964	M Schnelldorfer	Ger
1960	D Jenkins	USA

Year	Winner	
1956	H A Jenkins	USA
1952	R Button	USA
1948	R Button	USA
1936	K Schafer	Aut
1932	K Schafer	Aut
1928	G Grafstrom	Swe
1924	G Grafstrom	Swe
1920	G Grafstrom	Swe
1912	Not held	
1908	U Salchow	Swe

Women's Individual

Year	Winner	
1988	K Witt	GDR
1984	K Witt	GDR
1980	A Potzsch	GDR
1976	D Hamill	USA
1972	B Schuba	Aut
1968	P Fleming	USA
1964	S Dijkstra	Nld
1960	C Heiss	USA
1956	T Albright	USA
1952	J Altwegg	GB
1948	B Scott	Can
1936	S Henie	Nor
1932	S Henie	Nor
1928	S Henie	Nor
1924	H Szabo	Aut
1920	M Julin-Mauroy	Swe
1912	Not held	
1908	M Syers	GB

Pairs

Year	Winner	
1988	Y Gordeyeva &	
	S Grinkov	USSR
1984	Y Valova &	
	O Vasilev	USSR
1980	I Rodnina &	
	A Zaitsev	USSR
1976	I Rodnina &	
	A Zaitsev	USSR

Year	Winner	
1972	I Rodnina &	
	A Ulanov	USSR
1968	L Belousova &	
	O Protopopov	USSR
1964	L Belousova &	
	O Protopopov	USSR
1960	R Wagner & R Paul	Can
1956	E Schwarz &	
	K Oppelt	Aut
1952	R Falk & P Falk	FRG
1948	M Lannoy &	
	P Baugniet	Bel
1936	M Herber & E Baier	Ger
1932	A Brunet & P Brunet	Fra
1928	A Joly & P Brunet	Fra
1924	H Engelmann &	
	A Berger	Aut
1920	L Jakobsson &	
	W Jokobsson	Fin
1912	Not held	
1908	A Hubler & H Burger	Ger

Ice Dance

FIRST HELD 1976

Year	Winner	
1988	N Bestemianova &	
	A Bukin	USSR
1984	J Torvill & C Dean	GB
1980	N Linitshuck &	
	G Karponosov	USSR
1976	L Pakhomova &	
	A Gorshkov	USSR

SPEED SKATING
WORLD CHAMPIONS

FIRST HELD 1891

Year	Winner	
1991	J-O Koss	Nor

Year	Winner	
1990	J-O Koss	Nor
1989	L Visser	Nld
1988	E Flaim	Nld
1987	N Gulyayev	USSR
1986	H Vergeer	Nld
1985	H Vergeer	Nld
1984	O Bozyiev	USSR
1983	R Falk-Larssen	Nor
1982	H van der Duim	Nld
1981	A Sjobrend	Nor
1980	H van der Duim	Nld
1979	E Heiden	USA
1978	E Heiden	USA
1977	E Heiden	USA
1976	P Kleine	Nld
1975	H Kuipers	Nld
1974	S Stensen	Nor
1973	G Claesen	Swe
1972	A Schenk	Nld
1971	A Schenk	Nld
1970	A Schenk	Nld
1969	D Fornaess	Nor
1968	A Maier	Nor
1967	C Verkerk	Nld
1966	C Verkerk	Nld
1965	P I Moe	Nor
1964	K Johannesen	Nor
1963	J Nilsson	Swe
1962	V Kosichkin	USSR
1961	H van der Grift	Nld
1960	B Stenin	USSR
1959	J Jarvinen	Fin
1958	O Goncharenko	USSR
1957	K Johannesen	Nor
1956	O Goncharenko	USSR
1955	S Ericsson	Swe
1954	B Schilkov	USSR
1953	O Goncharenko	USSR
1952	H Andersen	Nor
1951	H Andersen	Nor
1950	H Andersen	Nor
1949	K Pajor	Hun
1948	O Lundberg	Nor
1947	L Parkkinen	Fin
1946/40	No Competition	
1939	B Wasenius	Fin

Year	Winner	
1938	I Ballangrud	Nor
1937	M Staksrud	Nor
1936	I Ballangrud	Nor
1935	M Staksrud	Nor
1934	B Evensen	Nor
1933	H Engnestangen	Nor
1932	I Ballangrud	Nor
1931	C Thunberg	Fin
1930	M Staksrud	Nor
1929	C Thunberg	Fin
1928	C Thunberg	Fin
1927	B Evensen	Nor
1926	I Ballangrud	Nor
1925	C Thunberg	Fin
1924	R Larsen	Nor
1923	C Thunberg	Fin
1922	H Strom	Nor
1921/15	No Competition	
1914	O Mathisen	Nor
1913	O Mathisen	Nor
1912	O Mathisen	Nor
1911	N Strunnikov	Rus
1910	N Strunnikov	Rus
1909	O Mathisen	Nor
1908	O Mathisen	Nor
1907/06	Not held	
1905	C de Koning	Nld
1904	S Mathisen	Nor
1903/02	Not held	
1901	F Wathen	Fin
1900	E Engelsaas	Nor
1899	P Oestlund	Nor
1898	P Oestlund	Nor
1897	J McCulloch	Can
1896	J Eden	Nld
1895	J Eden	Nld
1894	Not held	
1893	J Eden	Nld
1892	Not held	
1891	J Donoghue	USA

Women's Speed Skating

FIRST HELD 1936

Year	Winner	
1991	G Kleeman	Ger
1990	J Boerner	GDR
1989	C Moser	GDR
1988	K Kania	GDR
1987	K Kania	GDR
1986	K Kania	GDR
1985	A Schone	GDR
1984	K Enke	GDR
1983	A Schone	GDR
1982	K Enke	GDR
1981	N Petruseva	USSR
1980	N Petruseva	USSR
1979	B Heiden	USA
1978	T Averina	USSR
1977	V Bryndzey	USSR
1976	S Burka	Can
1975	K Kessow	GDR
1974	A Keulen-Deelstra	Nld
1973	A Keulen-Deelstra	Nld
1972	A Keulen-Deelstra	Nld
1971	N Statkevich	USSR
1970	A Keulen-Deelstra	Nld
1969	L Kauniste	USSR
1968	C Kaiser	Nld
1967	C Kaiser	Nld
1966	V Stenina	USSR
1965	I Artamonova	USSR
1964	L Skoblikova	USSR
1963	L Skoblikova	USSR
1962	I Artamonova	USSR
1961	V Stenina	USSR
1960	V Stenina	USSR
1959	T Rylova	USSR
1958	I Artamonova	USSR
1957	I Artamonova	USSR
1956	S Kondakova	USSR
1955	R Zhukova	USSR
1954	L Selikhova	USSR
1953	K Schegoleyeva	USSR
1952	L Selikhova	USSR
1951	E Huttunen	Fin
1950	M Isakova	USSR
1949	M Isakova	USSR

Year	Winner	
1948	M Isakova	USSR
1947	V Lesche	Fin
1946/40	No Competition	
1939	V Lesche	Fin
1938	L S Nilsen	Nor
1937	L S Nilsen	Nor
1936	K Klein	USA

Sprint Speed Skating

FIRST HELD 1970

Year	Winner	
1991	I Zhelezovski	USSR
1990	K T Bae	RoK
1989	I Zhelezovski	USSR
1988	D Jansen	USA
1987	A Kuroiwa	Jap
1986	I Zhelezovski	USSR
1985	I Zhelezovski	USSR
1984	G Boucher	Can
1983	A Kuroiwa	Jap
1982	S Khlebnikov	USSR
1981	F Romming	Nor
1980	E Heiden	USA
1979	E Heiden	USA
1978	E Heiden	USA
1977	E Heiden	USA
1976	J Granath	Swe
1975	A Safranov	USSR
1974	P Bjorang	Nor
1973	V Muratov	USSR
1972	L Linkovesi	Fin
1971	E Keller	FRG
1970	V Muratov	USSR

Women's Sprint Speed Skating

Year	Winner	
1991	M Garbrecht	Ger
1990	A Hauck	GDR
1989	B Blair	USA
1988	C Rothenburger	GDR
1987	K Kania	GDR

Year	Winner	
1986	K Kania	GDR
1985	C Rothenburger	GDR
1984	K Enke	GDR
1983	K Enke	GDR
1982	N Petruseva	USSR
1981	K Enke	GDR
1980	K Enke	GDR
1979	L Mueller	USA
1978	L Sadchikova	USSR
1977	S Burke	Can
1976	S Young	USA
1975	S Young	USA
1974	L Poulos	USA
1973	S Young	USA
1972	M Pflug	FRG
1971	R Schleiermacher	GDR
1970	L Titova	USSR

OLYMPIC CHAMPIONS
500 Metres

FIRST HELD 1924

Year	Winner	
1988	J Mey	GDR
1984	S Fokitchev	USSR
1980	E Heiden	USA
1976	Y Kulikov	USSR
1972	E Keller	FRG
1968	E Keller	FRG
1964	R McDermott	USA
1960	Y Grischin	USSR
1956	Y Grischin	USSR
1952	K Henry	USA
1948	F Helgesen	Nor
1936	I Ballangrud	Nor
1932	J Shea	USA
1928	C Thunberg	Fin
	B Evensen	Nor
1924	C Jewtraw	USA

1,000 Metres

FIRST HELD 1976

Year	Winner	
1988	N Gouliaev	USSR
1984	G Boucher	Can
1980	E Heiden	USA
1976	P Mueller	USA

1,500 Metres

FIRST HELD 1924

Year	Winner	
1988	A Hoffmann	GDR
1984	G Boucher	Can
1980	E Heiden	USA
1976	J Storholt	Nor
1972	A Schenk	Nld
1968	C Verkerk	Nld
1964	A Antson	USSR
1960	R Aas	Nor
	Y Grischin	USSR
1956	Y Grischin	USSR
	Y Michailov	USSR
1952	H Andersen	Nor
1948	S Farstad	Nor
1936	C Mathiesen	Nor
1932	J Shea	USA
1928	C Thunberg	Fin
1924	C Thunberg	Fin

5,000 Metres

FIRST HELD 1924

Year	Winner	
1988	T Gustafson	Swe
1984	T Gustafon	Swe
1980	E Heiden	USA
1976	S Stensen	Nor
1972	A Schenk	Nld
1968	A Maier	Nor
1964	K Johannesen	Nor
1960	Y Kositschkin	USSR
1956	B Schilkov	USSR

Year	Winner	
1952	H Andersen	Nor
1948	R Liaklev	Nor
1936	I Ballangrud	Nor
1932	I Jaffee	USA
1928	I Ballangrud	Nor
1924	C Thunberg	Fin

10,000 Metres

FIRST HELD 1924

Year	Winner	
1988	T Gustafson	Swe
1984	I Malkov	USSR
1980	E Heiden	USA
1976	P Kleine	Nld
1972	A Schenk	Nld
1968	J Hoglin	Swe
1964	J Nilsson	Swe
1960	K Johannesen	Nor
1956	S Ericsson	Swe
1952	H Andersen	Nor
1948	A Seyffarth	Swe
1936	I Ballangrud	Nor
1932	I Jaffee	USA
1928	Not held	
1924	J Skutnabb	Fin

Women's 500 Metres

FIRST HELD 1960

Year	Winner	
1988	B Blair	USA
1984	C Rothenburger	GDR
1980	K Enke	GDR
1976	S Young	USA
1972	A Henning	USA
1968	L Titova	USSR
1964	L Skoblikova	USSR
1960	H Haase	Ger

Women's 1,000 Metres

FIRST HELD 1960

Year	Winner	
1988	C Rothenburger	GDR
1984	K Enke	GDR
1980	N Petruseva	USSR
1976	T Averina	USSR
1972	M Pflug	FRG
1968	C Geijssen	Nld
1964	L Skoblikova	USSR
1960	K Guseva	USSR

Women's 1,500 Metres

FIRST HELD 1960

Year	Winner	
1988	Y Van Gennip	Nld
1984	K Enke	GDR
1980	A Borckink	Nld

Year	Winner	
1976	G Stepanskaya	USSR
1972	D Holum	USA
1968	K Mustonen	Fin
1964	L Skoblikova	USSR
1960	L Skoblikova	USSR

Women's 3,000 Metres

FIRST HELD 1960

Year	Winner	
1988	Y Van Gennip	Nld
1984	A Schoene	GDR
1980	B Jensen	Nor
1976	T Averina	USSR
1972	C Baas-Kaiser	Nld
1968	J Schut	Nld
1964	L Skoblikova	USSR
1960	L Skoblikova	USSR

JUDO

WORLD CHAMPIONS

Open

FIRST HELD 1956

Year	Winner	
1991	N Ogawa	Jap
1989	N Ogawa	Jap
1987	N Ogawa	Jap
1985	Y Masaki	Jap
1983	H Saito	Jap
1981	Y Yamashita	Jap
1979	S Endo	Jap
1975	H Uemura	Jap

Year	Winner	
1973	K Ninomiya	Jap
1971	M Shinomaki	Jap
1969	M Shinomaki	Jap
1967	M Matsunaga	Jap
1965	I Inokuma	Jap
1961	A Geesink	Nld
1958	K Sone	Jap
1956	S Natsui	Jap

Heavyweight

FIRST HELD 1965

Year	Winner	
1991	S Kosorotov	USSR
1989	N Ogawa	Jap
1987	G Vertichev	USSR
1985	Y C Cho	RoK
1983	Y Yamashita	Jap
1981	Y Yamashita	Jap
1979	Y Yamashita	Jap
1975	S Endo	Jap
1973	C Tagaki	Jap
1971	W Ruska	Nld
1969	S Suma	Jap
1967	W Ruska	Nld
1965	A Geesink	Nld

Light-Heavyweight

FIRST HELD 1967

Year	Winner	
1991	S Traineau	Fra
1989	K Kurtanidze	USSR
1987	H Sugai	Jap
1985	H Sugai	Jap
1983	V Divisenko	USSR
1981	T Khubuluri	USSR
1979	T Khubuluri	USSR
1975	J-L Rouge	Fra
1973	N Sato	Jap
1971	F Sasahara	Jap
1969	F Sasahara	Jap
1967	N Sato	Jap

Middleweight

FIRST HELD 1979

Year	Winner	
1991	H Okada	Jap
1989	F Canu	Fra
1987	F Canu	Fra
1985	P Seisenbacher	Aut
1983	D Ultsch	GDR

Year	Winner	
1981	B Tchoullouyan	Fra
1979	D Ultsch	GDR

Light-Middleweight

FIRST HELD 1965

Year	Winner	
1991	D Lascau	Ger
1989	Bying Ju Kim	RoK
1987	H Okada	Jap
1985	N Hikage	Jap
1983	N Hikage	Jap
1981	N Adams	GB
1979	S Fujii	Jap
1975	S Fujii	Jap
1973	S Fujii	Jap
1971	S Fujii	Jap
1969	E Sonoda	Jap
1967	E Maruki	Jap
1965	I Okano	Jap

Lightweight

FIRST HELD 1967

Year	Winner	
1991	T Koga	Jap
1989	T Koga	Jap
1987	M Swain	USA
1985	B K Ahn	RoK
1983	H Nakanishi	Jap
1981	C H Park	RoK
1979	K Katsuki	Jap
1975	V Nevzorov	USSR
1973	K Nomura	Jap
1971	H Tsuzawa	Jap
1969	H Minatoya	Jap
1967	H Minatoya	Jap

Featherweight

FIRST HELD 1965

Year	Winner	
1991	G Quellmalz	Ger
1989	D Becanovic	Yug
1987	Y Yamamoto	Jap
1985	Y Sokolov	USSR
1983	N Solodukhin	USSR
1981	K Kashiwazaki	Jap
1979	N Solodukhin	USSR
1975	Y Minami	Jap
1973	Y Minami	Jap
1971	T Kawaguchi	Jap
1969	Y Sonoda	Jap
1967	T Shigeoka	Jap
1965	H Minatoya	Jap

Bantamweight

FIRST HELD 1979

Year	Winner	
1991	T Koshino	Jap
1989	A Totikashvili	USSR
1987	K Jae-Yup	RoK
1985	S Hosokawa	Jap
1983	K Tletseri	USSR
1981	Y Moriwaki	Jap
1979	T Ray	Fra

FIRST HELD 1980

Women's Open

Year	Winner	
1991	Y Zhuang	CPR
1989	E Rodriguez	Cub
1987	F Gao	CPR
1986	I Berghmans	Bel
1984	I Berghmans	Bel
1982	I Berghmans	Bel
1980	I Berghmans	Bel

Women's Heavyweight

Year	Winner	
1991	M Ji-Yoon	RoK
1989	F Gao	CPR
1987	F Gao	CPR
1986	F Gao	CPR
1984	M Motta	Ita
1982	N Lupino	Fra
1980	M de Cal	Ita

Women's Light-Heavyweight

Year	Winner	
1991	K Mi-Jong	RoK
1989	I Berghmans	Bel
1987	I de Kok	Nld
1986	I de Kok	Nld
1984	I Berghmans	Bel
1982	B Classen	FRG
1980	J Triadou	Fra

Women's Middleweight

Year	Winner	
1991	I Pierantozzi	Ita
1989	I Pierantozzi	Ita
1987	A Schreiber	FRG
1986	B Deydier	Fra
1984	B Deydier	Fra
1982	B Deydier	Fra
1980	E Simon	Aut

Women's Light-Middleweight

Year	Winner	
1991	F Eickhoff	Ger
1989	C Fluery	Fra
1987	D Bell	GB
1986	D Bell	GB
1984	N Hernandez	Ven
1982	M Rothier	Fra
1980	A Staps	Nld

Women's Lightweight

Year	Winner	
1991	M Blasco	Spa
1989	C Arnaud	Fra
1987	C Arnaud	Fra
1986	A Hughes	GB
1984	A Burns	USA
1982	B Rodriguez	Fra
1980	G Winklbauer	Aut

Women's Featherweight

Year	Winner	
1991	A Giungi	Ita
1989	S Rendle	GB
1987	S Rendle	GB
1986	D Brun	Fra
1984	K Yamaguchi	Jap
1982	L Doyle	GB
1980	E Hrovat	Aut

Women's Bantamweight

Year	Winner	
1991	C Nowak	Fra
1989	K Briggs	GB
1987	Z Li	CPR
1986	K Briggs	GB
1984	K Briggs	GB
1982	K Briggs	GB
1980	J Bridge	GB

OLYMPIC CHAMPIONS

Open

FIRST HELD 1964

Year	Winner	
1988	Not held	
1984	Y Yamashita	Jap
1980	D Lorenz	GB

Year	Winner	
1976	H Uemura	Jap
1972	W Ruska	Nld
1968	Not held	
1964	A Geesink	Nld

Heavyweight

FIRST HELD 1964

Year	Winner	
1988	H Saito	Jap
1984	H Saito	Jap
1980	A Parisi	Fra
1976	S Novikov	USSR
1972	W Ruska	Nld
1968	Not held	
1964	I Inokuma	Jap

Light-Heavyweight

FIRST HELD 1972

Year	Winner	
1988	A Miguel	Bra
1984	H Z Ha	RoK
1980	R Van de Walle	Bel
1976	K Ninomiya	Jap
1972	S Chochoshvili	USSR

Middleweight

FIRST HELD 1964

Year	Winner	
1988	P Seisenbacher	Aut
1984	P Seisenbacher	Aut
1980	J Rothlisberger	Swi
1976	I Sonoda	Jap
1972	S Sekine	Jap
1968	Not held	
1964	I Okano	Jap

Light-Middleweight

FIRST HELD 1980

Year	Winner	
1988	W Legien	Pol
1984	F Wieneke	FRG
1980	S Khabaleri	USSR

Lightweight

FIRST HELD 1964

Year	Winner	
1988	M Alexandre	Fra
1984	B K Ahn	RoK
1980	E Gamba	Ita
1976	V Nevzorov	USSR
1972	T Nomura	Jap
1968	Not held	
1964	T Nakatani	Jap

Featherweight

FIRST HELD 1972

Year	Winner	
1988	L Kyung-Keun	RoK
1984	Y Matsuoka	Jap
1980	N Solodukhin	USSR
1976	H Rodriguez	Cub
1972	T Kawaguchi	Jap

Bantamweight

FIRST HELD 1980

Year	Winner	
1988	K Jae-Yup	RoK
1984	S Hosokawa	Jap
1980	T Rey	Fra

MODERN PENTATHLON

OLYMPIC CHAMPIONS
Individual

FIRST HELD 1912

Year	Winner	
1988	J Martinek	Hun
1984	D Masala	Ita
1980	A Starostin	USSR
1976	J Pyciak-Peciak	Pol
1972	A Balczo	Hun
1968	B Ferm	Swe
1964	F Torok	Hun
1960	F Nemeth	Hun
1956	L Hall	Swe

Year	Winner	
1952	L Hall	Swe
1948	W Grut	Swe
1936	G Handrick	Ger
1932	J G Oxenstierna	Swe
1928	S Thofelt	Swe
1924	B Lindman	Swe
1920	G Dryssen	Swe
1912	G Lilliehook	Swe

Team

FIRST HELD 1952

Year	Winner
1988	Hungary
1984	Italy
1980	USSR
1976	Great Britain
1972	USSR
1968	Hungary
1964	USSR
1960	Hungary
1956	USSR
1952	Hungary

WORLD CHAMPIONS

Individual

FIRST HELD 1949

Year	Winner	
1991	A Skrzypaszek	Pol
1990	G Tiberti	Ita
1989	L Fabian	Hun
1987	J Bouzou	Fra
1986	C Massullo	Ita
1985	A Mizser	Hun
1983	A Starostin	USSR
1982	D Masala	Ita
1981	J Pyciak-Peciak	Pol
1979	R Nieman	USA
1978	P Lednev	USSR
1977	J Pyciak-Peciak	Pol
1975	P Lednev	USSR
1974	P Lednev	USSR
1973	P Lednev	USSR
1971	B Onischenko	USSR
1970	P Kelemen	Hun
1969	A Balczo	Hun
1967	A Balczo	Hun
1966	A Balczo	Hun
1965	A Balczo	Hun
1963	A Balczo	Hun

Year	Winner	
1962	E Dobnikov	USSR
1961	I Novikov	USSR
1959	I Novikov	USSR
1958	I Novikov	USSR
1957	I Novikov	USSR
1955	K Salnikov	USSR
1954	B Thofelt	Swe
1953	G Benedek	Hun
1951	L Hall	Swe
1950	L Hall	Swe
1949	T Bjurefelt	Swe

Team

FIRST HELD 1949

Year	Winner
1991	USSR
1990	USSR
1989	Hungary
1987	Hungary
1986	Italy
1985	USSR
1983	USSR
1982	USSR
1981	Poland
1979	United States
1978	Poland
1977	Poland
1975	Hungary
1974	USSR
1973	USSR
1971	USSR
1970	Hungary
1969	USSR
1967	Hungary
1966	Hungary
1965	Hungary
1963	Hungary
1962	USSR
1961	USSR
1959	USSR
1958	USSR
1957	USSR
1955	Hungary

Year	Winner
1954	Hungary
1953	Sweden
1951	Sweden
1950	Sweden
1949	Sweden

Women's Individual

FIRST HELD 1981

Year	Winner	
1990	E Fjellerup	Den
1989	L Norwood	USA
1988	D Idzi	Pol
1987	I Kisselyeva	USSR
1986	I Kisselyeva	USSR
1985	B Kotowska	Pol
1984	S Jakovleva	USSR
1983	L Chernobrywy	Can

Year	Winner	
1982	W Norman	GB
1981	A Ahlgren	Swe

Women's Team

FIRST HELD 1981

Year	Winner
1990	Poland
1989	Poland
1988	Poland
1987	USSR
1986	France
1985	Poland
1984	USSR
1983	Great Britain
1982	Great Britain
1981	Great Britain

MOTOR CYCLING

WORLD CHAMPIONS

FIRST HELD 1949

500cc

Year	Winner		
1991	W Rainey	USA	Yamaha
1990	W Rainey	USA	Yamaha
1989	E Lawson	USA	Honda
1988	E Lawson	USA	Yamaha
1987	W Gardner	Aus	Honda
1986	E Lawson	USA	Yamaha
1985	F Spencer	USA	Honda
1984	E Lawson	USA	Yamaha
1983	F Spencer	USA	Honda
1982	F Uncini	Ita	Suzuki

Year	Winner		
1981	M Lucchinelli	Ita	Suzuki
1980	K Roberts	USA	Yamaha
1979	K Roberts	USA	Yamaha
1978	K Roberts	USA	Yamaha
1977	B Sheene	GB	Suzuki
1976	B Sheene	GB	Suzuki
1975	G Agostini	Ita	Yamaha
1974	P Read	GB	MV Augusta
1973	P Read	GB	MV Augusta
1972	G Agostini	Ita	MV Augusta
1971	G Agostini	Ita	MV Augusta
1970	G Agostini	Ita	MV Augusta
1969	G Agostini	Ita	MV Augusta
1968	G Agostini	Ita	MV Augusta
1967	G Agostini	Ita	MV Augusta
1966	G Agostini	Ita	MV Augusta
1965	M Hailwood	GB	MV Augusta
1964	M Hailwood	GB	MV Augusta
1963	M Hailwood	GB	MV Augusta
1962	M Hailwood	GB	MV Augusta
1961	G Hocking	Rho	MV Augusta
1960	J Surtees	GB	MV Augusta
1959	J Surtees	GB	MV Augusta
1958	J Surtees	GB	MV Augusta
1957	L Liberati	Ita	Gilera
1956	J Surtees	GB	MV Augusta
1955	G Duke	GB	Gilera
1954	G Duke	GB	Gilera
1953	G Duke	GB	Gilera
1952	U Masetti	Ita	Gilera
1951	G Duke	GB	Norton
1950	U Masetti	Ita	Gilera
1949	L Graham	GB	AJS

250cc

Year	Winner		
1991	L Cadalora	Ita	Honda
1990	J Kocinski	USA	Yamaha
1989	S Pons	Spa	Honda
1988	S Pons	Spa	Honda
1987	A Mang	FRG	Honda
1986	C Lavado	Ven	Yamaha
1985	F Spencer	USA	Honda
1984	C Sarron	Fra	Yamaha

Year	Winner		
1983	C Lavado	Ven	Yamaha
1982	J-L Tournadre	Fra	Yamaha
1981	A Mang	FRG	Kawasaki
1980	A Mang	FRG	Kawasaki
1979	K Ballington	SA	Kawasaki
1978	K Ballington	SA	Kawasaki
1977	M Lega	Ita	Morbidelli
1976	W Villa	Ita	Harley-Davidson
1975	W Villa	Ita	Harley-Davidson
1974	W Villa	Ita	Harley-Davidson
1973	D Braun	FRG	Yamaha
1972	J Saarinen	Fin	Yamaha
1971	P Read	GB	Yamaha
1970	R Gould	GB	Yamaha
1969	K Carruthers	Aus	Benelli
1968	P Read	GB	Yamaha
1967	M Hailwood	GB	Honda
1966	M Hailwood	GB	Honda
1965	P Read	GB	Yamaha
1964	P Read	GB	Yamaha
1963	J Redman	Rho	Honda
1962	J Redman	Rho	Honda
1961	M Hailwood	GB	Honda
1960	C Ubbiali	Ita	MV Augusta
1959	C Ubbiali	Ita	MV Augusta
1958	T Provini	Ita	MV Augusta
1957	C Sandford	GB	Mondial
1956	C Ubbiali	Ita	MV Augusta
1955	H Muller	FRG	NSU
1954	W Haas	FRG	NSU
1953	W Haas	FRG	NSU
1952	E Lorenzetti	Ita	Guzzi
1951	B Ruffo	Ita	Guzzi
1950	D Ambrosini	Ita	Benelli
1949	B Ruffo	Ita	Guzzi

125cc

Year	Winner		
1991	L Capirossi	Ita	Honda
1990	L Capirossi	Ita	Honda
1989	A Criville	Spa	Cobas
1988	J Martinez	Spa	Derbi
1987	F Gresini	Ita	Garelli
1986	L Cadalora	Ita	Garelli

Year	Winner		
1985	F Gresini	Ita	Garelli
1984	A Nieto	Spa	Garelli
1983	A Nieto	Spa	Garelli
1982	A Nieto	Spa	Garelli
1981	A Nieto	Spa	Minarelli
1980	P Bianchi	Ita	MBA
1979	A Nieto	Spa	Minarelli
1978	E Lazzarini	Ita	MBA
1977	P Bianchi	Ita	Morbidelli
1976	P Bianchi	Ita	Morbidelli
1975	P Pileri	Ita	Morbidelli
1974	K Andersson	Swe	Yamaha
1973	K Andersson	Swe	Yamaha
1972	A Nieto	Spa	Derbi
1971	A Nieto	Spa	Derbi
1970	D Braun	FRG	Suzuki
1969	D Simmonds	GB	Kawasaki
1968	P Read	GB	Yamaha
1967	B Ivy	GB	Yamaha
1966	L Taveri	Swi	Honda
1965	H Anderson	NZ	Suzuki
1964	L Taveri	Swi	Honda
1963	H Anderson	NZ	Suzuki
1962	L Taveri	Swi	Honda
1961	T Phillis	Aus	Honda
1960	C Ubbiali	Ita	MV Augusta
1959	C Ubbiali	Ita	MV Augusta
1958	C Ubbiali	Ita	MV Augusta
1957	T Provini	Ita	Mondial
1956	C Ubbiali	Ita	MV Augusta
1955	C Ubbiali	Ita	MV Augusta
1954	R Hollaus	Aut	NSU
1953	W Haas	FRG	NSU
1952	C Sandford	GB	MV Augusta
1951	C Ubbiali	Ita	Mondial
1950	B Ruffo	Ita	Mondial
1949	N Pagani	Ita	Mondial

Sidecar

Year	Winner		
1991	S Webster & G Simmons	GB	LCR Krauser
1990	A Michel (Fra) & S Birchall (GB)		LCR Krauser
1989	S Webster & T Hewitt	GB	LCR Krauser
1988	S Webster, T Hewitt & G Simmons	GB	LCR Krauser

Year	Winner		
1987	S Webster & T Hewitt	GB	LCR Krauser
1986	E Streuer & B Schnieders	Nld	LCR Yamaha
1985	E Streuer & B Schnieders	Nld	LCR Yamaha
1984	E Streuer & B Schnieders	Nld	LCR Yamaha
1983	R Biland & K Waltisberg	Swi	LCR Yamaha
1982	W Schwarzel & A Huber	Ger	Seymaz Yamaha
1981	R Biland & K Waltisberg	Swi	Yamaha
1980	J Taylor (GB) & B Johansson (Swe)		Yamaha
1979	R Biland & K Waltisberg	Swi	Yamaha
1978	R Biland (Swi) & K Williams (GB)		Yamaha
1977	G O'Dell, C Holland & K Arthur	GB	Yamaha
1976	R Steinhausen & J Huber	Ger	Busch Konig
1975	R Steinhausen & J Huber	Ger	Busch Konig
1974	K Enders & R Engelhardt	Ger	Busch Enders
1973	K Enders & R Engelhardt	Ger	BMW
1972	K Enders & R Engelhardt	Ger	BMW
1971	H Owesle (Ger) & P Rutterford (GB)		Munch URS
1970	K Enders & W Kalauch	Ger	BMW
1969	K Enders & R Engelhardt	Ger	BMW
1968	H Fath & W Kalauch	Ger	URS Fath
1967	K Enders & R Engelhardt	Ger	BMW
1966	F Scheidegger (Swi) & J Robinson (GB)		BMW
1965	F Scheidegger (Swi) & J Robinson (GB)		BMW
1964	M Deubel & E Horner	Ger	BMW
1963	M Deubel & E Horner	Ger	BMW
1962	M Deubel & E Horner	Ger	BMW
1961	M Deubel & E Horner	Ger	BMW
1960	H Fath & A Wohlgemuth	Ger	BMW
1959	W Schneider & H Strauss	Ger	BMW
1958	W Schneider & H Strauss	Ger	BMW
1957	F Hillebrand & M Grunwald	Ger	BMW
1956	W Noll & F Cron	Ger	BMW
1955	W Faust & K Remmert	Ger	BMW
1954	W Noll & F Cron	Ger	BMW
1953	E Oliver & S Dibben	GB	Norton
1952	C Smith & R Clements	GB	Norton
1951	E Oliver (GB) & L Dobelli (Ita)		Norton
1950	E Oliver (GB) & L Dobelli (Ita)		Norton
1949	E Oliver & D Jenkinson	GB	Norton

SENIOR TT CHAMPIONS

FIRST HELD 1911

Year	Winner		
1991	S Hislop	GB	Honda
1990	C Fogarty	GB	Honda
1989	S Hislop	GB	Honda
1988	J Dunlop	Ire	Honda
1987	J Dunlop	Ire	Honda
1986	R Burnett	GB	Honda
1985	J Dunlop	Ire	Honda
1984	R McElnea	GB	Suzuki
1983	R McElnea	GB	Suzuki
1982	N Brown	GB	Suzuki
1981	M Grant	GB	Suzuki
1980	G Crosby	NZ	Suzuki
1979	M Hailwood	GB	Suzuki
1978	T Herron	Ire	Suzuki
1977	P Read	GB	Suzuki
1976	T Herron	Ire	Yamaha
1975	M Grant	GB	Kawasaki
1974	P Carpenter	GB	Yamaha
1973	J Findlay	Aus	Suzuki
1972	G Agostini	Ita	MV Augusta
1971	G Agostini	Ita	MV Augusta
1970	G Agostini	Ita	MV Augusta
1969	G Agostini	Ita	MV Augusta
1968	G Agostini	Ita	MV Augusta
1967	M Hailwood	GB	MV Augusta
1966	M Hailwood	GB	MV Augusta
1965	M Hailwood	GB	MV Augusta
1964	M Hailwood	GB	MV Augusta
1963	M Hailwood	GB	MV Augusta
1962	G Hocking	Rho	MV Augusta
1961	M Hailwood	GB	Norton
1960	J Surtees	GB	MV Augusta
1959	J Surtees	GB	MV Augusta
1958	J Surtees	GB	MV Augusta
1957	R McIntyre	GB	Gilera
1956	J Surtees	GB	MV Augusta
1955	G Duke	GB	Gilera
1954	W R Amm	Rho	Norton
1953	W R Amm	Rho	Norton
1952	H R Armstrong	Ire	Norton
1951	G Duke	GB	Norton
1950	G Duke	GB	Norton

Year	Winner		
1949	H Daniell	GB	Norton
1948	A Bell	GB	Norton
1947	H Daniell	GB	Norton
1946/40	No Competition		
1939	G Meier	Ger	BMW
1938	H Daniell	GB	Norton
1937	F Frith	GB	Norton
1936	J Guthrie	GB	Norton
1935	S Woods	GB	Moto Guzzi
1934	J Guthrie	GB	Norton
1933	S Woods	GB	Norton
1932	S Woods	GB	Norton
1931	P Hunt	GB	Norton
1930	W Handley	GB	Rudge Whitworth
1929	C Dodson	GB	Sunbeam
1928	C Dodson	GB	Sunbeam
1927	A Bennett	Ire	Norton
1926	S Woods	GB	Norton
1925	H Davies	GB	HRD
1924	A Bennett	Ire	Norton
1923	T Sheard	GB	Douglas
1922	A Bennett	Ire	Sunbeam
1921	H Davies	GB	AJS
1920	T de la Hay	GB	Sunbeam
1919/15	No Competition		
1914	C Pullin	GB	Rudge
1913	H Wood	GB	Scott
1912	F Applebee	GB	Scott
1911	O Godfrey	GB	Indian

JUNIOR TT CHAMPIONS

FIRST HELD 1922

Year	Winner		
1991	R Dunlop	Ire	Yamaha
1990	I Lougher	GB	Yamaha
1989	J Rea	Ire	Yamaha
1988	J Dunlop	Ire	Honda
1987	E Laycock	Ire	EMC
1986	S Cull	Ire	Honda
1985	J Dunlop	Ire	Honda
1984	G McGregor	Aus	EMC
1983	C Law	GB	EMC
1982	C Law	GB	Waddon Ehrlich

Year	Winner		
1981	S Tonkin	GB	Armstrong CCM
1980	C Williams	GB	Yamaha
1979	C Williams	GB	Yamaha
1978	C Mortimer	GB	Yamaha
1977	C Williams	GB	Yamaha
1976	T Herron	Ire	Yamaha
1975	C Mortimer	GB	Yamaha
1974	C Williams	GB	Yamaha
1973	C Williams	GB	Yamaha
1972	P Read	GB	Yamaha
1971	P Read	GB	Yamaha
1970	K Carruthers	Aus	Yamaha
1969	K Carruthers	Aus	Benelli
1968	W Ivy	GB	Yamaha
1967	S Hailwood	GB	Honda
1966	S Hailwood	GB	Honda
1965	J Redman	Rho	Honda
1964	J Redman	Rho	Honda
1963	J Redman	Rho	Honda
1962	D Winter	GB	Honda
1961	S Hailwood	GB	Honda
1960	G Hocking	Rho	MV Augusta
1959	T Provini	Ita	MV Augusta
1958	T Provini	Ita	MV Augusta
1957	C Sandford	GB	Mondial
1956	C Ubbiali	Ita	MV Augusta
1955	W Lomas	GB	MV Augusta
1954	W Haas	FRG	NSU
1953	F Anderson	GB	Moto Guzzi
1952	F Anderson	GB	Moto Guzzi
1951	T Wood	GB	Moto Guzzi
1950	D Ambrosini	Ita	Benelli
1949	M Barrington	GB	Moto Guzzi
1948	M Cann	GB	Moto Guzzi
1947	M Barrington	GB	Moto Guzzi
1946/40	No Competition		
1939	E Mellors	GB	Benelli
1938	E Kludge	Ger	DKW
1937	O Tenni	Ita	Moto Guzzi
1936	A Foster	GB	New Imperial
1935	S Woods	GB	Moto Guzzi
1934	J Simpson	GB	Rudge
1933	S Gleave	GB	Excelsior
1932	L Davenport	GB	New Imperial
1931	G Walker	GB	Rudge
1930	J Guthrie	GB	AJS

Year	Winner		
1929	S Crabtree	GB	Excelsior
1928	F Longman	GB	O K Supreme
1927	W Handley	GB	Rex-Acme
1926	C Johnson	GB	Cotton
1925	E Twemlow	GB	New Imperial
1924	E Twemlow	GB	New Imperial
1923	J Porter	GB	New Gerrard
1922	G Davison	GB	Levis

MOTOR RACING

WORLD CHAMPIONS
Formula 1

FIRST HELD 1950

Year	Winner		
1990	A Senna	Bra	McLaren-Honda
1989	A Prost	Fra	McLaren-Honda
1988	A Senna	Bra	McLaren-Honda
1987	N Piquet	Bra	Williams-Honda
1986	A Prost	Fra	McLaren-TAG/Porsche
1985	A Prost	Fra	McLaren-TAG/Porsche
1984	N Lauda	Aut	McLaren-TAG/Porsche
1983	N Piquet	Bra	Brabham-BMW
1982	K Rosberg	Fin	Williams-Ford
1981	N Piquet	Bra	Brabham-Ford
1980	A Jones	Aus	Williams-Ford
1979	J Scheckter	SA	Ferrari
1978	M Andretti	USA	Lotus-Ford
1977	N Lauda	Aut	Ferrari
1976	J Hunt	GB	McLaren-Ford
1975	N Lauda	Aut	Ferrari
1974	E Fittipaldi	Bra	McLaren-Ford
1973	J Stewart	GB	Tyrrell-Ford
1972	E Fittipaldi	Bra	Lotus-Ford
1971	J Stewart	GB	Tyrrell-Ford
1970	J Rindt	Aut	Lotus-Ford
1969	J Stewart	GB	Matra-Ford

Year	Winner		
1968	G Hill	GB	Lotus-Ford
1967	D Hulme	NZ	Brabham-Repco
1966	J Brabham	Aus	Brabham-Repco
1965	J Clark	GB	Lotus-Climax
1964	J Surtees	GB	Ferrari
1963	J Clark	GB	Lotus-Climax
1962	G Hill	GB	BRM
1961	P Hill	USA	Ferrari
1960	J Brabham	Aus	Cooper-Climax
1959	J Brabham	Aus	Cooper-Climax
1958	M Hawthorn	GB	Ferrari
1957	J M Fangio	Arg	Maserati
1956	J M Fangio	Arg	Ferrari
1955	J M Fangio	Arg	Mercedes Benz
1954	J M Fangio	Arg	Maserati
1953	A Ascari	Ita	Ferrari
1952	A Ascari	Ita	Ferrari
1951	J M Fangio	Arg	Alfa Romeo
1950	N Farina	Ita	Alfa Romeo

CONSTRUCTORS CHAMPIONS

Formula 1

FIRST HELD 1958

Year	Winner	
1990	McLaren-Honda	GB
1989	McLaren-Honda	GB
1988	McLaren-Honda	GB
1987	Williams-Honda	GB
1986	Williams-Honda	GB
1985	McLaren-TAG/ Porsche	GB
1984	McLaren-TAG/ Porsche	GB
1983	Ferrari	Ita
1982	Ferrari	Ita
1981	Williams-Ford	GB
1980	Williams-Ford	GB
1979	Ferrari	Ita
1978	Lotus-Ford	GB
1977	Ferrari	Ita
1976	Ferrari	Ita

Year	Winner	
1975	Ferrari	Ita
1974	McLaren-Ford	GB
1973	Lotus-Ford	GB
1972	Lotus-Ford	GB
1971	Tyrrell-Ford	GB
1970	Lotus-Ford	GB
1969	Matra-Ford	Fra
1968	Lotus-Ford	GB
1967	Brabham-Repco	GB
1966	Brabham-Repco	GB
1965	Lotus-Climax	GB
1964	Ferrari	Ita
1963	Lotus-Climax	GB
1962	BRM	GB
1961	Ferrari	Ita
1960	Cooper-Climax	GB
1959	Cooper-Climax	GB
1958	Vanwall	GB

BRITISH GRAND PRIX

FIRST HELD 1950

Year	Winner			
1991	N Mansell	GB	Williams	Silverstone
1990	A Prost	Fra	Ferrari	Silverstone
1989	A Prost	Fra	McLaren	Silverstone
1988	A Senna	Bra	McLaren	Silverstone
1987	N Mansell	GB	Williams	Silverstone
1986	N Mansell	GB	Williams	Brands Hatch
1985	A Prost	Fra	McLaren	Silverstone
1984	N Lauda	Aut	McLaren	Brands Hatch
1983	A Prost	Fra	Renault	Silverstone
1982	N Lauda	Aut	McLaren	Brands Hatch
1981	J Watson	GB	McLaren	Silverstone
1980	A Jones	Aus	Williams	Brands Hatch
1979	C Regazzoni	Swi	Williams	Silverstone
1978	C Reutemann	Arg	Ferrari	Brands Hatch
1977	J Hunt	GB	McLaren	Silverstone
1976	N Lauda	Aut	Ferrari	Brands Hatch
1975	E Fittipaldi	Bra	McLaren	Silverstone
1974	J Scheckter	SA	Tyrrell	Brands Hatch
1973	P Revson	USA	McLaren	Silverstone
1972	E Fittipaldi	Bra	Lotus	Brands Hatch
1971	J Stewart	GB	Tyrrell	Silverstone
1970	J Rindt	Aut	Lotus	Brands Hatch
1969	J Stewart	GB	Matra	Silverstone
1968	J Siffert	Swi	Lotus	Brands Hatch
1967	J Clark	GB	Lotus	Silverstone
1966	J Brabham	Aus	Brabham	Brands Hatch
1965	J Clark	GB	Lotus	Silverstone
1964	J Clark	GB	Lotus	Brands Hatch
1963	J Clark	GB	Lotus	Silverstone
1962	J Clark	GB	Lotus	Aintree
1961	W von Trips	FRG	Ferrari	Aintree
1960	J Brabham	Aus	Cooper	Silverstone
1959	J Brabham	Aus	Cooper	Aintree
1958	P Collins	GB	Ferrari	Silverstone
1957	S Moss & T Brooks	GB	Vanwall	Aintree
1956	J M Fangio	Arg	Ferrari	Silverstone
1955	S Moss	GB	Mercedes-Benz	Aintree
1954	F Gonzalez	Arg	Ferrari	Silverstone
1953	A Ascari	Ita	Ferrari	Silverstone
1952	A Ascari	Ita	Ferrari	Silverstone
1951	F Gonzalez	Arg	Ferrari	Silverstone
1950	G Farina	Ita	Alfa-Romeo	Silverstone

INDIANAPOLIS 500

FIRST HELD 1911

Year	Winner		
1991	R Mears	USA	Penske
1990	A Luyendyk	Nld	Lola
1989	E Fittipaldi	Bra	Penske
1988	R Mears	USA	Penske
1987	A Unser	USA	March
1986	B Rahal	USA	March
1985	D Sullivan	USA	March
1984	R Mears	USA	March
1983	T Sneva	USA	March
1982	G Johncock	USA	Wildcat
1981	B Unser	USA	Penske
1980	J Rutherford	USA	Chaparral
1979	R Mears	USA	Penske
1978	A Unser	USA	Lola
1977	A J Foyt Jnr	USA	Coyote
1976	J Rutherford	USA	McLaren
1975	R Unser	USA	Eagle
1974	J Rutherford	USA	McLaren
1973	G Johncock	USA	Eagle
1972	M Donohue	USA	McLaren
1971	A Unser	USA	Johnny Lightning Special
1970	A Unser	USA	Johnny Lightning Special
1969	M Andretti	USA	STP Oil Treatment Special
1968	R Unser	USA	Rislone Special
1967	A J Foyt Jnr	USA	Sheraton-Thompson Special
1966	G Hill	GB	Lola
1965	J Clark	GB	Lotus
1964	A J Foyt Jnr	USA	Sheraton-Thompson Special
1963	P Jones	USA	Agajanian Special
1962	R Ward	USA	Leader Card 500
1961	A J Foyt Jnr	USA	Bowes Seal Special
1960	J Rathmann	USA	Ken-Paul Special
1959	R Ward	USA	Leader Card 500
1958	J Bryan	USA	Belond AP Special
1957	S Hanks	USA	Belond Exhaust Special
1956	P Flaherty	USA	John Zink Special
1955	B Sweikert	USA	John Zink Special
1954	B Vukovich	USA	Fuel Injection Special
1953	B Vukovich	USA	Fuel Injection Special
1952	T Ruttmann	USA	Agajanian Special
1951	L Wallard	USA	Belanger Special
1950	J Parsons	USA	Wynn's Special
1949	B Holland	USA	Blue Crown Special

	Winner		
1948	M Rose	USA	Blue Crown Special
1947	M Rose	USA	Blue Crown Special
1946	G Robson	USA	Thorne Engineering Special
1945/42	No Race		
1941	F Davis/M Rose	USA	Noc-Out Hose Special
1940	W Shaw	USA	Maserati
1939	W Shaw	USA	Maserati
1938	F Roberts	USA	Miller
1937	W Shaw	USA	Gilmore-Offenhauser
1936	L Meyer	USA	Miller
1935	K Petillo	USA	Miller
1934	B Cummings	USA	Miller
1933	L Meyer	USA	Miller
1932	F Frame	USA	Miller
1931	L Schneider	USA	Miller
1930	B Arnold	USA	Miller
1929	R Keech	USA	Miller
1928	L Meyer	USA	Miller
1927	G Souders	USA	Duesenberg
1926	F Lockhart	USA	Miller
1925	P DePaolo	USA	Duesenberg
1924	L Corum/J Boyer	USA	Duesenberg
1923	T Milton	USA	Miller
1922	J Murphy	USA	Duesenberg-Miller
1921	T Milton	USA	Frontenac
1920	G Chevrolet	USA	Monroe
1919	H Wilcox	USA	Peugeot
1918/17	No Race		
1916	D Resta	USA	Peugeot
1915	R DePalma	USA	Mercedes
1914	R Thomas	Fra	Delage
1913	J Goux	Fra	Peugeot
1912	J Dawson	USA	National
1911	R Harroun	USA	Marmon

LE MANS 24 HOUR RACE

FIRST HELD 1923

Year	Winner	
1991	V Weidler (Ger)/J Herbert (GB)/B Gachot (Bel)	Mazda
1990	J Neilsen (Den)/P Cobb (USA)/M Brundle (GB)	Jaguar
1989	S Dickens (Swe)/J Mass/M Reuter (FRG)	Mercedes
1988	J Lammers (Nld)/J Dumfries (GB)/ A Wallace (GB)	Jaguar
1987	H Stuck (FRG)/D Bell (GB)/A Holbert (USA)	Porsche
1986	H Stuck (FRG)/D Bell (GB)/A Holbert (USA)	Porsche
1985	K Ludwig (FRG)/P Barillo (Ita)/ J Winter (FRG)	Porsche
1984	K Ludwig (FRG)/H Pescarolo (Fra)	Porsche
1983	V Schuppan (Aut)/H Haywood (USA)/ A Holbert (USA)	Porsche
1982	J Ickx (Bel)/D Bell (GB)	Porsche
1981	J Ickx (Bel)/D Bell (GB)	Porsche
1980	J-P Jaussaud /J Rondeau (Fra)	Rondeau-Ford
1979	K Ludwig (FRG)/W Whittington/ D Whittington (USA)	Porsche
1978	J-P Jaussaud/D Pironi (Fra)	Renault Alpine
1977	J Ickx (Bel)/J Barth (FRG)/H Haywood (USA)	Porsche
1976	J Ickx (Bel)/G van Lennep (Nld)	Porsche
1975	J Ickx (Bel)/D Bell (GB)	Mirage-Ford
1974	H Pescarolo/G Larrousse (Fra)	Matra-Simca
1973	H Pescarolo/G Larrousse (Fra)	Matra-Simca
1972	H Pescarolo (Fra)/G Hill (GB)	Matra-Simca
1971	H Marko (Aut)/G van Lennep (Nld)	Porsche
1970	H Herrmann (FRG)/R Attwood (GB)	Porsche
1969	J Ickx (Bel)/J Oliver (GB)	Ford
1968	P Rodriguez (Mex)/L Bianchi (Bel)	Ford
1967	D Gurney/A J Foyt Jnr (USA)	Ford
1966	C Amon/B McLaren (NZ)	Ford
1965	J Rindt (Aut)/M Gregory (USA)	Ferrari
1964	J Guichet (Fra)/N Vaccarella (Ita)	Ferrari
1963	L Scarfiotti/L Bandini (Ita)	Ferrari
1962	O Gendebien (Bel)/P Hill (USA)	Ferrari
1961	O Gendebien (Bel)/P Hill (USA)	Ferrari
1960	O Gendebien/P Frere (Bel)	Ferrari
1959	C Shelby (USA)/R Salvadori (GB)	Aston Martin
1958	O Gendebien (Bel)/P Hill (USA)	Ferrari
1957	R Flockhart/I Bueb (GB)	Jaguar
1956	R Flockhart/N Sanderson (GB)	Jaguar
1955	M Hawthorn/I Bueb (GB)	Jaguar
1954	F Gonzalez (Arg)/M Trintignant (Fra)	Ferrari
1953	A Rolt/D Hamilton (GB)	Jaguar

Year	Winner	
1952	H Lang/K Riess (FRG)	Mercedes-Benz
1951	P Walker/P Whitehead (GB)	Jaguar
1950	L Rosier/J-L Rosier (Fra)	Talbot-Lago
1949	L Chinetti (Ita)/Lord P Selsdon (GB)	Ferrari
1948/40	No Race	
1939	J P Wimille/P Veyron (Fra)	Bugatti
1938	E Chaboud/J Tremoulet (Fra)	Delahaye
1937	J P Wimille/R Benoist (Fra)	Bugatti
1936	No Race	
1935	F Hindmarsh (GB)/L Fontes (Fra)	Lagonda
1934	L Chinetti (Ita)/P Etancelin (Fra)	Alfa Romeo
1933	R Sommer (Fra)/T Nuvolari (Ita)	Alfa Romeo
1932	R Sommer (Fra)/L Chinetti (Ita)	Alfa Romeo
1931	Lord Howe/H Birkin (GB)	Alfa Romeo
1930	W Barnato/G Kidston (GB)	Bentley
1929	W Barnato/H Birkin (GB)	Bentley
1928	W Barnato/B Rubin (GB)	Bentley
1927	Dr J Benjafield/S Davis (GB)	Bentley
1926	R Bloch/A Rossignol (Fra)	La Lorraine
1925	G de Courcelles/A Rossignol (Fra)	La Lorraine
1924	J Duff/F Clement (GB)	Bentley
1923	A Lagache/R Leonard (Fra)	Chenard & Walcker

WORLD SPORTS CAR CHAMPIONS

FIRST HELD 1953

Cars

Year	Winner	
1991	Jaguar	GB
1990	Mercedes	Ger
1989	Mercedes	Ger
1988	Jaguar	GB
1987	Jaguar	GB
1986	Brun Motorsport	Ger
1985	Porsche	Ger
1984	Porsche	Ger
1983	Porsche	Ger
1982	Porsche	Ger
1981	Porsche	Ger
1980	Lancia	Ita
1979	Porsche	Ger
1978	Porsche	Ger

Year	Winner	
1977	Porsche	Ger
1976	Porsche	Ger
1975	Alfa Romeo	Ita
1974	Matra-Simca	Fra
1973	Matra-Simca	Fra
1972	Ferrari	Ita
1971	Porsche	Ger
1970	Porsche	Ger
1969	Porsche	Ger
1968	Ford	GB
1967/62	Not held	
1961	Ferrari	Ita
1960	Ferrari	Ita
1959	Aston Martin	GB
1958	Ferrari	Ita
1957	Ferrari	Ita
1956	Ferrari	Ita
1955	Mercedes-Benz	Ger
1954	Ferrari	Ita
1953	Ferrari	Ita

Drivers

FIRST HELD 1981

Year	Winner		
1991	T Farbi	Ita	Jaguar
1990	J-L Schlesser (Fra) & M Baldi (Ita)		Mercedes
1989	J-L Schlesser	Fra	Mercedes
1988	M Brundle	GB	Jaguar
1987	R Boesel	Bra	Jaguar
1986	D Bell (GB) & H Stuck (FRG)		Porsche
1985	D Bell (GB) & H Stuck (FRG)		Porsche
1984	S Bellof	FRG	Porsche
1983	J Ickx	Bel	Porsche
1982	J Ickx	Bel	Porsche
1981	B Garretson	USA	Porsche

ORIENTEERING

WORLD CHAMPIONS

FIRST HELD 1966

Individual

Year	Winner	
1991	J Martensson	Swe
1989	P Thoresen	Nor
1987	K Olsson	Swe
1985	K Sallinen	Fin
1983	M Berglia	Nor
1981	O Thon	Nor
1979	O Thon	Nor
1978	E Johansen	Nor
1976	E Johansen	Nor
1974	B Frilen	Swe
1972	A Hadler	Nor
1970	S Berge	Nor
1968	K Johansson	Swe
1966	A Hadler	Nor

Team

Year	Winner
1991	Switzerland
1989	Norway
1987	Norway
1985	Norway
1983	Norway
1981	Norway
1979	Sweden
1978	Norway
1976	Sweden
1974	Sweden
1972	Sweden
1970	Norway
1968	Sweden
1966	Sweden

Women's Individual

Year	Winner	
1991	K Olah	Hun
1989	M Skogum	Swe
1987	A Hannus	Swe
1985	A Kringstad-Svensson	Swe
1983	A Kringstad-Svensson	Swe
1981	A Kringstad	Nor
1979	O Bergonstrom	Fin
1978	A Berit Eid	Nor
1976	L Veijalainen	Fin
1974	M Norgaard	Den
1972	S Monspart	Hun
1970	I Hadler	Nor
1968	U Lindquist	Swe
1966	U Lindquist	Swe

Women's Team

Year	Winner
1991	Sweden
1989	Sweden
1987	Norway
1985	Sweden
1983	Sweden
1981	Sweden
1979	Finland
1978	Finland
1976	Sweden
1974	Sweden
1972	Finland
1970	Sweden
1968	Norway
1966	Sweden

RACKETS

WORLD CHAMPIONS

Singles

FIRST HELD 1820

Played on a challenge basis

Year	Winner	
1988	J Male	GB
1986	J Prenn	GB
1984	W Boone	GB
1981	J Prenn	GB
1978	W Surtees	USA
1974	H Angus	GB
1972	W Surtees	USA
1954	G Atkins	GB

Year	Winner	
1947	J Dear	GB
1937	D Milford	GB
1928	C Williams	GB
1914	J Soutar	USA
1911	C Williams	GB
1903	J Jamsetjhi	Ind
1887	P Latham	GB
1878	J Gray	GB
1876	H B Fairs	GB
1866	W Gray	GB
1863	H Gray	GB
1862	W Hart-Dyke	GB
1860	F Erwood	GB
1846	L Mitchell	GB
1838	J Lamb	GB
1834	J Pittman	GB
1825	T Pittman	GB

Year	Winner	
1820	R Mackay	GB

Doubles

FIRST HELD 1990

Year	Winner	
1990	J Prenn & J Male	GB

BRITISH OPEN CHAMPIONS

Singles

FIRST HELD 1929

Year	Winner	
1991	J Male	GB
1990	N Smith	GB
1989	J Male	GB
1988	J Male	GB
1987	J Male	GB
1986	W Boone	GB
1985	J Prenn	GB
1984	W Boone	GB
1983	J Prenn	GB
1982	J Prenn	GB
1981	J Prenn	GB
1980	J Prenn	GB
1979	W Boone	GB
1978	H Angus	GB
1977	J Prenn	GB
1976	H Angus	GB
1975	H Angus	GB
1974	W Surtees	USA
1973	H Angus	GB

Year	Winner	
1972	H Angus	GB
1971	H Angus	GB
1971	H Angus	GB
1971	M Smith	GB
1970	C Swallow	GB
1967	J Leonard	GB
1964	G Atkins	GB
1961	G Atkins	GB
1960	J Dear	GB
1959	J Thompson	GB
1954	G Atkins	GB
1951	J Dear	GB
1946	J Dear	GB
1936	D Milford	GB
1934	A Cooper	GB
1933	I Akers-Douglas	GB
1932	Lord Aberdare	GB
1930	C Simpson	GB
1929	C Simpson	GB

Doubles

FIRST HELD 1981

Year	Winner	
1991	N Smith & S Hazell	GB
1990	J Prenn & J Male	GB
1989	J Prenn & J Male	GB
1988	J Prenn & J Male	GB
1987	J Prenn & J Male	GB
1986	J Prenn & J Male	GB
1985	W Boone & R Crawley	GB
1984	W Boone & R Crawley	GB
1983	W Boone & R Crawley	GB
1982	W Boone & R Crawley	GB
1981	W Boone & R Crawley	GB

RALLYING

WORLD RALLY CHAMPIONS

Cars

FIRST HELD 1968

Year	Winner	
1990	Lancia	Ita
1989	Lancia	Ita
1988	Lancia	Ita
1987	Lancia	Ita
1986	Peugeot	Fra
1985	Peugeot	Fra
1984	Audi	Ger
1983	Lancia	Ita
1982	Audi	Ger

Year	Winner	
1981	Talbot	Fra
1980	Fiat	Ita
1979	Ford	GB
1978	Fiat	Ita
1977	Fiat	Ita
1976	Lancia	Ita
1975	Lancia	Ita
1974	Lancia	Ita
1973	Alpine-Renault	Fra
1972	Lancia	Ita
1971	Alpine-Renault	Fra
1970	Porsche	Ger
1969	Ford (Europe)	
1968	Ford	GB

Drivers

FIRST HELD 1977

Year	Winner		
1990	C Sainz	Spa	Toyota
1989	M Biasion	Ita	Lancia
1988	M Biasion	Ita	Lancia
1987	J Kankkunen	Fin	Lancia
1986	J Kankkunen	Fin	Peugeot
1985	T Salonen	Fin	Peugeot
1984	S Blomqvist	Swe	Audi
1983	H Mikkola	Fin	Audi
1982	W Rohrl	FRG	Opel
1981	A Vatanen	Fin	Ford
1980	W Rohrl	FRG	Fiat
1979	B Waldegard	Swe	Ford
1978	M Alen	Fin	Fiat/Lancia
1977	S Munari	Ita	Lancia

MONTE CARLO RALLY

FIRST HELD 1911

Year	Winner	
1991	C Sainz & L Moya	Toyota
1990	D Auriol & B Occelli	Lancia
1989	M Biasion & T Siviero	Lancia
1988	B Saby & J Fauchille	Lancia
1987	M Biasion & T Siviero	Lancia Delta
1986	H Toivonen & S Cresto	Lancia Delta
1985	A Vatanen & T Harryman	Peugeot 205
1984	W Rohrl & C Geistdorfer	Audi Quattro
1983	W Rorhl & C Geistdorfer	Opel Ascona
1982	W Rorhl & C Geistdorfer	Opel Ascona
1981	J Ragnotti & J-M Andrie	Renault 5
1980	W Rohrl & C Geistdorfer	Fiat Abarth
1979	B Darniche & A Mahe	Lancia Stratos
1978	J-P Nicolas & V Laverne	Porsche Carrera
1977	S Munari & M Manucci	Lancia Stratos
1976	S Munari & S Maiga	Lancia Stratos
1975	S Munari & M Manucci	Lancia Stratos
1974	No Rally	
1973	J Andruet & M Petit	Alpine Renault
1972	S Munari & M Manucci	Lancia Fulvia
1971	O Anderson & D Stone	Alpine Renault
1970	B Waldegaard & L Helmer	Porsche
1969	B Waldegaard & L Helmer	Porsche
1968	V Elford & D Stone	Porsche
1967	R Aaltonen & H Liddon	Mini-Cooper
1966	P Toivonen & E Mikander	Citroen
1965	T Makinen & P Easter	Mini-Cooper
1964	P Hopkirk & H Liddon	Mini-Cooper
1963	E Carlsson & G Palm	Saab
1962	E Carlsson & G Haggbom	Saab
1961	M Martin & R Bateau	Panhard
1960	W Schock & R Moll	Mercedes Benz
1959	P Coltelloni & P Alexander	Citroen
1958	G Monraisse & J Feret	Renault
1957	No Rally	
1956	R Adams & F Bigger	Jaguar
1955	P Malling & G Fadum	Talbot
1954	L Chiron & G Basadonna	Lancia
1953	M Gastonides & P Worledge	Ford
1952	S Allard & G Warburton	Allard
1951	J Trevoux & R Crovetto	Delahaye
1950	M Becquart & H Secret	Hotchkiss
1949	J Trevoux & M Lesurque	Hotchkiss

Year	Winner	
1948/40	No Rally	
1939	J Trevoux & M Lesurque	Hotchkiss
1938	G Bakker Schut & K Ton	Ford
1937	R le Begue & J Quinlin	Delahaye
1936	I Zamfirescu & J Quinlin	Ford
1935	C Lahaye & R Quatresous	Renault
1934	J Trevoux & A Gas	Hotchkiss
1933	M Vasselle	Hotchkiss
1932	M Vasselle	Hotchkiss
1931	D Healey	Invicta
1930	H Petit	Licorne
1929	Dr S van Eijk	Graham-Paige
1928	J Bignan	Fiat
1927	J Lefebvre	Amilcar
1926	Hon V Bruce & W Brunell	A.C.Bristol
1925	F Repusseau	Renault
1924	J Ledure	Bignan
1923/13	No Rally	
1912	J Beutler	Berliet
1911	H Rougier	Turcat-Mery

SAFARI RALLY

FIRST HELD 1953

Year	Winner	
1991	J Kankkunen & J Piironen	Lancia
1990	B Waldegard & F Gallagher	Toyota
1989	M Biasion & T Siviero	Lancia
1988	M Biasion & T Siviero	Lancia
1987	H Mikkola & A Hertz	Audi
1986	B Waldegard & F Gallagher	Toyota
1985	J Kankkunen & F Gallagher	Toyota
1984	B Waldegard & H Thorszelius	Toyota
1983	A Vatanen & T Harryman	Opel
1982	S Mehta & M Doughty	Datsun
1981	S Mehta & M Doughty	Datsun
1980	S Mehta & M Doughty	Datsun
1979	S Mehta & M Doughty	Datsun
1978	J Nicolas & J Lefebvre	Peugeot
1977	B Waldegard & H Thorszelius	Ford
1976	J Singh & D Doig	Mitsubishi
1975	O Andersson & A Hertz	Peugeot
1974	J Singh & D Doig	Mitsubishi
1973	S Mehta & L Drews	Datsun

Year	Winner	
1972	H Mikkola & G Palm	Ford
1971	E Herrmann & H Schuller	Datsun
1970	E Herrmann & H Schuller	Datsun
1969	R Hillyer & J Aird	Ford
1968	N Nowicki & P Cliff	Peugeot
1967	B Shankland & C Rothwell	Peugeot
1966	B Shankland & C Rothwell	Peugeot
1965	J Singh & J Singh	Volvo
1964	P Hughes & B Young	Ford
1963	N Nowicki & P Cliff	Peugeot
1962	T Fjastad & B Schneider	Volkswagen
1961	J Manussis, B Coleridge & D Beckett	Mercedes
1960	B Fritschy & J Ellis	Mercedes
1959	B Fritschy & J Ellis	Mercedes
1958	No Winner	
1957	A Burton & A Hofmann	Volkswagen 1200
1956	E Cecil & T Vickers	DKW
1955	D Marwaha & V Preston	Ford Zephyr
1954	D Marwaha & V Preston	Volkswagen 1200
1953	A Dix & J Larsen	Volkswagen 1200

RAC RALLY

FIRST HELD 1951

Year	Winner	
1990	C Sainz & L Moya	Toyota
1989	P Airikala & R McNamee	Mitsubishi
1988	M Alen & I Kivimaki	Lancia
1987	J Kankkunen & J Piironen	Lancia
1986	T Salonen & S Harjanne	Peugeot
1985	H Toivenon & N Wilson	Lancia
1984	A Vatanen & T Harryman	Peugeot
1983	S Blomqvist & B Cederberg	Audi
1982	H Mikkola & A Hertz	Audi
1981	H Mikkola & A Hertz	Audi
1980	H Toivenon & P White	Talbot
1979	H Mikkola & A Hertz	Ford
1978	H Mikkola & A Hertz	Ford
1977	B Waldegard & H Thorszelius	Ford
1976	R Clark & S Pegg	Ford
1975	T Makinen & H Liddon	Ford
1974	T Makinen & H Liddon	Ford
1973	T Makinen & H Liddon	Ford
1972	R Clark & T Mason	Ford

Year	Winner	
1971	S Blomqvist & A Hertz	Saab
1970	H Kallstrom & G Haggbom	Lancia
1969	H Kallstrom & G Haggbom	Lancia
1968	S Lampinen & J Davenport	Saab
1967	No Rally	
1966	B Soderstrom & G Palm	Lotus-Ford
1965	R Aaltonen & T Ambrose	Mini-Cooper
1964	T Trana & G Thermanius	Volvo
1963	T Trana & S Lindstrom	Volvo
1962	E Carlsson & D Stone	Saab
1961	E Carlsson & J Brown	Saab
1960	E Carlsson & S Turner	Saab
1959	G Burgess & S Croft-Pearson	Ford
1958	P Harper & Dr E Deane	Sunbeam
1957	No Rally	
1956	L Sims, R Jones & T Ambrose	Aston Martin
1955	J Ray & B Horrocks	Standard
1954	J Wallwork & J Brooks	Triumph TR2
1953	I Appleyard & P Appleyard	Jaguar XK120
1952	G Imhof & Mrs B Fleming	Allard
1951	I Appleyard & P Appleyard	Jaguar XK120

REAL TENNIS

WORLD CHAMPIONS

FIRST HELD 1740

Played on a challenge basis

Year	Winner	
1987	W Davies	Aus
1981	C Ronaldson	GB
1976	H Angus	GB
1972	J Bostwick	USA
1969	G Bostwick	USA
1959	N Knox	USA
1957	A Johnson	GB

Year	Winner	
1955	J Dear	GB
1928	P Etchebaster	Fra
1916	G Covey	GB
1914	J Gould	USA
1912	G Covey	GB
1908	C Fairs	GB
1907	P Latham	GB
1905	C Fairs	GB
1895	P Latham	GB
1890	C Saunders	GB
1885	T Pettitt	USA
1871	G Lambert	GB
1862	E Tomkins	GB
1829	E Barre	Fra
1819	P Cox	GB

Year	Winner		Year	Winner	
1816	Marchesio	Ita	1970	H Angus	GB
1785	J Barcellon	Fra	1969	F Willis	GB
1765	R Masson	Fra	1968	H Angus	GB
1740	Clerge	Fra	1967	F Willis	GB
			1966	F Willis	GB
			1965	R Hughes	GB

BRITISH OPEN CHAMPIONS

Men's Singles

FIRST HELD 1965

Year	Winner	
1990	L Deuchar	Aus
1989	L Deuchar	Aus
1988	L Deuchar	Aus
1987	L Deuchar	Aus
1986	L Deuchar	Aus
1985	C Ronaldson	GB
1984	C Ronaldson	GB
1983	C Ronaldson	GB
1982	C Ronaldson	GB
1981	C Ronaldson	GB
1980	C Ronaldson	GB
1980	C Ronaldson	GB
1979	H Angus	GB
1978	C Ronaldson	GB
1977	H Angus	GB
1976	H Angus	GB
1975	C Ennis	GB
1974	H Angus	GB
1973	N Cripps	GB
1972	F Willis	GB
1971	N Cripps	GB
1970	F Willis	GB

Men's Doubles

FIRST HELD 1971

Year	Winner	
1990	W Davies & L Deuchar	Aus
1989	W Davies & L Deuchar	Aus
1988	W Davies & L Deuchar	Aus
1987	W Davies & L Deuchar	Aus
1986	W Davies & L Deuchar	Aus
1985	W Davies & L Deuchar	Aus
1984	W Davies & L Deuchar	Aus
1983	C Ronaldson & M Dean	GB
1982	N Cripps & A Lovell	GB
1981	C Ronaldson & M Dean	GB
1980	N Cripps & A Lovell	GB
1979	N Cripps & A Lovell	GB
1978	N Cripps & A Lovell	GB
1977	N Cripps & A Lovell	GB
1976	F Willis & D Cull	GB
1975	C Swallow & N Cripps	GB
1974	C Swallow & N Cripps	GB
1973	C Swallow & N Cripps	GB
1972	F Willis & C Ennis	GB
1971	R Hughes & N Cripps	GB

ROWING

OLYMPIC CHAMPIONS

Eights

FIRST HELD 1900

Year	Winner
1988	West Germany
1984	Canada
1980	East Germany
1976	East Germany
1972	New Zealand
1968	West Germany
1964	United States
1960	West Germany
1956	United States
1952	United States
1948	United States
1936	United States
1932	United States
1928	United States
1924	United States
1920	United States
1912	Great Britain
1908	Great Britain
1904	United States
1900	United States

Quadruple Sculls

FIRST HELD 1976

Year	Winner
1988	Italy
1984	West Germany
1980	East Germany
1976	East Germany

Coxed Fours

FIRST HELD 1900

Year	Winner
1988	East Germany
1984	Great Britain
1980	East Germany
1976	USSR
1972	West Germany
1968	New Zealand
1964	West Germany
1960	West Germany
1956	Italy
1952	Czechoslovakia
1948	United States
1936	Germany
1932	Germany
1928	Italy
1924	Switzerland
1920	Switzerland
1912	Germany
1908/04	Not held
1900	Germany

Coxless Fours

FIRST HELD 1900

Year	Winner
1988	East Germany
1984	New Zealand
1980	East Germany
1976	East Germany
1972	East Germany
1968	East Germany
1964	Denmark
1960	United States
1956	Canada
1952	Yugoslavia
1948	Italy
1936	Germany
1932	Great Britain

Year	Winner
1928	Great Britain
1924	Great Britain
1920/12	Not held
1908	Great Britain
1904	United States
1900	France

Coxed Pairs

FIRST HELD 1900

Year	Winner
1988	Italy
1984	Italy
1980	East Germany
1976	East Germany
1972	East Germany
1968	Italy
1964	United States
1960	West Germany
1956	United States
1952	France
1948	Denmark
1936	Germany
1932	United States
1928	Switzerland
1924	Switzerland
1920	Italy
1912/04	Not held
1900	Netherlands

Coxless Pairs

FIRST HELD 1904

Year	Winner	
1988	A Holmes & S Redgrave	GB
1984	P Iosub & V Toma	Rom
1980	B Landvoigt & J Landvoigt	GDR
1976	B Landvoigt & J Landvoigt	GDR

Year	Winner	
1972	S Brietzke & W Mager	GDR
1968	H-J Bothe & J Lucke	GDR
1964	G Hungerford & R Jackson	Can
1960	V Boreyko & O Golovanov	USSR
1956	J Fifer & D Hecht	USA
1952	C Logg & T Price	USA
1948	G Laurie & J Wilson	GB
1936	W Eichorn & H Strauss	Ger
1932	L Clive & A Edwards	GB
1928	K Moeschter & B Muller	Ger
1924	A Beijnen & W Rosingh	Nld
1920/12	No Competition	
1908	J Fenning & G Thomson	GB
1904	R Farnam & J Ryan	USA

Double Sculls

FIRST HELD 1904

Year	Winner	
1988	R Florijn & N Rienks	Nld
1984	B Lewis & P Enquist	USA
1980	J Dreifke & K Kroppelien	GDR
1976	A Hansen & F Hansen	Nor
1972	G Korshikov & A Timoshinin	USSR
1968	A Sass & A Timoshinin	USSR
1964	B Dubrovsky & O Tyurin	USSR
1960	V Kozak & P Schmidt	Cze
1956	A Berkutov & Y Tyukalov	USSR
1952	T Capozzo & E Guerrero	Arg

Year	Winner	
1948	R Burnell & H Bushnell	GB
1936	J Beresford & L Southwood	GB
1932	W Gilmore & K Myers	USA
1928	P Costello & C McIlvaine	USA
1924	P Costello & J Kelly	USA
1920	P Costello & J Kelly	USA
1912/08	No Competition	
1904	J Mulcahy & W Varley	USA

Single Sculls

FIRST HELD 1900

Year	Winner	
1988	T Lange	GDR
1984	P Karppinen	Fin
1980	P Karppinen	Fin
1976	P Karppinen	Fin
1972	Y Malishev	USSR
1968	H J Wienese	Nld
1964	V Ivanov	USSR
1960	V Ivanov	USSR
1956	V Ivanov	USSR
1952	Y Tyukalov	USSR
1948	M Wood	Aus
1936	G Schafer	Ger
1932	H Pearce	Aus
1928	H Pearce	Aus
1924	J Beresford	GB
1920	J Kelly	USA
1912	W Kinnear	GB
1908	H Blackstaffe	GB
1904	F Greer	USA
1900	H Barrelet	Fra

Women's Eights

FIRST HELD 1976

Year	Winner
1988	East Germany
1984	United States
1980	East Germany
1976	East Germany

Women's Quadruple Sculls

FIRST HELD 1976

Year	Winner
1988	East Germany
1984	Romania
1980	East Germany
1976	East Germany

Women's Coxed Fours

FIRST HELD 1976

Year	Winner
1988	East Germany
1984	Romania
1980	East Germany
1976	East Germany

Women's Coxless Pairs

FIRST HELD 1976

Year	Winner	
1988	O Homeghi & R Arba	Rom
1984	R Arba & E Horvat	Rom
1980	C Klier & U Steindorf	GDR
1976	S Grouitcheva & S Kelbetcheva	Bul

Women's Double Sculls

FIRST HELD 1976

Year	Winner	
1988	M Schroter & B Peter	GDR
1984	M Popescu & E Oleniuc	Rom
1980	Y Khlopsteva & L Popova	USSR
1976	S Otzetova & Z Yordanova	Bul

Women's Single Sculls

FIRST HELD 1976

Year	Winner	
1988	J Behrendt	GDR
1984	V Racila	Rom
1980	S Toma	Rom
1976	C Scheiblich	GDR

WORLD CHAMPIONS
Eights

FIRST HELD 1962

Year	Winner
1991	Germany
1990	West Germany
1989	West Germany
1987	United States
1986	Australia
1985	USSR
1983	New Zealand
1982	New Zealand
1981	USSR
1979	East Germany
1978	East Germany
1977	East Germany
1975	East Germany
1974	United States

Year	Winner
1970	East Germany
1966	West Germany
1962	West Germany

Quadruple Sculls

FIRST HELD 1974

Year	Winner
1991	USSR
1990	USSR
1989	Netherlands
1987	USSR
1986	USSR
1985	Canada
1983	West Germany
1982	East Germany
1981	East Germany
1979	East Germany
1978	East Germany
1977	East Germany
1975	East Germany
1974	East Germany

Coxed Fours

FIRST HELD 1962

Year	Winner
1991	Germany
1990	East Germany
1989	Romania
1987	East Germany
1986	East Germany
1985	USSR
1983	New Zealand
1982	East Germany
1981	East Germany
1979	East Germany
1978	East Germany
1977	East Germany
1975	USSR
1974	East Germany
1970	West Germany

Year	Winner
1966	East Germany
1962	West Germany

Coxless Fours

FIRST HELD 1962

Year	Winner
1991	Australia
1990	Australia
1989	East Germany
1987	East Germany
1986	United States
1985	West Germany
1983	West Germany
1982	Switzerland
1981	USSR
1979	East Germany
1978	USSR
1977	East Germany
1975	East Germany
1974	East Germany
1970	East Germany
1966	East Germany
1962	West Germany

Coxed Pairs

FIRST HELD 1962

Year	Winner
1991	Italy
1990	Italy
1989	Italy
1987	Italy
1986	Great Britain
1985	Italy
1983	East Germany
1982	Italy
1981	Italy
1979	East Germany
1978	East Germany
1977	Bulgaria
1975	East Germany

Year	Winner
1974	USSR
1970	Romania
1966	Netherlands
1962	West Germany

Coxless Pairs

FIRST HELD 1962

Year	Winner	
1991	S Redgrave & M Pinsent	GB
1990	T Jung & U Kellner	GDR
1989	T Jung & U Kellner	GDR
1987	A Holmes & S Redgrave	GB
1986	N Pimenov & Y Pimenov	USSR
1985	N Pimenov & Y Pimenov	USSR
1983	C Ertel & U Sauerbrey	GDR
1982	M Grepperud & S Loken	Nor
1981	Y Pimenov & N Pimenov	USSR
1979	B Landvoigt & J Landvoigt	FRG
1978	B Landvoigt & J Landvoigt	FRG
1977	V Yeliseyev & A Kulagin	USSR
1975	B Landvoigt & J Landvoigt	RG
1974	B Landvoigt & J Landvoigt	FRG
1970	P Gorny & W Klatt	GDR
1966	P Gorny & W Klatt	GDR
1962	D Bender & G Zumkeller	FRG

Double Sculls

FIRST HELD 1962

Year	Winner	
1991	H-J Zwolle & N Rienks	Nld
1990	A Jonke & C Zerbst	Aut
1989	L Bjoeness & R B Thorsen	Nor
1987	D Yordanov & V Radev	Bul
1986	A Belgori & I Pescalli	Ita
1985	T Lange & U Heppner	GDR
1983	T Lange & U Heppner	GDR
1982	A Hansen & R Thorsen	Nor
1981	K Kroppelien & J Dreifke	GDR
1979	A Hansen & F Hansen	Nor
1978	A Hansen & F Hansen	Nor
1977	C Baillieu & M Hart	GB
1975	A Hansen & F Hansen	Nor
1974	C Kreuziger & H Schmied	GDR
1970	J Engelbrecht & N Secher	Den
1966	M Burgin & M Studach	Swi
1962	R Duhamel & B Monnereau	Fra

Single Sculls

FIRST HELD 1962

Year	Winner	
1991	T Lange	Ger
1990	Y Yanson	USSR
1989	T Lange	GDR
1987	T Lange	GDR
1986	P-M Kolbe	FRG
1985	P Karpinnen	Fin
1983	P-M Kolbe	FRG
1982	R Reiche	GDR
1981	P-M Kolbe	FRG
1979	P Karpinnen	Fin

Year	Winner	
1978	P-M Kolbe	FRG
1977	J Dreifke	GDR
1975	P-M Kolbe	FRG
1974	W Honig	GDR
1970	A Demiddi	Arg
1966	D Spero	USA
1962	V Ivanov	USSR

Women's Eights

FIRST HELD 1974

Year	Winner
1991	Canada
1990	Romania
1989	Romania
1987	Romania
1986	USSR
1985	USSR
1983	USSR
1982	USSR
1981	USSR
1979	USSR
1978	USSR
1977	East Germany
1975	East Germany
1974	East Germany

Women's Quadruple Sculls

FIRST HELD 1974

Year	Winner
1991	Germany
1990	East Germany
1989	East Germany
1987	East Germany
1986	East Germany
1985	East Germany
1983	USSR
1982	USSR
1981	USSR
1979	East Germany
1978	Bulgaria

Year	Winner
1977	East Germany
1975	East Germany
1974	East Germany

Women's Coxed Fours

FIRST HELD 1974

Year	Winner
1991	Not held
1990	Not held
1989	Not held
1987	Romania
1986	Romania
1985	East Germany
1983	East Germany
1982	USSR
1981	USSR
1979	USSR
1978	East Germany
1977	East Germany
1975	East Germany
1974	East Germany

Women's Coxless Fours

FIRST HELD 1986

Year	Winner
1991	Canada
1990	Romania
1989	East Germany
1987	Not held
1986	United States

Women's Coxless Pairs

FIRST HELD 1974

Year	Winner	
1991	M McBean & K Heddle	Can

Year	Winner	
1990	S Werremeier & I Althoff	FRG
1989	K Haaker & J Zeidler	GDR
1987	R Arba & O Homeghi	Rom
1986	R Arba & O Homeghi	Rom
1985	R Arba & E Florea	Rom
1983	S Frohlich & M Sandig	GDR
1982	S Frohlich & M Sandig	GDR
1981	S Anders & I Rudolph	GDR
1979	C Bugel & U Steindorf	GDR
1978	C Bugel & U Steindorf	GDR
1977	S Dahne & A Noack	GDR
1975	S Dahne & A Noack	GDR
1974	M Ghita & C Neascu	Rom

Women's Double Sculls

FIRST HELD 1974

Year	Winner	
1991	K Boron & B Schramm	Ger
1990	K Boron & B Schramm	GDR
1989	J Sorgers & B Schramm	GDR
1987	S Madina & V Ninova	Bul
1986	S Schurabe & B Schramm	GDR
1985	S Schurabe & M Schroter	GDR
1983	J Scheck & M Schroter	GDR
1982	Y Braticko & A Makhina	USSR

Year	Winner	
1981	M Kokarevitha &	
	A Makhina	USSR
1979	C Linse &	
	H Westphal	GDR
1978	S Otzetova &	
	Z Yordanova	Bul
1977	A Borchmann &	
	R Zobelt	GDR
1975	Y Antonova &	
	G Yermoleyeva	USSR
1974	Y Antonova &	
	G Yermoleyeva	USSR

Women's Single Sculls

FIRST HELD 1974

Year	Winner	
1991	S Laumann	Can
1990	B Peter	GDR
1989	E Lipa	Rom
1987	M Georgieva	Bul
1986	J Hampe	GDR
1985	C Linse	GDR
1983	J Hampe	GDR
1982	I Fetissova	USSR
1981	S Toma	Rom
1979	S Toma	Rom
1978	C Hahn	GDR
1977	C Scheiblich	GDR
1975	C Scheiblich	GDR
1974	C Scheiblich	GDR

HENLEY REGATTA
Diamond Sculls

FIRST HELD 1844

Year	Winner	
1991	W Van Belleghem	Bel
1990	E Verdonk	NZ
1989	V Chalupa	Cze
1988	G McGlashan	Aus

Year	Winner	
1987	P-M Kolbe	FRG
1986	B Eltang	Den
1985	S Redgrave	Eng
1984	C Baillieu	Eng
1983	S Redgrave	Eng
1982	C Baillieu	Eng
1981	C Baillieu	Eng
1980	R Ibarra	Arg
1979	H Matheson	Eng
1978	T Crooks	Eng
1977	T Crooks	Eng
1976	E Hale	Aus
1975	S Drea	Ire
1974	S Drea	Ire
1973	S Drea	Ire
1972	A Timoschinin	USSR
1971	A Demiddi	Arg
1970	J Meissner	FRG
1969	H-J Bohmer	Ger
1968	H Wardell-Yerburgh	Eng
1967	M Studach	Swi
1966	A Hill	Ger
1965	D Spero	USA
1964	S Cromwell	USA
1963	G Kottman	Swi
1962	S Mackenzie	Aus
1961	S Mackenzie	Aus
1960	S Mackenzie	Aus
1959	S Mackenzie	Aus
1958	S Mackenzie	Aus
1957	S Mackenzie	Aus
1956	T Kocerka	Pol
1955	T Kocerka	Pol
1954	P Vlasic	Yug
1953	T Fox	Eng
1952	M Wood	Aus
1951	T Fox	Eng
1950	A-Rowe	Eng
1949	J Kelly Jnr	USA
1948	M Wood	Aus
1947	J Kelly Jnr	USA
1946	J Sepheriades	Fra
1945/40	No Competition	
1939	J Burk	USA
1938	J Burk	USA
1937	J Hasenohrl	Aut

Year	Winner		Year	Winner	
1936	E Rufli	Swi	1886	F Pitman	Eng
1935	E Rufli	Swi	1885	W Unwin	Eng
1934	H Buhtz	Ger	1884	W Unwin	Eng
1933	T Askwith	Eng	1883	J Lowndes	Eng
1932	H Buhtz	Ger	1882	J Lowndes	Eng
1931	R Pearce	Can	1881	J Lowndes	Eng
1930	J Guest	Can	1880	J Lowndes	Eng
1929	L Gunther	Nld	1879	J Lowndes	Eng
1928	J Wright	Can	1878	T Edwards-Moss	Eng
1927	R Lee	Eng	1877	T Edwards-Moss	Eng
1926	J Beresford	Eng	1876	F Playford	Eng
1925	J Beresford	Eng	1875	A Dicker	Eng
1924	J Beresford	Eng	1874	A Dicker	Eng
1923	M Morris	Eng	1873	A Dicker	Eng
1922	W Hoover	USA	1872	C Knollys	Eng
1921	F Eyken	Nld	1871	W Fawcus	Eng
1920	J Beresford	Eng	1870	J Close	Eng
1919/15	No Competition		1869	W Crofts	Eng
1914	G Sinigaglia	Ita	1868	W Stout	Eng
1913	C McVilly	Aus	1867	W Crofts	Eng
1912	E Powell	Eng	1866	E Michell	Eng
1911	W Kinnear	Eng	1865	E Michell	Eng
1910	W Kinnear	Eng	1864	W Woodgate	Eng
1909	A Stuart	Eng	1863	C Lawes	Eng
1908	A McCullock	Eng	1862	E Brickwood	Eng
1907	W Darell	Eng	1861	A Casamajor	Eng
1906	H Blackstaffe	Eng	1860	H Playford	Eng
1905	F Kelly	Eng	1859	E Brickwood	Eng
1904	L Scholes	Can	1858	A Casamajor	Eng
1903	F Kelly	Eng	1857	A Casamajor	Eng
1902	F Kelly	Eng	1856	A Casamajor	Eng
1901	C Fox	Eng	1855	A Casamajor	Eng
1900	E Hemmerde	Eng	1854	H Playford	Eng
1899	B Howell	Eng	1853	S Rippingall	Eng
1898	B Howell	Eng	1852	E Macnaghten	Eng
1897	E Ten Eyck	USA	1851	E Peacock	Eng
1896	Hon R Guinness	Eng	1850	T Bone	Eng
1895	Hon R Guinness	Eng	1849	T Bone	Eng
1894	G Nickalls	Eng	1848	W Bagshawe	Eng
1893	G Nickalls	Eng	1847	W Maule	Eng
1892	J Ooms	Nld	1846	E Moon	Eng
1891	V Nickalls	Eng	1845	S Wallace	Eng
1890	G Nickalls	Eng	1844	T Bumpsted	Eng
1889	G Nickalls	Eng			
1888	G Nickalls	Eng			
1887	J Gardner	Eng			

Grand Challenge Cup

FIRST HELD 1839

Year	Winner	
1991	Leander Club & Star	Eng
1990	RC Hansa Dortmund	FRG
1989	RC Hansa Dortmund	FRG
1988	Leander Club & Univ. of London	Eng
1987	Soviet Army	USSR
1986	Nautilus RC	Eng
1985	Harvard University	USA
1984	Leander Club & London RC	Eng
1983	London RC & Univ. of London	Eng
1982	Leander Club & London RC	Eng
1981	Oxford Univ. & Thames Tradesmen	Eng
1980	Charles River RA	USA
1979	Thames Tradesmen & London RC	Eng
1978	Trakia Club	Bul
1977	University of Washington	USA
1976	Thames Tradesmen	Eng
1975	Leander & Thames Tradesmen	Eng
1974	Trud Club	USSR
1973	Trud Kolomna	USSR
1972	WMF Moscow	USSR
1971	Tideway Scullers School	Eng
1970	Vorwarts Rostock	Ger
1969	Einheit Dresden	Ger
1968	University of London	Eng
1967	SCW Leipzig	Ger
1966	TSC, Berlin	Ger
1965	Ratzeburger RC	Ger
1964	CZ Viljnjus	USSR
1963	University of London	Eng
1962	USSR Navy, Moscow	USSR

Year	Winner	
1961	USSR Navy, Moscow	USSR
1960	Molesey BC	Eng
1959	Harvard University	USA
1958	Trud Leningrad	USSR
1956	CSFAF	Fra
1955	University of Penn	USA
1954	Krylia Sovetov	USSR
1953	Leander Club	Eng
1952	Leander Club	Eng
1951	Lady Margaret BC, Cambridge	Eng
1950	Harvard University	USA
1949	Leander Club	Eng
1948	Thames RC	Eng
1947	Jesus College, Cambridge	Eng
1946	Leander Club	Eng
1945/40	No Competition	
1939	Harvard University	USA
1938	London RC	Eng
1937	R G Wiking	Ger
1936	Zurich RC	Swi
1935	Pembroke College, Cambridge	Eng
1934	Leander Club	Eng
1933	London RC	Eng
1932	Leander Club	Eng
1931	London RC	Eng
1930	London RC	Eng
1929	Leander Club	Eng
1928	Thames RC	Eng
1927	Thames RC	Eng
1926	Leander Club	Eng
1925	Leander Club	Eng
1924	Leander Club	Eng
1923	Thames RC	Eng
1922	Leander Club	Eng
1921	Magdalen College, Oxford	Eng
1920	Magdalen College, Oxford	Eng
1919/15	No Competition	
1914	Harvard AA	USA
1913	Leander Club	Eng
1912	Sydney RC	Aus

Year	Winner		Year	Winner	
1911	Magdalen College, Oxford	Eng	1875	Leander Club	Eng
1910	Magdalen College, Oxford	Eng	1874	London RC	Eng
1909	RC Nautique Gand	Bel	1873	London RC	Eng
1908	Christ Church, Oxford	Eng	1872	London RC	Eng
1907	S Nautique Gand	Bel	1871	Etonian Club, Oxford	Eng
1906	C Nautique Gand	Bel	1870	Etonian Club, Oxford	Eng
1905	Leander Club	Eng	1869	Etonian Club, Oxford	Eng
1904	Leander Club	Eng	1868	London RC	Eng
1903	Leander Club	Eng	1867	Etonian Club, Oxford	Eng
1902	Third Trinity, Cambridge	Eng	1866	Etonian Club, Oxford	Eng
1901	Leander Club	Eng	1865	Kingston RC	Eng
1900	Leander Club	Eng	1864	Kingston RC	Eng
1899	Leander Club	Eng	1863	University College, Oxford	Eng
1898	Leander Club	Eng	1862	London RC	Eng
1897	New College, Oxford	Eng	1861	First Trinity, Cambridge	Eng
1896	Leander Club	Eng	1860	First Trinity, Cambridge	Eng
1895	Trinity Hall, Cambridge	Eng	1859	London RC	Eng
1894	Leander Club	Eng	1858	Cambridge University BC	Eng
1893	Leander Club	Eng	1857	London RC	Eng
1892	Leander Club	Eng	1856	Royal Chester RC	Eng
1891	Leander Club	Eng	1855	Cambridge University BC	Eng
1890	London RC	Eng	1854	First Trinity, Cambridge	Eng
1889	Thames RC	Eng	1853	Oxford University BC	Eng
1888	Thames RC	Eng	1852	Oxford University BC	Eng
1887	Trinity Hall, Cambridge	Eng	1851	Oxford University BC	Eng
1886	Trinity Hall, Cambridge	Eng	1850	Oxford University BC	Eng
1885	Jesus College, Cambridge	Eng	1849	Wadham College, Oxford	Eng
1884	London RC	Eng	1848	Oxford University BC	Eng
1883	London RC	Eng	1847	Oxford University BC	Eng
1882	Exeter College, Oxford	Eng	1846	Thames Club, London	Eng
1881	London RC	Eng	1845	Cambridge University BC	Eng
1880	Leander Club	Eng			
1879	Jesus College, Cambridge	Eng			
1878	Thames RC	Eng			
1877	London RC	Eng			
1876	Thames RC	Eng			

Year	Winner		Year	Winner
1844	Etonian Club, Oxford	Eng	1964	F Walker
1843	Oxford University		1963	D Allen
	BC	Eng	1962	C Dearsley
1842	Cambridge Sub.		1961	K Usher
	Rooms, London	Eng	1960	R Easterling
1841	Cambridge Sub.		1959	G Saunders
	Rooms, London	Eng	1958	R Crouch
1840	Leander Club	Eng	1957	K Collins
1839	Trinity College,		1956	C Williams
	Cambridge	Eng	1955	J Goulding
			1954	K Everest
			1953	R Bowles

DOGGETT'S COAT
AND BADGE

FIRST HELD 1715

Year	Winner		Year	Winner
			1952	G Green
			1951	M Martin
			1950	G Palmer
			1949	A Dymott
			1948	H Clark
			1947	J Palmer
			1946	J Anson
1991	L Neicho		1945	S Thomas
1990	S Collins		1944	F Ambler
1989	R A Humphrey		1943	E McGuinness
1988	G Hayes		1942	F Dott
1987	C Spencer		1941	G Bowles
1986	C Woodward Fisher		1940	E Lupton
1985	R Spencer		1939	D Thomas
1984	S McCarthy		1938	E H Phelps
1983	P Hickman		1937	W Silvester
1982	G Anness		1936	J Taylor
1981	W Hickman		1935	A Gobbett
1980	W Woodward Fisher		1934	H Smith
1979	F Bearwood		1933	E L Phelps
1978	A McPherson		1932	H T Silvester
1977	J Dwan		1931	T Harding
1976	P Prentice		1930	E A Phelps
1975	C Drury		1929	C Taylor
1974	R Lupton		1928	J Phelps
1973	R Prentice		1927	L Barry
1972	P Wilson		1926	T Green
1971	C Dwan		1925	H Barry
1970	M Spencer		1924	H Green
1969	L Grieves		1923	R Phelps
1968	J Lupton		1922	T Phelps
1967	C Briggs		1921	A Briggs
1966	D Stent		1920	H Hayes
1965	A Collins		1919	H Phelps

Year	Winner	Year	Winner
1918	A Gibbs	1872	T Green
1917	J Blackman	1871	T Mackinney
1916	F Pearce	1870	R Harding
1915	L West	1869	G Wright
1914	S Mason	1868	A Egalton
1913	G Gobbett	1867	H Maxwell
1912	L Francis	1866	A Iles
1911	W Woodward Fisher	1865	J Wood
1910	R Pocock	1864	D Coombes
1909	G Luck	1863	T Young
1908	J Graham	1862	J Messenger
1907	A Cook	1861	S Short
1906	E Brewer	1860	H Phelps
1905	H Sylvester	1859	C Farrow
1904	W Pizzey	1858	C Turner
1903	E Barry	1857	T White
1902	R Odell	1856	G Everson
1901	A Brewer	1855	H White
1900	J Turffrey	1854	D Hemmings
1899	J Lee	1853	J Finnis
1898	A Carter	1852	C Constable
1897	T Bullman	1851	G Wigget
1896	R Carter	1850	W Campbell
1895	J Gibson	1849	T Cole Jnr
1894	F Pearce	1848	J Ash
1893	J Harding	1847	W Ellis
1892	G Webb	1846	J Wing
1891	W Barry	1845	F Cobb
1890	J Sansom	1844	F Lett
1889	G Green	1843	J Fry
1888	C Harding	1842	J Liddey
1887	W East	1841	R Moore
1886	H Cole	1840	W Hawkins
1885	J Mackinney	1839	T Goodrum
1884	C Phelps	1838	S Bridge
1883	J Lloyd	1837	T Harrison
1882	H Audsley	1836	J Morris
1881	G Claridge	1835	W Dryson
1880	W Cobb	1834	W Tomlinson
1879	H Cordery	1833	G Maynard
1878	T Taylor	1832	R Waight
1877	J Tarryer	1831	R Oliver
1876	C Bulman	1830	W Butler
1875	W Phelps	1829	S Stubbs
1874	R Burwood	1828	R Mallett
1873	H Messum	1827	J Voss

Year	Winner	Year	Winner
1826	J Poett	1780	J Bradshaw
1825	G Staples	1779	W Boddington
1824	G Fogo	1778	H Pearson
1823	G Butcher	1777	J Pickering
1822	W Noulton	1776	W Price
1821	T Cole Snr	1775	Not known
1820	J Hartley	1774	Not known
1819	W Emery	1773	J Frovley
1818	W Nicholls	1772	H Briggs
1817	J Robson	1771	A Badmann
1816	T Tenham	1770	T Goddard
1815	J Scott	1769	Not known
1814	R Harris	1768	W Watson
1813	R Farson	1767	Not known
1812	R May	1766	Not known
1811	W Thornton	1765	R Eggleton
1810	J Smart	1764	J Morris
1809	F Jury	1763	S Eggleton
1808	G Newell	1762	W Wood
1807	J Evans	1761	W Penner
1806	J Goodwin	1760	E Wood
1805	T Johnson	1759	J Clarke
1804	C Gingle	1758	J Danby
1803	J Flower	1757	J White
1802	W Burns	1756	Not known
1801	J Curtis	1755	C Gill
1800	J Burgoyne	1754	A Marshall
1799	J Dixon	1753	N Sandford
1798	T Williams	1752	J Hogden
1797	J Hill	1751	J Earle
1796	J Thompson	1750	J Duncome
1795	W Parry	1749	H Hilden
1794	J Franklin	1748	T Wagdon
1793	A Haley	1747	J Joyner
1792	J Kettleby	1746	J White
1791	T Easton	1745	J Blasdale
1790	W Byers	1744	J Polton
1789	J Curtis	1743	A Wood
1788	T Radborne	1742	Not known
1787	B Rawlinson	1741	D Roberts
1786	J Nash	1740	J Wing
1785	Not known	1739	G Harrington
1784	J Davis	1738	J Oakes
1783	J Bowler	1737	J Heaver
1782	J Truckle	1736	W Hilliard
1781	E Reeves	1735	H Watford

Year	Winner
1734	J Bellows
1733	W Swabby
1732	R Adam
1731	J Aliss
1730	J Broughton
1729	J Bean
1728	J Gibbs
1727	Not known
1726	T Barrow
1725	Not known
1724	Not known
1723	E Howard
1722	W Morris
1721	C Gurney
1720	Not known

Year	Winner
1719	J Dolby
1718	Not known
1717	Not known
1716	E Bishop or E Guildford
1715	Not known

UNIVERSITY BOAT RACE

FIRST HELD 1829

Cambridge	69
Oxford	67
Deadheat	1 (1877)

RUGBY LEAGUE

WORLD CUP CHAMPIONS

FIRST HELD 1954

Year	Winner
1988	Australia
1977	Australia
1975	Australia
1972	Great Britain
1970	Australia
1968	Australia
1960	Great Britain
1957	Australia
1954	Great Britain

92 Aus.

RUGBY LEAGUE CHALLENGE CUP

FIRST HELD 1897

Year	Winner
1991	Wigan
1990	Wigan
1989	Wigan
1988	Wigan
1987	Halifax
1986	Castleford
1985	Wigan
1984	Widnes
1983	Featherstone Rovers
1982	Hull
1981	Widnes
1980	Hull Kingston Rovers
1979	Widnes
1978	Leeds
1977	Leeds

Year	Winner	Year	Winner
1976	St Helens	1930	Widnes
1975	Widnes	1929	Wigan
1974	Warrington	1928	Swinton
1973	Featherstone Rovers	1927	Oldham
1972	St Helens	1926	Swinton
1971	Leigh	1925	Oldham
1970	Castleford	1924	Wigan
1969	Castleford	1923	Leeds
1968	Leeds	1922	Rochdale Hornets
1967	Featherstone Rovers	1921	Leigh
1966	St Helens	1920	Huddersfield
1965	Wigan	1919/16	No Competition
1964	Widnes	1915	Huddersfield
1963	Wakefield Trinity	1914	Hull
1962	Wakefield Trinity	1913	Huddersfield
1961	St Helens	1912	Dewsbury
1960	Wakefield Trinity	1911	Broughton Rangers
1959	Wigan	1910	Leeds
1958	Wigan	1909	Wakefield Trinity
1957	Leeds	1908	Hunslet
1956	St Helens	1907	Warrington
1955	Barrow	1906	Bradford
1954	Warrington	1905	Warrington
1953	Huddersfield	1904	Halifax
1952	Workington Town	1903	Halifax
1951	Wigan	1902	Broughton Rangers
1950	Warrington	1901	Batley
1949	Bradford Northern	1900	Swinton
1948	Wigan	1899	Oldham
1947	Bradford Northern	1898	Batley
1946	Wakefield Trinity	1897	Batley
1945	Huddersfield		
1944	Bradford		
1943	Dewsbury		
1942	Leeds		
1941	Leeds		
1940	No Competition		
1939	Halifax		
1938	Salford		
1937	Widnes		
1936	Leeds		
1935	Castleford		
1934	Hunslet		
1933	Huddersfield		
1932	Leeds		
1931	Halifax		

PREMIERSHIP TROPHY

1st Division

FIRST HELD 1975

Year	Winner
1991	Hull
1990	Widnes
1989	Widnes
1988	Widnes
1987	Wigan

Year	Winner
1986	Warrington
1985	St Helens
1984	Hull Kingston Rovers
1983	Widnes
1982	Widnes
1981	Hull Kingston Rovers
1980	Widnes
1979	Leeds
1978	Bradford Northern
1977	St Helens
1976	St Helens
1975	Leeds

Play-off Winners

FIRST HELD 1906/07

Year	Winner
1973/74	Warrington
1972/73	Dewsbury
1971/72	Leeds
1970/71	St Helens
1969/70	St Helens
1968/69	Leeds
1967/68	Wakefield Trinity
1966/67	Wakefield Trinity
1965/66	St Helens
1964/65	Halifax
1963/64	No Play-off
1962/63	No Play-off
1961/62	Huddersfield
1960/61	Leeds
1959/60	Wigan
1958/59	St Helens
1957/58	Hull
1956/57	Oldham
1955/56	Hull
1954/55	Warrington
1953/54	Warrington
1952/53	St Helens
1951/52	Wigan
1950/51	Workington Town
1949/50	Wigan
1948/49	Huddersfield
1947/48	Warrington

Year	Winner
1946/47	Wigan
1945/46	Wigan
1944/45	Bradford Northern
1943/44	Wigan
1942/43	No Winner
1941/42	Dewsbury
1940/41	Bradford Northern
1939/40	Bradford Northern
1938/39	Salford
1937/38	Hunslet
1936/37	Salford
1935/36	Hull
1934/35	Swinton
1933/34	Wigan
1932/33	Salford
1931/32	St Helens
1930/31	Swinton
1929/30	Huddersfield
1928/29	Huddersfield
1927/28	Swinton
1926/27	Swinton
1925/26	Wigan
1924/25	Hull Kingston Rovers
1923/24	Batley
1922/23	Hull Kingston Rovers
1921/22	Wigan
1920/21	Hull
1919/15	No Competition
1919/20	Hull
1914/15	Huddersfield
1913/14	Salford
1912/13	Huddersfield
1911/12	Huddersfield
1910/11	Oldham
1909/10	Oldham
1908/09	Wigan
1907/08	Hunslet
1906/07	Halifax

League Leaders/Champions

FIRST HELD 1895/96

Year	Winner
1990/91	Wigan

Year	Winner	Year	Winner
1989/90	Wigan	1943/44	Wakefield Trinity
1988/89	Widnes	1942/43	Wigan
1987/88	Widnes	1941/42	Dewsbury
1986/87	Wigan	1940/41	Wigan (Lancs)
1985/86	Halifax	1940/41	Bradford Northern (Yorks)
1984/85	Hull Kingston Rovers	1939/40	Swinton (Lancs)
1983/84	Hull Kingston Rovers	1939/40	Bradford Northern (Yorks)
1982/83	Hull	1938/39	Salford
1981/82	Leigh	1937/38	Hunslet
1980/81	Bradford Northern	1936/37	Salford
1979/80	Bradford Northern	1935/36	Hull
1978/79	Hull Kingston Rovers	1934/35	Swinton
1977/78	Widnes	1933/34	Salford
1976/77	Featherstone Rovers	1932/33	Salford
1975/76	Salford	1931/32	Huddersfield
1974/75	St Helens	1930/31	Swinton
1973/74	Salford	1929/30	St Helens
1972/73	Warrington	1928/29	Huddersfield
1971/72	Leeds	1927/28	Swinton
1970/71	Wigan	1926/27	St Helens Recs
1969/70	Leeds	1925/26	Wigan
1968/69	Leeds	1924/25	Swinton
1967/68	Leeds	1923/24	Wigan
1966/67	Leeds	1922/23	Hull
1965/66	St Helens	1921/22	Oldham
1964/65	St Helens	1920/21	Hull Kingston Rovers
1963/64	Swinton	1919/20	Huddersfield
1962/63	Swinton	1918/19	Hull
1961/62	Wigan	1918/19	Rochdale Hornets
1960/61	Leeds	1918/15	No Competition
1959/60	St Helens	1914/15	Huddersfield
1958/59	St Helens	1913/14	Huddersfield
1957/58	Oldham	1912/13	Huddersfield
1956/57	Oldham	1911/12	Huddersfield
1955/56	Warrington	1910/11	Wigan
1954/55	Warrington	1909/10	Oldham
1953/54	Halifax	1908/09	Wigan
1952/53	St Helens	1907/08	Oldham
1951/52	Bradford Northern	1906/07	Halifax
1950/51	Warrington	1905/06	Leigh
1949/50	Wigan	1904/05	Oldham
1948/49	Warrington	1903/04	Bradford
1947/48	Wigan	1902/03	Halifax
1946/47	Wigan	1901/02	Broughton Rangers
1945/46	Wigan	1900/01	Oldham (Lancs)
1944/45	Bradford Northern	1900/01	Bradford (Yorks)

Year	Winner
1899/00	Runcorn (Lancs)
1899/00	Bradford (Yorks)
1898/99	Broughton Rangers (Lancs)
1898/99	Batley (Yorks)
1897/98	Oldham (Lancs)
1897/98	Hunslet (Yorks)
1896/97	Broughton Rangers (Lancs)
1896/97	Brighouse Rangers (Yorks)
1895/96	Manningham

REGAL TROPHY CHAMPIONS

FIRST HELD 1971/72

Year	Winner
1990/91	Warrington
1989/90	Wigan
1988/89	Wigan
1987/88	St Helens
1986/87	Wigan
1985/86	Wigan
1984/85	Hull Kingston Rovers
1983/84	Leeds
1982/83	Wigan
1981/82	Hull
1980/81	Warrington
1979/80	Bradford Northern
1978/79	Widnes
1977/78	Warrington
1976/77	Castleford
1975/76	Widnes
1974/75	Bradford Northern
1973/74	Warrington
1972/73	Leeds
1971/72	Halifax

SYDNEY PREMIERSHIP

Grand Final

FIRST HELD 1908

Year	Winner
1991	Penrith
1990	Canberra
1989	Canberra
1988	Canterbury-Bankstown
1987	Manly-Warringah
1986	Parramatta
1985	Canterbury-Bankstown
1984	Canterbury-Bankstown
1983	Parramatta
1982	Parramatta
1981	Parramatta
1980	Canterbury-Bankstown
1979	St George
1978	Manly-Warringah
1977	St George
1976	Manly-Warringah
1975	Eastern Suburbs
1974	Eastern Suburbs
1973	Manly-Warringah
1972	Manly-Warringah
1971	South Sydney
1970	South Sydney
1969	Balmain
1968	South Sydney
1967	South Sydney
1966	St George
1965	St George
1964	St George
1963	St George
1962	St George
1961	St George
1960	St George
1959	St George
1958	St George
1957	St George
1956	St George
1955	South Sydney
1954	South Sydney
1953	South Sydney
1952	Western Suburbs

Year	Winner	Year	Winner
1951	South Sydney	1929	South Sydney
1950	South Sydney	1928	South Sydney
1949	St George	1927	South Sydney
1948	Western Suburbs	1926	South Sydney
1947	Balmain	1925	South Sydney
1946	Balmain	1924	Balmain
1945	Eastern Suburbs	1923	Eastern Suburbs
1944	Balmain	1922	North Sydney
1943	Newtown	1921	North Sydney
1942	Canterbury-Bankstown	1920	Balmain
1941	St George	1919	Balmain
1940	Eastern Suburbs	1918	South Sydney
1939	Balmain	1917	Balmain
1938	Canterbury-Bankstown	1916	Balmain
1937	Eastern Suburbs	1915	Balmain
1936	Eastern Suburbs	1914	South Sydney
1935	Eastern Suburbs	1913	Eastern Suburbs
1934	Western Suburbs	1912	Eastern Suburbs
1933	Newtown	1911	Eastern Suburbs
1932	South Sydney	1910	Newtown
1931	South Sydney	1909	South Sydney
1930	Western Suburbs	1908	South Sydney

RUGBY UNION

WORLD CUP CHAMPIONS

FIRST HELD 1987

Year	Winner
1987	New Zealand

INTERNATIONAL CHAMPIONSHIP CHAMPIONS

FIRST HELD 1883

Year	Winner
1991	England
1990	Scotland
1989	France
1988	Wales/France
1987	France
1986	France/Scotland
1985	Ireland

Year	Winner	Year	Winner
1984	Scotland	1933	Scotland
1983	France/Ireland	1932	England/Wales/Ireland
1982	Ireland	1931	Wales
1981	France	1930	England
1980	England	1929	Scotland
1979	Wales	1928	England
1978	Wales	1927	Scotland/Ireland
1977	France	1926	Scotland/Ireland
1976	Wales	1925	Scotland
1975	Wales	1924	England
1974	Ireland	1923	England
1973	Wales/Scotland/Ireland/	1922	Wales
	England/France	1921	England
1972	Not completed	1920	England/Scotland/Wales
1971	Wales	1919/15	No Competition
1970	Wales/France	1914	England
1969	Wales	1913	England
1968	France	1912	England/Ireland
1967	France	1911	Wales
1966	Wales	1910	England
1965	Wales	1909	Wales
1964	Scotland/Wales	1908	Wales
1963	England	1907	Scotland
1962	France	1906	Ireland/Wales
1961	France	1905	Wales
1960	France/England	1904	Scotland
1959	France	1903	Scotland
1958	England	1902	Wales
1957	England	1901	Scotland
1956	Wales	1900	Wales
1955	Wales/France	1899	Ireland
1954	England/Wales/France	1898/97	Not completed
1953	England	1896	Ireland
1952	Wales	1895	Scotland
1951	Ireland	1894	Ireland
1950	Wales	1893	Wales
1949	Ireland	1892	England
1948	Ireland	1891	Scotland
1947	Wales/England	1890	England/Scotland
1946/40	No Competition	1889/88	Not completed
1939	England/Wales/Ireland	1887	Scotland
1938	Scotland	1886	England/Scotland
1937	England	1885	Not completed
1936	Wales	1884	England
1935	Ireland	1883	England
1934	England		

Grand Slam

FIRST HELD 1911

Year	Winner
1991	England
1990	Scotland
1987	France
1984	Scotland
1981	France
1980	England
1978	Wales
1977	France
1976	Wales
1971	Wales
1968	France
1957	England
1952	Wales
1950	Wales
1948	Ireland
1928	England
1925	Scotland
1924	England
1923	England
1921	England
1914	England
1913	England
1911	Wales

Triple Crown

FIRST HELD 1883

Year	Winner
1991	England
1990	Scotland
1988	Wales
1985	Ireland
1984	Scotland
1982	Ireland
1980	England
1979	Wales
1978	Wales
1977	Wales
1976	Wales
1971	Wales
1969	Wales

Year	Winner
1965	Wales
1960	England
1957	England
1954	England
1952	Wales
1950	Wales
1949	Ireland
1948	Ireland
1938	Scotland
1937	England
1934	England
1933	Scotland
1928	England
1925	Scotland
1924	England
1923	England
1921	England
1914	England
1913	England
1911	Wales
1909	Wales
1908	Wales
1907	Scotland
1905	Wales
1903	Scotland
1902	Wales
1901	Scotland
1900	Wales
1899	Ireland
1895	Scotland
1894	Ireland
1893	Wales
1892	England
1891	Scotland
1884	England
1883	England

COURAGE CLUBS CHAMPIONSHIP CHAMPIONS

FIRST HELD 1987/88

1st Division

Year	Winner
1990/91	Bath
1989/90	Wasps
1988/89	Bath
1987/88	Leicester

2nd Division

Year	Winner
1990/91	Rugby
1989/90	Northampton
1988/89	Saracens
1987/88	Rosslyn Park

3rd Division

Year	Winner
1990/91	West Hartlepool
1989/90	London Scottish
1988/89	Plymouth Albion
1987/88	Wakefield

PILKINGTON CUP

FIRST HELD 1972

Year	Winner
1991	Harlequins
1990	Bath
1989	Bath
1988	Harlequins
1987	Bath
1986	Bath
1985	Bath
1984	Bath

Year	Winner
1983	Bristol
1982	Gloucester
	Moseley
1981	Leicester
1980	Leicester
1979	Leicester
1978	Gloucester
1977	Gosforth
1976	Gosforth
1975	Bedford
1974	Coventry
1973	Coventry
1972	Gloucester

COUNTY CHAMPIONS

FIRST HELD 1889

Year	Winner
1991	Cornwall
1990	Lancashire
1989	Durham
1988	Lancashire
1987	Yorkshire
1986	Warwickshire
1985	Middlesex
1984	Gloucestershire
1983	Gloucestershire
1982	Lancashire
1981	Northumberland
1980	Lancashire
1979	Middlesex
1978	North Midlands
1977	Lancashire
1976	Gloucestershire
1975	Gloucestershire
1974	Gloucestershire
1973	Lancashire
1972	Gloucestershire
1971	Surrey
1970	Staffordshire
1969	Lancashire
1968	Middlesex
1967	Surrey
	Durham

Year	Winner	Year	Winner
1966	Middlesex	1910	Gloucestershire
1965	Warwickshire	1909	Durham
1964	Warwickshire	1908	Cornwall
1963	Warwickshire	1907	Devon
1962	Warwickshire		Durham
1961	Cheshire	1906	Devon
1960	Warwickshire	1905	Durham
1959	Warwickshire	1904	Kent
1958	Warwickshire	1903	Durham
1957	Devon	1902	Durham
1956	Middlesex	1901	Devon
1955	Lancashire	1900	Durham
1954	Middlesex	1899	Devon
1953	Yorkshire	1898	Northumberland
1952	Middlesex	1897	Kent
1951	East Midlands	1896	Yorkshire
1950	Cheshire	1895	Yorkshire
1949	Lancashire	1894	Yorkshire
1948	Lancashire	1893	Yorkshire
1947	Lancashire	1892	Yorkshire
1946/40	No Competition	1891	Lancashire
1939	Warwickshire	1890	Yorkshire
1938	Lancashire	1889	Yorkshire
1937	Gloucestershire		
1936	Hampshire		
1935	Lancashire		
1934	East Midlands		
1933	Hampshire		
1932	Gloucestershire		
1931	Gloucestershire		
1930	Gloucestershire		
1929	Middlesex		
1928	Yorkshire		
1927	Kent		
1926	Yorkshire		
1925	Leicestershire		
1924	Cumberland		
1923	Somerset		
1922	Gloucestershire		
1921	Gloucestershire		
1920	Gloucestershire		
1919/15	No Competition		
1914	Midlands		
1913	Gloucestershire		
1912	Devon		
1911	Devon		

WELSH LEAGUE CHAMPIONS

FIRST HELD 1990/91

Premier Division

Year	Winner
1990/91	Neath

1st Division

Year	Winner
1990/91	Newport

WELSH CUP

FIRST HELD 1972

Year	Winner
1991	Llanelli
1990	Neath
1989	Neath
1988	Llanelli
1987	Cardiff
1986	Cardiff
1985	Llanelli
1984	Cardiff
1983	Pontypool
1982	Cardiff
1981	Cardiff
1980	Bridgend
1979	Bridgend
1978	Swansea
1977	Newport
1976	Llanelli
1975	Llanelli
1974	Llanelli
1973	Llanelli
1972	Neath

McEWANS SCOTTISH CLUB CHAMPIONS

FIRST HELD 1973/74

Year	Winner
1990/91	Boroughmuir
1989/90	Melrose
1988/89	Kelso
1987/88	Kelso
1986/87	Hawick
1985/86	Hawick
1984/85	Hawick
1983/84	Hawick
1982/83	Gala
1981/82	Hawick
1980/81	Gala
1979/80	Gala

Year	Winner
1978/79	Heriot's FP
1977/78	Hawick
1976/77	Hawick
1975/76	Hawick
1974/75	Hawick
1973/74	Hawick

ALL-IRELAND LEAGUE CHAMPIONS

FIRST HELD 1990/91

Year	Winner
1990/91	Cork Constitution

THE MIDDLESEX SEVENS CHAMPIONS

FIRST HELD 1926

Year	Winner
1991	London Scottish
1990	Harlequins
1989	Harlequins
1988	Harlequins
1987	Harlequins
1986	Harlequins
1985	Wasps
1984	London Welsh
1983	Richmond
1982	Stewart's Melville FP
1981	Rosslyn Park
1980	Richmond
1979	Richmond
1978	Harlequins
1977	Richmond
1976	Loughborough Colleges
1975	Richmond
1974	Richmond
1973	London Welsh

Year	Winner
1972	London Welsh
1971	London Welsh
1970	Loughborough Colleges
1969	St Luke's College
1968	London Welsh
1967	Harlequins
1966	Loughborough Colleges
1965	London Scottish
1964	Loughborough Colleges
1963	London Scottish
1962	London Scottish
1961	London Scottish
1960	London Scottish
1959	Loughborough Colleges
1958	Blackheath
1957	St Luke's College
1956	London Welsh
1955	Richmond
1954	Rosslyn Park
1953	Richmond
1952	Wasps
1951	Richmond II
1950	Rosslyn Park
1949	Heriot's FP
1948	Wasps
1947	Rosslyn Park
1946	St Mary's Hospital
1945	Nottingham
1944	St Mary's Hospital
1943	St Mary's Hospital
1942	St Mary's Hospital
1941	Cambridge University
1940	St Mary's Hospital
1939	Cardiff
1938	Metropolitan Police
1937	London Scottish
1936	Sale
1935	Harlequins
1934	Barbarians
1933	Harlequins
1932	Blackheath
1931	London Welsh
1930	London Welsh
1929	Harlequins
1928	Harlequins
1927	Harlequins

Year	Winner
1926	Harlequins

NEW ZEALAND INTER-PROVINCIAL CHAMPIONS
Ranfurly Shield

FIRST HELD 1904

Played on a challenge basis

Year	Winner
1985	Auckland
1982	Canterbury
1981	Wellington
1980	Waikato
1979	Auckland
1978	North Auckland
1976	Manawatu
1974	Auckland
1974	Wellington
1974	South Canterbury
1973	Marlborough
1972	Canterbury
1972	Auckland
1971	North Auckland
1971	Auckland
1969	Canterbury
1966	Hawke's Bay
1966	Waikato
1965	Auckland
1963	Taranaki
1963	Wellington
1960	Auckland
1960	North Auckland
1959	Auckland
1959	Southland
1957	Taranaki
1957	Otago
1956	Wellington
1953	Canterbury
1953	Wellington
1952	Waikato

Year	Winner
1952	Auckland
1951	Waikato
1950	North Auckland
1950	South Canterbury
1950	Wairarapa
1950	Canterbury
1947	Otago
1938	Southland
1938	Otago
1937	Southland
1935	Otago
1935	Canterbury
1934	Auckland
1934	Hawke's Bay
1931	Canterbury
1930	Wellington
1929	Southland
1928	Wairarapa
1927	Canterbury
1927	Manawhenua
1927	Wairarapa
1922	Hawke's Bay
1921	Wellington
1920	Southland
1914	Wellington
1913	Taranaki
1905	Auckland
1904	Wellington

HONG KONG SEVENS CHAMPIONS

FIRST HELD 1976

Year	Winner
1991	Fiji
1990	Fiji
1989	New Zealand
1988	Australia
1987	New Zealand
1986	New Zealand
1985	Australia
1984	Fiji

Year	Winner
1983	Australia
1982	Australia
1981	Barbarians
1980	Fiji
1979	Australia
1978	Fiji
1977	Fiji
1976	Cantabrians

SYDNEY PREMIERSHIP
Grand Final

FIRST HELD 1900

Year	Winner
1991	Randwick
1990	Randwick
1989	Randwick
1988	Randwick
1987	Randwick
1986	Parramatta
1985	Parramatta
1984	Randwick
1983	Manly
1982	Randwick
1981	Randwick
1980	Randwick
1979	Randwick
1978	Randwick
1977	Parramatta
1976	Gordon
1975	Northern Suburbs
1974	Randwick
1973	Randwick
1972	University
1971	Randwick
1970	University
1969	Eastern Suburbs
1969	University
1968	University
1967	Randwick
1966	Randwick
1965	Randwick

Year	Winner	Year	Winner
1964	Northern Suburbs	1926	University
1963	Northern Suburbs	1925	Balmain
1962	University		Glebe
1961	University	1924	University
1960	Northern Suburbs	1923	University
1959	Randwick	1922	Manly
1958	Gordon	1921	Eastern Suburbs
1957	St George	1920	University
1956	Gordon	1919	University
1955	University	1918/15	No Competition
1954	University	1914	Glebe
1953	University	1913	Eastern Suburbs
1952	Gordon	1912	Glebe
1951	University	1911	Newtown
1950	Manly	1910	Newtown
1949	Gordon	1909	Glebe
1948	Randwick	1908	Newtown
1947	Eastern Suburbs	1907	Glebe
1946	Eastern Suburbs	1906	Glebe
1945	University	1905	South Sydney
1944	Eastern Suburbs	1904	University
1943	Manly	1903	Eastern Suburbs
1942	Manly	1902	Western Suburbs
1941	Eastern Suburbs	1901	Glebe
1940	Randwick		University
1939	University	1900	Glebe
1938	Randwick		
1937	University		
1936	Drummoyne		
1935	Northern Suburbs		
1934	Randwick		
1933	Northern Suburbs		
1932	Manly		
1931	Eastern Suburbs		
1930	Randwick		
1929	Western Suburbs		
1928	University		
1927	University		

THE VARSITY MATCH

FIRST HELD 1872

Cambridge	49
Oxford	48
Drawn	13

SHOOTING

OLYMPIC CHAMPIONS

Free Pistol

FIRST HELD 1896

Year	Winner	
1988	S Babii	Rom
1984	H Xu	CPR
1980	A Melentyev	USSR
1976	U Potteck	GDR
1972	R Skanakar	Swe
1968	G Kossykh	USSR
1964	V Markkanen	Fin
1960	A Gushchin	USSR
1956	P Linnosvuo	Fin
1952	H Benner	USA
1948	E Vazquez Cam	Per
1936	T Ullmann	Swe
1932/24	Not held	
1920	K Fredrick	USA
1912	A Lane	USA
1908/04	Not held	
1900	K Roderer	Swi
1896	S Paine	USA

Rapid-Fire Pistol

FIRST HELD 1896

Year	Winner	
1988	A Kouzmine	USSR
1984	T Kamachi	Jap
1980	C Ion	Rom
1976	N Klaar	GDR
1972	J Zapedzki	Pol
1968	J Zapedzki	Pol
1964	P Linnosvuo	Fin
1960	W McMillan	USA
1956	S Petrescu	Rom
1952	K Takacs	Hun

Year	Winner	
1948	K Takacs	Hun
1936	C van Oyen	Ger
1932	R Morigi	Ita
1928	Not held	
1924	P Bailey	USA
1920	G Paraense	Bra
1912	A Lane	USA
1908	P van Asbroeck	Bel
1904	Not held	
1900	M Larrouy	Fra
1896	J Phrangoudis	Gre

Small-Bore Rifle
Prone

FIRST HELD 1908

Year	Winner	
1988	M Varga	Cze
1984	E Etzel	USA
1980	K Varga	Hun
1976	K Smieszek	FRG
1972	H Jun Li	DPRK
1968	J Kurka	Cze
1964	L Hammerl	Hun
1960	P Kohnke	Ger
1956	G Ouellette	Can
1952	J Sarbu	Rom
1948	A Cook	USA
1936	W Rogeberg	Nor
1932	B Ronnmark	Swe
1928	Not held	
1924	P C de Lisle	Fra
1920	L Nuesslein	USA
1912	F Hird	USA
1908	A A Carnell	GB

Small-Bore Rifle
3 Positions

FIRST HELD 1952

Year	Winner	
1988	M Cooper	GB
1984	M Cooper	GB
1980	V Vlasov	USSR
1976	L Bassham	USA
1972	J Writer	USA
1968	B Klingner	FRG
1964	L Wigger	USA
1960	V Shamburkin	USSR
1956	A Bogdanov	USSR
1952	E Kongshaug	Nor

Running Game Target

FIRST HELD 1900

Year	Winner	
1988	T Heiestad	Nor
1984	Y Li	CPR
1980	I Solokov	USSR
1976	A Gazov	USSR
1972	L Zhelezniak	USSR
1968/04	Not held	
1900	L Debray	Fra

Skeet Shooting

FIRST HELD 1968

Year	Winner	
1988	A Wegner	GDR
1984	M Dryke	USA
1980	H K Rasmussen	Den
1976	J Panachek	Cze
1972	K Wirnhier	FRG
1968	E Petrov	USSR

Trap Shooting

FIRST HELD 1900

Year	Winner	
1988	D Monakov	USSR
1984	L Giovanetti	Ita
1980	L Giovanetti	Ita
1976	D Haldeman	USA
1972	A Scalzone	Ita
1968	R Braithwaite	GB
1964	E Mattarelli	Ita
1960	I Dumitrescu	Rom
1956	G Rossini	Ita
1952	G Genereux	Can
1948/28	Not held	
1924	G Halasy	Hun
1920	M Arie	USA
1912	J Graham	USA
1908	W Ewing	Can
1904	Not held	
1900	R de Barbarin	Fra

Air Pistol

FIRST HELD 1988

Year	Winner	
1988	T Kiriakov	Bul

Air Rifle

FIRST HELD 1984

Year	Winner	
1988	G Maksimovic	Yug
1984	P Herberle	Fra

Women's Sport Pistol

FIRST HELD 1984

Year	Winner	
1988	N Saloukvadze	USSR

Year	Winner	
1984	L Thom	Can

Women's Small-Bore Rifle

FIRST HELD 1984

Year	Winner	
1988	S Sperber	FRG
1984	X Wu	CPR

Women's Air Pistol

FIRST HELD 1988

Year	Winner	
1988	J Sekaric	Yug

Women's Air Rifle

FIRST HELD 1984

Year	Winner	
1988	I Chilova	USSR
1984	P Spurgin	USA

SKIING

ALPINE

WORLD CHAMPIONS

Men's Combined Alpine

FIRST HELD 1932

Year	Winner	
1991	S Eberharter	Aut
1989	M Girardelli	Lux
1987	M Girardelli	Lux
1985	P Zurbriggen	Swi
1982	M Vion	Fra
1980	P Mahre	USA
1978	A Wenzel	Lie
1976	G Thoeni	Ita
1974	F Klammer	Aut
1972	G Thoeni	Ita
1970	W Kidd	USA
1968	J-C Killy	Fra
1966	J-C Killy	Fra
1964	L Leitner	Ger

Year	Winner	
1962	K Schranz	Aut
1960	G Perillat	Fra
1958	A Sailer	Aut
1956	A Sailer	Aut
1954	S Eriksen	Nor
1952/40	No Competition	
1939	J Jennewein	Ger
1938	E Allais	Fra
1937	E Allais	Fra
1936	R Rominger	Aut
1935	A Seelos	Aut
1934	D Zogg	Swi
1933	A Seelos	Aut
1932	O Furrer	Swi

Downhill

FIRST HELD 1931

Year	Winner	
1991	F Heinzer	Swi

Year	Winner	
1989	H Tauscher	FRG
1987	P Muller	Swi
1985	P Zurbriggen	Swi
1982	H Weirather	Aut
1978	J Walcher	Aut
1974	D Zwilling	Aut
1970	B Russi	Swi
1966	J-C Killy	Fra
1962	K Schranz	Aut
1958	A Sailer	Aut
1954	C Pravda	Aut
1950	Z Colo	Ita
1949/40	No Competition	
1939	H Lantschner	Ger
1938	J Couttet	Fra
1937	E Allais	Fra
1936	R Rominger	Swi
1935	F Zingerle	Aut
1934	D Zogg	Swi
1933	W Prager	Swi
1932	G Lantschner	Aut
1931	W Prager	Swi

Slalom

FIRST HELD 1931

Year	Winner	
1991	M Girardelli	Lux
1989	R Nierlich	Aut
1987	F Worndl	FRG
1985	J Nilsson	Swe
1982	I Stenmark	Swe
1978	I Stenmark	Swe
1974	G Thoeni	Ita
1970	J Augert	Fra
1966	G Senoner	Ita
1962	C Bozon	Fra
1958	J Rieder	Aut
1954	S Eriksen	Nor
1950	G Schneider	Swi
1949/40	No Competition	
1939	R Rominger	Swi
1938	R Rominger	Swi
1937	E Allais	Fra

Year	Winner	
1936	R Matt	Aut
1935	A Seelos	Aut
1934	F Pfnur	Ger
1933	A Seelos	Aut
1932	F Dauber	Ger
1931	D Zogg	Swi

Giant Slalom

FIRST HELD 1950

Year	Winner	
1991	R Nierlich	Aut
1989	R Nierlich	Aut
1987	P Zurbriggen	Swi
1985	M Wasmeier	FRG
1982	S Mahre	USA
1978	I Stenmark	Swe
1974	G Thoeni	Ita
1970	K Schranz	Aut
1966	G Perillat	Fra
1962	E Zimmermann	Aut
1958	A Sailer	Aut
1954	S Eriksen	Nor
1950	Z Colo	Ita

Super-Giant Slalom

FIRST HELD 1987

Year	Winner	
1991	S Eberharter	Aut
1989	M Hangl	Swi
1987	P Zurbriggen	Swi

Combined Downhill

FIRST HELD 1991

Year	Winner	
1991	K Ghedina	Aut

Women's Combined

FIRST HELD 1931

Year	Winner	
1991	C Bournissen	Swi
1989	T McKinney	USA
1987	E Hess	Swi
1985	E Hess	Swi
1982	E Hess	Swi
1980	H Wenzel	Lie
1978	A Moser-Proll	Aut
1976	R Mittermaier	Ger
1974	F Serrat	Fra
1972	A Moser-Proll	Aut
1970	M Jacot	Can
1968	N Greene	Can
1966	M Goitschel	Fra
1964	M Goitschel	Fra
1962	M Goitschel	Fra
1960	A Heggtveit	Can
1958	F Danzer	Swi
1956	M Berthod	Swi
1954	I Schopfer	Swi
1952/40	No Competition	
1939	C Cranz	Ger
1938	C Cranz	Ger
1937	C Cranz	Ger
1936	E Pinching	GB
1935	C Cranz	Ger
1934	C Cranz	Ger
1933	I Lantschner	Aut
1932	R Streiff	Swi
1931	E Mackinnon	GB

Women's Downhill

FIRST HELD 1931

Year	Winner	
1991	P Kronberger	Aut
1989	M Walliser	Swi
1987	M Walliser	Swi
1985	M Figini	Swi
1982	G Sorensen	Can
1978	A Moser-Proll	Aut
1974	A Moser-Proll	Aut

Year	Winner	
1970	A Zyrd	Swi
1966	E Schinegger	Aut
1962	C Haas	Aut
1958	L Wheeler	Can
1954	I Schopfer	Swi
1950	T Beiser-Jochum	Aut
1949/40	No Competition	
1939	C Cranz	Ger
1938	L Resch	Ger
1937	C Cranz	Ger
1936	E Pinching	GB
1935	C Cranz	Ger
1934	A Ruegg	Swi
1933	I Lantschner	Aut
1932	P Wiesinger	Ita
1931	E Mackinnon	GB

Women's Slalom

FIRST HELD 1931

Year	Winner	
1991	V Schneider	Swi
1989	M Svet	Yug
1987	E Hess	Swi
1985	P Pelen	Fra
1982	E Hess	Swi
1978	L Solkner	Aut
1974	H Wenzel	Lie
1970	I Lafforgue	Fra
1966	A Famose	Fra
1962	M Jahn	Aut
1958	J Bjornbakken	Nor
1954	T Klecker	Aut
1950	D Rom	Aut
1947/40	No Competition	
1939	C Cranz	Ger
1938	C Cranz	Ger
1937	C Cranz	Ger
1936	G Paumgarten	Aut
1935	A Ruegg	Swi
1934	C Cranz	Ger
1933	I Lantschner	Aut
1932	R Streiff	Swi
1931	E Mackinnon	GB

Women's Giant Slalom

FIRST HELD 1950

Year	Winner	
1991	P Wiberg	Swe
1989	V Schneider	Swi
1987	V Schneider	Swi
1985	D Roffe	USA
1982	E Hess	Swi
1978	M Epple	FRG
1974	F Serrat	Fra
1970	B Clifford	Can
1966	M Goitschel	Fra
1962	M Jahn	Aut
1958	L Wheeler	Can
1954	L Schmitt	Fra
1950	D Rom	Aut

Women's Super-Giant Slalom

FIRST HELD 1987

Year	Winner	
1991	U Maier	Aut
1989	U Maier	Aut
1987	M Walliser	FRG

OLYMPIC CHAMPIONS

Men's Combined

FIRST HELD 1936

Year	Winner	
1988	H Strolz	Aut
1984/52	Not held	
1948	H Oreiller	Fra
1936	F Pfnur	Ger

Downhill

FIRST HELD 1948

Year	Winner	
1988	P Zurbriggen	Swi
1984	W Johnson	USA
1980	L Stock	Aut
1976	F Klammer	Aut
1972	B Russi	Swi
1968	J-C Killy	Fra
1964	E Zimmermann	Aut
1960	J Vuarnet	Fra
1956	A Sailer	Aut
1952	Z Colo	Ita
1948	H Oreiller	Fra

Slalom

FIRST HELD 1948

Year	Winner	
1988	A Tomba	Ita
1984	P Mahre	USA
1980	I Stenmark	Swe
1976	P Gros	Ita
1972	F Ochoa	Spa
1968	J-C Killy	Fra
1964	J Stiegler	Aut
1960	E Hinterseer	Aut
1956	A Sailer	Aut
1952	O Schneider	Aut
1948	E Reinalter	Swi

Giant Slalom

FIRST HELD 1952

Year	Winner	
1988	A Tomba	Ita
1984	M Julen	Swi
1980	I Stenmark	Swe
1976	H Hemmi	Swi
1972	G Thoeni	Ita
1968	J-C Killy	Fra
1964	F Boulieu	Fra

Year	Winner	
1960	R Staub	Swi
1956	A Sailer	Aut
1952	S Eriksen	Nor

Super-Giant Slalom

FIRST HELD 1988

Year	Winner	
1988	F Picard	Fra

Women's Combined

FIRST HELD 1936

Year	Winner	
1988	A Wachter	Aut
1984/52	Not held	
1948	T Beiser	Aut
1936	C Cranz	Ger

Women's Downhill

FIRST HELD 1948

Year	Winner	
1988	M Kiehl	FRG
1984	M Figini	Swi
1980	A Moser-Proll	Aut
1976	R Mittermaier	FRG
1972	M-T Nadig	Swi
1968	O Pall	Aut
1964	C Haas	Aut
1960	H Biebl	Ger
1956	M Berthod	Swi
1952	T Jochum-Beiser	Aut
1948	H Schlunegger	Swi

Women's Slalom

FIRST HELD 1948

Year	Winner	
1988	V Schneider	Swi
1984	P Magoni	Ita
1980	H Wenzel	Lie
1976	R Mittermaier	FRG
1972	B Cochran	USA
1968	M Goitschel	Fra
1964	C Goitschel	Fra
1960	A Heggtveit	Can
1956	R Colliard	Swi
1952	A Mead-Lawrence	USA
1948	G Fraser	USA

Women's Giant Slalom

FIRST HELD 1952

Year	Winner	
1988	V Schneider	Swi
1984	D Armstrong	USA
1980	H Wenzel	Lie
1976	K Kreiner	Can
1972	M-T Nadig	Swi
1968	N Greene	Can
1964	M Goitschel	Fra
1960	Y Ruegg	Swi
1956	O Reichert	Ger
1952	A Mead-Lawrence	USA

Women's Super-Giant Slalom

FIRST HELD 1988

Year	Winner	
1988	S Wolf	Aut

WORLD CUP CHAMPIONS

Men's Overall

FIRST HELD 1967

Year	Winner	
1991	M Girardelli	Lux
1990	P Zurbriggen	Swi
1989	M Girardelli	Lux
1988	P Zurbriggen	Swi
1987	P Zurbriggen	Swi
1986	M Girardelli	Lux
1985	M Girardelli	Lux
1984	P Zurbriggen	Swi
1983	P Mahre	USA
1982	P Mahre	USA
1981	P Mahre	USA
1980	A Wenzel	Lie
1979	P Luscher	Swi
1978	I Stenmark	Swe
1977	I Stenmark	Swe
1976	I Stenmark	Swe
1975	G Thoeni	Ita
1974	P Gros	Ita
1973	G Thoeni	Ita
1972	G Thoeni	Ita
1971	G Thoeni	Ita
1970	K Schranz	Aut
1969	K Schranz	Aut
1968	J-C Killy	Fra
1967	J-C Killy	Fra

Downhill

FIRST HELD 1967

Year	Winner	
1991	F Heinzer	Swi
1990	H Hoflehner	Aut
1989	M Girardelli	Lux
1988	P Zurbriggen	Swi
1987	P Zurbriggen	Swi
1986	P Wirnsberger	Aut
1985	H Hoflehner	Aut

Year	Winner	
1984	U Raber	Swi
1983	F Klammer	Aut
1982	S Podborski	Can
	P Muller	Swi
1981	H Weirather	Aut
1980	P Muller	Swi
1979	P Muller	Swi
1978	F Klammer	Aut
1977	F Klammer	Aut
1976	F Klammer	Aut
1975	F Klammer	Aut
1974	R Collombin	Swi
1973	R Collombin	Swi
1972	B Russi	Swi
1971	B Russi	Swi
1970	K Schranz	Aut
	K Cordin	Aut
1969	K Schranz	Aut
1968	G Nenning	Aut
1967	J-C Killy	Fra

Slalom

FIRST HELD 1967

Year	Winner	
1991	M Girardelli	Lux
1990	A Bittner	FRG
1989	A Bittner	FRG
1988	A Tomba	Ita
1987	B Krizaj	Yug
1986	R Petrovic	Yug
1985	M Girardelli	Lux
1984	M Girardelli	Lux
1983	I Stenmark	Swe
1982	P Mahre	Swe
1981	I Stenmark	Swe
1980	I Stenmark	Swe
1979	I Stenmark	Swe
1978	I Stenmark	Swe
1977	I Stenmark	Swe
1976	I Stenmark	Swe
1975	I Stenmark	Swe
1974	G Thoeni	Ita
1973	G Thoeni	Ita

Year	Winner	
1972	J Augert	Fra
1971	J Augert	Fra
1970	P Russel	Fra
	A Penz	Fra
1969	A Penz	Fra
	J Augert	Fra
	P Russel	Fra
1968	D Giovanoli	Swi
1967	J-C Killy	Fra

Giant Slalom

FIRST HELD 1967

Year	Winner	
1991	A Tomba	Ita
1990	O Furuseth	Nor
1989	O Furuseth	Nor
1988	A Tomba	Ita
1987	P Zurbriggen	Swi
1986	J Gaspoz	Swi
1985	M Girardelli	Lux
1984	I Stenmark	Swe
1983	P Mahre	USA
1982	P Mahre	USA
1981	I Stenmark	Swe
1980	I Stenmark	Swe
1979	I Stenmark	Swe
1978	I Stenmark	Swe
1977	H Hemmi	Swi
1976	I Stenmark	Swe
1975	I Stenmark	Swe
1974	P Gros	Ita
1973	H Hinterseer	Aut
1972	G Thoeni	Ita
1971	G Thoeni	Ita
	P Russel	Fra
1970	G Thoeni	Ita
1969	K Schranz	Aut
1968	J-C Killy	Fra
1967	J-C Killy	Fra

Super-Giant Slalom

FIRST HELD 1986

Year	Winner	
1991	F Heinzer	Swi
1990	P Zurbriggen	Swi
1989	P Zurbriggen	Swi
1988	P Zurbriggen	Swi
1987	P Zurbriggen	Swi
1986	M Wasmeier	FRG

Women's Overall

FIRST HELD 1967

Year	Winner	
1991	P Kronberger	Aut
1990	P Kronberger	Aut
1989	V Schneider	Swi
1988	M Figini	Swi
1987	M Walliser	Swi
1986	M Walliser	Swi
1985	M Figini	Swi
1984	E Hess	Swi
1983	T McKinney	USA
1982	E Hess	Swi
1981	M-T Nadig	Swi
1980	H Wenzel	Lie
1979	A Moser-Proll	Aut
1978	H Wenzel	Lie
1977	L Morerod	Swi
1976	R Mittermaier	FRG
1975	A Moser-Proll	Aut
1974	A Moser-Proll	Aut
1973	A Moser-Proll	Aut
1972	A Moser-Proll	Aut
1971	A Moser-Proll	Aut
1970	M Jacot	Fra
1969	G Gabl	Aut
1968	N Greene	Can
1967	N Greene	Can

Women's Downhill

FIRST HELD 1967

Year	Winner	
1991	C Bournissen	Swi
1990	K Gutensohn-Knopf	FRG
1989	M Figini	Swi
1988	M Figini	Swi
1987	M Figini	Swi
1986	M Walliser	Swi
1985	M Figini	Swi
1984	M Walliser	Swi
1983	D De Agostini	Swi
1982	C Gros-Gaudenier	Fra
1981	M-T Nadig	Swi
1980	M-T Nadig	Swi
1979	A Moser-Proll	Aut
1978	A Moser-Proll	Aut
1977	B Habersatter-Totschnig	Aut
1976	B Habersatter-Totschnig	Aut
1975	A Moser-Proll	Aut
1974	A Moser-Proll	Aut
1973	A Moser-Proll	Aut
1972	A Moser-Proll	Aut
1971	A Moser-Proll	Aut
1970	I Mir	Fra
1969	W Drexel	Aut
1968	I Mir	Fra
	O Pall	Aut
1967	M Goitschel	Fra

Women's Slalom

FIRST HELD 1967

Year	Winner	
1991	P Kronberger	Aut
1990	V Schneider	Swi
1989	V Schneider	Swi
1988	R Steiner	Aut
1987	C Schmidhauser	Swi
1986	R Steiner	Aut
1985	E Hess	Swi
1984	T McKinney	USA

Year	Winner	
1983	E Hess	Swi
1982	E Hess	Swi
1981	E Hess	Swi
1980	P Pelen	Fra
1979	R Sackl	Aut
1978	H Wenzel	Lie
1977	L Morerod	Swi
1976	L Morerod	Swi
1975	L Morerod	Swi
1974	C Zechmeister	FRG
1973	P Emonet	Fra
1972	B Laforgue	Fra
1971	B Laforgue	Fra
	B Clifford	Can
1970	I Laforgue	Fra
1969	G Gabl	Aut
1968	A Famose	Fra
1967	M Goitschel	Fra
	A Famose	Fra

Women's Giant Slalom

FIRST HELD 1967

Year	Winner	
1991	V Schneider	Swi
1990	A Wachter	Aut
1989	V Schneider	Swi
1988	M Svet	Yug
1987	M Walliser	Swi
	V Schneider	Swi
1986	V Schneider	Swi
1985	M Figini	Swi
	M Kiehl	FRG
1984	E Hess	Swi
1983	T McKinney	USA
1982	I Epple	FRG
1981	T McKinney	USA
1980	H Wenzel	Lie
1979	C Kinshoffer	Aut
1978	L Morerod	Swi
1977	L Morerod	Swi
1976	R Mittermaier	FRG
1975	A Moser-Proll	Aut
1974	H Wenzel	Lie

Year	Winner	
1973	M Kaserer	Aut
1972	A Moser-Proll	Aut
1971	A Moser-Proll	Aut
1970	M Jacot	Fra
	F Macchi	Fra
1969	M Cochran	USA
1968	N Greene	Can
1967	N Greene	Can

Women's Super-Giant Slalom

FIRST HELD 1986

Year	Winner	
1991	C Merle	Fra
1990	C Merle	Fra
1989	C Merle	Fra
1988	M Figini	Swi
1987	M Walliser	Swi
1986	M Kiehl	FRG

Nations Cup

FIRST HELD 1967

Year	Winner
1991	Austria
1990	Austria
1989	Switzerland
1988	Switzerland
1987	Switzerland
1986	Switzerland
1985	Switzerland
1984	Switzerland
1983	Switzerland
1982	Austria
1981	Austria
1980	Austria
1979	Austria
1978	Austria
1977	Austria
1976	Austria
1975	Austria

Year	Winner	
1974	Austria	
1973	Austria	
1972	France	
1971	France	
1970	France	
1969	Austria	
1968	France	
1967	France	

NORDIC WORLD CHAMPIONS

15 km Cross-Country – Classical

FIRST HELD 1954

Year	Winner	
1991	B Daehlie	Nor
1989	H Kirvesniemi	Fin
1987	M Albarello	Ita
1985	K Härkönen	Fin
1982	O Brä	Nor
1978	J Luszczek	Pol
1974	M Myrmo	Nor
1970	L-G Åslund	Swe
1966	G Eggen	Nor
1962	A Rönnlund	Sw
1958	V Hakulinen	Fin
1954	V Hakulinen	Fin

15 km Cross-Country – Freestyle

FIRST HELD 1989

Year	Winner	
1991	B Daehlie	Nor
1989	G Svan	Swe

18 km Cross-Country

FIRST HELD 1925

Year	Winner	
1950	K E Åstrom	Swe
1949/41	No Competition	
1939	J Kurikkala	Fin
1938	P Pitkanen	Fin
1937	L Bergendahl	Nor
1935	K Karppinen	Fin
1934	S Nurmela	Fin
1933	N Englund	Swe
1931	J Grottumsbraaten	Nor
1930	A Rudstadstuen	Nor
1929	V Saarinen	Fin
1927	J Lindgren	Swe
1926	J Grottumsbraaten	Nor
1925	O Nemecky	Cze

30 km Cross-Country

FIRST HELD 1926

Year	Winner	
1991	G Svan	Swe
1989	V Smirnov	USSR
1987	T Wassberg	Swe
1985	G Svan	Swe
1982	T Eriksson	Swe
1978	S Saveliev	USSR
1974	T Magnuson	Swe
1970	V Vedenin	USSR
1966	E Mäntyranta	Fin
1962	E Mäntyranta	Fin
1958	K Hämäläinen	Fin
1954	V Kusin	USSR
1950/27	No Competition	
1926	M Ravio	Fin

50 km Cross-Country

FIRST HELD 1925

Year	Winner	
1991	T Mogren	Swe

Year	Winner	
1989	G Svan	Swe
1987	M De Zolt	Ita
1985	G Svan	Swe
1982	T Wassberg	Swe
1978	S-Å Lundback	Swe
1974	G Grimmer	GDR
1970	K Oikarainen	Fin
1966	G Eggen	Nor
1962	S Jernberg	Swe
1958	S Jernberg	Swe
1954	V Kusin	USSR
1950	G Eriksson	Swe
1949/40	No Competition	
1939	L Bergendahl	Nor
1938	K Jalkanen	Fin
1937	P Niemi	Fin
1935	N Englund	Swe
1934	E Wiklund	Swe
1933	V Saarinen	Fin
1931	O Stenen	Nor
1930	S Utterstrom	Swe
1929	A Knuttila	Fin
1927	J Lindgren	Swe
1926	M Ravio	Fin
1925	F Donth	Cze

4 x 10 km Relay

FIRST HELD 1933

Year	Winner
1991	Norway
1989	Sweden
1987	Sweden
1985	Norway
1982	Norway
	USSR
1978	Sweden
1974	East Germany
1970	USSR
1966	Norway
1962	Sweden
1958	Sweden
1954	Finland
1950	Sweden

Year	Winner	
1949/40	No Competition	
1939	Finland	
1938	Finland	
1937	Norway	
1935	Finland	
1934	Finland	
1933	Sweden	

70 Metre Hill

FIRST HELD 1925

Year	Winner	
1991	H Kuttin	Aut
1989	J Weissflog	GDR
1987	J Parma	Cze
1985	J Weissflog	GDR
1982	A Kogler	Aut
1978	M Buse	GDR
1974	H-G Aschenbach	GDR
1970	G Napalkov	USSR
1966	B Wirkola	Nor
1962	T Engan	Nor
1958	J Kärkinen	Fin
1954	M Pietikäinen	Fin
1950	H Bjornstad	Nor
1949/41	No Competition	
1939	J Bradl	Ger
1938	A Ruud	Nor
1937	B Ruud	Nor
1935	B Ruud	Nor
1934	K Johansson	Nor
1933	M Reymond	Swi
1931	B Ruud	Nor
1930	G Andersen	Nor
1929	S Ruud	Nor
1927	T Edman	Swe
1926	J Tullin-Thams	Nor
1925	W Dick	Cze

90 Metre Hill

FIRST HELD 1962

Year	Winner	
1991	F Petek	Yug
1989	J Puikkonen	Fin
1987	A Felder	Aut
1985	P Bergerud	Nor
1982	M Nykyänen	Fin
1978	T Räisänen	Fin
1974	H-G Aschenbach	GDR
1970	G Napalkov	USSR
1966	B Wirkola	Nor
1962	H Recknagel	GDR

Men's Team Ski Jumping

FIRST HELD 1982

Year	Winner
1991	Austria
1989	Austria
1987	Finland
1985	Finland
1982	Norway

Nordic Combined

FIRST HELD 1925

Year	Winner	
1991	F-B Lundberg	Nor
1989	T E Elden	Nor
1987	T Lokken	Nor
1985	H Weinbuch	FRG
1982	T Sandberg	Nor
1978	K Winkler	GDR
1974	U Wehling	GDR
1970	L Rygl	Cze
1966	G Thoma	FRG
1962	A Larsen	Nor
1958	P Korhonen	Fin
1954	S Stenersen	Nor
1950	H Hasu	Fin
1949/40	No Competition	

Year	Winner	
1939	G Berauer	Ger
1938	O Hoffsbakken	Nor
1937	S Roen	Nor
1935	O Hagen	Nor
1934	O Hagen	Nor
1933	S Eriksson	Swe
1931	J Grottumsbraaten	Nor
1930	H Vinjarengen	Nor
1929	H Vinjarengen	Nor
1927	R Purkert	Cze
1926	J Grottumsbraaten	Nor
1925	O Nemecky	Cze

Men's Team Nordic Combined

FIRST HELD 1982

Year	Winner
1991	Austria
1989	Norway
1987	West Germany
1985	West Germany
1982	East Germany

Women's 5 km Cross-Country

FIRST HELD 1962

Year	Winner	
1991	T Dybendahl	Nor
1989	Not held	
1987	M Matikainen	Fin
1985	A Boe	Nor
1982	B Aunli	Nor
1978	H Takalo	Fin
1974	G Kulakova	USSR
1970	G Kulakova	USSR
1966	A Kolchina	USSR
1962	A Kolchina	USSR

Women's 10 km Cross-Country

FIRST HELD 1954

Year	Winner	
1991	E Valbe	USSR
1989	E Valbe	USSR
1987	A Jahren	Nor
1985	A Boe	Nor
1982	B Aunli	Nor
1978	Z Amosova	USSR
1974	G Kulakova	USSR
1970	A Oliunina	USSR
1966	K Boyarskikh	USSR
1962	A Kolchina	USSR
1958	A Kolchina	USSR
1954	L Kozyreva	USSR

Women's 15 km Cross-Country

FIRST HELD 1989

Year	Winner	
1991	E Valbe	USSR
1989	M Matikainen	Fin

Women's 20 km Cross-Country

FIRST HELD 1978

Year	Winner	
1987	M Westin	Swe
1985	G Nykkelmo	Nor
1982	R Smetanina	USSR
1980	V Hesse	GDR
1978	Z Amosova	USSR

Women's 30 km Cross-Country

FIRST HELD 1989

Year	Winner	
1991	L Egorova	USSR
1989	E Valbe	USSR

Women's 4 x 5 km Relay

FIRST HELD 1974

Year	Winner
1991	USSR
1989	Finland
1987	USSR
1985	USSR
1982	Norway
1978	Finland
1974	USSR

Women's 3 x 5 km Relay

FIRST HELD 1954

Year	Winner
1970	USSR
1966	USSR
1962	USSR
1958	USSR
1954	USSR

OLYMPIC CHAMPIONS
Combined

FIRST HELD 1924

Year	Winner	
1988	H Kempf	Swi
1984	T Sandberg	Nor
1980	U Wehling	GDR
1976	U Wehling	GDR
1972	U Wehling	GDR
1968	F Keller	FRG
1964	T Knutsen	Nor
1960	G Thoma	Ger
1956	S Stenersen	Nor
1952	S Slattvik	Nor
1948	H Hasu	Fin
1936	O Hagen	Nor
1932	J Grottumsbraaten	Nor
1928	J Grottumsbraaten	Nor
1924	T Haug	Nor

15 km Cross-Country

FIRST HELD 1924

Year	Winner	
1988	M Deviatiarov	USSR
1984	G Svan	Swe
1980	T Wassberg	Swe
1976	N Bajukov	Swe
1972	S Lundback	Swe
1968	H Gronningen	Nor
1964	E Mantyranta	Fin
1960	H Brusveen	Nor
1956	H Brenden	Nor
1952	H Brenden	Nor
1948	M Lundstrom	Swe
1936	E Larsson	Swe
1932	S Utterstrom	Swe
1928	J Grottumsbraaten	Nor
1924	T Haug	Nor

30 km Cross-Country

FIRST HELD 1956

Year	Winner	
1988	A Prokuorov	USSR
1984	N Zimyatov	USSR
1980	N Zimyatov	USSR
1976	S Savelyev	USSR
1972	V Vedenine	USSR

Year	Winner	
1968	F Nones	Ita
1964	E Mantyranta	Fin
1960	S Jernberg	Swe
1956	V Hakulinen	Fin

50 km Cross-Country

FIRST HELD 1924

Year	Winner	
1988	G Svan	Swe
1984	T Wassberg	Swe
1980	N Zimyatov	USSR
1976	I Formo	Nor
1972	P Tyldrum	Nor
1968	O Ellefsaeter	Nor
1964	S Jernberg	Swe
1960	K Hamamlainen	Fin
1956	S Jernberg	Swe
1952	V Hakulinen	Fin
1948	N Karlson	Swe
1936	E Wiklund	Swe
1932	V Saarinen	Fin
1928	P Hedlund	Swe
1924	T Haug	Nor

4 x 10 km Relay

FIRST HELD 1936

Year	Winner
1988	Sweden
1984	Sweden
1980	USSR
1976	Finland
1972	USSR
1968	Norway
1964	Sweden
1960	Finland
1956	USSR
1952	Finland
1948	Sweden
1936	Finland

70 Metre Hill

FIRST HELD 1924

Year	Winner	
1988	M Nykanen	Fin
1984	J Weissflog	GDR
1980	T Innauer	Aut
1976	H Aschenbach	GDR
1972	Y Kasaya	Jap
1968	J Raska	Cze
1964	V Kankkonen	Fin
1960	H Recknagel	Ger
1956	A Hyvarinen	Fin
1952	A Bergmann	Nor
1948	P Hugsted	Nor
1936	B Ruud	Nor
1932	B Ruud	Nor
1928	A Andersen	Nor
1924	J Tullin-Thams	Nor

90 Metre Hill

FIRST HELD 1964

Year	Winner	
1988	M Nykanen	Fin
1984	M Nykanen	Fin
1980	J Tormanen	Fin
1976	K Schnabl	Aut
1972	W Fortuna	Pol
1968	V Belousov	USSR
1964	T Engan	Nor

Women's 5 km Cross-Country

FIRST HELD 1964

Year	Winner	
1988	M Matikainen	Fin
1984	M Hamalainen	Fin
1980	R Smetanina	USSR
1976	H Takalo	Fin
1972	G Kulakova	USSR

Year	Winner	
1968	T Gustafsson	Swe
1964	K Boyarskikh	USSR

Women's 10 km Cross-Country

FIRST HELD 1952

Year	Winner	
1988	V Ventsene	USSR
1984	M Hamalainen	Fin
1980	B Petzold	GDR
1976	R Smetanina	USSR
1972	G Kulakova	USSR
1968	T Gustafsson	Swe
1964	K Boyarskikh	USSR
1960	M Gusakova	USSR
1956	L Kozyryeva	USSR
1952	L Wideman	Fin

Women's 20 km Cross-Country

FIRST HELD 1984

Year	Winner	
1988	T Tikhonova	USSR
1984	M Hamalainen	Fin

Women's 4 x 5 km Relay

FIRST HELD 1956

Year	Winner
1988	USSR
1984	Norway
1980	East Germany
1976	USSR
1972	USSR
1968	Norway
1964	USSR

Year	Winner
1960	Sweden
1956	Finland

WORLD CUP CHAMPIONS
Combined

FIRST HELD 1983

Year	Winner	
1991	F-B Lundberg	Nor
1990	K Sulzenbacher	Aut
1989	T Bredesen	Nor
1988	K Sulzenbacher	Aut
1987	T Lokken	Nor
1986	H Weinbuch	FRG
1985	G Andersen	Nor
1984	T Sandberg	Nor
1983	E Andersen	Nor

Cross-Country

FIRST HELD 1979

Year	Winner	
1991	V Smirnov	USSR
1990	V Ulvang	Nor
1989	G Svan	Swe
1988	G Svan	Swe
1987	T Mogren	Swe
1986	G Svan	Swe
1985	G Svan	Swe
1984	G Svan	Swe
1983	A Zavialov	USSR
1982	B Koch	USA
1981	A Zavialov	USSR
1980	J Mieto	Fin
1979	O Bra	Nor

Ski Jumping

FIRST HELD 1980

Year	Winner	
1991	A Felder	Aut
1990	A P Nikkola	Fin
1989	J Bokloev	Swe
1988	M Nykanen	Fin
1987	V Opaas	Nor
1986	M Nykanen	Fin
1985	M Nykanen	Fin
1984	J Weissflog	GDR
1983	M Nykanen	Fin
1982	A Kogler	Aut
1981	A Kogler	Aut
1980	H Neupert	Aut

Women's Cross-Country

FIRST HELD 1979

Year	Winner	
1991	E Valbe	USSR
1990	L Lazutina	USSR
1989	E Valbe	USSR
1988	M Matikainen	Fin
1987	M Matikainen	Fin
1986	M Matikainen	Fin
1985	A Boe	Nor
1984	M Hamalainen	Fin
1983	M Hamalainen	Fin
1982	B Aunli	Nor
1981	R Smetanina	USSR
1980	Not held	
1979	G Kulakova	USSR

SNOOKER

WORLD PROFESSIONAL CHAMPIONS

FIRST HELD 1927

Year	Winner	
1991	J Parrott	Eng
1990	S Hendry	Sco
1989	S Davis	Eng
1988	S Davis	Eng
1987	S Davis	Eng
1986	J Johnson	Eng
1985	D Taylor	Ire
1984	S Davis	Eng
1983	S Davis	Eng
1982	A Higgins	Ire
1981	S Davis	Eng
1980	C Thorburn	Can
1979	T Griffiths	Wal
1978	R Reardon	Wal
1977	J Spencer	Eng
1976	R Reardon	Wal
1975	R Reardon	Wal
1974	R Reardon	Wal
1973	R Reardon	Wal
1972	A Higgins	Ire
1970	J Spencer	Eng
1970	R Reardon	Wal
1969	J Spencer	Eng
1968	J Pulman	Eng
1966	J Pulman	Eng
1965	J Pulman	Eng
1964	J Pulman	Eng
1957	J Pulman	Eng
1956	F Davis	Eng
1955	F Davis	Eng
1954	F Davis	Eng
1953	F Davis	Eng

Year	Winner	
1952	F Davis	Eng
1951	F Davis	Eng
1950	W Donaldson	Sco
1949	F Davis	Eng
1948	F Davis	Eng
1947	W Donaldson	Sco
1946	J Davis	Eng
1945/41	No Competition	
1940	J Davis	Eng
1939	J Davis	Eng
1938	J Davis	Eng
1937	J Davis	Eng
1936	J Davis	Eng
1935	J Davis	Eng
1934	J Davis	Eng
1933	J Davis	Eng
1932	J Davis	Eng
1931	J Davis	Eng
1930	J Davis	Eng
1929	J Davis	Eng
1928	J Davis	Eng
1927	J Davis	Eng

WORLD AMATEUR CHAMPIONS

FIRST HELD 1963

Year	Winner	
1990	S O'Connor	Ire
1989	K Doherty	Ire
1988	J Wattana	Tha
1987	D Morgan	Wal
1986	P Mifsud	Mlt
1985	P Mifsud	Mlt
1984	O Agrawal	Ind
1982	T Parsons	Wal
1980	J White	Eng
1978	C Wilson	Wal
1976	D Mountjoy	Wal
1974	R Edmonds	Eng
1972	R Edmonds	Eng
1970	J Barron	Eng
1968	D Taylor	Eng

Year	Winner	
1966	G Owen	Eng
1963	G Owen	Eng

UK OPEN CHAMPIONS

FIRST HELD 1977

Year	Winner	
1990	S Hendry	Sco
1989	S Hendry	Sco
1988	D Mountjoy	Wal
1987	S Davis	Eng
1986	S Davis	Eng
1985	S Davis	Eng
1984	S Davis	Eng
1983	A Higgins	Ire
1982	T Griffiths	Wal
1981	S Davis	Eng
1980	S Davis	Eng
1979	J Virgo	Eng
1978	D Mountjoy	Wal
1977	P Fagan	Ire

BRITISH OPEN CHAMPIONS

FIRST HELD 1980

Year	Winner	
1991	S Hendry	Sco
1990	R Chaperon	Can
1989	T Meo	Eng
1988	S Hendry	Sco
1987	J White	Eng
1986	S Davis	Eng
1985	S Francisco	SA
1984	S Davis	Eng
1983	R Reardon	Eng
1982	S Davis	Eng
1981	S Davis	Eng
1980	A Higgins	Ire

ROTHMANS GRAND PRIX

FIRST HELD 1982

Year	Winner	
1990	S Hendry	Sco
1989	S Davis	Eng
1988	S Davis	Eng
1987	S Hendry	Sco
1986	J White	Eng
1985	S Davis	Eng
1984	D Taylor	Ire
1983	A Knowles	Eng
1982	R Reardon	Wal

BENSON & HEDGES MASTERS

FIRST HELD 1975

Year	Winner	
1991	S Hendry	Sco
1990	S Hendry	Sco

Year	Winner	
1989	S Hendry	Sco
1988	S Davis	Eng
1987	D Taylor	Ire
1986	C Thorburn	Can
1985	C Thorburn	Can
1984	J White	Eng
1983	C Thorburn	Can
1982	S Davis	Eng
1981	A Higgins	Ire
1980	T Griffiths	Wal
1979	P Mans	SA
1978	A Higgins	Ire
1977	D Mountjoy	Wal
1976	R Reardon	Wal
1975	J Spencer	Eng

WORLD MASTERS

FIRST HELD 1991

Year	Winner	
1991	J White	Eng

SPEEDWAY

WORLD CHAMPIONS
Individual

FIRST HELD 1936

Year	Winner	
1991	J O Pedersen	Den
1990	P Jonsson	Swe
1989	H Nielsen	Den
1988	E Gundersen	Den
1987	H Nielsen	Den

Year	Winner	
1986	H Nielsen	Den
1985	E Gundersen	Den
1984	E Gundersen	Den
1983	E Muller	FRG
1982	B Penhall	USA
1981	B Penhall	USA
1980	M Lee	Eng
1979	I Mauger	NZ
1978	O Olsen	Den
1977	I Mauger	NZ
1976	P Collins	Eng

Year	Winner	
1975	O Olsen	Den
1974	A Michanek	Swe
1973	J Szczakiel	Pol
1972	I Mauger	NZ
1971	O Olsen	Den
1970	I Mauger	NZ
1969	I Mauger	NZ
1968	I Mauger	NZ
1967	O Fundin	Swe
1966	B Briggs	NZ
1965	B Knutsson	Swe
1964	B Briggs	NZ
1963	O Fundin	Swe
1962	P Craven	Eng
1961	O Fundin	Swe
1960	O Fundin	Swe
1959	R Moore	NZ
1958	B Briggs	NZ
1957	B Briggs	NZ
1956	O Fundin	Swe
1955	P Craven	Eng
1954	R Moore	NZ
1953	F Williams	Wal
1952	J Young	Aus
1951	J Young	Aus
1950	F Williams	Wal
1949	T Price	Eng
1948/39	No Competition	
1938	B Wilkinson	Aus
1937	J Milne	USA
1936	L Van Praag	Aus

Pairs

FIRST HELD 1970

Year	Winner	
1991	H Nielsen & J O Pedersen	Den
1990	H Nielsen & J O Pedersen	Den
1989	H Nielsen & E Gundersen	Den
1988	H Nielsen & E Gundersen	Den

Year	Winner	
1987	H Nielsen & E Gundersen	Den
1986	H Nielsen & E Gundersen	Den
1985	E Gundersen & T Knudsen	Den
1984	P Collins & C Morton	Eng
1983	K Carter & P Collins	Eng
1982	D Sigalos & B Schwartz	USA
1981	B Penhall & B Schwartz	USA
1980	D Jessup & P Collins	Eng
1979	O Osen & H Nielsen	Den
1978	M Simmons & G Kennett	Eng
1977	P Collins & M Simmons	Eng
1976	J Louis & M Simmons	Eng
1975	A Michanek & T Jansson	Swe
1974	A Michanek & S Sjosten	Swe
1973	A Michanek & T Jansson	Swe
1972	R Wilson & T Betts	Eng
1971	J Szczakiel & A Wyglenda	Pol
1970	R Moore & I Mauger	NZ

Team

FIRST HELD 1960

Year	Winner
1991	Denmark
1990	United States
1989	England
1988	Denmark
1987	Denmark
1986	Denmark
1985	Denmark
1984	Denmark
1983	Denmark
1982	United States

Year	Winner
1981	Denmark
1980	England
1979	New Zealand
1978	Denmark
1977	England
1976	Australia
1975	England
1974	England
1973	Great Britain
1972	Great Britain
1971	Great Britain
1970	Sweden
1969	Poland
1968	Great Britain
1967	Sweden
1966	Poland
1965	Poland
1964	Sweden
1963	Sweden
1962	Sweden
1961	Poland
1960	Sweden

Long Track

FIRST HELD 1971

Year	Winner	
1991	G Riss	Ger
1990	S Wigg	Eng
1989	S Wigg	Eng
1988	K Maier	FRG
1987	K Maier	FRG
1986	E Gundersen	Den
1985	S Wigg	Eng
1984	E Gundersen	Den
1983	S Moran	USA
1982	K Maier	FRG
1981	M Lee	Eng
1980	K Maier	FRG
1979	A Weisbock	FRG
1978	E Muller	FRG
1977	A Michanek	Swe
1976	E Muller	FRG
1975	E Muller	FRG

Year	Winner	
1974	E Muller	FRG
1973	O Olsen	Den
1972	I Mauger	NZ
1971	I Mauger	NZ

BRITISH LEAGUE CHAMPIONS

FIRST HELD 1932

Year	Winner
1990	Reading
1989	Oxford
1988	Coventry
1987	Coventry
1986	Oxford
1985	Oxford
1984	Ipswich
1983	Cradley Heath
1982	Belle Vue
1981	Cradley Heath
1980	Reading
1979	Coventry
1978	Coventry
1977	White City
1976	Ipswich
1975	Ipswich
1974	Exeter
1973	Reading
1972	Belle Vue
1971	Belle Vue
1970	Belle Vue
1969	Poole
1968	Coventry
1967	Swindon
1966	Halifax
1965	West Ham
1964	Oxford
1963	Belle Vue
1962	Southampton
1961	Wimbledon
1960	Wimbledon
1959	Wimbledon

Year	Winner		Year	Winner
1958	Wimbledon		1947	Wembley
1957	Swindon		1946	Wembley
1956	Wimbledon		1945/40	No Competition
1955	Southampton		1939	Belle Vue
1954	Wimbledon		1938	New Cross
1953	Wembley		1937	West Ham
1952	Wembley		1936	Belle Vue
1951	Wembley		1935	Belle Vue
1950	Wembley		1934	Belle Vue
1949	Wembley		1933	Belle Vue
1948	New Cross		1932	Wembley

SQUASH

WORLD CHAMPIONS

FIRST HELD 1976

Men

Year	Winner	
1991	R Martin	Aus
1990	Jansher Khan	Pak
1989	Jansher Khan	Pak
1988	Jahangir Khan	Pak
1987	Jansher Khan	Pak
1986	R Norman	NZ
1985	Jahangir Khan	Pak
1984	Jahangir Khan	Pak
1983	Jahangir Khan	Pak
1982	Jahangir Khan	Pak
1981	Jahangir Khan	Pak
1980	G Hunt	Aus
1979	G Hunt	Aus
1978	Not held	
1977	G Hunt	Aus
1976	G Hunt	Aus

Women

Year	Winner	
1990	S Devoy	NZ
1989	M Le Moignan	GB
1987	S Devoy	NZ
1985	S Devoy	NZ
1983	V Cardwell	Aus
1981	R Thorne	Aus
1979	H McKay	Aus
1976	H McKay	Aus

BRITISH OPEN CHAMPIONS

Men

FIRST HELD 1930

Year	Winner	
1991	Jahangir Khan	Pak
1990	Jahangir Khan	Pak
1989	Jahangir Khan	Pak

Year	Winner	
1988	Jahangir Khan	Pak
1987	Jahangir Khan	Pak
1986	Jahangir Khan	Pak
1985	Jahangir Khan	Pak
1984	Jahangir Khan	Pak
1983	Jahangir Khan	Pak
1982	Jahangir Khan	Pak
1981	G Hunt	Aus
1980	G Hunt	Aus
1979	G Hunt	Aus
1978	G Hunt	Aus
1977	G Hunt	Aus
1976	G Hunt	Aus
1975	Q Zaman	Pak
1974	G Hunt	Aus
1973	J Barrington	GB
1972	J Barrington	GB
1971	J Barrington	GB
1970	J Barrington	GB
1969	G Hunt	Aus
1968	J Barrington	GB
1967	J Barrington	GB
1966	A Abou Taleb	Egy
1965	A Abou Taleb	Egy
1964	A Abou Taleb	Egy
1963	A Abou Taleb	Egy
1962	Mohibullah Khan	Pak
1961	Azam Khan	Pak
1960	Azam Khan	Pak
1959	Azam Khan	Pak
1958	Azam Khan	Pak
1957	Hashim Khan	Pak
1956	Roshan Khan	Pak
1955	Hashim Khan	Pak
1954	Hashim Khan	Pak
1953	Hashim Khan	Pak
1952	Hashim Khan	Pak
1951	Hashim Khan	Pak
1950	Hashim Khan	Pak
1949	M Karim	Egy
1948	M Karim	Egy
1947	M Karim	Egy
1946	M Karim	Egy
1945/39	No Competition	
1938	J Dear	GB
1937	A Bey	Egy

Year	Winner	
1936	A Bey	Egy
1935	A Bey	Egy
1934	A Bey	Egy
1933	A Bey	Egy
1932	A Bey	Egy
1931	D Butcher	GB
1930	D Butcher	GB

Women

FIRST HELD 1922

Year	Winner	
1991	L Opie	GB
1990	S Devoy	NZ
1989	S Devoy	NZ
1988	S Devoy	NZ
1987	S Devoy	NZ
1986	S Devoy	NZ
1985	S Devoy	NZ
1984	S Devoy	NZ
1983	V Cardwell	Aus
1982	V Cardwell	Aus
1981	V Hoffman	Aus
1980	V Hoffman	Aus
1979	B Wall	Aus
1978	S Newman	Aus
1977	H McKay	Aus
1976	H McKay	Aus
1975	H McKay	Aus
1974	H McKay	Aus
1973	H McKay	Aus
1972	H McKay	Aus
1971	H McKay	Aus
1970	H McKay	Aus
1969	H McKay	Aus
1968	H McKay	Aus
1967	H McKay	Aus
1966	H McKay	Aus
1965	H Blundell	Aus
1964	H Blundell	Aus
1963	H Blundell	Aus
1962	H Blundell	Aus
1961	F Marshall	GB
1960	S Macintosh	GB

Year	Winner		Year	Winner	
1959	Not held		1936	M Lumb	GB
1958	J Morgan	GB	1935	M Lumb	GB
1957	J Morgan	GB	1934	M Lumb	GB
1956	J Morgan	GB	1934	S Noel	GB
1955	J Morgan	GB	1933	S Noel	GB
1954	J Morgan	GB	1932	S Noel	GB
1953	J Morgan	GB	1931	C Fenwick	GB
1952	J Morgan	GB	1930	N Cave	GB
1951	J Morgan	GB	1929	N Cave	GB
1950	J Morgan	GB	1928	J Cave	GB
1949	J Curry	GB	1927	Not held	
1948	J Curry	GB	1926	C Fenwick	GB
1947	J Curry	GB	1925	C Fenwick	GB
1946/40	No Competition	·	1924	J Cave	GB
1939	M Lumb	GB	1923	N Cave	GB
1938	M Lumb	GB	1922	S Huntsman	GB
1937	M Lumb	GB	1922	J Cave	GB

SWIMMING

OLYMPIC CHAMPIONS

50 Metres Freestyle

FIRST HELD 1988

Year	Winner	
1988	M Biondi	USA

100 Metres Freestyle

FIRST HELD 1896

Year	Winner	
1988	M Biondi	USA
1984	A Gaines	USA
1980	J Woithe	GDR
1976	J Montgomery	USA

Year	Winner	
1972	M Spitz	USA
1968	M Wenden	Aus
1964	D Schollander	USA
1960	J Devitt	Aus
1956	J Henricks	Aus
1952	C Schloes	USA
1948	W Ris	USA
1936	F Csik	Hun
1932	Y Miyazaki	Jap
1928	J Weissmuller	USA
1924	J Weissmuller	USA
1920	D Kahanamoku	USA
1912	D Kahanamoku	USA
1908	C Daniels	USA
1904	Z Halmay	Hun
1900	Not held	
1896	A Hajos	Hun

200 Metres Freestyle

FIRST HELD 1900

Year	Winner	
1988	D Armstrong	Aus
1984	M Gross	FRG
1980	S Kopliakov	USSR
1976	B Furniss	USA
1972	M Spitz	USA
1968	M Wenden	Aus
1964/08	Not held	
1904	C Daniels	USA
1900	F Lane	Aus

400 Metres Freestyle

FIRST HELD 1896

Year	Winner	
1988	U Dassler	GDR
1984	G DiCarlo	USA
1980	V Salnikov	USSR
1976	B Goodell	USA
1972	B Cooper	Aus
1968	M Burton	USA
1964	D Schollander	USA
1960	M Rose	Aus
1956	M Rose	Aus
1952	J Boiteux	Fra
1948	W Smith	USA
1936	J Medica	USA
1932	B Crabbe	USA
1928	A Zorilla	Arg
1924	J Weissmuller	USA
1920	N Ross	USA
1912	G Hodgson	Can
1908	H Taylor	GB
1904	C Daniels	USA
1900	Not held	
1896	P Neumann	Aut

1500 Metres Freestyle

FIRST HELD 1896

Year	Winner	
1988	V Salnikov	USSR
1984	M O'Brien	USA
1980	V Salnikov	USSR
1976	B Goodell	USA
1972	M Burton	USA
1968	M Burton	USA
1964	R Windle	Aus
1960	J Konrads	Aus
1956	M Rose	Aus
1952	F Konno	USA
1948	J McLane	USA
1936	N Terada	Jap
1932	K Kitamura	Jap
1928	A Borg	Swe
1924	A Charlton	Aus
1920	N Ross	USA
1912	G Hodgson	Can
1908	H Taylor	GB
1904	E Rausch	Ger
1900	J Jarvis	GB
1896	A Hajos	Hun

100 Metres Backstroke

FIRST HELD 1904

Year	Winner	
1988	D Suzuki	Jap
1984	R Carey	USA
1980	B Baron	Swe
1976	J Naber	USA
1972	R Matthes	GDR
1968	R Matthes	GDR
1964	Not held	
1960	D Theile	Aus
1956	D Theile	Aus
1952	Y Oyakawa	USA
1948	A Stack	USA
1936	A Kiefer	USA
1932	M Kiyokawa	Jap
1928	G Kojac	USA
1924	W Kealoha	USA

Year	Winner	
1920	W Kealoha	USA
1912	H Hebner	USA
1908	A Bieberstein	Ger
1904	W Brack	Ger

200 Metres Backstroke

FIRST HELD 1900

Year	Winner	
1988	I Polianski	USSR
1984	R Carey	USA
1980	S Wladar	Hun
1976	J Naber	USA
1972	R Matthes	GDR
1968	R Matthes	GDR
1964	J Graef	USA
1960/04	Not held	
1900	E Hoppenberg	Ger

100 Metres Breaststroke

FIRST HELD 1968

Year	Winner	
1988	A Moorhouse	GB
1984	S Lundquist	USA
1980	D Goodhew	GB
1976	J Hencken	USA
1972	N Taguchi	Jap
1968	D McKenzie	USA

200 Metres Breaststroke

FIRST HELD 1908

Year	Winner	
1988	J Szabo	Hun
1984	V Davis	Can
1980	R Zhulpa	USSR
1976	D Wilkie	GB
1972	J Hencken	USA
1968	F Munoz	Mex

Year	Winner	
1964	I O'Brien	Aus
1960	W Mulliken	Can
1956	M Furukawa	Jap
1952	J Davies	Aus
1948	J Verdeur	USA
1936	T Hamuro	Jap
1932	Y Tsuruta	Jap
1928	Y Tsuruta	Jap
1924	R Skelton	USA
1920	H Malmroth	Swe
1912	W Bathe	Ger
1908	F Holman	GB

100 Metres Butterfly

FIRST HELD 1968

Year	Winner	
1988	A Nesty	Sur
1984	M Gross	FRG
1980	P Arvidsson	Swe
1976	M Vogel	USA
1972	M Spitz	USA
1968	D Russell	USA

200 Metres Butterfly

FIRST HELD 1956

Year	Winner	
1988	M Gross	FRG
1984	J Sieben	Aus
1980	S Fesenko	USSR
1976	M Bruner	USA
1972	M Spitz	USA
1968	C Robie	USA
1964	K Berry	Aus
1960	M Troy	USA
1956	W Yorzyk	USA

200 Metres Individual Medley

FIRST HELD 1968

Year	Winner	
1988	T Darnyi	Hun
1984	A Baumann	Can
1980/76	Not held	
1972	G Larsson	Swe
1968	C Hickcox	USA

400 Metres Individual Medley

FIRST HELD 1964

Year	Winner	
1988	T Darnyi	Hun
1984	A Baumann	Can
1980	A Sidorenko	USSR
1976	R Strachan	USA
1972	G Larsson	Swe
1968	C Hickcox	USA
1964	R Roth	USA

4 x 100 Metres Freestyle Relay

FIRST HELD 1964

Year	Winner
1988	United States
1984	United States
1980/76	No Competition
1972	United States
1968	United States
1964	United States

4 x 200 Metres Freestyle Relay

FIRST HELD 1908

Year	Winner
1988	United States
1984	United States
1980	USSR
1976	United States
1972	United States
1968	United States
1964	United States
1960	United States
1956	Australia
1952	United States
1948	United States
1936	Japan
1932	Japan
1928	United States
1924	United States
1920	United States
1912	Australasia
1908	Great Britain

4 x 100 Metres Medley Relay

FIRST HELD 1960

Year	Winner
1988	United States
1984	United States
1980	Australia
1976	United States
1972	United States
1968	United States
1964	United States
1960	United States

Women's 50 Metres Freestyle

FIRST HELD 1988

Year	Winner	
1988	K Otto	GDR

Women's 100 Metres Freestyle

FIRST HELD 1912

Year	Winner	
1988	K Otto	GDR
1984	C Steinseifer	USA
	N Hogshead	USA
1980	B Krause	GDR
1976	K Ender	GDR
1972	S Neilson	USA
1968	J Henne	USA
1964	D Fraser	Aus
1960	D Fraser	Aus
1956	D Fraser	Aus
1952	K Szoke	Hun
1948	G Andersen	Den
1936	H Mastenbroek	Nld
1932	H Madison	USA
1928	A Osipowich	USA
1924	E Lackie	USA
1920	E Bleibtrey	USA
1912	F Durack	Aus

Women's 200 Metres Freestyle

FIRST HELD 1968

Year	Winner	
1988	H Friedrich	GDR
1984	M Wayte	USA
1980	B Krause	GDR
1976	K Ender	GDR
1972	S Gould	Aus
1968	D Meyer	USA

Women's 400 Metres Freestyle

FIRST HELD 1920

Year	Winner	
1988	J Evans	USA

Year	Winner	
1984	T Cohen	USA
1980	I Diers	GDR
1976	P Thuemer	GDR
1972	S Gould	Aus
1968	D Meyer	USA
1964	V Duenkel	USA
1960	C von Saltza	USA
1956	L Crapp	Aus
1952	V Gyenge	Hun
1948	A Curtis	USA
1936	H Mastenbroek	Nld
1932	H Madison	USA
1928	M Norelius	USA
1924	M Norelius	USA
1920	E Bleibtrey	USA

Women's 800 Metres Freestyle

FIRST HELD 1968

Year	Winner	
1988	J Evans	USA
1984	T Cohen	USA
1980	M Ford	Aus
1976	P Thuemer	GDR
1972	K Rothhammer	USA
1968	D Meyer	USA

Women's 100 Metres Backstroke

FIRST HELD 1924

Year	Winner	
1988	K Otto	GDR
1984	T Andrews	USA
1980	R Reinisch	GDR
1976	U Richter	GDR
1972	M Belote	USA
1968	K Hall	USA
1964	C Ferguson	USA
1960	L Burke	USA
1956	J Grinham	GB

Year	Winner	
1952	J Harrison	SA
1948	K Harup	Den
1936	D Senff	Nld
1932	E Holm	USA
1928	M Braun	Nld
1924	S Bauer	USA

Women's 200 Metres Backstroke

FIRST HELD 1968

Year	Winner	
1988	K Egerszegi	Hun
1984	J de Rover	Nld
1980	R Reinisch	GDR
1976	U Richter	GDR
1972	M Belote	USA
1968	P Watson	USA

Women's 100 Metres Breaststroke

FIRST HELD 1968

Year	Winner	
1988	T Dangalakova	Bul
1984	P Van Staveren	Nld
1980	U Geweniger	GDR
1976	H Anke	GDR
1972	C Carr	USA
1968	D Bjedov	Yug

Women's 200 Metres Breaststroke

FIRST HELD 1924

Year	Winner	
1988	S Hoerner	GDR
1984	A Ottenbrite	Can
1980	L Kachushite	USSR
1976	M Kosheveya	USSR

Year	Winner	
1972	B Whitfield	Aus
1968	S Wichman	USA
1964	G Prozumenshchi-kova	USSR
1960	A Lonsbrough	GB
1956	U Happe	FRG
1952	E Szekely	Hun
1948	P van Vliet	Nld
1936	H Maehata	Jap
1932	C Dennis	Aus
1928	H Schrader	Ger
1924	L Morton	GB

Women's 100 Metres Butterfly

FIRST HELD 1956

Year	Winner	
1988	K Otto	GDR
1984	M Meagher	USA
1980	C Metschuck	GDR
1976	K Ender	GDR
1972	M Aoki	Jap
1968	L McClements	Aus
1964	S Stouder	USA
1960	C Schuler	USA
1956	S Mann	USA

Women's 200 Metres Butterfly

FIRST HELD 1968

Year	Winner	
1988	K Nord	GDR
1984	M Meagher	USA
1980	I Geissler	GDR
1976	A Pollack	GDR
1972	K Moe	USA
1968	A Kok	Nld

Women's 200 Metres Individual Medley

FIRST HELD 1968

Year	Winner	
1988	D Hunger	GDR
1984	T Caulkins	USA
1980/76	Not held	
1972	S Gould	Aus
1968	C Kolb	USA

Women's 400 Metres Individual Medley

FIRST HELD 1964

Year	Winner	
1988	J Evans	USA
1984	T Caulkins	USA
1980	P Schneider	GDR
1976	U Tauber	GDR
1972	G Neall	Aus
1968	C Kolb	USA
1964	D De Varona	USA

Women's 4 x 100 Metres Freestyle Relay

FIRST HELD 1912

Year	Winner
1988	East Germany
1984	United States
1980	East Germany
1976	United States
1972	United States
1968	United States
1964	United States
1960	United States
1956	Australia
1952	Hungary
1948	United States
1936	Netherlands
1932	United States

Year	Winner
1928	United States
1924	United States
1920	United States
1912	Great Britain

Women's 4 x 100 Metres Medley Relay

FIRST HELD 1960

Year	Winner
1988	East Germany
1984	United States
1980	East Germany
1976	East Germany
1972	United States
1968	United States
1964	United States
1960	United States

Women's Synchronised Swimming – Solo

FIRST HELD 1984

Year	Winner	
1988	C Waldo	Can
1984	T Ruiz	USA

Women's Synchronised Swimming – Duet

FIRST HELD 1984

Year	Winner	
1988	M Cameron & C Waldo	Can
1984	C Costie & T Ruiz	USA

WORLD CHAMPIONS

50 Metres Freestyle

FIRST HELD 1986

Year	Winner	
1991	T Jager	USA
1986	T Jager	USA

FIRST HELD 1973

100 Metres Freestyle

Year	Winner	
1991	M Biondi	USA
1986	M Biondi	USA
1982	J Woithe	GDR
1978	D McCagg	USA
1975	A Coan	USA
1973	J Montgomery	USA

200 Metres Freestyle

Year	Winner	
1991	G Lamberti	Ita
1986	M Gross	FRG
1982	M Gross	FRG
1978	W Forrester	USA
1975	T Shaw	USA
1973	J Montgomery	USA

400 Metres Freestyle

Year	Winner	
1991	J Hoffmann	Ger
1986	R Henkel	FRG
1982	V Salnikov	USSR
1978	V Salnikov	USSR
1975	T Shaw	USA
1973	R DeMont	USA

1500 Metres Freestyle

Year	Winner	
1991	J Hoffmann	Ger
1986	R Henkel	FRG
1982	V Salnikov	USSR
1978	V Salnikov	USSR
1975	T Shaw	USA
1973	S Holland	Aus

100 Metres Backstroke

Year	Winner	
1991	J Rouse	USA
1986	I Polianski	USSR
1982	D Richter	GDR
1978	R Jackson	USA
1975	R Matthes	GDR
1973	R Matthes	GDR

200 Metres Backstroke

Year	Winner	
1991	M Lopez-Zubero	Spa
1986	I Polianski	USSR
1982	R Carey	USA
1978	J Vassallo	USA
1975	Z Verraszto	Hun
1973	R Matthes	GDR

100 Metres Breaststroke

Year	Winner	
1991	N Rozsa	Hun
1986	V Davis	Can
1982	S Lundquist	USA
1978	W Kusch	GDR
1975	D Wilkie	GB
1973	J Hencken	USA

200 Metres Breaststroke

Year	Winner	
1991	M Barrowman	USA
1986	J Szabo	Hun
1982	V Davis	Can
1978	N Nevid	USA
1975	D Wilkie	GB
1973	D Wilkie	GB

100 Metres Butterfly

Year	Winner	
1991	A Nesty	USA
1986	P Morales	USA
1982	M Gribble	USA
1978	J Bottom	USA
1975	G Jagenburg	USA
1973	B Robertson	Can

200 Metres Butterfly

Year	Winner	
1991	M Stewart	USA
1986	M Gross	FRG
1982	M Gross	FRG
1978	M Bruner	USA
1975	W Forrester	USA
1973	R Backhaus	USA

200 Metres Individual Medley

Year	Winner	
1991	T Darnyi	Hun
1986	T Darnyi	Hun
1982	A Sidorenko	USSR
1978	G Smith	Can
1975	A Hargitay	Hun
1973	G Larsson	Swe

400 Metres Individual Medley

Year	Winner	
1991	T Darnyi	Hun
1986	T Darnyi	Hun
1982	R Prado	Bra
1978	J Vassallo	USA
1975	A Hargitay	Hun
1973	A Hargitay	Hun

4 x 100 Metres Freestyle Relay

Year	Winner
1991	United States
1986	United States
1982	United States
1978	United States
1975	United States
1973	United States

4 x 200 Metres Freestyle Relay

Year	Winner
1991	Germany
1986	East Germany
1982	United States
1978	United States
1975	West Germany
1973	United States

4 x 100 Metres Medley Relay

Year	Winner
1991	United States
1986	United States
1982	United States
1978	United States
1975	United States
1973	United States

Women's 50 Metres Freestyle

FIRST HELD 1986

Year	Winner	
1991	Z Yong	CPR
1986	T Costache	Rom

FIRST HELD 1973

Women's 100 Metres Freestyle

Year	Winner	
1991	N Haislett	USA
1986	K Otto	GDR
1982	B Meineke	GDR
1978	B Krause	GDR
1975	K Ender	GDR
1973	K Ender	GDR

Women's 200 Metres Freestyle

Year	Winner	
1991	H Lewis	Aus
1986	H Friedrich	GDR
1982	A Verstappen	Nld
1978	C Woodhead	USA
1975	S Babashoff	USA
1973	K Rothhammer	USA

Women's 400 Metres Freestyle

Year	Winner	
1991	J Evans	USA
1986	H Friedrich	GDR
1982	C Schmidt	GDR
1978	T Wickham	Aus
1975	S Babashoff	USA
1973	H Greenwood	USA

Women's 800 Metres Freestyle

Year	Winner	
1991	J Evans	USA
1986	A Strauss	GDR
1982	K Lineham	USA
1978	T Wickham	Aus
1975	J Turrall	Aus
1973	N Calligaris	Ita

Women's 100 Metres Backstroke

Year	Winner	
1991	K Egerszegi	Hun
1986	B Mitchell	USA
1982	K Otto	GDR
1978	L Jezek	USA
1975	U Richter	GDR
1973	U Richter	GDR

Women's 200 Metres Backstroke

Year	Winner	
1991	K Egerszegi	Hun
1986	C Sirch	GDR
1982	C Sirch	GDR
1978	L Jezek	USA
1975	B Treiber	GDR
1973	M Belote	USA

Women's 100 Metres Breaststroke

Year	Winner	
1991	L Frame	Aus
1986	S Gerasch	GDR
1982	U Geweniger	GDR
1978	Y Bogdanova	USSR
1975	H Anke	GDR
1973	R Vogel	GDR

Women's 200 Metres Breaststroke

Year	Winner	
1991	Y Volkova	USSR
1986	S Horner	GDR
1982	S Varganova	USSR
1978	L Kachushite	USSR
1975	H Anke	GDR
1973	R Vogel	GDR

Women's 100 Metres Butterfly

Year	Winner	
1991	Q Hong	CPR
1986	K Gressler	GDR
1982	M Meagher	USA
1978	M Pennington	USA
1975	K Ender	GDR
1973	K Ender	GDR

Women's 200 Metres Butterfly

Year	Winner	
1991	S Sanders	USA
1986	M Meagher	USA
1982	I Geissler	GDR
1978	T Caulkins	USA
1975	R Kother	GDR
1973	R Kother	GDR

Women's 200 Metres Individual Medley

Year	Winner	
1991	L Li	CPR
1986	K Otto	GDR
1982	P Schneider	GDR
1978	T Caulkins	USA
1975	K Heddy	USA
1973	A Hubner	GDR

Women's 400 Metres Individual Medley

Year	Winner	
1991	L Li	CPR
1986	K Nord	GDR
1982	P Schneider	GDR
1978	T Caulkins	USA
1975	U Tauber	GDR
1973	G Wegner	GDR

Women's 4 x 100 Metres Freestyle Relay

Year	Winner
1991	United States
1986	East Germany
1982	East Germany
1978	United States
1975	East Germany
1973	East Germany

Women's 4 x 100 Metres Medley Relay

Year	Winner
1991	United States
1986	East Germany
1982	East Germany
1978	United States
1975	East Germany
1973	East Germany

Women's 4 x 200 Metres Freestyle Relay

FIRST HELD 1986

Year	Winner
1991	Germany
1986	East Germany

FIRST HELD 1973

Women's Synchronised Swimming – Solo

Year	Winner	
1991	S Frechette	Can
1986	C Waldo	Can
1982	T Ruiz	USA
1978	H Vanderburg	Can
1975	G Buzonas	USA
1973	T Andersen	USA

Women's Synchronised Swimming – Duet

Year	Winner	
1991	S & K Josephson	USA
1986	C Waldo & M Cameron	Can

Year	Winner	
1982	K Kryczka & S Hambrook	Can
1978	M Calkins & H Vanderburg	Can
1975	R Curren & A Norrish	USA
1973	T Andersen & G Johnson	USA

Women's Synchronised Swimming – Team

Year	Winner
1991	United States
1986	Canada
1982	Canada
1978	United States
1975	United States
1973	United States

TABLE TENNIS

WORLD CHAMPIONS
Men's Singles

FIRST HELD 1927

Year	Winner	
1991	J Persson	Swe
1989	J Waldner	Swe
1987	J Jialiang	CPR
1985	J Jialiang	CPR
1983	G Yue-Hua	CPR
1981	G Yue-Hua	CPR
1979	S Ono	Jap
1977	M Kohno	Jap
1975	I Jonyer	Hun

Year	Winner	
1973	H En-ting	CPR
1971	S Bengtsson	Swe
1969	S Ito	Jap
1967	N Hasegawa	Jap
1965	C Tse-tung	CPR
1963	C Tse-tung	CPR
1961	C Tse-tung	CPR
1959	J Kuo-tuan	CPR
1957	T Tanaka	Jap
1956	I Ogimura	Jap
1955	T Tanaka	Jap
1954	I Ogimura	Jap
1953	F Sido	Hun
1952	H Satoh	Jap
1951	J Leach	GB

Year	Winner	
1950	R Bergmann	GB
1949	J Leach	GB
1948	R Bergmann	GB
1947	B Vana	Cze
1946/40	No Competition	
1939	R Bergmann	Aut
1938	B Vana	Cze
1937	R Bergmann	Aut
1936	S Kolar	Cze
1935	V Barna	Hun
1934	V Barna	Hun
1933	V Barna	Hun
1932	V Barna	Hun
1931	M Szabados	Hun
1930	V Barna	Hun
1929	F Perry	GB
1928	Z Mechlovits	Hun
1927	R Jacobi	Hun

Men's Doubles

FIRST HELD 1927

Year	Winner	
1991	P Karlsson & T von Scheele	Swe
1989	J Rosskopf & S Fetzner	FRG
1987	C Longcan & W Qingguang	CPR
1985	M Appelgren & U Carlsson	Swe
1983	D Surbek & Z Kalinic	Yug
1981	C Zhen-Hua & L Zhen-Shi	CPR
1979	D Surbek & A Stipancic	Yug
1977	L Zhenshi & L Geliang	CPR
1975	G Gergely & I Jonyer	Hun
1973	S Bengtsson & K Johansson	Swe
1971	I Jonyer & T Klampar	Hun
1969	H Alser & K Johansson	Swe
1967	H Alser & K Johansson	Swe
1965	C Tse-Tung & H Yin-Sheng	CPR
1963	C Shih-Lin & W Chih-Liang	CPR
1961	N Hoshino & K Kimura	Jap
1959	I Ogimura & T Murakami	Jap
1957	L Andreadis & L Stipek	Cze
1956	I Ogimura & Y Tomita	Jap
1955	I Andreadis & L Stipek	Cze
1954	V Harangozo & Z Dolinar	Yug
1953	J Koczian & F Sido	Hun
1952	N Fujii & T Hayashi	Jap
1951	B Vana & I Andreadis	Cze
1950	F Sido & F Soos	Hun
1949	F Tokar & I Andreadis	Cze
1948	B Vana & L Stipek	Cze
1947	B Vana & A Slar	Cze
1946/40	No Competition	
1939	V Barna (Hun) & R Bergmann (Aut)	
1938	S Schiff & J McClure	USA
1937	R Blattner & J McClure	USA
1936	R Blattner & J McClure	USA
1935	V Barna & M Szabados	Hun
1934	V Barna & M Szabados	Hun
1933	V Barna & S Glancz	Hun
1932	V Barna & M Szabados	Hun
1931	V Barna & M Szabados	Hun

Year	Winner	
1930	V Barna &	
	M Szabados	Hun
1929	V Barna &	
	M Szabados	Hun
1928	A Liebster & R Thum	Aut
1927	R Jacobi & D Pesci	Hun

Year	Winner	
1935	M Kettnerova	Cze
1934	M Kettnerova	Cze
1933	A Sipos	Hun
1932	A Sipos	Hun
1931	M Mednyanszky	Hun
1930	M Mednyanszky	Hun
1929	M Mednyanszky	Hun
1928	M Mednyanszky	Hun
1927	M Mednyanszky	Hun

Women's Singles

FIRST HELD 1927

Year	Winner	
1991	D Yaping	CPR
1989	Q Hong	CPR
1987	H Zhili	CPR
1985	C Yan-Hua	CPR
1983	C Yan-Hua	CPR
1981	T Ling	CPR
1979	K Hsin-Ai	CPR
1977	P Yung-Sun	DPRK
1975	P Yung-Sun	DPRK
1973	Hu Yu-Lan	CPR
1971	L Hui-Ching	CPR
1969	T Kowada	Jap
1967	S Morisawa	Jap
1965	N Fukazu	Jap
1963	K Matsuzaki	Jap
1961	C Chung-hui	CPR
1959	K Matsuzaki	Jap
1957	F Eguchi	Jap
1956	T Okawa	Jap
1955	A Rozeanu	Rom
1954	A Rozeanu	Rom
1953	A Rozeanu	Rom
1952	A Rozeanu	Rom
1951	A Rozeanu	Rom
1950	A Rozeanu	Rom
1949	G Farkas	Hun
1948	G Farkas	Hun
1947	G Farkas	Hun
1946/40	No Competition	
1939	V Depetrisova	Cze
1938	T Pritzi	Aut
1937	Not completed	
1936	R Aarons	USA

Women's Doubles

FIRST HELD 1928

Year	Winner	
1991	C Zihe & G Jun	CPR
1989	Q Hong & D Yaping	CPR
1987	Y Young-Ja &	
	H Jung-Hua	RoK
1985	D Lili & G Lijuan	CPR
1983	S Jianping & D Lili	CPR
1981	C Yan-Hua &	
	Z Deijing	CPR
1979	Z Li & Z Deijing	CPR
1977	P Yong Ok (DPRK) &	
	Y Yin (CPR)	
1975	M Alexandru (Rom) &	
	S Takashima (Jap)	
1973	M Alexandru (Rom) &	
	M Hamada (Jap)	
1971	C Min-Chih &	
	L Hui-Ching	CPR
1969	S Grinberg &	
	Z Rudnova	USSR
1967	S Hirota &	
	S Morisawa	Jap
1965	C Min-Chih &	
	L Hui-Ching	CPR
1963	K Matsuzaki & M Seki	Jap
1961	M Alexandru &	
	G Pitica	Rom
1959	T Namba &	
	K Yamaizumi	Jap
1957	L Mosoczy &	
	A Simon	Hun

Year	Winner	
1956	A Rozeanu & F Zeller	Rom
1955	A Rozeanu & F Zeller	Rom
1954	D Rowe & R Rowe	GB
1953	G Farkas (Hun) & A Rozeanu (Rom)	
1952	S Narahara & T Nishimura	Jap
1951	D Rowe & R Rowe	GB
1950	D Beregi & H Elliot	GB
1949	H Elliot (GB) & G Farkas (Hun)	
1948	V Thomas & M Franks	GB
1947	G Farkas (Hun) & T Pritzi (Aut)	
1946/40	No Competition	
1939	T Pritzi & H Bussmann	Aut
1938	V Depetrisova & V Votrubcova	Cze
1937	V Depetrisova & V Votrubcova	Cze
1936	M Kettnerova & M Smidova	Cze
1935	M Mednyanszky & A Sipos	Hun
1934	M Mednyanszky & A Sipos	Hun
1933	M Mednyanszky & A Sipos	Hun
1932	M Mednyanszky & A Sipos	Hun
1931	M Mednyanszky & A Sipos	Hun
1930	M Mednyanszky & A Sipos	Hun
1929	E Metzger & E Ruester	Ger
1928	M Mednyanszky (Hun) & F Flamm (Aut)	

Mixed Doubles

FIRST HELD 1927

Year	Winner	
1991	W Tao & L Wei	CPR
1989	H Jung-Hwa & Yoo Nam-Kyu	RoK
1987	G Lijuan & H Lun	CPR
1985	C Yan-Hua & C Zhenhua	CPR
1983	N Xialin & G Yue-Hua	CPR
1981	H Junquin & X Saike	CPR
1979	K Hsin-Ai & L Geliang	CPR
1977	C Bergeret & J Secretin	Fra
1975	A Ferdman & S Gomozkov	USSR
1973	Li Li & L Geliang	CPR
1971	L Hui-Ching & C Shih-Lin	CPR
1969	Y Konno & N Hasegawa	Jap
1967	N Yamanaka & N Hasegawa	Jap
1965	M Seki & K Kimura	Jap
1963	K Ito & K Kimura	Jap
1961	K Matsuzaki & I Ogimura	Jap
1959	F Eguchi & I Ogimura	Jap
1957	F Eguchi & I Ogimura	Jap
1956	L Neuberger & E Klein	USA
1955	E Koczian & K Szepesi	Hun
1954	G Farkas (Hun) & I Andeadis (Cze)	
1953	A Rozeanu (Rom) & F Sido (Hun)	
1952	A Rozeanu (Rom) & F Sido (Hun)	
1951	A Rozeanu (Rom) & B Vana (Cze)	
1950	G Farkas & S Sido	Hun
1949	G Farkas & S Sido	Hun

Year	Winner		Year	Winner
1948	T Thall & R Miles	USA	1971	China
1947	G Farkas & F Soos	Hun	1969	Japan
1946/40	No Competition		1967	Japan
1939	V Votrubcova & B Vana	Cze	1965	China
1938	W Woodhead (GB) & L Bellak (Hun)		1963	China
1937	V Votrubcova & B Vana	Cze	1961	China
1936	G Kleinova & M Hamr	Cze	1959	Japan
1935	A Sipos & V Barna	Hun	1957	Japan
1934	M Mednyanszky & M Szabados	Hun	1956	Japan
1933	M Mednyanszky & I Kelen	Hun	1955	Japan
1932	A Sipos & V Barna	Hun	1954	Japan
1931	M Mednyanszky & M Szabados	Hun	1953	England
1930	M Mednyanszky & M Szabados	Hun	1952	Hungary
1929	A Sipos & I Kelen	Hun	1951	Czechoslovakia
1928	M Mednyanszky & Z Mechlovits	Hun	1950	Czechoslovakia
1927	M Mednyanszky & Z Mechlovits	Hun	1949	Hungary
			1948	Czechoslovakia
			1947	Czechoslovakia
			1946/40	No Competition
			1939	Czechoslovakia
			1938	Hungary
			1937	United States
			1936	Austria
			1935	Hungary
			1934	Hungary
			1933	Hungary
			1932	Czechoslovakia
			1931	Hungary
			1930	Hungary
			1929	Hungary
			1928	Hungary
			1927	Hungary

SWAYTHLING CUP

Men's World Team Champions

FIRST HELD 1927

Year	Winner
1991	Sweden
1989	Sweden
1987	China
1985	China
1983	China
1981	China
1979	Hungary
1977	China
1975	China
1973	Sweden

CORBILLON CUP

Women's World Team Champions

FIRST HELD 1934

Year	Winner
1991	Korea
1989	China
1987	China
1985	China

Year	Winner
1983	China
1981	China
1979	China
1977	China
1975	China
1973	South Korea
1971	Japan
1969	USSR
1967	Japan
1965	China
1963	Japan
1961	Japan
1958	Japan
1957	Japan
1956	Romania
1955	Romania
1954	Japan
1953	Romania
1952	Japan
1951	Romania
1950	Romania
1949	United States
1948	England
1947	England
1946/40	No Competition
1939	Germany
1938	Czechoslovakia
1937	United States
1936	Czechoslovakia
1935	Czechoslovakia
1934	Germany

OLYMPIC CHAMPIONS

FIRST HELD 1988

Men's Singles

Year	Winner	
1988	Yoo Nam-Kyu	RoK

Men's Doubles

Year	Winner	
1988	C Longcan & W Qingguang	CPR

Women's Singles

Year	Winner	
1988	Chen Jing	CPR

Women's Doubles

Year	Winner	
1988	H Jung-Hwa & Y Young-Ja	RoK

TENNIS

ALL-ENGLAND CHAMPIONS

Men's Singles

FIRST HELD 1877

Year	Winner	
1991	M Stich	Ger
1990	S Edberg	Swe
1989	B Becker	FRG
1988	S Edberg	Swe
1987	P Cash	Aus
1986	B Becker	FRG
1985	B Becker	FRG
1984	J McEnroe	USA
1983	J McEnroe	USA
1982	J Connors	USA
1981	J McEnroe	USA
1980	B Borg	Swe
1979	B Borg	Swe
1978	B Borg	Swe
1977	B Borg	Swe
1976	B Borg	Swe
1975	A Ashe	USA
1974	J Connors	USA
1973	J Kodes	Cze
1972	S Smith	USA
1971	J Newcombe	Aus
1970	J Newcombe	Aus
1969	R Laver	Aus
1968	R Laver	Aus
1967	J Newcombe	Aus
1966	M Santana	Spa
1965	R Emerson	Aus
1964	R Emerson	Aus
1963	C McKinley	USA
1962	R Laver	Aus
1961	R Laver	Aus
1960	N Fraser	Aus
1959	A Olmedo	USA
1958	A Cooper	Aus
1957	L Hoad	Aus
1956	L Hoad	Aus

Year	Winner	
1955	M A Trabert	USA
1954	J Drobny	Egy
1953	E V Seixas	USA
1952	F Sedgman	Aus
1951	R Savitt	USA
1950	J E Patty	USA
1949	F Schroeder	USA
1948	R Falkenburg	USA
1947	J Kramer	USA
1946	Y Petra	Fra
1945/40	No Competition	
1939	R Riggs	USA
1938	J D Budge	USA
1937	J D Budge	USA
1936	F Perry	GB
1935	F Perry	GB
1934	F Perry	GB
1933	J Crawford	Aus
1932	E Vines	USA
1931	S Wood	USA
1930	W Tilden	USA
1929	H Cochet	Fra
1928	R Lacoste	Fra
1927	H Cochet	Fra
1926	J Borotra	Fra
1925	R Lacoste	Fra
1924	J Borotra	Fra
1923	W Johnston	USA
1922	G Patterson	Aus
1921	W Tilden	USA
1920	W Tilden	USA
1919	G Patterson	Aus
1918/15	No Competition	
1914	N Brookes	Aus
1913	A Wilding	NZ
1912	A Wilding	NZ
1911	A Wilding	NZ
1910	A Wilding	NZ
1909	A W Gore	GB
1908	A W Gore	GB
1907	N Brookes	Aus
1906	H L Doherty	GB

Year	Winner	
1905	H L Doherty	GB
1904	H L Doherty	GB
1903	H L Doherty	GB
1902	H L Doherty	GB
1901	A W Gore	GB
1900	R F Doherty	GB
1899	R F Doherty	GB
1898	R F Doherty	GB
1897	R F Doherty	GB
1896	H Mahoney	GB
1895	W Baddeley	GB
1894	J Pim	GB
1893	J Pim	GB
1892	W Baddeley	GB
1891	W Baddeley	GB
1890	W Hamilton	GB
1889	W Renshaw	GB
1888	E Renshaw	GB
1887	H F Lawford	GB
1886	W Renshaw	GB
1885	W Renshaw	GB
1884	W Renshaw	GB
1883	W Renshaw	GB
1882	W Renshaw	GB
1881	W Renshaw	GB
1880	Rev J T Hartley	GB
1879	Rev J T Hartley	GB
1878	P F Hadow	GB
1877	S W Gore	GB

Men's Doubles

FIRST HELD 1879

Year	Winner	
1991	J Fitzgerald (Aus) & A Jarryd (Swe)	
1990	R Leach & J Pugh	USA
1989	J Fitzgerald (Aus) & A Jarryd (Swe)	
1988	K Flach & R Seguso	USA
1987	K Flach & R Seguso	USA
1986	J Nystrom & M Wilander	Swe
1985	H Gunthardt (Swi) & B Taroczy (Hun)	

Year	Winner	
1984	P Fleming & J McEnroe	USA
1983	P Fleming & J McEnroe	USA
1982	P McNamara & P McNamee	Aus
1981	P Fleming & J McEnroe	USA
1980	P McNamara & P McNamee	Aus
1979	P Fleming & J McEnroe	USA
1978	R Hewitt & F McMillan	SA
1977	R Case & G Masters	Aus
1976	B Gottfried (USA) & R Ramirez (Mex)	
1975	V Gerulaitis & A Mayer	USA
1974	J Newcombe & A Roche	Aus
1973	J Connors (USA) & I Nastase (Rom)	
1972	R Hewitt & F McMillan	SA
1971	R Emerson & R Laver	Aus
1970	J Newcombe & A Roche	Aus
1969	J Newcombe & A Roche	Aus
1968	J Newcombe & A Roche	Aus
1967	R Hewitt & F McMillan	SA
1966	K Fletcher & J Newcombe	Aus
1965	J Newcombe & A Roche	Aus
1964	R Hewitt & F Stolle	Aus
1963	R Osuna & A Palafox	Mex
1962	R Hewitt & F Stolle	Aus
1961	R Emerson & N Fraser	Aus

Year	Winner		Year	Winner	
1960	R Osuna (Mex) &		1927	F Hunter &	
	R D Ralston (USA)			W Tilden	USA
1959	R Emerson &		1926	J Brugnon &	
	N Fraser	Aus		H Cochet	Fra
1958	S Davidson &		1925	J Borotra &	
	U Schmidt	Swe		R Lacoste	Fra
1957	G Mulloy &		1924	F Hunter &	
	J E Patty	USA		V Richards	USA
1956	L Hoad &		1923	L Godfree & R Lycett	GB
	K Rosewall	Aus	1922	J Anderson (Aus) &	
1955	R Hartwig & L Hoad	Aus		R Lycett (GB)	
1954	R Hartwig & M Rose	Aus	1921	R Lycett &	
1953	L Hoad & K Rosewall	Aus		M Woosnam	GB
1952	K McGregor &		1920	C Garland &	
	F Sedgman	Aus		R Williams	USA
1951	K McGregor &		1919	P O'Hara-Wood &	
	F Sedgman	Aus		R Thomas	Aus
1950	J Bromwich &		1918/15	No Competition	
	A Quist	Aus	1914	N Brookes (Aus) &	
1949	R Gonzales &			A Wilding (NZ)	
	F Parker	USA	1913	C Dixon &	
1948	J Bromwich &			H Roper Barrett	GB
	F Sedgman	Aus	1912	C Dixon &	
1947	R Falkenburg &			H Roper Barrett	GB
	J Kramer	USA	1911	M Decugis &	
1946	T Brown &			A Gobert	Fra
	J Kramer	USA	1910	M Ritchie (GB) &	
1945/40	No Competition			A Wilding (NZ)	
1939	E Cooke & R Riggs	USA	1909	A Gore &	
1938	J D Budge &			H Roper Barrett	GB
	G Mako	USA	1908	M Ritchie (GB) &	
1937	J D Budge &			A Wilding (NZ)	
	G Mako	USA	1907	N Brookes (Aus) &	
1936	G Hughes &			A Wilding (NZ)	
	C Tuckey	GB	1906	F Riseley & S Smith	GB
1935	J Crawford & A Quist	Aus	1905	H L Doherty &	
1934	G Lott & L Stoefen	USA		R F Doherty	GB
1933	J Borotra & J Brugnon	Fra	1904	H L Doherty &	
1932	J Borotra & J Brugnon	Fra		R F Doherty	GB
1931	G Lott & J Van Ryn	USA	1903	H L Doherty &	
1930	W Allison &			R F Doherty	GB
	J Van Ryn	USA	1902	F Riseley & S Smith	GB
1929	W Allison &		1901	H L Doherty &	
	J Van Ryn	USA		R F Doherty	GB
1928	J Brugnon &		1900	H L Doherty &	
	H Cochet	Fra		R F Doherty	GB

Year	Winner	
1899	H L Doherty & R F Doherty	GB
1898	H L Doherty & R F Doherty	GB
1897	H L Doherty & R F Doherty	GB
1896	H Baddeley & W Baddeley	GB
1895	H Baddeley & W Baddeley	GB
1894	H Baddeley & W Baddeley	GB
1893	J Pim & F Stoker	GB
1892	H Barlow & E Lewis	GB
1891	H Baddeley & W Baddeley	GB
1890	J Pim & F Stoker	GB
1889	E Renshaw & W Renshaw	GB
1888	E Renshaw & W Renshaw	GB
1887	P Bowes-Lyon & H Wilberforce	GB
1886	E Renshaw & W Renshaw	GB
1885	E Renshaw & W Renshaw	GB
1884	E Renshaw & W Renshaw	GB
1883	C Grinstead & C Weldon	GB
1882	Rev J T Hartley & R Richardson	GB
1881	E Renshaw & W Renshaw	GB
1880	E Renshaw & W Renshaw	GB
1879	L Erskine & H Lawford	GB

Women's Singles

FIRST HELD 1884

Year	Winner	
1991	S Graf	Ger
1990	M Navratilova	USA
1989	S Graf	FRG
1988	S Graf	FRG
1987	M Navratilova	USA
1986	M Navratilova	USA
1985	M Navratilova	USA
1984	M Navratilova	USA
1983	M Navratilova	USA
1982	M Navratilova	USA
1981	C Evert-Lloyd	USA
1980	E Cawley	Aus
1979	M Navratilova	Cze
1978	M Navratilova	Cze
1977	V Wade	GB
1976	C Evert	USA
1975	B J King	USA
1974	C Evert	USA
1973	B J King	USA
1972	B J King	USA
1971	E Goolagong	Aus
1970	M Court	Aus
1969	A Jones	GB
1968	B J King	USA
1967	B J King	USA
1966	B J King	USA
1965	M Smith	Aus
1964	M Bueno	Bra
1963	M Smith	Aus
1962	K Susman	USA
1961	A Mortimer	GB
1960	M Bueno	Bra
1959	M Bueno	Bra
1958	A Gibson	USA
1957	A Gibson	USA
1956	S Fry	USA
1955	A L Brough	USA
1954	M Connolly	USA
1953	M Connolly	USA
1952	M Connolly	USA
1951	D Hart	USA
1950	A L Brough	USA
1949	A L Brough	USA

Year	Winner	
1948	A L Brough	USA
1947	M Osborne	USA
1946	P Betz	USA
1945/40	No Competition	
1939	A Marble	USA
1938	H Moody	USA
1937	D Round	GB
1936	H Jacobs	USA
1935	H Moody	USA
1934	D Round	GB
1933	H Moody	USA
1932	H Moody	USA
1931	C Aussem	Ger
1930	H Moody	USA
1929	H Wills	USA
1928	H Wills	USA
1927	H Wills	USA
1926	K Godfree	GB
1925	S Lenglen	Fra
1924	K McKane	GB
1923	S Lenglen	Fra
1922	S Lenglen	Fra
1921	S Lenglen	Fra
1920	S Lenglen	Fra
1919	S Lenglen	Fra
1918/15	No Competition	
1914	D Lambert Chambers	GB
1913	D Lambert Chambers	GB
1912	E Larcombe	GB
1911	D Lambert Chambers	GB
1910	D Lambert Chambers	GB
1909	D Boothby	GB
1908	C Sterry	GB
1907	M Sutton	USA
1906	D Douglass	GB
1905	M Sutton	USA
1904	D Douglass	GB
1903	D Douglass	GB
1902	M Robb	GB
1901	C Sterry	GB
1900	B Hillyard	GB
1899	B Hillyard	GB
1898	C Cooper	GB
1897	B Hillyard	GB
1896	C Cooper	GB
1895	C Cooper	GB

Year	Winner	
1894	B Hillyard	GB
1893	C Dod	GB
1892	C Dod	GB
1891	C Dod	GB
1890	H Rice	GB
1889	B Hillyard	GB
1888	C Dod	GB
1887	C Dod	GB
1886	B Bingley	GB
1885	M Watson	GB
1884	M Watson	GB

Women's Doubles

FIRST HELD 1913

Year	Winner	
1991	L Savchenko & N Zvereva	USSR
1990	J Novotna & H Sukova	Cze
1989	J Novotna & H Sukova	Cze
1988	S Graf (FRG) & G Sabatini (Arg)	
1987	C Kohde-Kilsch (FRG) & H Sukova (Cze)	
1986	M Navratilova & P Shriver	USA
1985	K Jordan (USA) & E Smylie (Aus)	
1984	M Navratilova & P Shriver	USA
1983	M Navratilova & P Shriver	USA
1982	M Navratilova & P Shriver	USA
1981	M Navratilova (Cze) & P Shriver (USA)	
1980	K Jordan & A Smith	USA
1979	B J King (USA) & M Navratilova (Cze)	
1978	K Reid & W Turnbull	Aus
1977	E Cawley (Aus) & J Russell (USA)	

Year	Winner	
1976	C Evert (USA) &	
	M Navratilova (Cze)	
1975	A Kiyomura (USA) &	
	K Sawamatsu (Jap)	
1974	E Goolagong (Aus) &	
	M Michel (USA)	
1973	R Casals & B J King	USA
1972	B J King (USA) &	
	B Stove (Ndl)	
1971	R Casals & B J King	USA
1970	R Casals & B J King	USA
1969	M Court & J Tegart	Aus
1968	R Casals & B J King	USA
1967	R Casals & B J King	USA
1966	M Bueno (Bra) &	
	N Richey (USA)	
1965	M Bueno (Bra) &	
	B J Moffitt (USA)	
1964	M Smith & L Turner	Aus
1963	M Bueno (Bra) &	
	D Hard (USA)	
1962	K Susman &	
	B J Moffitt	USA
1961	K Hantze &	
	B J Moffitt	USA
1960	M Bueno (Bra) &	
	D Hard (USA)	
1959	J Arth & D Hard	USA
1958	M Bueno (Bra) &	
	A Gibson (USA)	
1957	A Gibson & D Hard	USA
1956	A Buxton (GB) &	
	A Gibson (USA)	
1955	A Mortimer &	
	J Shilcock	GB
1954	A L Brough &	
	M du Pont	USA
1953	S Fry & D Hart	USA
1952	S Fry & D Hart	USA
1951	S Fry & D Hart	USA
1950	A L Brough &	
	M du Pont	USA
1949	A L Brough &	
	M du Pont	USA
1948	A L Brough &	
	M du Pont	USA

Year	Winner	
1947	D Hart & P Todd	USA
1946	A L Brough &	
	M Osborne	USA
1945/40	No Competition	
1939	S Fabyan &	
	A Marble	USA
1938	S Fabyan &	
	A Marble	USA
1937	S Mathieu (Fra) &	
	A Yorke (GB)	
1936	F James &	
	K Stammers	GB
1935	F James &	
	K Stammers	GB
1934	S Mathieu (Fra) &	
	E Ryan (USA)	
1933	S Mathieu (Fra) &	
	E Ryan (USA)	
1932	D Metaxa (Fra) &	
	J Sigart (Bel)	
1931	D Shepherd-Barron &	
	P Mudford	GB
1930	H Moody & E Ryan	USA
1929	L Mitchell &	
	M Watson	GB
1928	P Saunders &	
	M Watson	GB
1927	H Wills & E Ryan	USA
1926	M Browne & E Ryan	USA
1925	S Lenglen (Fra) &	
	E Ryan (USA)	
1924	H Wightman &	
	H Wills	USA
1923	S Lenglen (Fra) &	
	E Ryan (USA)	
1922	S Lenglen (Fra) &	
	E Ryan (USA)	
1921	S Lenglen (Fra) &	
	E Ryan (USA)	
1920	S Lenglen (Fra) &	
	E Ryan (USA)	
1919	S Lenglen (Fra) &	
	E Ryan (USA)	
1918/15	No Competition	
1914	A Morton (GB) &	
	E Ryan (USA)	

Year	Winner	
1913	R McNair & D Boothby	GB

Mixed Doubles

FIRST HELD 1913

Year	Winner	
1991	J Fitzgerald & E Smylie	Aus
1990	R Leach & Z Garrison	USA
1989	J Pugh (USA) & J Novotna (Cze)	
1988	S Stewart & Z Garrison	USA
1987	J Bates & J Durie	GB
1986	K Flach & K Jordan	USA
1985	P McNamee (Aus) & M Navratilova (USA)	
1984	J Lloyd (GB) & W Turnbull (Aus)	
1983	J Lloyd (GB) & W Turnbull (Aus)	
1982	K Curren (SA) & A Smith (USA)	
1981	F McMillan (SA) & B Stove (Ndl)	
1980	J Austin & T Austin	USA
1979	R Hewitt & G Stevens	SA
1978	F McMillan (SA) & B Stove (Ndl)	
1977	R Hewitt & G Stevens	SA
1976	A Roche (Aus) & F Durr (Fra)	
1975	M Reissen (USA) & M Court (Aus)	
1974	O Davidson (Aus) & B J King (USA)	
1973	O Davidson (Aus) & B J King (USA)	
1972	I Nastase (Rom) & R Casals (USA)	
1971	O Davidson (Aus) & B J King (USA)	
1970	I Nastase (Rom) & R Casals (USA)	
1969	F Stolle (Aus) & A Jones (GB)	
1968	K Fletcher & M Court	Aus
1967	O Davidson (Aus) & B J King (USA)	
1966	K Fletcher & M Smith	Aus
1965	K Fletcher & M Smith	Aus
1964	F Stolle & L Turner	Aus
1963	K Fletcher & M Smith	Aus
1962	N Fraser (Aus) & M du Pont (USA)	
1961	F Stolle & L Turner	Aus
1960	R Laver (Aus) & D Hard (USA)	
1959	R Laver (Aus) & D Hard (USA)	
1958	R Howe & L Coghlan	Aus
1957	M Rose (Aus) & D Hard (USA)	
1956	E V Seixas & S Fry	USA
1955	E V Seixas & D Hart	USA
1954	E V Seixas & D Hart	USA
1953	E V Seixas & D Hart	USA
1952	F Sedgman (Aus) & D Hart (USA)	
1951	F Sedgman (Aus) & D Hart (USA)	
1950	E Sturgess (SA) & A L Brough (USA)	
1949	E Sturgess & S Summers	SA
1948	J Bromwich (Aus) & A L Brough (USA)	
1947	J Bromwich (Aus) & A L Brough (USA)	
1946	T Brown & A L Brough	USA
1945/40	No Competition	
1939	R Riggs & A Marble	USA

Year	Winner	
1938	J D Budge &	
	A Marble	USA
1937	J D Budge &	
	A Marble	USA
1936	F Perry & D Round	GB
1935	F Perry & D Round	GB
1934	R Miki (Jap) &	
	D Round (GB)	
1933	G von Cramm &	
	H Krahwinkel	Ger
1932	E Maier (Spa) &	
	E Ryan (USA)	
1931	G Lott & A Harper	USA
1930	J Crawford (Aus) &	
	E Ryan (USA)	
1929	F Hunter & H Wills	USA
1928	P Spence (SA) &	
	E Ryan (USA)	
1927	F Hunter & E Ryan	USA
1926	L Godfree &	
	K Godfree	GB
1925	J Borotra & S Lenglen	Fra
1924	J Gilbert &	
	K McKane	GB
1923	R Lycett (GB) &	
	E Ryan (USA)	
1922	P O'Hara-Wood (Aus) &	
	S Lenglen (Fra)	
1921	R Lycett (GB) &	
	E Ryan (USA)	
1920	G Patterson (Aus) &	
	S Lenglen (Fra)	
1919	R Lycett (GB) &	
	E Ryan (USA)	
1918/15	No Competition	
1914	J Parke & E Larcombe	GB
1913	H Crisp & A Tuckey	GB

UNITED STATES CHAMPIONS

Men's Singles

FIRST HELD 1881

Year	Winner	
1991	S Edberg	Swe
1990	P Sampras	USA
1989	B Becker	FRG
1988	M Wilander	Swe
1987	I Lendl	Cze
1986	I Lendl	Cze
1985	I Lendl	Cze
1984	J McEnroe	USA
1983	J Connors	USA
1982	J Connors	USA
1981	J McEnroe	USA
1980	J McEnroe	USA
1979	J McEnroe	USA
1978	J Connors	USA
1977	G Vilas	Arg
1976	J Connors	USA
1975	M Orantes	Spa
1974	J Connors	USA
1973	J Newcombe	Aus
1972	I Nastase	Rom
1971	S Smith	USA
1970	K Rosewall	Aus
1969	R Laver (Open)	Aus
1969	S Smith (Amateur)	USA
1968	A Ashe (Amateur)	USA
1968	A Ashe (Open)	USA
1967	J Newcombe	Aus
1966	F Stolle	Aus
1965	M Santana	Spa
1964	R Emerson	Aus
1963	R Osuna	Mex
1962	R Laver	Aus
1961	R Emerson	Aus
1960	N Fraser	Aus
1959	N Fraser	Aus
1958	A Cooper	Aus
1957	M Anderson	Aus
1956	K Rosewall	Aus
1955	M A Trabert	USA
1954	E V Seixas	USA

Year	Winner		Year	Winner	
1953	M A Trabert	USA	1907	W Larned	USA
1952	F Sedgman	Aus	1906	W Clothier	USA
1951	F Sedgman	Aus	1905	B Wright	USA
1950	A Larsen	USA	1904	H Ward	USA
1949	R Gonzales	USA	1903	H L Doherty	GB
1948	R Gonzales	USA	1902	W Larned	USA
1947	J Kramer	USA	1901	W Larned	USA
1946	J Kramer	USA	1900	M Whitman	USA
1945	F Parker	USA	1899	M Whitman	USA
1944	F Parker	USA	1898	M Whitman	USA
1943	J Hunt	USA	1897	R Wrenn	USA
1942	F Schroeder	USA	1896	R Wrenn	USA
1941	R Riggs	USA	1895	F Hovey	USA
1940	W McNeill	USA	1894	R Wrenn	USA
1939	R Riggs	USA	1893	R Wrenn	USA
1938	J D Budge	USA	1892	O Campbell	USA
1937	J D Budge	USA	1891	O Campbell	USA
1936	F Perry	GB	1890	O Campbell	USA
1935	W Allison	USA	1889	H Slocum	USA
1934	F Perry	GB	1888	H Slocum	USA
1933	F Perry	GB	1887	R Sears	USA
1932	H Vines	USA	1886	R Sears	USA
1931	H Vines	USA	1885	R Sears	USA
1930	J Doeg	USA	1884	R Sears	USA
1929	W Tilden	USA	1883	R Sears	USA
1928	H Cochet	Fra	1882	R Sears	USA
1927	R Lacoste	Fra	1881	R Sears	USA
1926	R Lacoste	Fra			
1925	W Tilden	USA			
1924	W Tilden	USA			
1923	W Tilden	USA		Men's Doubles	
1922	W Tilden	USA			
1921	W Tilden	USA	**FIRST HELD 1881**		
1920	W Tilden	USA	Year	Winner	
1919	W Johnston	USA			
1918	R Murray	USA	1991	J Fitzgerald (Aus) & A Jarryd (Swe)	
1917	Not held				
1916	R Williams	USA	1990	P Aldrich & D Visser	SA
1915	W Johnston	USA	1989	J McEnroe (USA) & M Woodforde (Aus)	
1914	R Williams	USA			
1913	M McLoughlin	USA	1988	S Casal & E Sanchez	Spa
1912	M McLoughlin	USA	1987	S Edberg & A Jarryd	Swe
1911	W Larned	USA	1986	A Gomez (Ecu) & S Zivojinovic (Yug)	
1910	W Larned	USA			
1909	W Larned	USA	1985	K Flach & R Seguso	USA
1908	W Larned	USA			

Men's Doubles

FIRST HELD 1881

Year	Winner	
1984	J Fitzgerald (Aus) & T Smid (Cze)	
1983	P Fleming & J McEnroe	USA
1982	K Curren (SA) & S Denton (USA)	
1981	P Fleming & J McEnroe	USA
1980	R Lutz & S Smith	USA
1979	P Fleming & J McEnroe	USA
1978	R Lutz & S Smith	USA
1977	R Hewitt & F McMillan	SA
1976	T Okker (Nld) & M Riessen (USA)	
1975	J Connors (USA) & I Nastase (Rom)	
1974	R Lutz & S Smith	USA
1973	O Davidson & J Newcombe	Aus
1972	C Drysdale (SA) & R Taylor (GB)	
1971	J Newcombe (Aus) & R Taylor (GB)	
1970	P Barthes (Fra) & N Pilic (Yug)	
1969	R Crealy & A Stone (Amateur)	Aus
1969	K Rosewall & F Stolle (Open)	Aus
1968	R Lutz & S Smith (Amateur)	USA
1968	R Lutz & S Smith (Open)	USA
1967	J Newcombe & A Roche	Aus
1966	R Emerson & F Stolle	Aus
1965	R Emerson & F Stolle	Aus
1964	C McKinley & R D Ralston	USA
1963	C McKinley & R D Ralston	USA
1962	R Osuna & R Palafox	Mex

Year	Winner	
1961	C McKinley & R D Ralston.	USA
1960	R Emerson & N Fraser	Aus
1959	R Emerson & N Fraser	Aus
1958	A Olmedo & H Richardson	USA
1957	A Cooper & N Fraser	Aus
1956	L Hoad & K Rosewall	Aus
1955	K Kano & A Miyagi	Jap
1954	E V Seixas & M A Trabert	USA
1953	R Hartwig & M Rose	Aus
1952	M Rose (Aus) & E V Seixas (USA)	
1951	K McGregor & F Sedgman	Aus
1950	J Bromwich & F Sedgman	Aus
1949	J Bromwich & O Sidwell	Aus
1948	G Mulloy & W Talbert	USA
1947	J Kramer & F Schroeder	USA
1946	G Mulloy & W Talbert	USA
1945	G Mulloy & W Talbert	USA
1944	R Falkenburg & D McNeill	USA
1943	J Kramer & F Parker	USA
1942	G Mulloy & W Talbert	USA
1941	J Kramer & F Schroeder	USA
1940	J Kramer & F Schroeder	USA
1939	J Bromwich & A Quist	Aus
1938	J D Budge & G Mako	USA
1937	H Henkel & G von Cramm	Ger

Year	Winner		Year	Winner	
1936	J D Budge &		1911	F Little &	
	G Mako	USA		G Touchard	USA
1935	W Allison &		1910	F Alexander &	
	J Van Ryn	USA		H Hackett	USA
1934	G Lott & L Stoefen	USA	1909	F Alexander &	
1933	G Lott & L Stoefen	USA		H Hackett	USA
1932	K Gledhill &		1908	F Alexander &	
	H Vines	USA		H Hackett	USA
1931	W Allison &		1907	F Alexander &	
	J Van Ryn	USA		B Wright	USA
1930	J Doeg & G Lott	USA	1906	H Ward & B Wright	USA
1929	J Doeg & G Lott	USA	1905	H Ward & B Wright	USA
1928	J Hennessey &		1904	H Ward & B Wright	USA
	G Lott	USA	1903	R F Doherty &	
1927	F Hunter &			H L Doherty	GB
	W Tilden	USA	1902	R F Doherty &	
1926	V Richards &			H L Doherty	GB
	R Williams	USA	1901	H Ward & D Davis	USA
1925	V Richards &		1900	H Ward & D Davis	USA
	R Williams	USA	1899	H Ward & D Davis	USA
1924	H Kinsey &		1898	L Ware & P Sheldon	USA
	R Kinsey	USA	1897	L Ware & P Sheldon	USA
1923	B Norton (SA) &		1896	C Neel & S Neel	USA
	W Tilden (USA)		1895	M Chase &	
1922	V Richards &			R Wrenn	USA
	W Tilden	USA	1894	C Hobart & F Hovey	USA
1921	V Richards &		1893	C Hobart & F Hovey	USA
	W Tilden	USA	1892	O Campbell &	
1920	W Johnston &			R Huntingdon	USA
	C Griffin	USA	1891	O Campbell &	
1919	N Brookes &			R Huntingdon	USA
	G Patterson	Aus	1890	V Hall & C Hobart	USA
1918	V Richards &		1889	H Slocum &	
	W Tilden	USA		H Taylor	USA
1917	Not held		1888	O Campbell &	
1916	W Johnston &			V Hall	USA
	C Griffin	USA	1887	R Sears & J Dwight	USA
1915	W Johnston &		1886	R Sears & J Dwight	USA
	C Griffin	USA	1885	R Sears & J Clark	USA
1914	M McLoughlin &		1884	R Sears & J Dwight	USA
	T Bundy	USA	1883	R Sears & J Dwight	USA
1913	M McLoughlin &		1882	R Sears & J Dwight	USA
	T Bundy	USA	1881	C Clark & F Taylor	USA
1912	M McLoughlin &				
	T Bundy	USA			

Women's Singles

FIRST HELD 1887

Year	Winner	
1991	M Seles	Yug
1990	G Sabatini	Arg
1989	S Graf	FRG
1988	S Graf	FRG
1987	M Navratilova	USA
1986	M Navratilova	USA
1985	H Mandlikova	Cze
1984	M Navratilova	USA
1983	M Navratilova	USA
1982	C Evert-Lloyd	USA
1981	T Austin	USA
1980	C Evert-Lloyd	USA
1979	T Austin	USA
1978	C Evert	USA
1977	C Evert	USA
1976	C Evert	USA
1975	C Evert	USA
1974	B J King	USA
1973	M Court	USA
1972	B J King	USA
1971	B J King	USA
1970	M Court	Aus
1969	M Court (Amateur)	Aus
1969	M Court (Open)	Aus
1968	M Court (Amateur)	Aus
1968	V Wade (Open)	GB
1967	B J King	USA
1966	M Bueno	Bra
1965	M Smith	Aus
1964	M Bueno	Bra
1963	M Bueno	Bra
1962	M Smith	Aus
1961	D Hard	USA
1960	D Hard	USA
1959	M Bueno	Bra
1958	A Gibson	USA
1957	A Gibson	USA
1956	S Fry	USA
1955	D Hart	USA
1954	D Hart	USA
1953	M Connolly	USA
1952	M Connolly	USA
1951	M Connolly	USA

Year	Winner	
1950	M du Pont	USA
1949	M du Pont	USA
1948	M du Pont	USA
1947	A L Brough	USA
1946	P Betz	USA
1945	S Cooke	USA
1944	P Betz	USA
1943	P Betz	USA
1942	P Betz	USA
1941	S Cooke	USA
1940	A Marble	USA
1939	A Marble	USA
1938	A Marble	USA
1937	A Lizana	Chi
1936	A Marble	USA
1935	H Jacobs	USA
1934	H Jacobs	USA
1933	H Jacobs	USA
1932	H Jacobs	USA
1931	H Moody	USA
1930	B Nuthall	GB
1929	H Wills	USA
1928	H Wills	USA
1927	H Wills	USA
1926	M Mallory	USA
1925	H Wills	USA
1924	H Wills	USA
1923	H Wills	USA
1922	M Mallory	USA
1921	M Mallory	USA
1920	M Mallory	USA
1919	H Wightman	USA
1918	M Bjurstedt	USA
1917	Not held	
1916	M Bjurstedt	USA
1915	M Bjurstedt	USA
1914	M Browne	USA
1913	M Browne	USA
1912	M Browne	USA
1911	H Hotchkiss	USA
1910	H Hotchkiss	USA
1909	H Hotchkiss	USA
1908	M Barger-Wallach	USA
1907	E Sears	USA
1906	H Homans	USA
1905	E Moore	USA

Year	Winner	
1904	M Sutton	USA
1903	E Moore	USA
1902	M Jones	USA
1901	E Moore	USA
1900	M McAteer	USA
1899	M Jones	USA
1898	J Atkinson	USA
1897	J Atkinson	USA
1896	E Moore	USA
1895	J Atkinson	USA
1894	H Helwig	USA
1893	A Terry	USA
1892	M Cahill	Ire
1891	M Cahill	Ire
1890	E Roosevelt	USA
1889	B Townsend	USA
1888	B Townsend	USA
1887	E Hansell	USA

Women's Doubles

FIRST HELD 1890

Year	Winner	
1991	P Shriver (USA) & N Zvereva (USSR)	
1990	M Navratilova (USA) & G Fernandez (PR)	
1989	H Mandlikova (Aus) & M Navratilova (USA)	
1988	G Fernandez (PR) & R White (USA)	
1987	M Navratilova & P Shriver	USA
1986	M Navratilova & P Shriver	USA
1985	C Kohde-Kilsch (FRG) & H Sukova (Cze)	
1984	M Navratilova & P Shriver	USA
1983	M Navratilova & P Shriver	USA
1982	R Casals (USA) & W Turnbull (Aus)	
1981	K Jordan & A Smith	USA

Year	Winner	
1980	B J King (USA) & M Navratilova (Cze)	
1979	B Stove (Nld) & W Turnbull (Aus)	
1978	B J King (USA) & M Navratilova (Cze)	
1977	M Navratilova (Cze) & B Stove (Nld)	
1976	L Boshoff & I Kloss	SA
1975	M Court (Aus) & V Wade (GB)	
1974	R Casals & B J King	USA
1973	M Court (Aus) & V Wade (GB)	
1972	F Durr (Fra) & B Stove (Nld)	
1971	R Casals (USA) & J Dalton (Aus)	
1970	M Court & J Dalton	Aus
1969	F Durr (Fra) & D Hard (USA) (Open)	
1969	M Court (Aus) & V Wade (GB) (Amateur)	
1968	M Bueno (Bra) & M Court (Aus) (Open)	
1968	M Bueno (Bra) & M Court (Aus) (Amateur)	
1967	R Casals & B J King	USA
1966	M Bueno (Bra) & N Richey (USA)	
1965	N Richey & C Graebner	USA
1964	K Susman & B J Moffitt	USA
1963	R Ebbern & M Smith	Aus
1962	D Hard (USA) & M Bueno (Bra)	
1961	D Hard (USA) & L Turner (Aus)	
1960	D Hard (USA) & M Bueno (Bra)	
1959	D Hard & J Arth	USA
1958	D Hard & J Arth	USA
1957	A L Brough & M du Pont	USA
1956	A L Brough & M du Pont	USA

Year	Winner	
1955	A L Brough & M du Pont	USA
1954	S Fry & D Hart	USA
1953	S Fry & D Hart	USA
1952	S Fry & D Hart	USA
1951	S Fry & D Hart	USA
1950	A L Brough & M du Pont	USA
1949	A L Brough & M du Pont	USA
1948	A L Brough & M du Pont	USA
1947	A L Brough & M Osborne	USA
1946	A L Brough & M Osborne	USA
1945	A L Brough & M Osborne	USA
1944	A L Brough & M Osborne	USA
1943	A L Brough & M Osborne	USA
1942	A L Brough & M Osborne	USA
1941	S Cooke & M Osborne	USA
1940	S Fabyan & A Marble	USA
1939	S Fabyan & A Marble	USA
1938	S Fabyan & A Marble	USA
1937	S Fabyan & A Marble	USA
1936	M Van Ryn & C Babcock	USA
1935	H Jacobs & S Fabyan	USA
1934	H Jacobs & S Palfrey	USA
1933	B Nuthall & F James	GB
1932	H Jacobs & S Palfrey	USA
1931	B Nuthall & E Whittingstall	GB
1930	B Nuthall (GB) & S Palfrey (USA)	
1929	P Michell & P Watson	GB

Year	Winner	
1928	H Wightman & H Wills	USA
1927	E Harvey & K Godfree	GB
1926	E Goss & E Ryan	USA
1925	M Browne & H Wills	USA
1924	H Wightman & H Wills	USA
1923	P Covell & K McKane	GB
1922	H Wills & M Jessup	USA
1921	M Browne & R Williams	USA
1920	E Goss & M Zinderstein	USA
1919	E Goss & M Zinderstein	USA
1918	E Goss & M Zinderstein	USA
1917	Not held	
1916	M Bjurstedt & E Sears	USA
1915	H Wightman & E Sears	USA
1914	M Browne & R Williams	USA
1913	M Browne & R Williams	USA
1912	M Browne & D Green	USA
1911	H Hotchkiss & E Sears	USA
1910	H Hotchkiss & E Rotch	USA
1909	H Hotchkiss & E Rotch	USA
1908	M Curtis & E Sears	USA
1907	C Neely & M Weimer	USA
1906	L Coe & D Platt	USA
1905	H Homans & C Neely	USA
1904	M Hall & M Sutton	USA
1903	E Moore & C Neely	USA
1902	J Atkinson & M Jones	USA

Year	Winner	
1901	J Atkinson & M McAteer	USA
1900	H Champlin & E Parker	USA
1899	J Craven & M McAteer	USA
1898	J Atkinson & K Atkinson	USA
1897	J Atkinson & K Atkinson	USA
1896	J Atkinson & E Moore	USA
1895	J Atkinson & H Helwig	USA
1894	J Atkinson & H Helwig	USA
1893	A Terry & H Butler	USA
1892	M Cahill (Ire) & A McKinley (USA)	
1891	M Cahill (Ire) & F Morgan (USA)	
1890	E Roosevelt & G Roosevelt	USA

Mixed Doubles

FIRST HELD 1892

Year	Winner	
1991	M Bollegraf & T Nijssen	Nld
1990	T Woodbridge & E Smylie	Aus
1989	S Cannon & R White	USA
1988	J Pugh (USA) & J Novotna (Cze)	
1987	E Sanchez (Spa) & M Navratilova (USA)	
1986	S Casal (Spa) & R Reggi (Ita)	
1985	H Gunthardt (Swi) & M Navratilova (USA)	
1984	T Gullikson (USA) & M Maleeva (Bul)	

Year	Winner	
1983	J Fitzgerald & E Sayers	Aus
1982	K Curren (SA) & A Smith (USA)	
1981	K Curren (SA) & A Smith (USA)	
1980	M Riessen & W Turnbull	USA
1979	R Hewitt & G Stevens	SA
1978	F McMillan (SA) & B Stove (Nld)	
1977	F McMillan (SA) & B Stove (Nld)	
1976	P Dent (Aus) & B J King (USA)	
1975	D Stockton & R Casals	USA
1974	G Masters (Aus) & Teeguarden (USA)	
1973	O Davidson (Aus) & J King (USA)	
1972	M Riessen (USA) & M Court (Aus)	
1971	O Davidson (Aus) & J King (USA)	
1970	M Riessen (USA) & M Court (Aus)	
1969	M Riessen (USA) & M Court (Aus) (Open)	
1969	P Sullivan & P Hogan (Amateur)	USA
1968	P Curtis (GB) & M-A Eisel (USA)	
1967	O Davidson (Aus) & B J King (USA)	
1966	O Davidson (Aus) & D Fales (USA)	
1965	F Stolle & M Smith	Aus
1964	J Newcombe & M Smith	Aus
1963	K Fletcher & M Smith	Aus
1962	F Stolle & M Smith	Aus
1961	R Mark & M Smith	Aus
1960	N Fraser (Aus) & M du Pont (USA)	

Year	Winner	
1959	N Fraser (Aus) & M du Pont (USA)	
1958	N Fraser (Aus) & M du Pont (USA)	
1957	K Nielsen (Den) & A Gibson (USA)	
1956	K Rosewall (Aus) & M du Pont (USA)	
1955	E V Seixas & D Hart	USA
1954	E V Seixas & D Hart	USA
1953	E V Seixas & D Hart	USA
1952	F Sedgman (Aus) & D Hart (USA)	
1951	F Sedgman (Aus) & D Hart (USA)	
1950	K McGregor (Aus) & M du Pont (USA)	
1949	E Sturgess (SA) & A L Brough (USA)	
1948	T Brown & A L Brough	USA
1947	J Bromwich (Aus) & A L Brough (USA)	
1946	W Talbert & M Osborne	USA
1945	W Talbert & M Osborne	USA
1944	W Talbert & M Osborne	USA
1943	W Talbert & M Osborne	USA
1942	F Schroeder & A L Brough	USA
1941	J Kramer & S Cooke	USA
1940	R Riggs & A Marble	USA
1939	H Hopman (Aus) & A Marble (USA)	
1938	J D Budge & A Marble	USA
1937	J D Budge & S Fabyan	USA
1936	G Mako & A Marble	USA
1935	E Maier (Spa) & S Fabyan (USA)	
1934	G Lott & H Jacobs	USA
1933	E Vines & E Ryan	USA

Year	Winner	
1932	F Perry (GB) & S Palfrey (USA)	
1931	G Lott (USA) & B Nuthall (GB)	
1930	W Allison & E Cross	USA
1929	G Lott (USA) & B Nuthall (GB)	
1928	J Hawkes (Aus) & H Wills (USA)	
1927	H Cochet (Fra) & E Bennett (GB)	
1926	J Borotra (Fra) & E Ryan (USA)	
1925	J Hawkes (Aus) & K McKane (GB)	
1924	V Richards & H Wills	USA
1923	W Tilden & M Mallory	USA
1922	W Tilden & M Mallory	USA
1921	W Johnston & M Browne	USA
1920	W Johnson & H Wightman	USA
1919	V Richards & M Zinderstein	USA
1918	I Wright & H Wightman	USA
1917	Not held	
1916	W Davis & E Sears	USA
1915	H Johnson & H Wightman	USA
1914	W Tilden & M Browne	USA
1913	W Tilden & M Browne	USA
1912	R Williams & M Browne	USA
1911	W Johnson & H Hotchkiss	USA
1910	J Carpenter & H Hotchkiss	USA
1909	W Johnson & H Hotchkiss	USA
1908	N Niles & E Rotch	USA

Year	Winner	
1907	W Johnson &	
	M Sayres	USA
1906	E Dewhurst &	
	S Coffin	USA
1905	C Hobart &	
	C Hobart	USA
1904	W Grant & E Moore	USA
1903	H Allen &	
	H Chapman	USA
1902	W Grant & E Moore	USA
1901	F Little & M Jones	USA
1900	A Codman &	
	M Hunnewell	USA
1899	A Hoskins &	
	E Rastall	USA
1898	E Fischer & C Neely	USA
1897	D Magruder &	
	L Henson	USA
1896	E Fischer &	
	J Atkinson	USA
1895	E Fischer &	
	J Atkinson	USA
1894	E Fischer &	
	J Atkinson	USA
1893	C Hobart &	
	E Roosevelt	USA
1892	C Hobart (USA) &	
	M Cahill (Ire)	

FRENCH CHAMPIONS

Men's Singles

FIRST HELD 1891

Year	Winner	
1991	J Courier	USA
1990	A Gomez	Ecu
1989	M Chang	USA
1988	M Wilander	Swe
1987	I Lendl	Cze
1986	I Lendl	Cze
1985	M Wilander	Swe
1984	I Lendl	Cze

Year	Winner	
1983	Y Noah	Fra
1982	M Wilander	Swe
1981	B Borg	Swe
1980	B Borg	Swe
1979	B Borg	Swe
1978	B Borg	Swe
1977	G Vilas	Arg
1976	A Panatta	Ita
1975	B Borg	Swe
1974	B Borg	Swe
1973	I Nastase	Rom
1972	A Gimeno	Spa
1971	J Kodes	Cze
1970	J Kodes	Cze
1969	R Laver	Aus
1968	K Rosewall	Aus
1967	R Emerson	Aus
1966	A Roche	Aus
1965	F Stolle	Aus
1964	M Santana	Spa
1963	R Emerson	Aus
1962	R Laver	Aus
1961	M Santana	Spa
1960	N Pietrangeli	Ita
1959	N Pietrangeli	Ita
1958	M Rose	Aus
1957	S Davidson	Swe
1956	L Hoad	Aus
1955	M A Trabert	USA
1954	M A Trabert	USA
1953	K Rosewall	Aus
1952	J Drobny	Egy
1951	J Drobny	Egy
1950	J E Patty	USA
1949	F Parker	USA
1948	F Parker	USA
1947	J Asboth	Hun
1946	M Bernard	Fra
1945/40	No Competition	
1939	W McNeill	USA
1938	J D Budge	USA
1937	H Henkel	Ger
1936	G von Cramm	Ger
1935	F Perry	GB
1934	G von Cramm	Ger
1933	J Crawford	Aus

Year	Winner	
1932	H Cochet	Fra
1931	J Borotra	Fra
1930	H Cochet	Fra
1929	R Lacoste	Fra
1928	H Cochet	Fra
1927	R Lacoste	Fra
1926	H Cochet	Fra
1925	R Lacoste	Fra
1924	J Borotra	Fra
1923	P Blanchy	Fra
1922	H Cochet	Fra
1921	J Samarzeuilh	Fra
1920	A Gobert	Fra
1919/15	No Competition	
1914	M Decugis	Fra
1913	M Decugis	Fra
1912	M Decugis	Fra
1911	A Gobert	Fra
1910	M Germot	Fra
1909	M Decugis	Fra
1908	M Decugis	Fra
1907	M Decugis	Fra
1906	M Germot	Fra
1905	M Germot	Fra
1904	M Decugis	Fra
1903	M Decugis	Fra
1902	M Vacherot	Fra
1901	A Vacherot	Fra
1900	P Ayme	Fra
1899	P Ayme	Fra
1898	P Ayme	Fra
1897	P Ayme	Fra
1896	A Vacherot	Fra
1895	A Vacherot	Fra
1894	A Vacherot	Fra
1893	L Riboulet	Fra
1892	J Schopfer	Fra
1891	J Briggs	GB

Men's Doubles

FIRST HELD 1906

Year	Winner	
1991	A Jarryd (Swe) & J Fitzgerald (Aus)	
1990	S Casal & E Sanchez	Spa
1989	J Grabb & P McEnroe	USA
1988	A Gomez (Ecu) & E Sanchez (Spa)	
1987	A Jarryd (Swe) & R Seguso (USA)	
1986	J Fitzgerald (Aus) & T Smid (Cze)	
1985	M Edmondson & K Warwick	Aus
1984	H Leconte & Y Noah	Fra
1983	A Jarryd & H Simonsson	Swe
1982	S Stewart & F Taygan	USA
1981	H Gunthardt (Swi) & B Taroczy (Hun)	
1980	V Amaya & H Pfister	USA
1979	G Mayer & A Mayer	USA
1978	G Mayer & H Pfister	USA
1977	B Gottfried (USA) & R Ramirez (Mex)	
1976	F McNair & S Stewart	USA
1975	B Gottfried (USA) & R Ramirez (Mex)	
1974	R Crealy (Aus) & O Parun (NZ)	
1973	J Newcombe (Aus) & T Okker (Nld)	
1972	R Hewitt & F McMillan	SA
1971	A Ashe & M Riessen	USA
1970	I Nastase & I Tiriac	Rom
1969	J Newcombe & A Roche	Aus
1968	K Rosewall & F Stolle	Aus
1967	J Newcombe & A Roche	Aus

Year	Winner		Year	Winner	
1966	C Graebner &		1935	J Crawford & A Quist	Aus
	R D Ralston	USA	1934	J Borotra & J Brugnon	Fra
1965	R Emerson & F Stolle	Aus	1933	G Hughes & F Perry	GB
1964	R Emerson &		1932	H Cochet &	
	K Fletcher	Aus		J Brugnon	Fra
1963	R Emerson (Aus) &		1931	G Lott & J Van Ryn	USA
	M Santana (Spa)		1930	H Cochet &	
1962	R Emerson &			J Brugnon	Fra
	N Fraser	Aus	1929	J Borotra & R Lacoste	Fra
1961	R Emerson &		1928	J Borotra & J Brugnon	Fra
	R Laver	Aus	1927	H Cochet &	
1960	R Emerson &			J Brugnon	Fra
	N Fraser	Aus	1926	V Richards &	
1959	N Pietrangeli &			H Kinsey	USA
	O Sirola	Ita	1925	J Borotra & R Lacoste	Fra
1958	A Cooper & N Fraser	Aus	1924	J Borotra & R Lacoste	Fra
1957	M Anderson &		1923	P Blanchy &	
	A Cooper	Aus		J Samarzeuilh	Fra
1956	D Candy (Aus) &		1922	J Brugnon &	
	R Perry (USA)			M Dupont	Fra
1955	E V Seixas &		1921	A Gobert &	
	M A Trabert	USA		W Laurentz	Fra
1954	E V Seixas &		1920	M Decugis &	
	M A Trabert	USA		M Germot	Fra
1953	L Hoad & K Rosewall	Aus	1919/15	No Competition	
1952	K McGregor &		1914	M Decugis &	
	F Sedgman	Aus		M Germot	Fra
1951	K McGregor &		1913	M Decugis &	
	F Sedgman	Aus		M Germot	Fra
1950	W Talbert &		1912	M Decugis &	
	M A Trabert	USA		M Germot	Fra
1949	R Gonzales &		1911	M Decugis &	
	F Parker	USA		M Germot	Fra
1948	L Bergelin (Swe) &		1910	M Decugis &	
	J Drobny (Cze)			M Germot	Fra
1947	E Fannin & E Sturgess	SA	1909	M Decugis &	
1946	M Bernard & Y Petra	Fra		M Germot	Fra
1945/40	No Competition		1908	M Decugis &	
1939	W McNeill &			M Germot	Fra
	C Harris	USA	1907	M Decugis &	
1938	B Destremau &			M Germot	Fra
	Y Petra	Fra	1906	M Decugis &	
1937	G von Cramm &			M Germot	Fra
	H Henkel	Ger			
1936	J Borotra &				
	M Bernard	Fra			

Women's Singles

FIRST HELD 1897

Year	Winner	
1991	M Seles	Yug
1990	M Seles	Yug
1989	A Sanchez-Vicaro	Spa
1988	S Graf	FRG
1987	S Graf	FRG
1986	C Evert-Lloyd	USA
1985	C Evert-Lloyd	USA
1984	M Navratilova	USA
1983	C Evert-Lloyd	USA
1982	M Navratilova	USA
1981	H Mandlikova	Cze
1980	C Evert-Lloyd	USA
1979	C Evert-Lloyd	USA
1978	V Ruzici	Rom
1977	M Jausovec	Yug
1976	S Barker	GB
1975	C Evert	USA
1974	C Evert	USA
1973	M Court	Aus
1972	B J King	USA
1971	E Goolagong	Aus
1970	M Court	Aus
1969	M Court	Aus
1968	N Richey	USA
1967	F Durr	Fra
1966	A Jones	GB
1965	L Turner	Aus
1964	M Smith	Aus
1963	L Turner	Aus
1962	M Smith	Aus
1961	A Haydon	GB
1960	D Hard	USA
1959	C Truman	GB
1958	S Kormoczy	Hun
1957	S Bloomer	GB
1956	A Gibson	USA
1955	A Mortimer	GB
1954	M Connolly	USA
1953	M Connolly	USA
1952	D Hart	USA
1951	S Fry	USA
1950	D Hart	USA
1949	M du Pont	USA

Year	Winner	
1948	N Landry	Fra
1947	P Todd	USA
1946	M Osborne	USA
1945/40	No Competition	
1939	S Mathieu	Fra
1938	S Mathieu	Fra
1937	H Sperling	Ger
1936	H Sperling	Ger
1935	H Sperling	Ger
1934	M Scriven	GB
1933	M Scriven	GB
1932	H Moody	USA
1931	C Aussem	Ger
1930	H Moody	USA
1929	H Wills	USA
1928	H Wills	USA
1927	K Bouman	Nld
1926	S Lenglen	Fra
1925	S Lenglen	Fra
1924	D Vlasto	Fra
1923	S Lenglen	Fra
1922	S Lenglen	Fra
1921	S Lenglen	Fra
1920	S Lenglen	Fra
1919/15	No Competition	
1914	M Broquedis	Fra
1913	M Broquedis	Fra
1912	J Mattey	Fra
1911	J Mattey	Fra
1910	J Mattey	Fra
1909	J Mattey	Fra
1908	K Fenwick	Fra
1907	Mme de Kermel	Fra
1906	K Fenwick	Fra
1905	K Gillou	Fra
1904	K Gillou	Fra
1903	C Masson	Fra
1902	C Masson	Fra
1901	P Girod	Fra
1900	C Prevost	Fra
1899	C Masson	Fra
1898	C Masson	Fra
1897	C Masson	Fra

Women's Doubles

FIRST HELD 1925

Year	Winner	
1991	J Novotna (Cze) & G Fernandez (USA)	
1990	J Novotna & H Sukova	Cze
1989	L Savchenko & N Zvereva	USSR
1988	M Navratilova & P Shriver	USA
1987	M Navratilova & P Shriver	USA
1986	M Navratilova (USA) & A Temesvari (Hun)	
1985	M Navratilova & P Shriver	USA
1984	M Navratilova & P Shriver	USA
1983	R Fairbank (SA) & C Reynolds (USA)	
1982	M Navratilova & A Smith	USA
1981	R Fairbank & T Harford	SA
1980	K Jordan & A Smith	USA
1979	B Stove (Nld) & W Turnbull (Aus)	
1978	M Jausovec (Yug) & V Ruzici (Rom)	
1977	R Marsikova (Cze) & P Teeguarden (USA)	
1976	F Bonicelli (Uru) & G Lovera (Fra)	
1975	C Evert (USA) & M Navratilova (Cze)	
1974	C Evert (USA) & O Morozova (USSR)	
1973	M Court (Aus) & V Wade (GB)	
1972	B J King (USA) & B Stove (Nld)	
1971	F Durr & G Chanfreau	Fra
1970	F Durr & G Chanfreau	Fra

Year	Winner	
1969	F Durr (Fra) & A Jones (GB)	
1968	F Durr (Fra) & A Jones (GB)	
1967	F Durr (Fra) & G Sheriff (Aus)	
1966	M Smith & J Tegart	Aus
1965	M Smith & L Turner	Aus
1964	M Smith & L Turner	Aus
1963	A Jones (GB) & R Schuurman (SA)	
1962	S Price & R Schuurman	SA
1961	S Reynolds & R Schuurman	SA
1960	M Bueno (Bra) & D Hard (USA)	
1959	S Reynolds & R Schuurman	SA
1958	Y Ramirez & R Reyes	Mex
1957	S Bloomer (GB) & D Hard (USA)	
1956	A Buxton (GB) & A Gibson (USA)	
1955	B Fleitz & D Hard	USA
1954	M Connolly (USA) & N Hopman (Aus)	
1953	S Fry & D Hart	USA
1952	S Fry & D Hart	USA
1951	S Fry & D Hart	USA
1950	S Fry & D Hart	USA
1949	A L Brough & M du Pont	USA
1948	D Hart & P Todd	USA
1947	A L Brough & M Osborne	USA
1946	A L Brough & M Osborne	USA
1945/40	No Competition	
1939	S Mathieu (Fra) & J Jedrzedjowska (Pol)	
1938	S Mathieu (Fra) & A Yorke (USA)	
1937	S Mathieu (Fra) & A Yorke (USA)	
1936	S Mathieu (Fra) & A Yorke (USA)	

Year	Winner	
1935	M Scriven & K Stammers	GB
1934	S Mathieu (Fra) & E Ryan (USA)	
1933	S Mathieu (Fra) & E Ryan (USA)	
1932	H Moody & E Ryan	USA
1931	E Whittingstall & B Nuthall	GB
1930	H Moody & E Ryan	USA
1929	E de Alvarez (Spa) & K Bouman (Nld)	
1928	P Watson & E Bennett	GB
1927	G Peacock (Ind) & E Heine (SA)	
1926	S Lenglen & D Vlasto	Fra
1925	S Lenglen & D Vlasto	Fra

Mixed Doubles

FIRST HELD 1925

Year	Winner	
1991	C Suk & H Sukova	Cze
1990	J Lozano (Mex) & A Sanchez-Vicario (Spa)	
1989	T Nijssen & M Bollegraf	Nld
1988	J Lozano (Mex) & L McNeil (USA)	
1987	E Sanchez (Spa) & P Shriver (USA)	
1986	K Flach & K Jordan	USA
1985	H Gunthardt (Swi) & M Navratilova (USA)	
1984	D Stockton & A Smith	USA
1983	E Teltscher & B Jordan	USA
1982	J Lloyd (GB) & W Turnbull (Aus)	
1981	J Arias & A Jaeger	USA
1980	W Martin & A Smith	USA
1979	R Hewitt (SA) & W Turnbull (Aus)	

Year	Winner	
1978	P Slozil & R Tomanova	Cze
1977	J McEnroe & M Carillo	USA
1976	K Warwick (Aus) & I Kloss (SA)	
1975	T Koch (Bra) & F Bonicelli (Uru)	
1974	I Molina (Col) & M Navratilova (Cze)	
1973	J Barclay & F Durr	Fra
1972	K Warwick & E Goolagong	Aus
1971	J Barclay & F Durr	Fra
1970	R Hewitt (SA) & B J King (USA)	
1969	M Riessen (USA) & M Court (Aus)	
1968	J Barclay & F Durr	Fra
1967	O Davidson (Aus) & B J King (USA)	
1966	F McMillan & A Van Zyl	SA
1965	K Fletcher & M Smith	Aus
1964	K Fletcher & M Smith	Aus
1963	K Fletcher & M Smith	Aus
1962	R Howe (Aus) & R Schuurman (SA)	
1961	R Laver (Aus) & D Hard (USA)	
1960	R Howe (Aus) & M Bueno (Bra)	
1959	W Knight (GB) & Y Ramirez (Mex)	
1958	N Pietrangeli (Ita) & S Bloomer (GB)	
1957	J Javorsky & V Puzejova	Cze
1956	L Ayala (Chi) & T Long (Aus)	
1955	G Forbes (SA) & D Hard (USA)	

Year	Winner	
1954	L Hoad (Aus) & M Connolly (USA)	
1953	E V Seixas & D Hart	USA
1952	F Sedgman (Aus) & D Hart (USA)	
1951	F Sedgman (Aus) & D Hart (USA)	
1950	E Morea (Arg) & B Scofield (USA)	
1949	E Sturgess & S Summers	SA
1948	J Drobny (Cze) & P Todd (USA)	
1947	E Sturgess & S Summers	SA
1946	J E Patty & P Betz	USA
1945/40	No Competition	
1939	E Cooke & S Fabyan	USA
1938	D Mitic (Yug) & S Mathieu (Fra)	
1937	Y Petra & S Mathieu	Fra
1936	M Bernard (Fra) & A Yorke (GB)	
1935	M Bernard (Fra) & L Payot (Swi)	
1934	J Borotra & C Rosambert	Fra
1933	J Crawford (Aus) & M Scriven (GB)	
1932	F Perry & B Nuthall	GB
1931	P Spence (SA) & B Nuthall (GB)	
1930	W Tilden (USA) & C Aussem (Ger)	
1929	H Cochet (Fra) & E Bennett (GB)	
1928	H Cochet (Fra) & E Bennett (GB)	
1927	J Borotra & M Bordes	Fra
1926	J Brugnon & S Lenglen	Fra
1925	J Brugnon & S Lenglen	Fra

AUSTRALIAN CHAMPIONS

Men's Singles

FIRST HELD 1905

Year	Winner	
1991	B Becker	Ger
1990	I Lendl	Cze
1989	I Lendl	Cze
1988	M Wilander	Swe
1987	S Edberg	Swe
1986	Not held	
1985	S Edberg	Swe
1984	M Wilander	Swe
1983	M Wilander	Swe
1982	J Kriek	SA
1981	J Kriek	SA
1980	B Teacher	USA
1979	G Vilas	Arg
1978	G Vilas	Arg
1977	V Gerulaitis	USA
1977	R Tanner	USA
1976	M Edmondson	Aus
1975	J Newcombe	Aus
1974	J Connors	USA
1973	J Newcombe	Aus
1972	K Rosewall	Aus
1971	K Rosewall	Aus
1970	A Ashe	USA
1969	R Laver	Aus
1968	W Bowrey	Aus
1967	R Emerson	Aus
1966	R Emerson	Aus
1965	R Emerson	Aus
1964	R Emerson	Aus
1963	R Emerson	Aus
1962	R Laver	Aus
1961	R Emerson	Aus
1960	R Laver	Aus
1959	A Olmedo	USA
1958	A Cooper	Aus
1957	A Cooper	Aus
1956	L Hoad	Aus
1955	K Rosewall	Aus
1954	M Rose	Aus
1953	K Rosewall	Aus

Year	Winner	
1952	K McGregor	Aus
1951	R Savitt	USA
1950	F Sedgman	Aus
1949	F Sedgman	Aus
1948	A Quist	Aus
1947	D Pails	Aus
1946	J Bromwich	Aus
1945/41	No Competition	
1940	A Quist	Aus
1939	J Bromwich	Aus
1938	J D Budge	USA
1937	V McGrath	Aus
1936	A Quist	Aus
1935	J Crawford	Aus
1934	F Perry	GB
1933	J Crawford	Aus
1932	J Crawford	Aus
1931	J Crawford	Aus
1930	E Moon	Aus
1929	J Gregory	GB
1928	J Borotra	Fra
1927	G Patterson	Aus
1926	J Hawkes	Aus
1925	J Anderson	Aus
1924	J Anderson	Aus
1923	P O'Hara-Wood	Aus
1922	J Anderson	Aus
1921	R Gemmell	Aus
1920	P O'Hara-Wood	Aus
1919	A Kingscote	GB
1918/16	No Competition	
1915	F Lowe	GB
1914	A O'Hara-Wood	Aus
1913	E Parker	Aus
1912	J Parke	GB
1911	N Brookes	Aus
1910	R Heath	Aus
1909	A Wilding	NZ
1908	F Alexander	USA
1907	H Rice	Aus
1906	A Wilding	NZ
1905	R Heath	Aus

Men's Doubles

FIRST HELD 1905

Year	Winner	
1991	S Davis & D Pate	USA
1990	P Aldrich & D Visser	SA
1989	R Leach & J Pugh	USA
1988	R Leach & J Pugh	USA
1987	S Edberg & A Jarryd	Swe
1986	Not held	
1985	P Annacone (USA) & C Van Rensberg (SA)	
1984	M Edmondson (Aus) & S Stewart (USA)	
1983	M Edmondson & P McNamee	Aus
1982	J Alexander & J Fitzgerald	Aus
1981	M Edmondson & K Warwick	Aus
1980	M Edmondson & K Warwick	Aus
1979	P McNamara & P McNamee	Aus
1978	W Fibak (Pol) & K Warwick (Aus)	
1977	R Ruffels & A Stone	Aus
1977	A Ashe (USA) & A Roche (Aus)	
1976	J Newcombe & A Roche	Aus
1975	J Alexander & P Dent	Aus
1974	R Case & G Masters	Aus
1973	M Anderson & J Newcombe	Aus
1972	O Davidson & K Rosewall	Aus
1971	J Newcombe & A Roche	Aus
1970	R Lutz & S Smith	USA
1969	R Emerson & R Laver	Aus
1968	R Crealy & A Stone	Aus
1967	J Newcombe & A Roche	Aus
1966	R Emerson & F Stolle	Aus

Year	Winner	
1965	J Newcombe & A Roche	Aus
1964	R Hewitt & F Stolle	Aus
1963	R Hewitt & F Stolle	Aus
1962	R Emerson & N Fraser	Aus
1961	R Laver & R Mark	Aus
1960	R Laver & R Mark	Aus
1959	R Laver & R Mark	Aus
1958	A Cooper & N Fraser	Aus
1957	N Fraser & L Hoad	Aus
1956	L Hoad & K Rosewall	Aus
1955	E V Seixas & M A Trabert	USA
1954	R Hartwig & M Rose	Aus
1953	L Hoad & K Rosewall	Aus
1952	F Sedgman & K McGregor	Aus
1951	F Sedgman & K McGregor	Aus
1950	A Quist & J Bromwich	Aus
1949	A Quist & J Bromwich	Aus
1948	A Quist & J Bromwich	Aus
1947	A Quist & J Bromwich	Aus
1946	A Quist & J Bromwich	Aus
1945/41	No Competition	
1940	A Quist & J Bromwich	Aus
1939	A Quist & J Bromwich	Aus
1938	A Quist & J Bromwich	Aus
1937	A Quist & D Turnbull	Aus
1936	A Quist & D Turnbull	Aus
1935	J Crawford & V McGrath	Aus
1934	F Perry & G Hughes	GB
1933	H Vines & K Gledhill	USA
1932	J Crawford & E Moon	Aus

Year	Winner	
1931	C Donohoe & R Dunlop	Aus
1930	J Crawford & H Hopman	Aus
1929	J Crawford & H Hopman	Aus
1928	J Borotra & J Brugnon	Fra
1927	G Patterson & J Hawkes	Aus
1926	G Patterson & J Hawkes	Aus
1925	G Patterson & P O'Hara-Wood	Aus
1924	N Brookes & J Anderson	Aus
1923	P O'Hara-Wood & C St John	Aus
1922	G Patterson & J Hawkes	Aus
1921	R Gemmell & S Eaton	Aus
1920	P O'Hara-Wood & R Thomas	Aus
1919	P O'Hara-Wood & R Thomas	Aus
1918/16	No Competition	
1915	H Rice & C Todd	Aus
1914	A Campbell & G Patterson	Aus
1913	E Parker & A Hedemann	Aus
1912	J Parke & C Dixon	GB
1911	R Heath (Aus) & R Lycett (GB)	
1910	H Rice & A Campbell	Aus
1909	E Parker & J Keane	Aus
1908	F Alexander (USA) & A Dunlop (Aus)	
1907	H Parker (NZ) & W Gregg (Aus)	
1906	A Wilding (NZ) & R Heath (Aus)	
1905	T Tachell (Aus) & R Lycett (GB)	

Women's Singles

FIRST HELD 1922

Year	Winner	
1991	M Seles	Yug
1990	S Graf	FRG
1989	S Graf	FRG
1988	S Graf	FRG
1987	H Mandlikova	Cze
1986	Not held	
1985	M Navratilova	USA
1984	C Evert-Lloyd	USA
1983	M Navratilova	USA
1982	C Evert-Lloyd	USA
1981	M Navratilova	USA
1980	H Mandlikova	Cze
1979	B Jordan	USA
1978	C O'Neill	Aus
1977	E Cawley	Aus
1977	K Reid	Aus
1976	E Cawley	Aus
1975	E Goolagong	Aus
1974	E Goolagong	Aus
1973	M Court	Aus
1972	V Wade	GB
1971	M Court	Aus
1970	M Court	Aus
1969	M Court	Aus
1968	B J King	USA
1967	N Richey	USA
1966	M Smith	Aus
1965	M Smith	Aus
1964	M Smith	Aus
1963	M Smith	Aus
1962	M Smith	Aus
1961	M Smith	Aus
1960	M Smith	Aus
1959	M Reitano	Aus
1958	A Mortimer	GB
1957	S Fry	USA
1956	M Carter	Aus
1955	B Penrose	Aus
1954	T Long	Aus
1953	M Connolly	USA
1952	T Long	Aus
1951	N Bolton	Aus
1950	A L Brough	USA
1949	D Hart	USA
1948	N Bolton	Aus
1947	N Bolton	Aus
1946	N Bolton	Aus
1945/41	No Competition	
1940	N Bolton	Aus
1939	V Westacott	Aus
1938	M Bundy	USA
1937	N Wynne	Aus
1936	J Hartigan	Aus
1935	D Round	GB
1934	J Hartigan	Aus
1933	J Hartigan	Aus
1932	C Buttsworth	Aus
1931	C Buttsworth	Aus
1930	D Akhurst	Aus
1929	D Akhurst	Aus
1928	D Akhurst	Aus
1927	E Boyd	Aus
1926	D Akhurst	Aus
1925	D Akhurst	Aus
1924	S Lance	Aus
1923	M Molesworth	Aus
1922	M Molesworth	Aus

Women's Doubles

FIRST HELD 1922

Year	Winner	
1991	P Fendick & M J Fernandez	USA
1990	J Novotna & H Sukova	Cze
1989	M Navratilova & P Shriver	USA
1988	M Navratilova & P Shriver	USA
1987	M Navratilova & P Shriver	USA
1986	Not held	
1985	M Navratilova & P Shriver	USA
1984	M Navratilova & P Shriver	USA

Year	Winner		Year	Winner	
1983	M Navratilova &		1957	S Fry & A Gibson	USA
	P Shriver	USA	1956	M Hawton & T Long	Aus
1982	M Navratilova &		1955	M Hawton &	
	P Shriver	USA		B Penrose	Aus
1981	K Jordan & A Smith	USA	1954	M Hawton &	
1980	B Nagelsen (USA) &			B Penrose	Aus
	M Navratilova (Cze)		1953	M Connolly &	
1979	J Chaloner (NZ) &			J Sampson	USA
	D Evers (Aus)		1952	T Long & N Bolton	Aus
1978	B Nagelsen (USA) &		1951	T Long & N Bolton	Aus
	R Tomanova (Cze)		1950	A L Brough &	
1977	E Cawley & R Cawley	Aus		D Hart	USA
	M Guerrant (USA) &		1949	T Long & N Bolton	Aus
	K Reid (Aus)		1948	T Long & N Bolton	Aus
1977	D Fromholtz &		1947	T Long & N Bolton	Aus
	H Gourlay	Aus	1946	M Bevis & J Fitch	Aus
1976	E Cawley &		1945/41	No Competition	
	H Gourlay	Aus	1940	T Coyne & N Bolton	Aus
1975	E Goolagong (Aus) &		1939	T Coyne & N Wynne	Aus
	M Michel (USA)		1938	T Coyne & N Wynne	Aus
1974	E Goolagong (Aus) &		1937	T Coyne & N Wynne	Aus
	M Michel (USA)		1936	T Coyne & N Wynne	Aus
1973	M Court (Aus) &		1935	E Dearman & E Lyle	GB
	V Wade (GB)		1934	M Molesworth &	
1972	H Gourlay &			V Westacott	Aus
	K Harris	Aus	1933	M Molesworth &	
1971	M Court &			V Westacott	Aus
	E Goolagong	Aus	1932	C Buttsworth &	
1970	M Court & J Dalton	Aus		M Crawford	Aus
1969	M Court & J Tegart	Aus	1931	L Bickerton &	
1968	K Krantzcke &			D Cozens	Aus
	K Melville	Aus	1930	E Hood &	
1967	J Tegart & L Turner	Aus		M Molesworth	Aus
1966	C Graebner &		1929	D Akhurst &	
	N Richey	USA		L Bickerton	Aus
1965	M Smith & L Turner	Aus	1928	D Akhurst & E Boyd	Aus
1964	J Tegart & L Turner	Aus	1927	L Bickerton &	
1963	R Ebbern & M Smith	Aus		P O'Hara Wood	Aus
1962	R Ebbern & M Smith	Aus	1926	E Boyd &	
1961	M Reitano &			P O'Hara Wood	Aus
	M Smith	Aus	1925	D Akhurst &	
1960	M Bueno (Bra) &			S Harper	Aus
	C Truman (GB)		1924	D Akhurst & S Lance	Aus
1959	S Reynolds &		1923	E Boyd & S Lance	Aus
	R Schuurman	SA	1922	E Boyd &	
1958	M Hawton & T Long	Aus		M Mountain	Aus

Mixed Doubles

FIRST HELD 1922

Year	Winner	
1991	J Bates & J Durie	GB
19?0	J Pugh (USA) & N Zvereva (USSR)	
89	J Pugh (USA) & J Novotna (Cze)	
1988	J Pugh (USA) & J Novotna (Cze)	
1987	S Stewart & Z Garrison	USA
1986/70	No Competition	
1969	M Riessen (USA) & M Court (Aus)	
	F Stolle (Aus) & A Jones (GB)	
1968	R Crealy (Aus) & B J King (USA)	
1967	O Davidson & L Turner	USA
1966	A Roche & J Tegart	Aus
1965	J Newcombe & M Smith	Aus
	O Davidson & L Turner	Aus
1964	K Fletcher & M Smith	Aus
1963	K Fletcher & M Smith	Aus
1962	F Stolle & L Turner	Aus
1961	R Hewitt & J Lehane	Aus
1960	T Fancutt (SA) & J Lehane (Aus)	
1959	R Mark (Aus) & S Reynolds (SA)	
1958	R Howe & M Hawton	Aus
1957	M Anderson & F Muller	Aus
1956	N Fraser & B Penrose	Aus
1955	G Worthington & T Long	Aus
1954	R Hartwig & T Long	Aus
1953	R Hartwig (Aus) & J Sampson (USA)	

Year	Winner	
1952	G Worthington & T Long	Aus
1951	G Worthington & T Long	Aus
1950	F Sedgman (Aus) & D Hart (USA)	
1949	F Sedgman (Aus) & D Hart (USA)	
1948	C Long & N Bolton	Aus
1947	C Long & N Bolton	Aus
1946	C Long & N Bolton	Aus
1945/41	No Competition	
1940	C Long & N Wynne	Aus
1939	H Hopman & N Hopman	Aus
1938	J Bromwich & M Wilson	Aus
1937	H Hopman & N Hopman	Aus
1936	H Hopman & N Hopman	Aus
1935	C Boussus (Fra) & L Bickerton (Aus)	
1934	E Moon & J Hartigan	Aus
1933	J Crawford & M Crawford	Aus
1932	J Crawford & M Crawford	Aus
1930	H Hopman & N Hall	Aus
1929	E Moon & D Akhurst	Aus
1928	J Borotra (Fra) & D Akhurst (Aus)	
1927	J Hawkes & E Boyd	Aus
1926	J Hawkes & E Boyd	Aus
1925	J Willard & D Akhurst	Aus
1924	J Willard & D Akhurst	Aus
1923	H Rice & S Lance	Aus
1922	J Hawkes & E Boyd	Aus

GRAND PRIX MASTERS CHAMPIONS

FIRST HELD 1970

Men's Singles

Year	Winner	
1989	S Edberg	Swe
1988	B Becker	FRG
1987	I Lendl	Cze
1986	I Lendl	Cze
1985	J McEnroe	USA
1984	J McEnroe	USA
1983	I Lendl	Cze
1982	I Lendl	Cze
1981	B Borg	Swe
1980	B Borg	Swe
1979	J McEnroe	USA
1978	J Connors	USA
1977	Not held	
1976	M Orantes	Spa
1975	I Nastase	Rom
1974	G Vilas	Arg
1973	I Nastase	Rom
1972	I Nastase	Rom
1971	I Nastase	Rom
1970	S Smith	USA

Men's Doubles

Year	Winner	
1989	J Grabb & P McEnroe	USA
1988	R Leach & J Pugh	USA
1987	M Mecir & T Smid	Cze
1986	A Jarryd & S Edberg	Swe
1985	P Fleming & J McEnroe	USA
1984	P Fleming & J McEnroe	USA
1983	P Fleming & J McEnroe	USA
1982	P Fleming & J McEnroe	USA
1981	P Fleming & J McEnroe	USA
1980	P Fleming & J McEnroe	USA
1979	P Fleming & J McEnroe	USA
1978	R Hewitt & F McMillan	SA
1977	Not held	
1976	F McNair & S Stewart	USA
1975	J Gisbert & M Orantes	Spa
1974/71	Not held	
1970	S Smith & A Ashe	USA

ATP TOUR WORLD CHAMPIONS

Men's Singles

FIRST HELD 1990

Year	Winner	
1990	A Agassi	USA

GRAND SLAM CUP CHAMPIONS

Men's Singles

FIRST HELD 1990

Year	Winner	
1990	P Sampras	USA

DAVIS CUP

FIRST HELD 1900

Year	Winner
1990	United States

Year	Winner
1989	West Germany
1988	West Germany
1987	Sweden
1986	Australia
1985	Sweden
1984	Sweden
1983	Australia
1982	United States
1981	United States
1980	Czechoslovakia
1979	United States
1978	United States
1977	Australia
1976	Italy
1975	Sweden
1974	South Africa
1973	Australia
1972	United States
1971	United States
1970	United States
1969	United States
1968	United States
1967	Australia
1966	Australia
1965	Australia
1964	Australia
1963	United States
1962	Australia
1961	Australia
1960	Australia
1959	Australia
1958	United States
1957	Australia
1956	Australia
1955	Australia
1954	United States
1953	Australia
1952	Australia
1951	Australia
1950	Australia
1949	United States
1948	United States
1947	United States
1946	United States
1945/40	No Competition
1939	Australia

Year	Winner
1938	United States
1937	United States
1936	Great Britain
1935	Great Britain
1934	Great Britain
1933	Great Britain
1932	France
1931	France
1930	France
1929	France
1928	France
1927	France
1926	United States
1925	United States
1924	United States
1923	United States
1922	United States
1921	United States
1920	United States
1919	Australasia
1918/15	No Competition
1914	Australasia
1913	United States
1912	Great Britain
1911	Australasia
1910	No Challenge
1909	Australasia
1908	Australasia
1907	Australasia
1906	Great Britain
1905	Great Britain
1904	Great Britain
1903	Great Britain
1902	United States
1901	No Challenge
1900	United States

FEDERATION CUP

FIRST HELD 1963

Year	Winner
1991	Spain
1990	United States
1989	United States

Year	Winner
1988	Czechoslovakia
1987	West Germany
1986	United States
1985	Czechoslovakia
1984	Czechoslovakia
1983	Czechoslovakia
1982	United States
1981	United States
1980	United States
1979	United States
1978	United States
1977	United States
1976	United States
1975	Czechoslovakia
1974	Australia
1973	Australia
1972	South Africa
1971	Australia
1970	Australia
1969	United States
1968	Australia
1967	United States
1966	United States
1965	Australia
1964	Australia
1963	United States

OLYMPIC CHAMPIONS

Men's Singles

FIRST HELD 1896

Year	Winner	
1988	M Mecir	Cze
1984/28	Not held	
1924	V Richards	USA
1920	L Raymond	SA
1912	C L Winslow	SA
1908	M J G Ritchie	GB
1904	B Wright	USA
1900	H L Doherty	GB
1896	J Boland	Ire

Men's Doubles

FIRST HELD 1896

Year	Winner	
1988	K Flach & R Seguso	USA
1984/28	Not held	
1924	V Richards & F T Hunter	USA
1920	O G N Turnbull & M Woosnam	GB
1912	C L Winslow & H A Kitson	SA
1908	R F Doherty & G W Hillyard	GB
1904	B Wright & E W Leonard	USA
1900	H L Doherty & R F Doherty	GB
1896	J Boland (Ire) & F Traun (Ger)	

Women's Singles

FIRST HELD 1900

Year	Winner	
1988	S Graf	FRG
1984/28	Not held	
1924	H Wills	USA
1920	S Lenglen	Fra
1912	M Broquedis	Fra
1908	D Chambers	GB
1904	Not held	
•1900	C Cooper	GB

Women's Doubles

FIRST HELD 1920

Year	Winner	
1988	P Shriver & Z Garrison	USA
1984/28	Not held	

Year	Winner	
1924	H Wills &	
	H Wightman	USA
1920	K McKane &	
	R J McNair	GB

VOLLEYBALL

WORLD CHAMPIONS

Men

FIRST HELD 1949

Year	Winner
1990	Italy
1986	United States
1982	USSR
1978	USSR
1974	Poland
1970	East Germany
1966	Czechoslovakia
1962	USSR
1960	USSR
1956	Czechoslovakia
1952	USSR
1949	USSR

Women

FIRST HELD 1952

Year	Winner
1990	USSR
1986	China
1982	China
1978	Cuba
1974	Japan
1970	USSR

Year	Winner
1966	Japan
1962	Japan
1960	USSR
1956	USSR
1952	USSR

OLYMPIC CHAMPIONS

FIRST HELD 1964

Men

Year	Winner
1988	United States
1984	United States
1980	USSR
1976	Poland
1972	Japan
1968	USSR
1964	USSR

Women

Year	Winner
1988	USSR
1984	China
1980	USSR
1976	Japan

Year	Winner
1972	USSR
1968	USSR
1964	Japan

WATER POLO

OLYMPIC CHAMPIONS

FIRST HELD 1900

Year	Winner
1988	Yugoslavia
1984	Yugoslavia
1980	USSR
1976	Hungary
1972	USSR
1968	Yugoslavia
1964	Hungary
1960	Italy
1956	Hungary
1952	Hungary
1948	Italy
1936	Hungary
1932	Hungary
1928	Germany
1924	France
1920	Great Britain
1912	Great Britain
1908	Great Britain
1904	United States
1900	Great Britain

WORLD CHAMPIONS

FIRST HELD 1973

Year	Winner
1991	Yugoslavia
1986	Yugoslavia
1982	USSR
1978	Italy
1975	USSR
1973	Hungary

WOMEN'S WORLD CHAMPIONS

FIRST HELD 1986

Year	Winner
1991	Netherlands
1986	Australia

WATER SKIING

WORLD CHAMPIONS

Overall

FIRST HELD 1949

Year	Winner	
1991	P Martin	Fra
1989	P Martin	Fra
1987	S Duvall	USA
1985	S Duvall	USA
1983	S Duvall	USA
1981	S Duvall	USA
1979	J McClintock	Can
1977	M Hazelwood	GB
1975	C Suarez	Ven
1973	G Athans	Can
1971	G Athans	Can
1969	M Suyderhoud	USA
1967	M Suyderhoud	USA
1965	R Hillier	USA
1963	B Spencer	USA
1961	B Zaccardi	Ita
1959	C Stearns	USA
1957	J Cash	USA
1955	A Mendoza	USA
1953	A Mendoza	USA
1950	D Pope Jnr	USA
1949	G de Clerq	Bel
	C Jourdan	Fra

Tricks

FIRST HELD 1949

Year	Winner	
1991	P Martin	Fra
1989	A Benet	Fra
1987	P Martin	Fra
1985	B LaPoint	USA
1983	C Pickos	USA

Year	Winner	
1981	C Pickos	USA
1979	P Martin	Fra
1977	C Suarez	Ven
1975	W Grimditch	USA
1973	W Grimditch	USA
1971	R McCormick	USA
1969	B Cockburn	Aus
1967	A Kempton	USA
1965	K White	USA
1963	B Spencer	USA
1961	J Muller	Fra
1959	P Logut	Fra
1957	M Amsbury	USA
1955	S Scott	USA
1953	W Witherall	USA
1950	J Andresen	USA
1949	P Gouin	Fra

Slalom

FIRST HELD 1949

Year	Winner	
1991	L Lowe	USA
1989	A Mapple	GB
1987	B LaPoint	USA
1985	P Martin	Fra
1983	B LaPoint	USA
1981	A Mapple	GB
1979	B LaPoint	USA
1977	B LaPoint	USA
1975	R Zucchi	Ita
1973	G Athans	Can
1971	M Suyderhoud	USA
1969	V Palomo	Spa
1967	T Antunano	Mex
1965	R Hillier	USA
1963	B Spencer	USA
1961	J Jackson	USA
1959	C Stearns	USA
1957	J Cash	USA

Year	Winner	
1955	A Mendoza	USA
1953	C Blackwell	Can
1950	D Pope Jnr	USA
1949	C Jourdan	Fra

Jumping

FIRST HELD 1949

Year	Winner	
1991	B Neville	Aus
1989	G Carrington	Aus
1987	S Duvall	USA
1985	G Carrington	Aus
1983	S Duvall	USA
1981	M Hazelwood	GB
1979	M Hazelwood	GB
1977	M Suyderhoud	USA
1975	R McCormick	USA
1973	R McCormick	USA
1971	M Suyderhoud	USA
1969	W Grimditch	USA
1967	A Kempton	USA
1965	L Penacho	USA
1963	J Jackson	USA
1961	L Penacho	USA
1959	B McCalla	USA
1957	J Muller	Fra
1955	A Mendoza	USA
1953	A Mendoza	USA
1950	G de Clerq	Bel
1949	G de Clerq	Bel

Women's Overall

FIRST HELD 1949

Year	Winner	
1991	K Neville	Aus
1989	D Mapple	USA
1987	D Brush	USA
1985	K Neville	Aus
1983	A Carrasco	Ven
1981	K Roberge	USA

Year	Winner	
1979	C Todd	USA
1977	C Todd	USA
1975	L Allan-Shetter	USA
1973	L St John	USA
1971	C Weir	USA
1969	L Allan	USA
1967	J Stewart-Wood	GB
1965	L Allan	USA
1963	J Brown	USA
1961	S Hulsemann	Lux
1959	V Van Hook	USA
1957	M Doria	Swi
1955	W Worthington-McGuire	USA
1953	L Rawls	USA
1950	W Worthington-McGuire	USA
1949	W Worthington	USA

Women's Tricks

FIRST HELD 1949

Year	Winner	
1991	T Larsen	USA
1989	T Larsen	USA
1987	N Rumiantseva	USSR
1985	J McClintock	USA
1983	N Ponomareva	USSR
1981	A Carrasco	Ven
1979	N Rumiantseva	USSR
1977	M Carrasco	Ven
1975	M Carrasco	Ven
1973	M Carrasco	Ven
1971	W Stahle	Nld
1969	L Allan	USA
1967	D Duflot	Fra
1965	D Duflot	Fra
1963	G Dalle	Fra
1961	S Hulsemann	Lux
1959	P Castlevetri	Ita
1957	M Doria	Swi
1955	M Doria	Swi
1953	L Rawls	USA

Year	Winner	
1950	W Worthington-McGuire	USA
1949	M Bouteiller	Fra

Women's Slalom

FIRST HELD 1949

Year	Winner	
1991	H Kjellander	Swe
1989	K Laskoff	USA
1987	K Laskoff	USA
1985	C Duvall	USA
1983	C Todd	USA
1981	C Todd	USA
1979	P Messner	Can
1977	C Todd	USA
1975	L Allan-Shetter	USA
1973	S Maurial	Fra
1971	C Freeman	USA
1969	L Allan	USA
1967	L Allan	USA
1965	B Cooper-Clark	USA
1963	J Brown	USA
1961	J Kirtley	USA
1959	V Van Hook	USA
1957	M Doria	Swi
1955	W Worthington-McGuire	USA
1953	E Wolford	USA
1950	E Wolford	USA
1949	W Worthington	USA

Women's Jumping

FIRST HELD 1949

Year	Winner	
1991	S Slone	USA
1989	D Mapple	USA
1987	D Brush	USA
1985	D Brush	USA
1983	C Todd	USA
1981	D Brush	USA

Year	Winner	
1979	C Todd	USA
1977	L Giddens	USA
1975	L Allan-Shetter	USA
1973	L Allan-Shetter	USA
1971	C Weir	USA
1969	L Allan	USA
1967	J Stewart-Wood	GB
1965	L Allan	USA
1963	R Hansluvka	Aut
1961	R Hansluvka	Aut
1959	N Rideout	USA
1957	N Rideout	USA
1955	W Worthington-McGuire	USA
1953	S Swaney	USA
1950	J Kirkpatrick	USA
1949	W Worthington	USA

Team

FIRST HELD 1957

Year	Winner
1991	Canada
1989	United States
1987	United States
1985	United States
1983	United States
1981	United States
1979	United States
1977	United States
1975	United States
1973	United States
1971	United States
1969	United States
1967	United States
1965	United States
1963	United States
1961	United States
1959	United States
1957	United States

WEIGHTLIFTING

WORLD CHAMPIONS
Super-Heavyweight

FIRST HELD 1969

Year	Winner	
1990	L Taranenko	USSR
1989	A Kurlovich	USSR
1987	A Kurlovich	USSR
1986	A Krastev	Bul
1985	A Krastev	Bul
1983	A Pisarenko	USSR
1982	A Pisarenko	USSR
1981	A Pisarenko	USSR
1979	S Rakhmanov	USSR
1978	J Heuser	GDR
1977	V Alekseyev	USSR
1975	V Alekseyev	USSR
1974	V Alekseyev	USSR
1973	V Alekseyev	USSR
1971	V Alekseyev	USSR
1970	V Alekseyev	USSR
1969	J Dube	USA

Year	Winner	
1975	V Khristov	Bul
1974	V Ustyuzhin	USSR
1973	P Pervushin	USSR
1971	Y Kozin	USSR
1970	J Talts	USSR
1969	R Bednarski	USA
1966	L Zhabotinskiy	USSR
1965	L Zhabotinskiy	USSR
1963	Y Vlasov	USSR
1962	Y Vlasov	USSR
1961	Y Vlasov	USSR
1959	Y Vlasov	USSR
1958	A Medvedev	USSR
1957	A Medvedev	USSR
1955	P Anderson	USA
1954	N Schemansky	USA
1953	D Hepburn	Can
1951	J Davis	USA
1950	J Davis	USA
1949	J Davis	USA
1947	J Davis	USA
1946	J Davis	USA
1945/39	No Competition	
1938	J Manger	Ger
1937	J Manger	Ger

Heavyweight

FIRST HELD 1937

Year	Winner	
1990	S Botev	Bul
1989	S Botev	Bul
1987	Y Zakharevich	USSR
1986	Y Zakharevich	USSR
1985	Y Zakharevich	USSR
1983	V Klokov	USSR
1982	S Arakelov	USSR
1981	V Kravchuk	USSR
1979	S Arakelov	USSR
1978	Y Zaitsev	USSR
1977	V Khristov	Bul

Up to 100 kg

FIRST HELD 1977

Year	Winner	
1990	N Vlad	Rom
1989	P Stefanov	Bul
1987	P Kuznyetsov	USSR
1986	N Vlad	Rom
1985	S Szanyi	Hun
1983	P Kuznyetsov	USSR
1982	V Sots	USSR
1981	V Sots	USSR
1979	P Sirchin	USSR

Year	Winner	
1978	D Rigert	USSR
1977	A Kozlov	USSR

Middle Heavyweight

FIRST HELD 1951

Year	Winner	
1990	A Khrapaty	USSR
1989	A Khrapaty	USSR
1987	A Khrapaty	USSR
1986	A Khrapaty	USSR
1985	A Khrapaty	USSR
	V Solodov	USSR
1983	B Blagoyev	Bul
1982	B Blagoyev	Bul
1981	B Blagoyev	Bul
1979	G Bessonov	USSR
1978	R Milser	FRG
1977	S Poltoratskiy	USSR
1975	D Rigert	USSR
1974	D Rigert	USSR
1973	D Rigert	USSR
1971	D Rigert	USSR
1970	V Kolotov	USSR
1969	K Kangasniemi	Fin
1966	G Toth	Hun
1965	L Martin	GB
1963	L Martin	GB
1962	L Martin	GB
1961	I Palinski	Pol
1959	L Martin	GB
1958	A Vorobyev	USSR
1957	A Vorobyev	USSR
1955	A Vorobyev	USSR
1954	A Vorobyev	USSR
1953	N Schemansky	USA
1951	N Schemansky	USA

Light Heavyweight

FIRST HELD 1937

Year	Winner	
1990	A Orazourdyev	USSR
1989	K Kunev	Bul
1987	L Barsi	Hun
1986	A Zlatev	Bul
1985	Y Vardanyan	USSR
1983	Y Vardanyan	USSR
1982	A Zlatev	Bul
1981	Y Vardanyan	USSR
1979	Y Vardanyan	USSR
1978	Y Vardanyan	USSR
1977	G Bessonov	USSR
1975	V Shariy	USSR
1974	T Stoychev	Bul
1973	V Rizhenkov	USSR
1971	B Pavlov	USSR
1970	G Ivanchenko	USSR
1969	M Ohuchi	Jap
1966	V Belyayev	USSR
1965	N Osimek	Pol
1963	G Veres	Hun
1962	G Veres	Hun
1961	R Plukfelder	USSR
1959	R Plukfelder	USSR
1958	T Lomakin	USSR
1957	T Lomakin	USSR
1955	T Kono	USA
1954	T Kono	USA
1953	A Vorobyev	USSR
1951	S Stanczyk	USA
1950	S Stanczyk	USA
1949	S Stanczyk	USA
1947	J Terpak	USA
1946	G Novak	USSR
1945/39	No Competition	
1938	J Davis	USA
1937	F Haller	Aut

Middleweight

FIRST HELD 1937

Year	Winner	
1990	F Kassapu	USSR
1989	A Orazourdyev	USSR
1987	B Guidikov	Bul
1986	A Varbanov	Bul
1985	A Varbanov	Bul
1983	A Varbanov	Bul
1982	Y Rusev	Bul
1981	Y Rusev	Bul
1979	R Urrutia	Cub
1978	R Urrutia	Cub
1977	Y Vardanyan	USSR
1975	P Wenzel	GDR
1974	N Kolev	Bul
1973	N Kolev	Bul
1971	V Kanygin	USSR
1970	V Kurentsov	USSR
1969	V Kurentsov	USSR
1966	V Kurentsov	USSR
1965	V Kurentsov	USSR
1963	A Kurinov	USSR
1962	A Kurinov	USSR
1961	A Kurinov	USSR
1959	T Kono	USA
1958	T Kono	USA
1957	T Kono	USA
1955	P George	USA
1954	P George	USA
1953	T Kono	USA
1951	P George	USA
1950	K El Touni	Egy
1949	K El Touni	Egy
1947	S Stanczyk	USA
1946	K El Touni	Egy
1945/39	No Competition	
1938	A Wagner	Ger
1937	J Terpak	USA

Lightweight

FIRST HELD 1937

Year	Winner	
1990	Kim Myong Nam	DPRK
1989	I Militossian	USSR
1987	M Petrov	Bul
1986	M Petrov	Bul
1985	M Petrov	Bul
1983	J Kunz	GDR
1982	P Mandra	Pol
1981	J Kunz	GDR
1979	Y Rusev	Bul
1978	Y Rusev	Bul
1977	R Urrutia	Cub
1975	P Korol	USSR
1974	P Korol	USSR
1973	M Kirzhinov	USSR
1971	Z Kaczmarek	Pol
1970	Z Kaczmarek	Pol
1969	W Baszanowski	Pol
1966	Y Katsura	USSR
1965	W Baszanowski	Pol
1963	M Zielinski	Pol
1962	V Kaplunov	USSR
1961	W Baszanowski	Pol
1959	V Bushuyev	USSR
1958	V Bushuyev	USSR
1957	V Bushuyev	USSR
1955	N Kostilyev	Irn
1954	D Ivanov	USSR
1953	P George	USA
1951	I Shams	Egy
1950	J Pitman	USA
1949	I Shams	Egy
1947	P George	USA
1946	S Stanczyk	USA
1945/39	No Competition	
1938	A Terlazzo	USA
1937	A Terlazzo	USA

Featherweight

FIRST HELD 1937

Year	Winner	
1990	N Peshalov	Bul
1989	N Suleymanoglu	Tur
1987	S Topourov	Bul
1986	N Suleymanoglu	Bul
1985	N Suleymanoglu	Bul
1983	Y Sarkisyan	USSR
1982	Y Sarkisyan	USSR
1981	B Manolov	Bul
1979	M Severyn	USSR
1978	N Kolesnikov	USSR
1977	N Kolesnikov	USSR
1975	G Todorov	Bul
1974	G Todorov	Bul
1973	D Shanidze	USSR
1971	Y Miyake	Jap
1970	M Novak	Pol
1969	Y Miyake	Jap
1966	Y Miyake	Jap
1965	Y Mikaye	Jap
1963	Y Miyake	Jap
1962	Y Minayev	USSR
1961	I Berger	USA
1959	M Zielinski	Pol
1958	I Berger	USA
1957	Y Minayev	USSR
1955	R Chimiskyan	USSR
1954	R Chimiskyan	USSR
1953	N Saksonov	USSR
1951	S Gouda	Egy
1950	M Fayad	Egy
1949	M Fayad	Egy
1947	R Higgins	USA
1946	A Andersson	Swe
1945/39	No Competition	
1938	G Liebsch	Ger
1937	G Liebsch	Ger

Bantamweight

FIRST HELD 1947

Year	Winner	
1990	Liu Shoubin	CPR
1989	H Suleimanov	Bul
1987	N Terziyski	Bul
1986	M Grablev	Bul
1985	N Terziyski	Bul
1983	O Mirzoyan	USSR
1982	A Kodiabashev	Bul
1981	A Kodiabashev	Bul
1979	A Kodiabashev	Bul
1978	D Nunez	Cub
1977	J Hosotani	Jap
1975	A Kirov	USSR
1974	A Kirov	USSR
1973	A Kirov	USSR
1971	G Chetin	USSR
1970	M Nassiri	Irn
1969	M Nassiri	Irn
1966	A Vakhonin	USSR
1965	I Foldi	Hun
1963	A Vakhonin	USSR
1962	Y Miyake	Jap
1961	V Stogov	USSR
1959	V Stogov	USSR
1958	V Stogov	USSR
1957	V Stogov	USSR
1955	V Stogov	USSR
1954	B Farhutdinov	USSR
1953	I Udodov	USSR
1951	M Namdjou	Irn
1950	M Namdjou	Irn
1949	M Namdjou	Irn
1947	J de Pietro	USA

Flyweight

FIRST HELD 1969

Year	Winner	
1990	I Ivanov	Bul
1989	I Ivanov	Bul
1987	S Marinov	Bul
1986	S Marinov	Bul

Year	Winner	
1985	S Marinov	Bul
1983	N Terziyski	Bul
1982	S Leletko	Pol
1981	K Osmonalyev	USSR
1979	K Osmonalyev	USSR
1978	K Osmonalyev	USSR
1977	A Voronin	USSR
1975	Z Smalcerz	Pol
1974	M Nassiri	Irn
1973	M Nassiri	Irn
1971	Z Smalcerz	Pol
1970	S Holczreiter	Hun
1969	V Krishchisin	USSR

OLYMPIC CHAMPIONS

Super-Heavyweight

FIRST HELD 1972

Year	Winner	
1988	A Kurlovich	USSR
1984	D Lukin	Aus
1980	S Rakhmanov	USSR
1976	V Alexeyev	USSR
1972	V Alexeyev	USSR

Heavyweight

FIRST HELD 1896

Year	Winner	
1988	Y Zakharevich	USSR
1984	N Oberburger	Ita
1980	L Taranenko	USSR
1976	Y Zaitsev	USSR
1972	J Talts	USSR
1968	L Zhabotinsky	USSR
1964	L Zhabotinsky	USSR
1960	Y Vlasov	USSR
1956	P Anderson	USA
1952	J Davis	USA
1948	J Davis	USA

Year	Winner	
1936	J Manger	Aut
1932	J Skobla	Cze
1928	J Strassberger	Ger
1924	G Tonani	Ita
1920	F Bottino	Ita
1912/08	Not held	
1904	P Kakousis	Gre
1900	Not held	
1896	V Jensen	Den

Up to 100 kg

FIRST HELD 1980

Year	Winner	
1988	P Kouznetsov	USSR
1984	R Milser	FRG
1980	O Zaremba	Cze

Middle Heavyweight

FIRST HELD 1952

Year	Winner	
1988	A Khrapaty	USSR
1984	N Vlad	Rom
1980	P Baczako	Hun
1976	D Rigert	USSR
1972	A Nikolov	Bul
1968	K Kangasniemi	Fin
1964	V Golovanov	USSR
1960	A Vorobyev	USSR
1956	A Vorobyev	USSR
1952	N Schemansky	USA

Light Heavyweight

FIRST HELD 1920

Year	Winner	
1988	I Arsamakov	USSR
1984	P Becheru	Rom
1980	Y Vardanyan	USSR

Year	Winner	
1976	V Shary	USSR
1972	L Jenssen	Nor
1968	B Selitsky	USSR
1964	R Plukfelder	USSR
1960	I Palinski	Pol
1956	T Kono	USA
1952	T Lomakin	USSR
1948	S Stanczyk	USA
1936	L Hostin	Fra
1932	L Hostin	Fra
1928	S Nosseir	Egy
1924	C Rigoulot	Fra
1920	E Cadine	Fra

Middleweight

FIRST HELD 1920

Year	Winner	
1988	B Guidikov	Bul
1984	K-H Radschinsky	FRG
1980	A Zlatev	Bul
1976	Y Mitkov	Bul
1972	Y Bikov	Bul
1968	V Kurentsov	USSR
1964	H Zdrazila	Cze
1960	A Kurinov	USSR
1956	F Bogdanovski	USSR
1952	P George	USA
1948	F Spellman	USA
1936	K El Thouni	Egy
1932	R Ismayr	Ger
1928	R Francois	Fra
1924	C Galimberti	Ita
1920	H Gance	Fra

Lightweight

FIRST HELD 1920

Year	Winner	
1988	J Kunz	GDR
1984	Yao Jingyuan	CPR
1980	Y Rusev	Bul

Year	Winner	
1976	P Korol	USSR
1972	M Kirzhinov	USSR
1968	W Baszanowski	Pol
1964	W Baszanowski	Pol
1960	V Bushuyev	USSR
1956	I Rybak	USSR
1952	T Kono	USA
1948	I Shams	Egy
1936	A M Mesbah	Egy
	R Fein	Aut
1932	R Duverger	Fra
1928	K Helbig	Ger
	H Haas	Aut
1924	E Decottignies	Fra
1920	A Neuland	Est

Featherweight

FIRST HELD 1920

Year	Winner	
1988	N Suleymanoglu	Tur
1984	Chen Weiqiang	CPR
1980	V Mazin	USSR
1976	N Kolesnikov	USSR
1972	N Nurikyan	Bul
1968	Y Miyake	Jap
1964	Y Miyake	Jap
1960	Y Minayev	USSR
1956	I Berger	USA
1952	R Chimishkyan	USSR
1948	M Fayad	Egy
1936	A Terlazzo	USA
1932	R Suvigny	Fra
1928	F Andrysek	Aut
1924	P Gabetti	Ita
1920	F de Haes	Bel

Bantamweight

FIRST HELD 1948

Year	Winner	
1988	O Mirzoian	USSR
1984	Wu Shude	CPR
1980	D Nunez	Cub
1976	N Nurikyan	Bul
1972	I Foldi	Hun
1968	M Nassiri	Irn
1964	A Vakhonin	USSR
1960	C Vinci	USA
1956	C Vinci	USA
1952	I Udodov	USSR
1948	J de Pietro	USA

Flyweight

FIRST HELD 1972

Year	Winner	
1988	S Marinov	Bul
1984	Z Guoqiang	CPR
1980	K Osmonoliev	USSR
1976	A Voronin	USSR
1972	Z Smalcerz	Pol

WRESTLING

OLYMPIC CHAMPIONS – FREE-STYLE

Super-Heavyweight

FIRST HELD 1972

Year	Winner	
1988	D Gobedjichvili	USSR
1984	B Baumgartner	USA
1980	S Andiyev	USSR
1976	S Andiyev	USSR
1972	A Medved	USSR

Heavyweight

FIRST HELD 1904

Year	Winner	
1988	V Puscasu	Rom
1984	L Banach	USA
1980	I Mate	Yug
1976	I Yarygin	USSR
1972	I Yarygin	USSR
1968	A Medved	USSR
1964	A Ivanitsky	USSR
1960	W Dietrich	Ger
1956	H Kaplan	Tur
1952	A Mekokishvili	USSR
1948	G Bobis	Hun
1936	K Palusalu	Est
1932	J Richthoff	Swe
1928	J Richthoff	Swe
1924	H Steele	USA
1920	R Roth	Swi
1912	Not held	
1908	G O'Kelly	GB
1904	B Hansen	USA

Light-Heavyweight

FIRST HELD 1920

Year	Winner	
1988	M Khadartsev	USSR
1984	E Banach	USA
1980	S Oganesyan	USSR
1976	L Tediashvili	USSR
1972	B Peterson	USA
1968	A Ayik	Tur
1964	A Medved	USSR
1960	I Atli	Tur
1956	G R Tahkti	Irn
1952	W Palm	Swe
1948	H Wittenberg	USA
1936	K Fridell	Swe
1932	P Mehringer	USA
1928	T Sjostedt	Swe
1924	J Spellman	USA
1920	A Larsson	Swe

Middleweight

FIRST HELD 1908

Year	Winner	
1988	Han Myung-Woo	RoK
1984	M Schultz	USA
1980	I Abilov	Bul
1976	J Peterson	USA
1972	L Tediashvili	USSR
1968	B Gurevich	USSR
1964	P Gardschev	Bul
1960	H Gungor	Tur
1956	N Stantschev	Bul
1952	D Tsimakuridze	USSR
1948	G Brand	USA
1936	E Poilve	Fra
1932	I Johansson	Swe
1928	E Kyburz	Swi
1924	F Hagmann	Swi
1920	E Leino	Fin
1912	Not held	
1908	S Bacon	GB

Welterweight

FIRST HELD 1904

Year	Winner	
1988	K Monday	USA
1984	D Schultz	USA
1980	V Raitchev	Bul
1976	J Date	Jap
1972	W Wells	USA
1968	M Atalay	Tur
1964	I Ogan	Tur
1960	D Blubaugh	USA
1956	M Ikeda	Jap
1952	W Smith	USA
1948	Y Dogu	Tur
1936	F Lewis	USA
1932	J van Bebber	USA
1928	A Haavisto	Fin
1924	H Gehri	Swi
1920/08	Not held	
1904	C Erickson	USA

Lightweight

FIRST HELD 1904

Year	Winner	
1988	A Fadzeyev	USSR
1984	In-Tak You	RoK
1980	S Absaidov	USSR
1976	P Pinigin	USSR
1972	D Gable	USA
1968	A M Ardabili	Irn
1964	E Valtschev	Bul
1960	S Wilson	USA
1956	E Habibi	Irn
1952	O Anderberg	Swe
1948	C Atik	Tur
1936	K Karpati	Hun
1932	C Pacome	Fra
1928	O Kapp	Est
1924	R Vis	USA
1920	K Anttila	Fin
1912	Not held	
1908	G de Relwyskow	GB
1904	O Roehm	USA

Featherweight

FIRST HELD 1904

Year	Winner	
1988	J Smith	USA
1984	R Lewis	USA
1980	M Abushev	USSR
1976	Jung-Mo Yang	RoK
1972	Z Abdulbekov	USSR
1968	M Kaneko	Jap
1964	O Watanabe	Jap
1960	M Dagistanli	Tur
1956	S Sasahara	Jap
1952	B Sit	Tur
1948	G Bilge	Tur
1936	K Pihlajamaki	Fin
1932	H Pihlajamaki	Fin
1928	A Morrison	USA
1924	R Reed	USA
1920	C Ackerly	USA
1912	Not held	
1908	G Dole	USA
1904	B Bradshaw	USA

Bantamweight

FIRST HELD 1904

Year	Winner	
1988	S Beloglazov	USSR
1984	H Tomiyama	Jap
1980	S Beloglazov	USSR
1976	V Yumin	USSR
1972	H Yanagide	Jap
1968	Y Uetake	Jap
1964	Y Uetake	Jap
1960	T McCann	USA
1956	M Dagistanli	Tur
1952	S Ishii	Jap
1948	N Akar	Tur
1936	O Zombori	Hun

Year	Winner	
1932	R Pearce	USA
1928	K Makinen	Fin
1924	K Pihlajamaki	Fin
1920/12	Not held	
1908	G Mehnert	USA
1904	I Niflot	USA

Flyweight

FIRST HELD 1904

Year	Winner	
1988	M Sato	Jap
1984	S Trstena	Yug
1980	A Beloglazov	USA
1976	Y Takada	Jap
1972	K Kato	Jap
1968	S Nakata	Jap
1964	Y Yoshida	Jap
1960	A Bilek	Tur
1956	M Tsalkalamanidze	USSR
1952	H Gemici	Tur
1948	L Viitala	Fin
1936/08	No Competition	
1904	G Mehnert	USA

Light-Flyweight

FIRST HELD 1904

Year	Winner	
1988	T Kobayashi	Jap
1984	R Weaver	USA
1980	C Pollio	Ita
1976	K Issaev	Bul
1972	R Dmitriev	USA
1968/08	Not held	
1904	R Curry	USA

OLYMPIC CHAMPIONS – GRECO-ROMAN

Super-Heavyweight

FIRST HELD 1972

Year	Winner	
1988	A Karelin	USSR
1984	J Blatnick	USA
1980	A Kolchinsky	USSR
1976	A Kolchinsky	USSR
1972	A Roschin	USSR

Heavyweight

FIRST HELD 1896

Year	Winner	
1988	A Wronski	Pol
1984	V Andrei	Rom
1980	G Raikov	Bul
1976	N Bolboshin	USSR
1972	N Martinescu	Rom
1968	I Kozma	Hun
1964	I Kozma	Hun
1960	I Bogdan	USSR
1956	A Parfenov	USSR
1952	J Kotkas	USSR
1948	A Kirecci	Tur
1936	K Palusalu	Est
1932	C Westergren	Swe
1928	R Svensson	Swe
1924	H Deglane	Fra
1920	A Lindfors	Fin
1912	Y Saarela	Fin
1908	R Weisz	Hun
1904/00	Not held	
1896	C Schuhmann	Ger

Light-Heavyweight

FIRST HELD 1908

Year	Winner	
1988	A Komchev	Bul
1984	S Fraser	USA
1980	N Novenyi	Hun
1976	V Rezantsev	USSR
1972	V Rezantsev	USSR
1968	B Radev	Bul
1964	B Radev	Bul
1960	T Kis	Tur
1956	V Nikolayev	USSR
1952	K Grondahl	Fin
1948	K Nilsson	Swe
1936	A Cadier	Swe
1932	R Svensson	Swe
1928	I Moustafa	Egy
1924	C Westergren	Swe
1920	C Johansson	Swe
1912	No gold medal awarded	
1908	V Weckman	Fin

Middleweight

FIRST HELD 1908

Year	Winner	
1988	M Mamiachvili	USSR
1984	I Draica	Rom
1980	G Korban	USSR
1976	M Petkovic	Yug
1972	C Hegedus	Hun
1968	L Metz	GDR
1964	B Simic	Yug
1960	D Dobrev	Bul
1956	G Kartoziya	USSR
1952	A Gronberg	Swe
1948	A Gronberg	Swe
1936	I Johansson	Swe
1932	V Kokkinen	Fin
1928	V Kokkinen	Fin
1924	E Westerlund	Fin
1920	C Westergren	Swe
1912	C Johansson	Swe
1908	F Martensson	Swe

Welterweight

FIRST HELD 1932

Year	Winner	
1988	Kim Young-Nam	RoK
1984	J Salomaki	Fin
1980	F Kocsis	Hun
1976	A Bykov	USSR
1972	V Macha	Cze
1968	R Vesper	GDR
1964	A Kolesov	USSR
1960	M Bayrak	Tur
1956	M Bayrak	Tur
1952	M Szilvasi	Hun
1948	G Andersson	Swe
1936	R Svedberg	Swe
1932	I Johansson	Swe

Lightweight

FIRST HELD 1908

Year	Winner	
1988	L Djoufalakian	USSR
1984	V Lisjak	Yug
1980	S Rusu	Rom
1976	S Nalbandyan	USSR
1972	S Khisamutdinov	USSR
1968	M Mumemura	Jap
1964	K Ayvaz	Tur
1960	A Koridze	USSR
1956	K Lehtonen	Fin
1952	S Safin	USSR
1948	G Freij	Swe
1936	L Kosekela	Fin
1932	E Malmberg	Swe
1928	L Keresztes	Hun
1924	O Friman	Fin
1920	E Ware	Fin
1912	E Ware	Fin
1908	E Porro	Ita

Featherweight

FIRST HELD 1912

Year	Winner	
1988	K Madjidov	USSR
1984	Weon-Kee Kim	RoK
1980	S Migiakis	Gre
1976	K Lipien	Pol
1972	G Markov	Bul
1968	R Rurua	USSR
1964	I Polyak	Hun
1960	M Sille	Tur
1956	R Makinen	Fin
1952	Y Punkin	USSR
1948	M Oktav	Tur
1936	Y Erkan	Tur
1932	G Gozzi	Ita
1928	V Vali	Est
1924	K Antila	Fin
1920	O Friman	Fin
1912	K Koskelo	Fin

Bantamweight

FIRST HELD 1924

Year	Winner	
1988	A Sike	Hun
1984	P Passarelli	FRG
1980	S Serikov	USSR
1976	P Ukkola	Fin
1972	R Kazakov	USSR
1968	J Varga	Hun
1964	M Ichiguchi	Jap
1960	O Karavayev	USSR
1956	K Vyrupayev	USSR
1952	I Hodos	Hun
1948	K Pettersen	Swe
1936	M Lorincz	Hun
1932	J Brendel	Ger
1928	K Leucht	Ger
1924	E Putsep	Est

Flyweight

FIRST HELD 1948

Year	Winner	
1988	J Ronningen	Nor
1984	A Miyahara	Jap
1980	V Blagidze	USSR
1976	V Konstantinov	USSR
1972	P Kirov	Bul
1968	P Kirov	Bul
1964	T Hanahara	Jap
1960	D Pirvulescu	Rom
1956	N Solovyov	USSR
1952	B Gurevich	USSR
1948	P Lombardi	Ita

Light-Flyweight

FIRST HELD 1972

Year	Winner	
1988	V Maenza	Ita
1984	V Maenza	Ita
1980	Z Ushkempirov	USSR
1976	A Shumakov	USSR
1972	G Berceanu	Rom

WORLD CHAMPIONS – FREE-STYLE

Super-Heavyweight

FIRST HELD 1969

Year	Winner	
1990	D Gobedjichvili	USSR
1989	A Soleimani	Irn
1987	A Khadartzev	USSR
1986	B Baumgartner	USA
1985	D Gobedjichvili	USSR
1983	S Khasimikov	USSR
1982	S Khasimikov	USSR
1981	S Khasimikov	USSR

Year	Winner	
1979	S Khasimikov	USSR
1977	S Andiyev	USSR
1975	S Andiyev	USSR
1974	S Ladislav	Rom
1973	S Andiyev	USSR
1971	A Medved	USSR
1970	A Medved	USSR
1969	A Medved	USSR

Heavyweight

FIRST HELD 1951

Year	Winner	
1990	L Khabelov	USSR
1989	A Atavov	USSR
1987	L Khabelov	USSR
1986	A Khadartzev	USSR
1985	L Khabelov	USSR
1983	A Khadartzev	USSR
1982	I Mate	USSR
1981	R Gehrke	GDR
1979	I Mate	USSR
1978	H Buttner	GDR
1977	A Bisultanov	USSR
1975	K Bayanminkh	Mgl
1974	V Gulyutkin	USSR
1973	I Yarygin	USSR
1971	S Lomidze	USSR
1970	V Gulyutkin	USSR
1969	S Lomidze	USSR
1967	A Medved	USSR
1966	A Ivanitskiy	USSR
1965	A Ivanitskiy	USSR
1963	A Ivanitskiy	USSR
1962	A Ivanitskiy	USSR
1961	W Dietrich	FRG
1959	L Ahmedov	Bul
1957	H Kaplan	Tur
1954	A Mekokishvili	USSR
1953	L Akhmedov	Bul
1951	B Antonsson	Swe

Light-Heavyweight

FIRST HELD 1951

Year	Winner	
1990	M Khadartsev	USSR
1989	M Khadartsev	USSR
1987	M Khadartsev	USSR
1986	M Khadartsev	USSR
1985	B Sherr	USA
1983	P Naneyev	USSR
1982	U Neupert	GDR
1981	S Oganesyan	USSR
1979	K Ortzuyev	USSR
1978	U Neupert	GDR
1977	A Prokopchuk	USSR
1975	L Tediashvili	USSR
1974	L Tediashvili	USSR
1973	L Tediashvili	USSR
1971	R Petrov	Bul
1970	G Strakhov	USSR
1969	B Gurevich	USSR
1967	A Ayik	Tur
1966	A Medved	USSR
1965	A Ayik	Tur
1963	A Medved	USSR
1962	A Medved	USSR
1961	G Takhti	Irn
1959	G Takhti	Irn
1957	M Petkov	Bul
1954	A Englas	USSR
1953	A Albul	USSR
1951	Y Dogu	Tur

Middleweight

FIRST HELD 1951

Year	Winner	
1990	J Lohyna	Cze
1989	E Jabraylov	USSR
1987	M Schultz	USA
1986	V Modosyan	USSR
1985	M Schultz	USA
1983	T Dzgoev	USSR
1982	T Dzgoev	USSR
1981	C Campbell	USA

Year	Winner	
1979	I Kovacs	Hun
1978	M Aratsilov	USSR
1977	A Seger	FRG
1975	A Seger	FRG
1974	V Novozhilov	USSR
1973	V Syulzhin	USSR
1971	L Tediashvili	USSR
1970	Y Shakhmuradov	USSR
1969	F Fozzard	USA
1967	B Gurevich	USSR
1966	P Gardschev	Bul
1965	M Mehdizadeh	Irn
1963	P Gardschev	Bul
1962	M Mehdizadeh	Irn
1961	M Mehdizadeh	Irn
1959	G Shkirtladze	USSR
1957	N Sorouri	Irn
1954	A Zandi	Irn
1953	H Gungor	Tur
1951	H Zafer	Tur

Welterweight

FIRST HELD 1951

Year	Winner	
1990	R Sofiyadi	Bul
1989	K Monday	USA
1987	A Vareyev	USSR
1986	R Cascaret	Cub
1985	R Cascaret	Cub
1983	D Schultz	USA
1982	L Kemp	USA
1981	M Knosp	FRG
1979	L Kemp	USA
1978	L Kemp	USA
1977	S Dzidezic	USA
1975	R Ashuraliyev	USSR
1974	R Ashuraliyev	USSR
1973	M Barzegar	Irn
1971	Y Gusov	USSR
1970	W Wells	USA
1969	Z Beriashvili	USSR
1967	D Robin	Fra
1966	M Atalay	Tur

Year	Winner	
1965	G Sagaradze	USSR
1963	G Sagaradze	USSR
1962	E Habibi	Irn
1961	E Habibi	Irn
1959	E Habibi	Irn
1957	V Balavadze	USSR
1954	V Balavadze	USSR
1953	I Ogan	Tur
1951	C Atik	Tur

Lightweight

FIRST HELD 1951

Year	Winner	
1990	A Fadzeyev	USSR
1989	B Bovdayev	USSR
1987	A Fadzeyev	USSR
1986	A Fadzeyev	USSR
1985	A Fadzeyev	USSR
1983	A Fadzeyev	USSR
1982	M Kharachura	USSR
1981	S Absaidov	USSR
1979	M Kharachura	USSR
1978	P Pinigin	USSR
1977	P Pinigin	USSR
1975	P Pinigin	USSR
1974	N Nasrullayev	USSR
1973	L Keaser	USA
1971	D Gable	USA
1970	A M Ardabili	Irn
1969	A M Ardabili	Irn
1967	A M Ardabili	Irn
1966	A M Ardabili	Irn
1965	A M Ardabili	Irn
1963	I Horiuchi	Jap
1962	E Valtchev	Bul
1961	M Sanatkaram	Irn
1959	V Sinyavskiy	USSR
1957	A Bestayev	USSR
1954	D Toyfighe	Irn
1953	V Sinyavskiy	USSR
1951	O Anderberg	Swe

Featherweight

FIRST HELD 1951

Year	Winner	
1990	J Smith	USA
1989	J Smith	USA
1987	J Smith	USA
1986	H Isayev	USSR
1985	V Alekseyev	USSR
1983	V Alekseyev	USSR
1982	S Beloglazov	USSR
1981	S Sterev	Bul
1979	V Yumin	USSR
1978	V Yumin	USSR
1977	V Yumin	USSR
1975	Z Oydov	Mgl
1974	I Zeveg	Mgl
1973	Z Abdulbekov	USSR
1971	Z Abdulbekov	USSR
1970	S Seyed-Abbassi	Irn
1969	T Morita	Jap
1967	M Kaneko	Jap
1966	M Kaneko	Jap
1965	M Saidabadi	Irn
1963	O Watanabe	Jap
1962	O Watanabe	Jap
1961	V Rubashvili	USSR
1959	M Dagistanli	Tur
1957	M Dagistanli	Tur
1954	S Sasahara	Jap
1953	H Moucheguian	USSR
1951	H Zafer	Tur

Bantamweight

FIRST HELD 1951

Year	Winner	
1990	A Puertos	Cub
1989	Y Sik-Kim	DPRK
1987	S Beloglazov	USSR
1986	S Beloglazov	USSR
1985	S Beloglazov	USSR
1983	S Beloglazov	USSR
1982	A Beloglazov	USSR

Year	Winner	
1981	S Beloglazov	USSR
1979	H Tomiyama	Jap
1978	H Tomiyama	Jap
1977	T Sasaki	Jap
1975	M Arai	Jap
1974	V Yumin	USSR
1973	M Farahvashi-Fashandi	Irn
1971	H Yanagida	Jap
1970	H Yanagida	Jap
1969	T Tanaki	Jap
1967	A Aliyev	USSR
1966	A Aliyev	USSR
1965	T Fukada	Jap
1963	A Ibragimov	USSR
1962	H Akbas	Tur
1961	M Saidabadi	Irn
1959	H Akbas	Tur
1957	H Akbas	Tur
1954	M Dagistanli	Tur
1953	H Akbas	Tur
1951	N Akar	Tur

Flyweight

FIRST HELD 1951

Year	Winner	
1990	M Torkan	Irn
1989	V Jordanov	Bul
1987	V Jordanov	Bul
1986	Kim-Yong Sik	DPRK
1985	V Jordanov	Bul
1983	V Jordanov	Bul
1982	H Reich	GDR
1981	T Asakura	Jap
1979	Y Takada	Jap
1978	A Beloglazov	USSR
1977	Y Takada	Jap
1975	Y Takada	Jap
1974	Y Takada	Jap
1973	E Javadpour	Irn
1971	M Ghorbani	Irn
1970	R Ali	Tur
1969	R Sanders	USA

Year	Winner	
1967	S Nakata	Jap
1966	C Chang	RoK
1965	Y Yoshida	Jap
1963	Y Cemal	Tur
1962	A Aliyev	USSR
1961	A Aliyev	USSR
1959	A Aliyev	USSR
1957	M Kartel	Tur
1954	H Akbas	Tur
1953	G Saydov	USSR
1951	K Yucel	Tur

Light-Flyweight

FIRST HELD 1969

Year	Winner	
1990	A Martinez	Cub
1989	Kim Jong-Shin	RoK
1987	Li Yae-Sik	DPRK
1986	Li Yae-Sik	DPRK
1985	Hwan Kim-Chol	RoK
1983	Hwan Kim-Chol	RoK
1982	S Kornilayev	USSR
1981	S Kornilayev	USSR
1979	S Kornilayev	USSR
1978	S Kornilayev	USSR
1977	A Beloglazov	USA
1975	H Issaev	Bul
1974	H Murselov	Bul
1973	R Dmitriyev	USSR
1971	E Javadpour	Irn
1970	E Javadpour	Irn
1969	E Javadpour	Irn

WORLD CHAMPIONS – GRECO-ROMAN

Super-Heavyweight

FIRST HELD 1969

Year	Winner	
1990	A Karelin	USSR
1989	A Karelin	USSR
1987	I Rostozotsky	USSR
1986	T Johansson	Swe
1985	I Rostozotsky	USSR
1983	J Artiochin	USSR
1982	N Dinev	Bul
1981	R Memisevic	Yug
1979	A Tomov	Bul
1978	A Kolinchsky	USSR
1977	N Dinev	Bul
1975	A Tomov	Bul
1974	A Tomov	Bul
1973	A Tomov	Bul
1971	P Svensson	Swe
1970	A Roshin	USSR
1969	A Roshin	USSR

Heavyweight

FIRST HELD 1921

Year	Winner	
1990	S Demiaschkievich	USSR
1989	G Himmel	FRG
1987	C Guedekhouri	USSR
1986	T Gaspar	Hun
1985	A Dmitrov	Bul
1983	A Dmitrov	Bul
1982	R Wroclawski	Pol
1981	M Saladze	USSR
1979	N Balboshin	USSR
1978	N Balboshin	USSR
1977	N Balboshin	USSR
1975	K Losano	Bul
1974	N Balboshin	USSR
1973	N Balboshin	USSR

Year	Winner	
1971	N Martinescu	Rom
1970	P Svensson	Swe
1969	N Yakovenko	USSR
1967	I Kozma	Hun
1966	I Kozma	Hun
1965	N Shmakov	USSR
1963	A Rochin	USSR
1962	I Kozma	Hun
1961	I Bogdan	USSR
1958	I Bogdan	USSR
1955	A Mazur	USSR
1953	B Antonsson	Swe
1950	B Antonsson	Swe
1949/23	No Championships	
1922	E Nilsson	Swe
1921	J Salila	Fin

Light-Heavyweight

FIRST HELD 1921

Year	Winner	
1990	M Bullmann	Ger
1989	M Bullmann	GDR
1987	V Popov	USSR
1986	A Malina	Pol
1985	M Houk	USA
1983	I Kanygin	USSR
1982	F Andersson	Swe
1981	I Kanygin	USSR
1979	F Andersson	Swe
1978	S Nikolov	Bul
1977	F Andersson	Swe
1975	V Rezantsev	USSR
1974	V Rezantsev	USSR
1973	V Rezantsev	USSR
1971	V Rezantsev	USSR
1970	V Rezantsev	USSR
1969	A Yurkevich	USSR
1967	N Yakovenko	USSR
1966	B Radev	Bul
1965	J Anisimov	USSR
1963	R Abashidze	USSR
1962	R Abashidze	USSR
1961	G Gurics	Hun

Year	Winner	
1958	R Abashidze	USSR
1955	V Nikolayev	USSR
1953	A Englas	USSR
1950	M Candas	Tur
1949/23	No Championships	
1922	E Rosenquist	Fin
1921	E Rosenquist	Fin

Middleweight

FIRST HELD 1921

Year	Winner	
1990	P Farkas	Hun
1989	T Komaromi	Hun
1987	T Komaromi	Hun
1986	No gold medal awarded	
1985	B Daras	Pol
1983	T Abkhasava	USSR
1982	T Abkhasava	USSR
1981	G Korban	USSR
1979	G Korban	USSR
1978	I Draica	Rom
1977	V Cheboskarov	USSR
1975	A Nazarenko	USSR
1974	A Nazarenko	USSR
1973	L Liberman	USSR
1971	C Hegedus	Hun
1970	A Nazarenko	USSR
1969	P Kroumov	Bul
1967	L Sillai	Hun
1966	V Olenik	USSR
1965	R Bogdanas	USSR
1963	T Kis	Tur
1962	T Kis	Tur
1961	V Zenin	USSR
1958	G Kartozlya	USSR
1955	G Kartozlya	USSR
1953	G Kartozlya	USSR
1950	A Gronberg	Swe
1949/23	No Championships	
1922	C Westergren	Ger
1921	T Tamminen	Fin

Welterweight

FIRST HELD 1950

Year	Winner	
1990	M Iskamdarian	USSR
1989	D Tourlykhanov	USSR
1987	J Ilomaki	Fin
1986	M Mamiachvili	USSR
1985	M Mamiachvili	USSR
1983	M Mamiachvili	USSR
1982	S Rusu	Rom
1981	A Kudryavtsev	USSR
1979	F Kocsis	Hun
1978	A Niftulayev	USSR
1977	V Macha	Cze
1975	A Bykov	USSR
1974	V Macha	Cze
1973	I Kolev	Bul
1971	V Igumenov	USSR
1970	V Igumenov	USSR
1969	V Igumenov	USSR
1967	V Igumenov	USSR
1966	V Igumenov	USSR
1965	A Kolesov	USSR
1963	A Kolesov	USSR
1962	A Kolesov	USSR
1961	V Bularca	Rom
1958	K Ayvaz	Tur
1955	V Maneyev	USSR
1953	G Chatvorjan	USSR
1950	M Simanainen	Fin

Lightweight

FIRST HELD 1921

Year	Winner	
1990	I Duguchiev	USSR
1989	C Passarelli	FRG
1987	A Abayev	USSR
1986	L Djoufalakian	USSR
1985	S Negrisan	Rom
1983	T Sipila	Fin
1982	G Yermilov	USSR
1981	G Yermilov	USSR

Year	Winner	
1979	A Supron	Pol
1978	S Rusu	Rom
1977	H Wehling	GDR
1975	S Khisamutdinov	USSR
1974	N Davidyan	USSR
1973	S Khisamutdinov	USSR
1971	S Damyanovic	Yug
1970	R Rurua	USSR
1969	S Popescu	Rom
1967	E Tapio	Fin
1966	S Horvat	Yug
1965	G Supanov	USSR
1963	S Horvat	Yug
1962	K Ayvaz	Tur
1961	A Koridze	USSR
1958	R Dogan	Tur
1955	G Gamarnik	USSR
1953	G Freij	Swe
1950	J Gal	Hun
1949/23	No Championships	
1922	E Westerlund	Fin
1921	O Friman	Fin

Featherweight

FIRST HELD 1921

Year	Winner	
1990	M Olivares	Cub
1989	K Madjidov	USSR
1987	J Vanguelov	Bul
1986	K Madjidov	USSR
1985	J Vanguelov	Bul
1983	H Lahtinen	Fin
1982	R Swierad	Pol
1981	I Toth	Hun
1979	I Toth	Hun
1978	B Kramarenko	USSR
1977	L Reczi	Hun
1975	N Davidyan	USSR
1974	K Lipien	Pol
1973	K Lipien	Pol
1971	G Markov	Bul
1970	H Fujimoto	Jap
1969	R Rurua	USA

Year	Winner	
1967	R Rurua	USA
1966	R Rurua	USA
1965	Y Grigoryev	USSR
1963	G Sapunov	USSR
1962	I Polyak	Hun
1961	M Mansour	Egy
1958	I Polyak	Hun
1955	I Polyak	Hun
1953	O Anderberg	Swe
1950	O Anderberg	Swe
1949/23	No Championships	
1922	K Anttila	Fin
1921	K Anttila	Fin

Bantamweight

FIRST HELD 1921

Year	Winner	
1990	R Yildiz	Ger
1989	E Ivanov	Bul
1987	P Mourier	Fra
1986	E Ivanov	Bul
1985	S Balov	Bul
1983	E Masaki	Jap
1982	P Mikhalik	Pol
1981	P Passarelli	FRG
1979	S Serikov	USSR
1978	S Serikov	USSR
1977	P Ukkola	Fin
1975	F Mustafin	USSR
1974	F Mustafin	USSR
1973	J Lipien	Pol
1971	R Kazakov	USSR
1970	J Varga	Hun
1969	R Kazakov	USSR
1967	I Baciu	Rom
1966	F Strange	FRG
1965	I Chernya	USSR
1963	J Varga	Hun
1962	M Ichiguchi	Jap
1961	O Karavayev	USSR
1958	O Karavayev	USSR
1955	V Stashevich	USSR
1953	A Teryan	USSR

Year	Winner	
1950	A Hassan	Egy
1949/23	No Championships	
1922	F Svensson	Swe
1921	V Ikonen	Fin

Flyweight

FIRST HELD 1950

Year	Winner	
1990	A Ignatenko	USSR
1989	A Ignatenko	USSR
1987	P Roque	Cub
1986	S Dyudyayev	USSR
1985	J Ronningen	Nor
1983	B Pashayan	USSR
1982	B Pashayan	USSR
1981	V Blagidze	USSR
1979	L Racz	Hun
1978	V Blagidze	USSR
1977	N Ginga	Rom
1975	V Konstantinov	USSR
1974	P Kirov	USSR
1973	G Guergue	Rom
1971	P Kirov	Bul
1970	P Kirov	Bul
1969	F Aluzadeh	Irn
1967	V Bakulin	USSR
1966	A Kerezov	Bul
1965	S Rybalko	USSR

Year	Winner	
1963	B Vukov	Yug
1962	S Rybalko	USSR
1961	A Saydov	USSR
1958	B Gurevich	USSR
1955	I Fabra	Ita
1953	B Gurevich	USSR
1950	B Johansson	Swe

Light-Flyweight

FIRST HELD 1969

Year	Winner	
1990	O Koutcherenko	USSR
1989	O Koutcherenko	USSR
1987	M Allakhverdiev	USSR
1986	M Allakhverdiev	USSR
1985	M Allakhverdiev	USSR
1983	B Tsenov	Bul
1982	T Karashvili	USSR
1981	Z Ushkempirov	USSR
1978	C Alexandru	Rom
1977	A Shumakov	USSR
1975	V Zubkov	USSR
1974	V Zubkov	USSR
1973	V Zubkov	USSR
1971	V Zubkov	USSR
1970	G Berceanu	Rom
1969	G Berceanu	Rom

YACHTING

OLYMPIC CHAMPIONS

470 Class

FIRST HELD 1976

Year	Winner	
1988	T Peponnet & L Pillot	Fra
1984	J-L Doreste & R Molina	Spa
1980	M Soares & E Penido	Bra
1976	F Hubner & H Bode	FRG

Star

FIRST HELD 1932

Year	Winner	
1988	M McIntyre & B Vaile	GB
1984	W Buchan & S Erickson	USA
1980	V Mankin & A Muzychenko	USSR
1976	Not held	
1972	D Forbes & J Anderson	Aus
1968	L North & P Barrett	USA
1964	D Knowles & C Cooke	Bah
1960	T Pinegin & F Shutkov	USSR
1956	H Williams & L Lowe	USA
1952	A Straulino & N Rode	Ita
1948	H Smart & P Smart	USA
1936	P Bischoff & H J Weise	Ger
1932	G Gray & A Libano	USA

Soling

FIRST HELD 1972

Year	Winner
1988	East Germany
1984	United States
1980	Denmark
1976	Denmark
1972	United States

Flying Dutchman

FIRST HELD 1960

Year	Winner	
1988	J Bojsen-Moeller & C Gronberg	Den
1984	J McKee & C Buchan	USA
1980	A Abascal & M Noguer	Spa
1976	J Diesch & E Diesch	FRG
1972	R Pattisson & C Davies	GB
1968	R Pattisson & I Macdonald-Smith	GB
1964	H Pedersen & E Wells	NZ
1960	P Lunde & B Bergvall	Nor

Finn

FIRST HELD 1924

Year	Winner	
1988	J-L Doreste	Spa
1984	R Coutts	NZ
1980	E Rechardt	Fin
1976	J Schumann	GDR
1972	S Maury	Fra
1968	V Mankin	USSR
1964	W Kuhweide	Ger
1960	P Elvstrom	Den
1956	P Elvstrom	Den

Year	Winner	
1952	P Elvstrom	Den
1948	P Elvstrom	Den
1936	D Kagchelland	Nld
1932	J Lebrun	Fra
1928	S Thorell	Swe
1924	L Huybrechts	Bel

Tornado

FIRST HELD 1976

Year	Winner	
1988	N Henard & J-Y Le Deroff	Fra
1984	R Sellers & C Timms	NZ
1980	A Welter & L Bjorkstrom	Bra
1976	R White & J Osborn	GB

Windsurfing

FIRST HELD 1984

Year	Winner	
1988	B Kendall	NZ
1984	S Van den Berg	Nld

Women's 470 Class

FIRST HELD 1988

Year	Winner	
1988	L Jewell & A Jolly	USA

AMERICA'S CUP

FIRST HELD 1870

Year	Winner		
1988	D Conner	USA	Stars & Stripes
1987	D Conner	USA	Stars & Stripes
1983	J Bertrand	Aus	Australia II
1980	D Conner	USA	Freedom
1977	T Turner	USA	Courageous
1974	T Hood	USA	Courageous
1970	B Ficker	USA	Intrepid
1967	E Mosbacher	USA	Intrepid
1964	B Bavier	USA	Constellation
1962	E Mosbacher	USA	Weatherly
1958	B Cunningham	USA	Columbia
1937	H Vanderbilt	USA	Ranger
1934	H Vanderbilt	USA	Rainbow
1930	H Vanderbilt	USA	Enterprise
1920	C Adams	USA	Resolute
1903	C Barr	USA	Reliance
1901	C Barr	USA	Columbia
1899	C Barr	USA	Columbia
1895	H Haff	USA	Defender

Year	Winner		
1893	W Hansen	USA	Vigilant
1887	H Haff	USA	Volunteer
1886	M Stone	USA	Mayflower
1885	A Crocker	USA	Puritan
1881	N Clock	USA	Mischief
1876	J Williams	USA	Madeleine
1871	N Comstock	USA	Columbia
	S Greeenwood	USA	Sappho
1870	A Comstock	USA	Magic

ADMIRAL'S CUP

FIRST HELD 1957

Year	Winner
1991	France
1989	Great Britain
1987	New Zealand
1985	West Germany
1983	West Germany
1981	Great Britain
1979	Australia
1977	Great Britain
1975	Great Britain
1973	West Germany
1971	Great Britain
1969	United States
1967	Australia
1965	Great Britain
1963	Great Britain
1961	United States
1959	Great Britain
1957	Great Britain

WHITBREAD ROUND THE WORLD RACE

FIRST HELD 1973/74

Year	Winner		
1989/90	P Blake	NZ	Steinlager 2
1985/86	P Fehlmann	Swi	UBS Switzerland
1981/82	C van Rietschoten	Nld	Flyer II
1977/78	C van Rietschoten	Nld	Flyer
1973/74	R Carlin	Mex	Sayula II

PLAYFAIR CRICKET ANNUAL 1991 Bill Frindall £2.50
PLAYFAIR FOOTBALL ANNUAL 1991–92 Jack Rollin £2.99
PLAYFAIR NON-LEAGUE FOOTBALL ANNUAL 1991–92
   Bruce Smith £3.50
THE SPORTING DECADE: 1980s Chris Dighton £6.99

Queen Anne Press offers an exciting range of quality titles by both
established and new authors. All of the books in this series are
available from:
Queen Anne Press Paperbacks
Cash Sales Department,
P.O. Box 11,
Falmouth,
Cornwall TR10 9EN.

Alternatively you may fax your order to the above address. Fax No.
0326 76423.

Payments can be made as follows: Cheque, postal order (payable to
Macdonald & Co (Publishers) Ltd) or by credit cards, Visa/Access.
Do not send cash or currency. UK customers: please send a cheque or
postal order (no currency) and allow 80p for postage and packing for
the first book plus 20p for each additional book up to a maximum
charge of £2.00.

B.F.P.O. customers please allow 80p for the first book plus 20p for
each additional book.

Overseas customers including Ireland, please allow £1.50 for postage
and packing for the first book, £1.00 for the second book, and 30p for
each additional book.

NAME (Block Letters) —————————————————————

ADDRESS —————————————————————————

————————————————————————————————————

I enclose my remittance for ————————————

I wish to pay by Access/Visa Card

Number ————————————————————

Card Expiry Date ————————————